Mario Merz

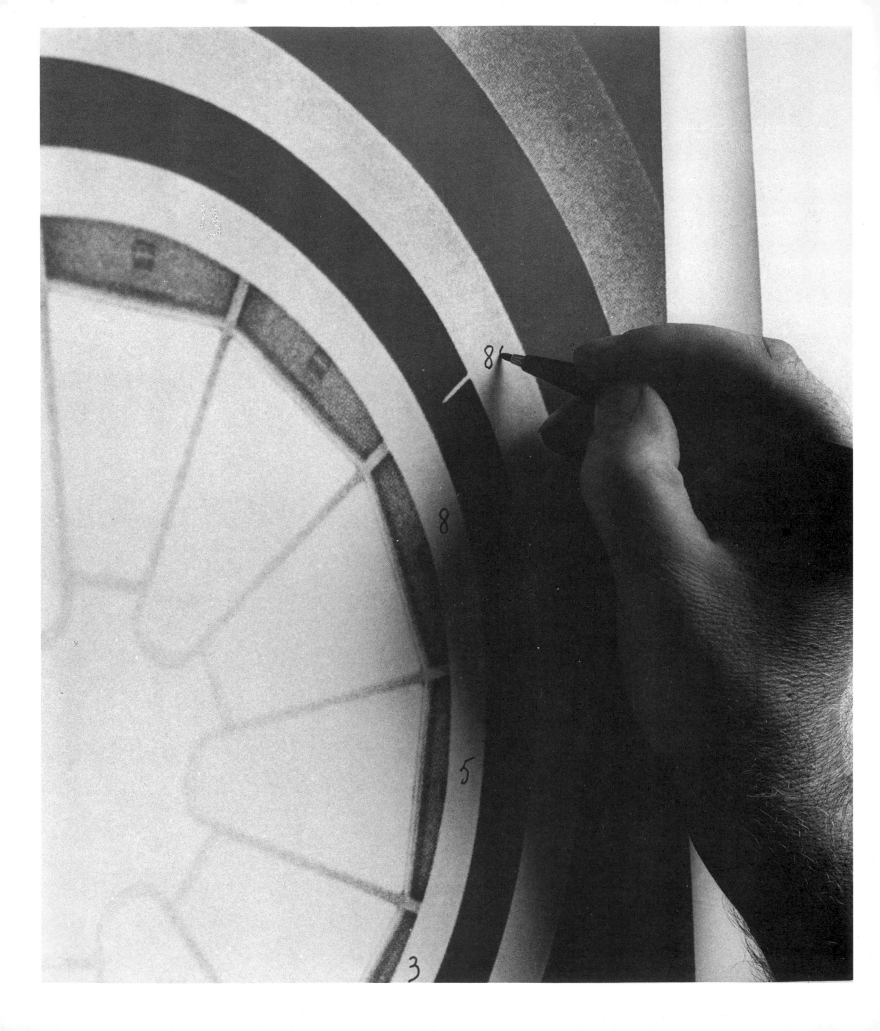

Germano Celant

This exhibition is made possible
in collaboration with apparel
and fashion group Gruppo GFT
and The Rivetti Art Foundation.

Mario Merz

Solomon R.
Guggenheim Museum
New York

Rizzoli, New York

Mario Merz
Solomon R. Guggenheim
Museum, New York
September 28 - November 26, 1989

**Project organization
and production**

Curator
Germano Celant

Project Management
Michael Govan

Coordination
Thomas Padon

Research, Europe
Luisa De Vettor

Research
Nancy Spector
Jennifer Blessing
Richard Roller

Editorial
Carol Fuerstein
Diana Murphy

Translation
Joachim Neugroschel

Design
Pierluigi Cerri
with Andrea Lancellotti

Installation
Scott Wixon
Dennis Schoelerman
Peter Costa
Timothy Ross
Guggenheim Operations
and Preparation staff
Mariano Boggia
and Ryoichi Hayashi,
artist's assistants

Registrar
Victoria Hertz

Public Relations
Glory Jones

Events
Linda Gering
Maria Masciotti

Interns
Thomas Seydoux
Paula Billingsley
Patricia de Alvear
Jeanhee Kim

ISBN 0-8478-1213-8
LC 89 64077
Printed in Italy
© 1989 by The Solomon R. Guggenheim
Foundation, New York
and by Electa, Milan
Elemond Arte
Elemond Editori Associati
English translations © 1989
by Joachim Neugroschel

Distributed exclusively in the United States
and Canada by Rizzoli International Publications, INC.
300 Park Avenue South, New York, NY 10010

Table of Contents

Lenders to the Exhibition

Guido Accornero
Angelo Baldasarre, Bari
Udo and Anette Brandhorst
Liliane and Michel Durand-Dessert,
Paris
Giulio Einaudi Editore S.p.A.,
A.S., Turin
Gerald S. Elliott, Chicago
Konrad Fischer, Düsseldorf
The Frito-Lay Collection,
Plano, Texas
The Arthur and Carol Goldberg
Collection
Raymond J. Learsy
Marcello Levi, Turin
Marisa Lombardi, Milan
Mario Merz
Metzeler Collection, Düsseldorf
The Rivetti Art Foundation, Turin
Giuliana and Tommaso Setari, Rome
Sonnabend Collection, New York
Christian Stein, Turin
Elisabeth and Ealan Wingate,
New York

Art Gallery of Ontario, Toronto
Bonnefantenmuseum, Maastricht,
The Netherlands
Castello di Rivoli, Museo d'Arte
Contemporanea, Rivoli (Turin)
Musée d'Art Moderne, Saint-Etienne
Musée National d'Art Moderne,
Centre Georges Pompidou, Paris
Museo d'Arte Contemporanea,
Palazzo Reale, Milan
Museo Civico di Torino, Galleria
d'Arte Moderna, Turin
The Museum of Modern Art,
New York
Rijksmuseum Kröller-Müller, Otterlo
Stedelijk Museum, Amsterdam

Galleria Salvatore Ala, Milan
and New York
Thomas Ammann Fine Art AG,
Zürich
Jean Bernier Gallery, Athens
Galerie Liliane et Michel
Durand-Dessert, Paris
Willy d'Huysser Gallery, Brussels
and Knokke, Belgium
Anthony d'Offay Gallery, London
Galleria Pieroni, Rome
Galleria Antonio Tucci Russo, Turin
Sonnabend Gallery, New York
Pietro Sparta Gallery, Chagny
Sperone Westwater, New York
Galleria Christian Stein, Milan
and Turin

Acknowledgments

An exhibition of work by Mario Merz is by its very nature a complicated endeavor. The variety of scale, the fragility and the often poignant ephemerality of the materials Merz employs in his art must be considered a challenge to the routine of the institution. Works by Merz can never be installed the same way twice. For all of these reasons and more, the present retrospective, involving the entire Frank Lloyd Wright spiral, is a singular achievement, the product of the enormous labor, patience and dedication of the staff of the Guggenheim and of others who participated in its making.

First, it must be emphasized that while this exhibition includes Mario Merz's work from the 1950s to the present, attaching the term "retrospective" to it is provisional at best. Merz's continual recombination of elements from different works and the organic mutation of one sculpture into another make his objects difficult to date or even to distinguish from one another. Thus, like most of his installations, this retrospective is a unique event that has required and depended on Mario Merz himself, and also on the collaboration of Marisa Merz, in every way. In embodying Merz's vital contribution to our culture, it may in itself be considered one of his greatest works. Projects of this scale and quality cannot be produced without sponsorship. In the case of Gruppo GFT and The Rivetti Art Foundation, cofounders of the present undertaking, sponsorship must be considered partnership. Marco Rivetti, with Roberto Balma and Anna Martina of GFT, has supported the exhibition in every phase of its planning and execution. Marco Rivetti's personal attention and commitment to contemporary art, and the encouragement he, his company and his foundation have given to artists and institutions are rare indeed, and the Guggenheim is grateful for its association with Mr. Rivetti and Gruppo GFT. Mario Merz's work is sought worldwide. We are fortunate to have had the encouragement and collaboration of lending sister institutions who, like the Guggenheim, are entrusted with the care and preservation of objects of cultural importance.

The greatest risks in terms of supporting contemporary art and bringing it to the attention of the public are often taken not by public institutions but by private collectors and galleries. Christian Stein and Gianfranco Benedetti of Galleria Christian Stein of Milan and Turin, and Barbara Gladstone and her gallery in New York have been exceptionally generous in their personal and financial commitment to Merz and this exhibition project. Several significant new works could not have been constructed without their assistance. Ileana Sonnabend, whose ongoing support of major artists and movements of the last thirty years is legendary, was an early champion of Merz's work. Along with Antonio Homem, she was crucial to the realization of the exhibition. Antonio Tucci Russo of Turin and Sperone Westwater Gallery of New York were also involved from the project's beginning. My thanks go as well to all of the collectors and galleries making generous loans to the exhibition. A project of this scale touches the entire staff of the Museum and consumes the full attention of many. Thomas Padon professionally and delicately managed, overall, the significant curatorial and logistical problems posed by every aspect of the exhibition; he was ably assisted by interns Thomas Seydoux, Paula Billingsley and Patricia de Alvear. Luisa De Vettor, assistant to Germano Celant in Genoa, who has worked over the long term on the forthcoming systematic catalogue of Merz's work, has contributed research to the present publication. This catalogue was brought to fruition in a precious few months by a dedicated and indefatigable team. Nancy Spector, Assistant Curator for Research, with Jennifer Blessing, in collaboration with Manager of Information Systems Richard Roller, assembled, computerized, researched and shaped the sizable documentation. We also express our gratitude to The Museum of Modern Art Library, which has been exceptionally generous with its resources. The publication itself is the product of the acumen, precision and resilience of Editor Carol Fuerstein and Assistant Editor Diana Murphy, who received essential help from intern Jeanhee Kim. Thanks

also are due Joachim Neugroschel for his facility with the Italian tongue and his sensitivity to the subtleties of the text. In Milan, Pierluigi Cerri, with Andrea Lancellotti, applied his intuition and imagination to the design and concept of the catalogue and posters. The staff of Electa, with Tiziana Quirico, likewise lent its energies to the production of the book.

As the only exhibition of a single living artist ever to occupy the entirety of the Wright spiral, its actual installation has been an extraordinarliy complicated task. That Merz's work sustains a provocative and compatible dialogue with Wright's elegant but formidable building is certainly due in large part to the artist's and architect's shared desire to balance organic forms and industrial materials. Yet this dialogue could not have been achieved without the superb preparation and installation crew that made the exhibition a reality. Scott Wixon, Dennis Schoelerman, Timothy Ross, Peter Costa and Ani Rivera, as well as the artist's assistants Mariano Boggia and Ryoichi Hayashi, led a skillful, patient and tireless team. The works and various materials that comprise them were shepherded to the Museum from international sites under the deft guidance of Assistant Registrar Victoria Hertz. Finally, it is an unusual dynamic between the institution and the individuals who comprise it that makes a historic event like this possible. The exhibition is in a real sense the result of the imagination and devotion of Germano Celant, Guggenheim Curator of Contemporary Art. As a critic and proponent of contemporary art for the last twenty-five years, Celant has provided much more than insightful commentary; he has helped to shape the field of play. As the Guggenheim moves towards the end of the century whose art it has set out to document, Germano Celant will be a key shaper of the institution's future purpose.

Thomas Krens

The Organic Flow of Art

Mario Merz's Kitchen, Fibonacci series from 1 to 5 (Cucina di Mario Merz, Serie di Fibonacci da 1 a 5). 1968
Neon tubes
Courtesy Gian Enzo Sperone, Turin

Merz at the Guggenheim Museum, New York, 1989. Photo by Hugh Hales-Tooke

Nomadic Cartography

In 1945, at the end of the war, I was in prison for political reasons, and I did a portrait of another prisoner, a man with a huge, red beard.... I never once lifted the pencil from the paper.... When I left prison, I went straight to the countryside to do some drawings of grass, the same way I did the portrait. But this time, I went outdoors in the morning and headed for the field. The period of drawing in the field was the period of marking, which continued from dawn to dusk, and always with the same method: I never once removed the pencil from the paper. I stopped towards sundown, and the fact that I had spent all day drawing that endlessly convoluted line, like a tangle of intestines, and never lifted the pencil, allowed me to think. I had spent the whole day thinking, following my thoughts and everything happening around me – for example, the twittering birds, the falling leaves, the distant rumble of a van. All these things entered the drawing, not in a natural way, of course, but as time, as a recording, as if the pencil lead were the point of certain instruments registering on a sheet of paper: the point keeps rotating, it records the humidity, the temperature, the noises, the sounds.[1]

In order to understand Mario Merz's artistic explorations, we must first review the ideas that molded his earliest works, earliest procedures, earliest impulses. By affirming the basic value of his linguistic matrices and process matrices, we can make his scope and horizon comprehensible. We have to start with his imprisonment for anti-Fascist views, during which time and afterwards he ventured into the labyrinth of drawing. In his drawings, he deposited, as if on a photographic plate, the results of his feelings about the world and himself. His exercises and practice brought forth a "portrait" and then a "landscape," both of which he drew without lifting his pencil from the paper. Together with subsequent equally important pieces, such as the 1952 *Leaf (Foglia)* paintings and the great 1963 painting *Crustacean (Crostaceo)*, done in Pisa, those drawings set up an ensemble of meanings which, when made evident, can define the future coordinates of Merz's artistic evolution.

More than anything, the combination of social commitment with the search for a personal and different language reveals a desire to participate directly in the liberation from various current ways of thinking and communicating. Merz intended to forge new perspectives. On the one hand, after joining the partisan group *Giustizia e Libertà* (Justice and Liberty) in the struggle against Fascist ideology and oppression, he was arrested and imprisoned. On the other hand, inspired by the same radical principles, he turned to painting in order to appropriate an alternative way of seeing. The correspondence between those two aspects already indicates a possible coalescence of political and cultural involvement, which led to a consciousness of the historical and individual situation. In this way, Merz achieved an identity as an intellectual and an artist, who, while not forsaking the truly personal, kept confronting or dissenting, relating to or synchronizing with the culture of his era.

The discovery of the cultural or artistic dimension, as historically determined by interaction with the "situation" and hence with everyday life, is confirmed by works that Merz did during his imprisonment or immediately afterwards, during the days of the Liberation. (Unfortunately, those pieces were lost or destroyed.) Still, the artist speaks of drawings he executed on any paintable or drawable surface that he managed to find in prison: wrapping paper, tissue paper, newsprint. He would draw figures or faces moved by internal agitation and a linear seething. These images, which gradually overflowed into Merz's surviving paintings of the 1950s, reveal a Surrealistic and Expressionistic conviction, typical of postwar painting, when Italian and European art tried to overcome its dilemma of being trapped between the extremes of Realism and Abstraction. That was the time of the Neorealist cinema of Roberto Rossellini and Luchino Visconti and the illustrational, propagandistic and narrative vision of a Marxian Socialist Realism. These approaches were confronted and challenged by the chromatic and linear essentialism of abstract art, which was starting to unmoor itself from the teleology of design and pure form, when the Bauhaus closed shop and turned into industrial technologism.

Merz attempted to sidestep the two risks by practicing his own form of brinkmanship between them: "1945: Is art a solitary

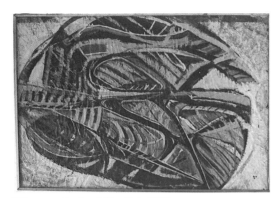

*Cat. no. 1, *Leaf (Foglia)*. 1952

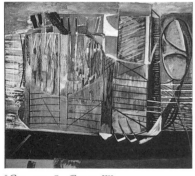

*Cat. no. 5, *Gypsy Wagon (Carrozzone)*. 1953

*Cat. no. 3, *Seed in the Wind (Seme nel vento)*. 1953

solution? Is art a public solution? Did art actually manage to unite two highly diverse ways of acting and achieve a compromise?''[2] Merz's prison ''portrait'' and his subsequent ''landscape'' stake off a territory in which his art seems to assimilate his environment: the prisoner among prisoners or the field in which the painter stations himself. The radius of action is entered by a contingent force, which is vital, because the artist has looked around and recorded his experience. But what is the method of his recording? Merz finds it in the seismographic process of drawing and painting: a face situated in a condition, closed or open, is transformed into a sensitive registering device, a sort of seismometer that can record or transmit, on paper or canvas, the emotional and environmental earthquakes that stimulate it.

This kind of immersion in everyday experience can last for whole days, resulting in just a single drawing, tortuous and intricate, made up of continuous lines and contours, translating the artist's inner changes, his reactions to a context. The arabesque is not planned; hence it is born not a priori but a posteriori, emerging as it does from the creative experience. In this way, it is characterized by its total subjectivity (the artist is the fulcrum of the sensorial and sensitive registration) and by its necessary objectivity (registration and recording), both of which are integrated and realized. The threshold of contact between the two is present time, so that the criterion of artistic implementability resides not in a future dimension of infinity and utopia, but in the contingency and necessity of the hic et nunc.

This invention of the landscape sinks its roots into the landscape itself, almost as if the artist were a nomad feeding on everyday life and living off the mobility of the territory he traverses. It is no fluke that Merz's line on the paper goes on almost infinitely, disrupted only by sunset and weather, and giving shape to a labyrinth that becomes an image. This demonstrates that the act of drawing, of making art, is ''existence in motion,'' a continuous moving and straying that involve the appropriation and deepening of the surrounding space – a *Verwinding*, to use a Heideggerian term. This anarchic and liberating passage led to the 1953 painting *Gypsy Wagon*

(Carrozzone) – a visual metaphor for a Gypsy attitude, which sees vagabonding through the world as a way of life.

According to this notion, art, for Merz, can be neither a transcendental and metaphysical representation nor a psychological reflection; rather, it is a passage from material to material, from the same to the same, in which the present and the occasion count, as does meeting oneself in motion.

A further deepening of the essence of this nomadism, in a ''time [that] continues and never stops...which binds up everything,''[3] was assigned to the *Leaf* paintings, done in 1952 and first exhibited that year at the Galleria d'Arte La Bussola, Turin. Such works, put in relation to the content and the historical moment in Italy, are large-format canvases, in which the oil paint is dense and fleshy, practically a living bark. Merz's technique is to create impastos that conjure up the entanglements of life. Those same colors form tortuous and intricate lines; they seem vulnerable to constant change, interweaving into small natural and vegetable entities such as rocks and sawdust. They signal a ''where'' composed of materials and signs, whose value is intrinsic, in the action of the hand or in its radius of intervention. Furthermore, the configuration of the image, the leaf, dissolves into the structure; hence it seems intent on exposing the skeleton and the veins and arteries rather than the vegetable surface. It is as if, for Merz, painting, the making of art, means acting in a void in order to fill it and thereby fill one's own existence. The artist is looking for existential organicity in the architectural and social structures. In fact, according to Merz's definition, ''the leaf had become a symbol; the symbol of the organic whole'';[4] it even adapts itself, as a real bark, to the structure of a wall:

Thus, leaves were enormous only because I realized that walls were big and leaves were attaching themselves to walls. I wanted to do a painting that would relate to the wall, not just to its internal image; and so the internal image adapted itself to the external relationship.[5]

And if the outside is adjusted to the inside, then painting too will follow gravitational forces, it will remain suspended on the wall like a creeping vine or it will rise from the ground, following the force of the wind:

My paintings should not necessarily be hung

The Welder (Il saldatore). 1956
Oil on canvas, 39 3/16 × 27 3/8"
(70 × 100 cm.)
Private Collection, Turin

on the wall, they can be placed on the floor or attached to the ceiling.... It's good for paintings to start occupying a position in space, just like a chair or a table, which are useful in everyday life.[6]

The cyclical and dialectical character of the leaf painting celebrates the degree of energy absorption in Merz's art, which strives to catalyze the field of sensations and environmental stimuli in which it is inscribed. His works thus reflect a development that assimilates the surrounding totality, linking up with the notion of growth and death, becoming a raw material of germination and proliferation. Rethought in terms of a contemporary perspective, which includes the igloo and the spiral table, the leaf painting is a perimeter or enclosure; it stakes off a territory made up of flakes and fragments, soils and colors, blending into a "bark," a surface of isolation and shelter, which, however, grows progressively, like a spiral.

In 1963, Merz executed that same surface of progressive growth on a canvas, a true catalyst of material and experience, by reversing and spreading out all the pigments he had bought in the city of Pisa during the course of a year. The accumulation produced a painting bark "fifteen centimeters [six inches] thick,"[7] which was scheduled to be shown at the Promotrice delle Belle Arti in Turin; unfortunately, it shattered. This opus testified both to the passage of time, one year, and to the artist's activity during that period. The consequence was a painting qua vortex, taking in all external and internal factors, traversed by stratifying data and visions that canceled one another out, transcending and negating one another. It was a black hole in space and time, where nothing was static or conscious. The viewer had to enter it and lose his way in order to verify it as an always open transmission network traversed by energies and signs: the pulsation of neon, with its discharge of light, which would pass through the jutting canvases and everyday objects, was affirmed several years later.

Nevertheless, before going on to Merz's great three-dimensional and architectural works, we have to deal with another background factor: the theme of light as a flux that illuminates and joins opposite polarities in order to create a unified physical and intellectual field.

In 1956, Merz painted several versions of *The Welder (Il saldatore)*, the figure of a nocturnal worker, illuminated by the whooshing blowtorch, which shoots out fire and cuts rails. The depicted light energy stands for motion and its speed; it traverses space and connects two instants or two positions, signaling an interval or making the duration and distance between two facts intelligible. Hence, it is a major instrument of consciousness; in fact, it "illuminates," it institutes the trajectory linking two points, fusing them into a compromise and making them participants in the same continuum.

This total field is a kind of energy cloud: "I see all my output of 1950," says Merz, "almost like premedieval painting, from an era in which painting, for the medieval world, meant entering a cloud...."[8] Here, the artist moves, finding the equivalence, the equalizing, of abstraction and figuration. The infinite possibilities of form are then explored from *Seed in the Wind (Seme nel vento)* to *Tree (Albero)*, both painted in 1953, which pass from Vasily Kandinsky's cult of the nonobjective image to Jean Dubuffet's figurative discursiveness.

The incursion across the frontier between figuration and abstraction helps us to imagine indistinct territories teeming with confused things, between painting and sculpture – things like branches and fronds, forests and trees, chestnuts and twigs. Every entity moves amid similar entities, yet is different because it presents an autonomous form and position while sharing the same osmotic pressure. Every entity has an umbilical cord, which ties it to the next one, placing it in sequence as in a series of numbers: we are approaching the neon numbers, according to the Fibonacci proliferation.

From the viewpoint of art history, the search for a continuum in Mario Merz's oeuvre from 1945 to 1963 not only reveals a harmony, an identification with the typical material of Dubuffet and Jean Fautrier; in its quest for organicity with the territory of experience and contingency, that phase of Merz's work evinces a clear analogy with the positions of Situationism, a politico-cultural movement that charged through Europe from 1948 to 1957, making strong headway in Italy, especially Turin.[9] In particular, his awareness of Situationism

Merz in his studio in via Santa Giulia, Turin. Behind the artist: *Untitled*, 1967
Canvas-lined wood, neon tube and metal, each element 94 1/2 × 78 3/4 × 31 1/2'' (240 × 200 × 80 cm.). Collection of the artist

came from his frenzied discussions, starting in 1960, with Pinot Gallizio, an artist from Alba. Previously, in 1955, Gallizio, who had already met Asger Jorn, had founded the International Movement for an Imagist Bauhaus, which advocated an antifunctionalism close to Guy Debord's Situationist propositions.

Merz has always refused to identify his paintings with the Surrealist and Informel figurations of Jorn and Karel Appel, Constant and Gallizio. He claims that his referent during that period was Jackson Pollock, saying that if you consider Pollock it's like Boccioni, but if you consider Appel, its like a certain degeneration of late Picasso, an Existentialism of the surface. Nevertheless, a certain correspondence with the methods of Situationism is obvious in Merz. A distinct rapport can be found in their mutual interest in the interaction between motion and the urban territory. In fact, in 1956, Debord spoke of the "drift" — a process of random and unplanned movement across various spaces, a movement also defined as psychogeographic. The idea is to identify a method of lucidly and dynamically accentuating an urban drawing, reacting to it in terms of the found situation. It is a process of letting go in a random field of energy, a street or a house, outside or inside, in order to find a possible appointment with a mental situation, that of an "experience" on which, subsequently, one can build a new habitat. This motoric denouement within a process of experiencing, of feeling found things in situ is, as we have seen, also shared by Merz; except that he does not express himself in kilometric paintings, like Gallizio, or in radiating and polycentric paintings, like Jorn. For Merz, making art consists of sowing a forest of inextricable and indistinguishable signs, giving life to a throng of words from the flow of inconstancy, in which gestures and things, put in circulation by the artist, have something of a winding motion that does not differentiate among the various energies. These can sometimes become perceptible and recognizable, in the guise of uncertain and changing figures (a leaf, a tree, the human shape, a Gypsy wagon, a flowery rock, a seed in the wind and so on). Nevertheless, the ultimate result will trace a strange and sometimes hazardous geography, delimiting a territory in which oppo-

sites, such as day and night, matter and concept, conscious and unconscious, are able to coexist.

Merz's paintings from 1949 to 1963 — emblems of his organic rapport with the world and the things around him — are verified even in terms of the artistic activities of that era: for example, European Informel as well as American Action Painting and Abstract Expressionism. What distinguishes Merz's works? Let us focus on a few telling examples.

While Fautrier's *Hostages*, 1944, and Dubuffet's *Texturologies*, 1957, with their materials and drips, try to evoke social phenomena, from Nazi massacres of prisoners to the teeming of urban crowds, Mario Merz's paintings insist on the values inherent in the everyday life of the solitary individual. Contrary to a known and familiar reality, Merz's paintings pursue the unfamiliar in everyday experience, the erotic, sensual osmosis with the environmental conduit found during his own journey. Fautrier and Dubuffet "document" a historical course, the rhythm of a life that, with a dramatic or candid, a critical or ironic eye, derives from the events of a culture. On the other hand, Merz, using himself as a sensitive needle, tries to draw a map in which the archetypes of the individual's feeling and living solidify as they move through differentiated territories. Thus, art for Merz is not a narrative; rather, it bears witness to an instantaneousness of time, which can last for days or even months: in a field or in the city of Pisa. Hence, the absence of any swift, rapid gestures that pour or trace signs on a canvas, à la Pollock and Lucio Fontana; instead, we find an obsessive repetition of a linear and chromatic drawing that tends to stop only "towards sundown." According to that attitude, the work is translated into a crucible, a vessel — two-dimensional until 1963; then, as of 1964, three-dimensional and architectural — in which are solidified the puffs and variations of natural and human energies surrounding the artist: these can be the figure of a prisoner, a leaf, or all the pigments bought during a year in Pisa. Unlike Dubuffet or Willem de Kooning, Merz is not trying to evoke the cruel or ironical enticement of landscapes and female bodies; rather, he wants to produce upon the canvas a trail of chromatic lava,

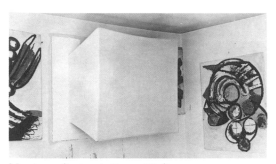

Merz's studio in via Santa Giulia,
Turin, 1965
In center: *Untitled*, 1964
Canvas and wood, 51 3/16 × 63 × 31
1/2'' (131 × 160 × 15 cm.)
Courtesy Galleria Gian Enzo
Sperone, Turin

Cat. no. 109, *Prehistoric Wind from
the Frozen Mountains (Vento
preistorico dalle montagne gelate)*.
1966+79

which, in its process of thickening, speaks of fullnesses and voids, of lines and networks, of visual diastoles and systoles, as registered in the course of a day by the seismograph/artist.

The resulting cartography is neither the fabulous and monstrous sensuality of a female body, again as in Dubuffet and de Kooning, nor the political tragedy of Fautrier or the anguished signs of Francis Bacon; instead, we have a flow of utterly undiscriminated color: a tangle of existential waves, in which Merz takes refuge – a habitat. When the latter becomes three-dimensional, the term for defining it is the igloo.

A final element distinguishes Merz from the artists of Informel and Action Painting: the fusion of the body of the artifice with the canvas is never disrupted. The contact is given not by dry, nervous gestures, like a Fontana slash or a Pollock drip, but by linear actions that tend to remain intact (the hand never leaves the drawing), as if they were united by a natural destiny. For Merz, art is thus intensified life, it unrolls with the forces of existence. It is a "breath from below," to quote Antonin Artaud,[10] a breath in which are stratified the energy currents that activate the vital contexts. Merz populates space and occupies the vacuum, evincing a silence of thoughts and sensations; he accumulates signs in order to set off an explosion of their comptemporary and cohesive force. He works on the field of energy in order to form groups of meaning, which take in even the insane moments of life. He unites or assembles their unusual and contradictory directions, giving them an unforeseen and astonishing fixity, which defines the work of art.

As of 1963: Crucibles of Earth and Light

It was in terms of the growth of condensation and solidification that the artist demanded a growth from the canvas. In 1963, he concentrated a six-inch layer of pigments on the surface. The painting jutted out; but, having become a bark or a crust of earth, it developed cracks and fissures, foreshadowing the clay igloo, which forms cracks upon drying. Merz thus had to abandon his system in order to make room for a different kind of jutting. He achieved this in 1964 when he constructed the *Untitled* series: white or colored canvases or wicker on

wood structures, from which shaped canvases jutted out in the form of a cube or truncated pyramid or roof-covered three-dimensional triangle. Of these "jutting forms," in white canvas or wicker two photographs remain;[11] they were taken in Merz's studio on via Santa Giulia, in Turin, which I had the good fortune to visit during that period. Vestiges of those paintings are extant, because the artist recycled them in later works: for example, *Prehistoric Wind from the Frozen Mountains (Vento preistorico dalle montagne gelate)*, 1965+78, painted yellow and traversed by a neon tube; and *Prehistoric Wind from the Frozen Mountains*, 1966+79, its surface painted dark brown on one side and silver on the other, pierced by a neon tube and placed on a heap of twigs, with Fibonacci numbers. Done in both white and colder colors, such works must be regarded as painting/sculptures, halfway between the two media. Their roots obviously go back to Merz's Pisa canvas, except that these painting/sculptures evince a growth and organic development, taking the form of a structure or volume that juts out towards the viewer. Technically, Merz executed these pieces by blocking a plane/surface on the ground and, with the help of steel clamps,[12] setting up regular or irregular stretchers covered with canvas or wicker. That same year, 1965, Merz exhibited them along with paintings in order to make them easier to read and to clarify their artistic process:

The works I made after everything else – the jutting structures – were determined by the presence of flat works. In the latter, the black sign, summary and flaking, functioned as a margin, and as such, it delimited the planes of the various colored surfaces, showing the need for further development. Thus, in dealing with the operative situation of form expanding into space, the flat paintings were like blueprints for works that are still to be carried out.[13]

The pictorial surface rises, forming a relief; it is experienced as a leap through space. Its rise indicates the pleasure of the fermentation that always activates creative energy, from dawn till dusk, and once again the next morning, and so on, from day to day. The sculpture, with its volume, thus surges from the painting, with its surface; and from this point on, it is impossible for Merz to separate them.

Cat. no. 18, *Untitled*. 1966

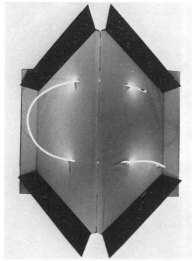

Cat. no. 22, *On the Street (Nella strada)*. 1967

Furthermore, the dilation of the painting in a convexity accentuates the impatient fullness of its growth. By 1965, the wealth of sensations that were initially registered by the line and the color could no longer be contained; these sensations kept swelling and tended to seek an epidermic fullness that produced effervescences, which Merz fixed in truncated pyramids or jutting triangles. This process seems to reflect the attempt of the painting – a blind and illusory window on the world – to open its shutters and let the light through.

Take *Untitled*, 1966, with its jutting shape, which is made of interwoven reeds: a fisherman's net basket, which has captured a neon tube, leans against the extreme end of the triangle formed by the shutters. In the *Untitled* series of 1965, which eventually was inserted into pieces done during the 1970s, the two lateral surfaces are painted with strips and stripes in such a way that the color glides from one to the next, both against and across it, thereby creating an effect that looks like rain, a natural phenomenon, like color, as an instrument for registering the environment. Both comparisons suggest a naturalistic reading of Mario Merz's art; but, as a closer inspection reveals, they are due to the subject matter, leaves and trees, that he used during the 1950s. It would be more interesting to point out that the material and natural metaphor prefigures an organic link between the Baroque discipline of a Borromini and the modernist cosmology of a Gaudí. For Merz, as we have noted, the artwork crystallizes from a trajectory or a parabola: it is based on two points, in space and in time. "My forms," says Merz, "have neither a before nor an after, even if each one of them is the history of what has been; moreover, in its potential for modification, each form is open to the future."[14] It results from a curve of the fall of the material, color, and so on, which produces an open design, as suggested by the movement. Here, space, as in the Baroque, is "that of travel, repetitiousness.... It dwells on the unusual, validates the ephemeral, threatens the perpetuity of order."[15]

The reference to Baroque methods helps us to understand the emergence of a linguistic elipsis in Merz's work, with the two centers, painting and sculpture; it also enables us to anticipate the favoring of the unwonted

decentralizing of things and elements (canvas + neon + reeds + color, and so on) and to announce the dynamics of the circle, in the igloo, with its possibilities of elasticity and multiplication.

But let us go back to *Untitled*, 1966, in which the elements reveal an energetic density, making it totally different from Merz's earlier pieces. Above all, we note that beyond the interweaving of the jutting structure, the wicker and the neon, this work has other peculiarities. The lateral surfaces have holes covered with scotch tape and revealing haloes that seem to indicate the use of fire. A similar physical and mental vertigo characterizes the installation *On the Street (Nella strada)*, 1967. The jutting form is no longer colored or made of wicker; now, it is a white and very tense canvas, ripped and traversed by a wavy neon line and framed above and below by metal bands. The osmosis between the parts is no longer based on the stratification of colors or the expansion of forms into space; it now derives from a transfer: the neon penetrates the volume, leaving rips on the surface and producing a strong energy contrast.

Both pieces thus concretize the work of an assemblage; they combine different symbolic and metaphorical materials, various meanings, allowing different realities to coexist. Ultimately, they produce a new vortex, which gathers various products of Merz's artistic language. These are extremely important balancing acts, confirming past motifs and introducing new values, partly in relation to artistic events that characterize Italy, especially Turin.

We must now look at the visual and linguistic aspect of Merz's work. The encounter of unities of discourse fusing into a whole that becomes a different object is part of the process of dislocation and disorientation triggered by the discourse of historical vanguards, from Dadaism to Surrealism. Flouting the orthodoxy of the Weltanschauung, it favors an iconoclastic and marginal vision. Furthermore, the recourse to constructed things (the jutting forms, the neon lines) or found things (the fishing basket) expresses a shift towards surprise, but in a contrary way. Augmenting the strategy of assemblage and interweaving, the focus thus swings towards a new texture of reality, bringing forth a different

Installation, Galerie Sonnabend,
Paris, April 1969, including
from right to left:
Sitin. 1968
Metal tubes, wire mesh, wax and
neon tubes, 7 1/4 × 21 5/8 × 25
1/2" (18.5 × 55 × 64.8 cm.)
Courtesy Kunsthalle, Düsseldorf
Untitled. 1969
Metal tubes, twigs and lamp,
70 7/8 × 70 7/8 × 39 3/8"
(180 × 180 × 100 cm.)
Collection of the artist
*Cat. no. 21, Horse Theater
(Teatro cavallo). 1967*

Installation, Galleria Gian Enzo
Sperone, Turin. January 1968,
including from right to left:
Carrier Cone (Cono portante). 1967
Wood and neon tube, 31 1/2
× 86 1/8" d. (80 × 220 cm.)
Collection of the artist.
*Cat. no. 21, Horse Theater
(Teatro cavallo). 1967*
Untitled. 1967
Bottle, neon tube and rubber,
27 9/16 × 19 11/16 × 9 11/16"
(70 × 50 × 50 cm.)
Collection of the artist
Cat. no. 26, Hamper (Cestone).
1967

sensibility, which is based on new relationships. The dynamism thereby obtained moves other meanings, which are based on the metamorphoses of things, changes and identities. The resulting effect is that of a semantic instability of substances and elements, as if plural meanings, shifts and performances in perpetual motion opened up before each object. The work becomes an active site of encounter, a metaphor for the conjunction of and penetration by signs, the birthplace of something new.

But in which direction does the crisscrossing of Merz's signs achieve its configuration? What is its cradle? How is it different from the Neo-Dada and Pop ensembles that circulated during the 1960s? The answers lie in the before and after of an Italian phenomenon: as of 1963, Turin saw the launchings of new information enterprises, such as Gian Enzo Sperone's Galleria Il Punto. While the Galleria Civica d'Arte Moderna had presented major retrospectives of the works of Franz Kline and Bacon in 1962 and 1963, these new galleries added Roy Lichtenstein, Andy Warhol, Robert Rauschenberg, Jim Dine and James Rosenquist to the artistic panorama experienced by Merz. The triumph of these artists in Italy was due to the Venice Biennale of 1964, which awarded its first prize to Rauschenberg. Along with them, articles on Minimalism in *Artforum* and *Art News* helped to bring an international context to the Turin art world. For decades Turin had mediated between Italy and France, concretizing its activities in exhibitions and cultural centers, such as Michel Tapié's Centre de Recherche Estétique in Turin. But now the Turinese focus shifted from Paris to New York. In this way, the dialogue highlighted a scene that was shared by or imbued with both Pop and Minimalism, yet conscious of possessing an inalienable European identity that was irreconcilable with any other.

The year 1966 marked the debut of Arte Povera, the theory of which was defined in 1967, with a search for continuous metamorphoses of languages, accompanied by a transmutation and proliferation that are different from any forms. The goal was to deviate from the absolutism of mass-media icons, those of popular culture, and to challenge in order to shatter the abstract and linear images of industrial, reductive and Minimalist perfection. Basically, this new

movement opposed a monolithic culture that excludes ambiguity and confusion, explosion and deconstruction, irresponsibility and material chaos, with all the psycho-physical reversals that these terms imply. The essence of this shift was the scattering of a potential of figures and images that could circulate in all directions, with no apparent coherence, aside from the iconoclasm of incoherence, as a method of working and creating.

The dissemination commenced in Turin during 1966 and 1967. In the course of one year, the Gian Enzo Sperone, Christian Stein and Notizie galleries held solo exhibitions of the work of Michelangelo Pistoletto, Pino Pascali, Alighiero Boetti, Luciano Fabro, Marisa Merz, Giulio Paolini and Gilberto Zorio, and group shows including the same artists as well as Mario Merz and Jannis Kounellis.[16]

In 1966, Mario Merz began responding and contributing to this new linguistic climate, with the concrete presence of the above-mentioned ensembles, such as *Untitled*, 1966, and *On the Street*, 1967. Their fullness was intensified not only by the interweaving of discordant entities, but also by the addition of a concrete subject – light in the guise of neon, as a disruptive energy. The theme of light, say fire or a radiant substance, iconographically present in Merz's *The Welder*, 1956, was a common legacy of Italian artists from Futurism to Spatialism. But it was only with Fontana's *Structure for the Ninth Milan Triennial*, 1961, that neon, with its coldness, entered the art system, to be followed in 1963 by Dan Flavin's gold fluorescent tube. These two artists defined a different use of light as subject matter.

In 1949, Fontana, following the premises of Giacomo Balla and Umberto Boccioni, introduced light as a new device, in *Spatial Environment*; akin to the cut or the hole in the canvas, light helped to create a space or route of maximum flexibility. It is a fluctuating substance, unlimited, unbounded, which the artist, with a gesture, uses to cross the environment. It therefore aimed at upsetting the pictorial space, turning it into a traversable phenomenon. However, Flavin's statements refer to the tautological value of light as an icon, an "anonymous and inglorious" entity, presented by means of fluorescent tubes, their monochromes

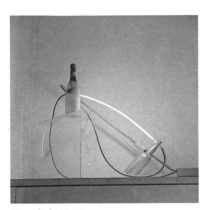

Untitled. 1967
Bottles, rubber, neon tube and spray
paint, 23 5/8 × 27 9/16 × 15 3/4"
(60 × 70 × 40 cm.)
Collection of the artist; Courtesy
Gian Enzo Sperone, Turin

Cat. no. 20, *Horse Theater
(Teatro cavallo).* 1967

ranging from gold to pink, from cool white to red and blue. They are technological totems, virtually endless columns (*Gold Diagonal* was initially dedicated to Constantin Brancusi, hence to his *Endless Column*), which, consistent with Marshall McLuhan's theory, are paeans to the discovery of light as pure information.

For Merz, in contrast, light is a fire, creating combustions, altering the composition of the elements, producing tensions by piercing and ripping. Moreover, according to the natural symbolism accompanying it, light/fire renews the alchemy of the parts, to become an instrument of penetrating knowledge (in 1972, the Fibonacci numbers were written in neon) and a motor of periodic regeneration. On the other hand, it is also a vehicle, putting the parts in contact with each other, uniting them, suggesting new totalities.

The summary nature of two discordant entities was confirmed in another *Untitled*, 1966, which I saw in Merz's studio on via Santa Giulia. This piece consisted of two jutting shapes on triangular bases; made of wicker, they were placed near one another, thus constituting a sequence, both of them linked by a horizontal neon tube, which pierced one shape, the space between them, and then the second shape. Aside from aligning the objects and making them visually compact (fire is an alchemical *coniunctio* accompanying all processes of modification of material), light has a pictorial character, altering the colors of things: *The neon, which casts its violent light on the canvas shapes, also has a sense of violence, which alters the very colors of the materials of paintings. It is not the problem of color per se that interests me, even though the neon changes the colors of various materials without transposing the image, which is what happens in paintings.*[17]

Fascination with light is always evoked by a concrete and material anti-illusionist vision. It releases a true gaze by revealing the resources of the materials and their performance. It strikes the surfaces and activates them, qualifying their essentiality, giving them life, naming them, and thereby turning them into writing. (*Objet cache-toi, Sitin* and *Solitary Solidarity [Solitario solidale]* were done in 1968, one year after *On the Street*.)

If the principal goal is to interweave

multiplicity in order to release its wandering energy, Merz's 1968 show at the Galleria Gian Enzo Sperone, Turin, revealed the vast breath of the artist's new course in relation to objects. He exhibited works dated 1966 and 1967; two of them, *Horse Theater (Teatro cavallo)* and *Hamper (Cestone)* contained jutting forms, while others, *Carrier Cone (Cono portante), Lance (Lancia)* and *Untitled,* involving bottles and neon, did without them completely. The use of the word "theater" makes *Horse Theater* a presage of a future evolution that will introduce a continuous variability and mutation into the movements of the actors, that is, the components of a work. Nevertheless, those features associated with the word "horse" retain something animal-like, something natural: a feeling that anchors them to an uncontrolled vital sensibility. In addition, the word "theater" also implies the directorial role of the artist, who is called upon to prearrange an activity that celebrates energy and movement, images and performances. The ensemble is formed by a pillow painted red (in other versions, it either is white or disappears altogether), an uncovered iron structure (recalling the jutting forms of the paintings of 1966-67) and two neon lights, a wavy tube on the wall and a linear one on the structure.

The materialization of a whole, producing a "theater," inspired Merz to look for a "dramatization" that would open variants to the kaleidoscope of combinations and grafts on the wall. The "performers" demonstrated agility and movement, dropping down and propping themselves on the floor. They practiced a relationship with the totality of the environment, crossing it without becoming entrenched. "In my opinion," says Merz, "art is the only thing that allows us to get through things and to be a process of traversing rather than an arrival."[18] *Horse Theater* thus unhooks the work from the wall and defines an independent space that has removed the canvas, hence the genre of painting, from the jutting structure, and that tries to put greater emphasis on the encounter of figures of neon light and the figures of the everyday object, the pillow.

Indeed, that same exhibition included *Untitled*, 1967, which consists of a bottle leaning against a plexiglass cube and pierced by a neon tube. This complex object

Pierced Glass and Bottle (Bicchiere e bottiglia trapassati). 1967
Bottle, glass, plant, spray paint and neon tube on wood, 9 13/16 × 35 7/16 × 13" (25 × 90 × 33 cm.)
Collection Pierluigi Pero, Milan

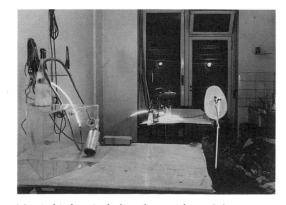

Merz's kitchen including from right to left:
Untitled. 1966-67
Chamber pot, clamps and neon tubes, 27 9/16 × 15 3/4 × 11 13/16" (70 × 40 × 30 cm.)
Collection Angelo Baldessarre, Bari
Untitled. 1967
Bottles, rubber, neon tubes and spray paint, 23 5/8 × 27 9/16 × 15 3/4" (60 × 70 × 40 cm.)
Collection of the artist

is part of a series of 1967 installations in which neon joined forces with an umbrella, a glass and a bottle, a raincoat and a chamber pot. These pieces are blocks, which, by suggesting a different system of associating things, draws different meanings from them.

Top priority was still given to the continuity of energy, already present in the paintings done in 1953: "I think that in nature, the elements all crisscross one another."[19] Almost as important was the theme of lightning, which electrifies things, placing them in a field of different energy. However, lightning also transfixes; it resembles a *Lance*, 1967, penetrating bodies and modifying them internally.

A further meaning originates in the encounter of two registers: the object and the neon light. They have to yield the meaning that is theater and the representation of a coupling in which each loses and gains identity. Everything moves along a line of dialectics: on the one side, marginal objects tied to an organic and corporeal functionality, which speaks of drinking, urinating, dressing, getting soaked by rain – in sum, living in a daily and common rhythm; and on the other side, the cold, technological abstraction of light, an instrument for exploring the dark, a scientific and sacred device. Both possess ample virtualities of signification between conscious and unconscious, material and immaterial, being and nonbeing – the legacy of an ambiguity sought by historical vanguards from Pablo Picasso to Marcel Duchamp, from Kurt Schwitters to Salvador Dalí.

However, as we can note, Merz does not pick a strange and unusual object, selected for its exotic character or industrial force; he prefers objects found at home or in a corner to those coming from somewhere else. He circulates his everyday devices, such as his raincoat, then his car, as aids for living. Indeed, as in his drawings of 1945 to 1949, he is always the center and fulcrum of aggregation and sensory elaboration in an external stage decoration: the spectacle arises from the trajectories traced by *his* objects.

Ultimately, in this network of associations, the object and the neon light are invested with a flurry of meanings that make them oscillate between dream and reality, painting and sculpture, libido and concept.

...for instance, the empty wine bottle traversed by neon. It was something of an invention – that emerging spurt of wine represented by light, instead of painting. Rather than painting that spurt, I emphasized the effect of explosion and flight. It became very sensual, but also nonsensual, because it was reduced to a line.[20]

At times, either the neon, or the tip of the lance, or the bottle is covered with red pigment. For Merz, sculptures always remain paintings, but his colors continue to evoke a mobile and active vital force. Red recalls fire, coursing blood and wine. It again implies the process of modification and generation, inciting to action and warming up the interiors of bodies. It is also a symbol of warrior ability as well as passion and sensuality.

In *Raincoat (Impermeabile)*, 1967, the two intersecting neon tubes that perforate the raincoat (which Merz discarded after using it) were covered with touches of red pigment. They thus evince the artist's inner force and energy as well as his explosion on the outside. This is an artist who identifies himself in the artwork as his habitation and habitat, the raincoat, but who is ready to leave it or set it aside, like a nomad, in order to reach new things. The force of this raincoat is poised disquietingly for all of Merz's creative activity so far. It is his shadow and his imprint. If he left it behind, he would be virtually removing his gaze from the territory of his body, in order to ignore its temporal course. The raincoat thus becomes a presence, dropping from period to period into the work, emphasizing the artist's mobile body, which leaves enigmatic clues in space. A neat, meticulous reflected image emerges in 1972, 1979, 1981, up to the recent *Turbine (Turbina)*, 1988, displaying the estrangement that grazes the artist when he tries to manifest the place of his experience: the body of life. The raincoat is the echo of this body, which is reborn and finds itself again, made recognizable because it is still traversed by energy: the light that is a continuous awakening and illumination.

Merz's view differs from that of Bruce Nauman. Both began using neon in 1966, but with diverse goals. The California artist thinks in terms of decorative culture, he refers to advertising slogans and the cityscape filled with luminous writings. He

What's To Be Done? (Che fare?). 1968
Metal pot, wax and neon
5 13/16 × 19 11/16 × 7 7/8"
(cm. 15 × 50 × 20.21)
Collection Musée Departemental
des Vosges, Epinal

Sitin. 1968
Metal tubes, wire mesh, wax and
neon tubes, 7 1/4 × 21 5/8 × 25
1/2" (18.5 × 55 × 64.8 cm.)
Courtesy Kunsthalle, Düsseldorf

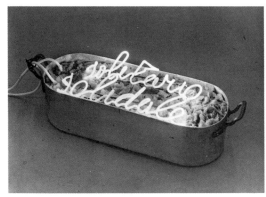

Cat. no. 35, *Solitary Solidarity
(Solitario solidale).* 1968

listens to Las Vegas as a place of energy and attempts a poetic response, which places the artist at the center; his statements and writing which relate to the street signs and street advertisements:[21] *The True Artist Helps the World by Revealing Mystic Truth,* 1967, designed for a window or a wall sign, or else for an extraterrestrial slogan that exalts the artist himself, in *My Name as Though It Were Written on the Surface of the Moon,* 1968. Thus, neon is utilized as a potency for information and publicity, able to accept any and all messages. Rather than accelerating the energy, neon cools it down, triggering an implosion of meaning, producing an evanescence of the medium itself for a circularity of the artist's lyrical and poetic thought. Nauman works on his transformism, opting for a writing that, in a world of nonexistence, such as advertising, reintroduces the corporal existence of an artistic being. This is the very opposite of Merz, who uses that being in order to transcend the distinction between a world of shadow and a world of substance so as to join them together and unite them. Hence, it is not employed as a phantom or absence, but as a gestural and vital presence (the course always seems free and subordinate to the gesture of the hand, as in a drawing); it injects an erotic component, a passage between various bodies with different sensualities. It is something in between, an intermediary that unites and provokes a libidinal spark, a pleasure that passes through the individual subjectivity. That is why Merz's neon is put to an amorous use, conquering or conquered. It is both ephemeral and solid. It fuses grace and strength, fatness and skinniness, satisfying all experiences. It guarantees the circulation of pleasure between lovers, because it makes the boiling of sensual energy pass from one body to the other.

The Gentle Movement of the Igloos

This is the same boiling found under *Hamper,* 1967, shown in Amalfi for the exhibition *Arte povera + Azioni povere:* a pot of water boiling under a cut cone of wicker. Akin to light, water runs; hence, it recurs in Merz's oeuvre as in *What's To Be Done? (Che fare?),* 1969, shown at L'Attico in Rome, and *The Drop of Water (La goccia d'acqua),* 1987, shown in Bordeaux. Water, here, symbolizes regeneration, raw materi-

al, vitality, incessant movement. Side by side with neon/fire, it creates a sharp polarity, a contrast, thereby producing yet another fertile pair. However, it was also a political boiling in 1968 that disrupted civil society, triggering a crisis in behaviors and languages, in attitudes towards power and the family, and inflicting a deep wound on a static society, making it mobile and filling it with conflict. That was the year in which the old social contradictions fused with the revolt against the authoritarian power of one generation over another. The year 1968 brought the explosive rejection of a philistine culture, which failed to recognize the "other" – from the female to the homosexual. This phenomenon, leaving its imprint on all cultural models, had a worldwide diffusion. People spoke of a revolutionary imagination, an image of power and a universal renewal. The references were to all languages, so that art, too, was affected, undergoing a tremendous but salutary shock. It opened up to multiplicity, no longer categorizing itself as painting or sculpture; it went into the streets and into the deserts, calling its adventures Arte Povera, Land Art, Body Art, Conceptual Art. It was a period of feverish experimentation, which liberalized the creative processes.

Merz, too, experienced the abundance of that time and, as a good seismograph, he registered the situation, integrating it in his work, for example, in *Sitin,* 1968, and *Solitary Solidarity,* both 1968 – titles deriving directly from actions, events and graffiti of the May uprising in France.

The meaning was politico-existential, the writings were inserted on a wax stratum, which filled up, or a net or in a pot. That is why they were the nutriments, both intellectual and physical, of a society as well as an individual. At the same time, the writing, when placed upon the object, dominated it, tried to make it disappear. It was almost as if the idea and the utopia, the project and the dream, written but not experienced, betrayed sensitivity and delicacy. Merz's reading was meticulous: illusion crumbled, because it was mental, cerebral, and not experienced; it remained an *Unreal City (Città irreale),* 1968.

Still, we are left with the awareness that the idea or the written commitment can annul the world, so that words replace reality,

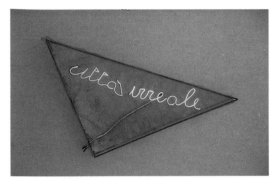

*Cat. no. 40, *Unreal City*
(Città irreale). 1968*

Cat. no. 31, *Giap Igloo – If the Enemy Masses His
Forces, He Loses Ground; If He Scatters, He Loses
Strength (Igloo di Giap – Se il nemico si concentra
perde terreno se si disperde perde forza). 1968*

occupying it until it ultimately disappears. Merz feels the danger of opening art to the dominion of the thinker and the ideologue, which was emphasized by the arrival of Conceptual Art on the visual scene. Merz reacted by minimizing the efficacy of the idea qua word, which could easily devour the object, and by constructing a real world: the gallery.

I made the igloo for three overlapping reasons. First in order discard the jutting plane or wall plane and create a space independent of the process of hanging things on the wall or nailing them to the wall and putting them on a table. Hence, the idea of the igloo as the idea of absolute and self-contained space: it is not modeled; it is a hemisphere placed on the ground. I wanted the hemisphere to be nongeometrical, so the hemispherical shape created by a metallic structure was covered with sacks or shapeless pieces of material such as soil, clay or glass. Then I began the work of writing on this structure. I felt it was so important to be able to write in an absolutely static form like neon.[22]

Linkable to the cabins and domes of primitive and historical structures, the igloo[23] reveals the essential function of delimiting a territory or an environment between inner space and outer space. It works with limits, such as the perimeter of a painting, marking the boundary between full and empty. It is a magnet, accumulating tensions and weights, thoughts and gestures, whose osmosis is energetically defined with the breath of the circumference, which, being elastic, vibrates under the pressures of clay or glass. As a den and a cathedral of survival, shielding against winds and artistic stress, the igloo is the image of the nomad and the vagabond, who believes not so much in a secure object as in a dynamic and contradictory existence. As we have already emphasized in regard to Merz's works of the 1905s: for the nomad, existence means moving in a context and reinventing for oneself an osmosis with food and nature, landscape and local people, without crystallizing as anything definite or stable. By the same token, his structures are not likely to endure; rather, they emerge from the accumulation of items necessary for his survival. Merz, a nomad in painting, became a builder of igloos:

You have to construct in a way that is antithetical to present-day models. Construct with processes of development and withdrawal, by deploying willpower and subduing will power, in a natural breath, day and night. The materials are chosen from one time to the next, dictated by fate, by the location, by the adjacency of other elements, by the plants.... Constructing is an hour-by-hour and day-by-day need to fuse your will with everything that is dispersive in life.[24]

Accordingly, construction becomes an interpretation and humanization of territories; it is no longer felt as a place of passage and parking, but as a field of sensibilities. The erection of the igloo thus responds to personal and social needs, while remaining open to symbolic and cosmic interpretations. The dimension of the igloo is mythical and moves through time, which is why its re-creation preserves the engima of an active but spent life. Thus, the clamps and arches forming its bark or defensive crust can bear painted glass and mats, bite and fix canvases and twigs, gather stone slabs and glass, car doors and wax surfaces. Everything is reduced to the enigma and magma of nomadic energy, in which signs form images that combine miserable yet vital and present materials.

The earliest igloos, *Objet cache-toi* and *Giap Igloo (Igloo di Giap)* were made in 1968 and were installed that same year at the Deposito d'Arte Presente, Turin. *Giap Igloo* bore the sentence *"Se il nemico si concentra perde terreno, se si disperde perde forza"* (If the enemy masses his forces, he loses ground; if he scatters he loses strength). The first igloo was a semicircular structure bearing a net on which Merz had placed lumps of clay that eventually dried; the words *"objet cache-toi"* (object, conceal yourself) were written on the clay. The second igloo was made of lumps of clay held together by cellophane bearing the Giap script. In the system of political and sensory hopes created that year, 1968, the mutual support between the affirmation of a closed and compact hemispherical world, the metaphor for an individual habitat, and the assumption of a collective consciousness by means of the harmony of writing demonstrated that, for Merz, art has never been a happy island, an art for art's sake that does not participate even minimally in the historical parabola; rather, it is a speaking and

Merz incising *Traces (Tracce)* on wall in San Benedetto del Tronto, 1969

Traces (Tracce). 1969
Incisions on wall in San Benedetto del Tronto

*Cat. no. 49, *Igloo Fibonacci.* 1970

acting, the responsible occupation of space that does not indicate the risk and danger typical of strategy. Giap, a Vietnamese general, and the artist, both of whom think of mounting an attack on all the structures of political or visual oppression, not simply in terms of violence, but in terms of force in a dialectical relationship with the enemy and the context.

As a place of salvation and energetic declaration, the igloo is a pure testimony to trust amid insecurity. Merz regards the artist's destiny as an essentially anarchic enterprise, which rejects any kind of authority or set of rules, proliferating where there is no security. It is a way of life and thought, it can proceed lightly and swiftly, it is a double skin that shields the artist's ideal body.

The igloo is the ideal organic shape. It is both a world and a small house. What interests me in the igloo is that it exists in the mind prior to being implemented: an organic idea is not yet organic in the absolute; it first has to be realized. Next comes the problem of organizing a structure that is as simple as possible. Architecture is a construction for refuge, for giving human beings a total dimension.... The igloo is a synthesis, a complex image, since I thoroughly torment the elementary image of an igloo, which I carry inside myself.[25]

Merz manages to define the dwelling-less place that gives rise to the solitary consciousness of a unique and complex self-expression that is not tied to any norms aside from that of a process of growth and grafting on the root stock of the cultural plant; in so doing, Merz lends lightness and clarity to that cultural plant. In *Never Has Stone Been Raised on Stone (Mai alzato pietra su pietra)*, 1968, the lumps of clay are replaced by lumps of cloth, while the writing places art outside the realm of brutal physical work, transforming art into a delicate, sensual activity with a strong female component; after all, the idea of the lumps came from Marisa Merz, whose presence henceforth fundamentally marked her husband's oeuvre.

If indeed the igloo is a starting point for fantastic and energetic radiation as well as self-absorption, its image can magnetize all sensibilities. It repels gazes in order to defend itself, but takes them in for a dialogue, turning opaque or transparent, rigid or dry, covering itself with glass and twigs, delicate and frail when clad in wax or canvas, defensive and aggressive when coated with broken glass. Hence, the igloo is an open entity, which accepts the fact that inside and outside are one and the same, just like love and hate, friendship and enmity. The dialectics introduced into Merz's first drawing ultimately became architecture, a habitable vessel, functioning as the same alembic of sensations and experiences; it is a cup (an upside-down cup) that gathers the dust of its wanderings upon its shell.

The igloo is a subject devoted to a relationship with architecture and landscape. It gathers a place and a time, but since it does not put them in order, it is drawn to chance and disorder. It works on blendings and it shatters the habitual configurations of Cartesian thought, because it brings out unforeseen articulations. It is a passerby, living the rhythm of the city and its chaos. Its existence is made up of vestiges and fragments, and it never admits the phenomenological rigor of Minimalist objectivity. The greater attention paid by Merz to his environmental situation is thus not free of sensorial effluvia, it touches the world in its flesh and bone. The igloo is an experienced scrap.

In opposition to the rigorous enunciation of Minimalism, the igloo establishes a gnoseological and mental contact with space and architecture, devoid of smudges and imprecisions. During those same years, the sculptures of Donald Judd and Carl Andre, the environments of Sol LeWitt and Flavin resisted any interference. They culminated in pure signs and volumes, imbued with an absolute industrial and geometric sublimation. Minimalism followed a phenomenological doctrine, describing, as it did, constructive modalities and the procedures of appearances. It purified the results of art, reducing them to their formal essentiality, relating them to their primary generality. The study of such eidetic phenomena leads to an awareness of artistic method and process, but reduces them to sheer appearance, thereby almost eliminating the difference between shadow and substance.

Merz secures himself against that risk, utilizing a primary form (the sphere), but not relying on its metaphysical purity or its conceptuality. He loads it with the imprints

Installation, Walker Art Center,
Minneapolis, January 1972

*Cat. no. 55, *Iguana*. 1971

of a precarious and delirious truth, transforming it into concrete but also enigmatic knowledge. For the Italian artist, the notion and phenomenon of a form, its logic and conceptuality are momentary factors. Together with Franz Kafka and Marcel Proust, authors whom Merz read as a teenager, he believes that evanescent and ephemeral data guarantee a greater intensity. Thus, he opposes the maximum topographical precision of Minimalism with a maximum openness to the accidents and randomness of a trip through the things of everyday life and nature.

In 1969, an utterly frail and dissonant location was offered by the Galleria L'Attico in Rome, where Merz exhibited pieces involving glass, twigs, wax and stucco. Each work participated in the unique environment: an old garage revamped into a gallery, where Kounellis had presented his live horses. In this space, Merz installed ten pieces, including: *Wood Shavings (Truccioli)*, 1967-69, a bale of hay with a neon tube; *Small Parcel (Il pacchetto),* 1969, a sequence of dusty panes illuminated from behind; *Nugget (Lingotto),* 1969, a truncated pyramidal structure surrounded by twigs, its peak occupied by a block of wax; and *Automobile Pierced by Neon (Automobile trapassata dal neon)*, 1969, a gray Simca 1000, with a Swiss license plate, which, after being driven by Merz for years, wound up as an artwork (like the raincoat), with a neon tube stuck into its roof.

Compared with the previous show in Turin, the images displayed in Rome tended towards liquefaction, moving from the transparency of glass to the frailty of stucco and wax. In their thrust towards a dissipation of the object, these works introduced nets and twigs, hay and bamboo, and brought back water (*What's To Be Done*), while presenting the constant leitmotif of the nomad, this time in the avator of a car. The effect was that of a discharge into a bright, windy, airborne landscape of leaves and shrubs. These were floating transparent entities, which, nevertheless, formed a territory, whose memory quivered with rural poetry, that of Italy and the Piedmont, as described by Cesare Pavese.

The calm presence of the twigs running under *The Bridge (Il ponte)* of bamboo and glass formed a throng that surrounded the wax nest in *Nugget*, introducing a subsequent naturalistic metaphor for the course of life as well as the flow of the seasons. The latter affirmed the value of transience, the eternal return of a beauty of absolute temporality.

The awareness of finding an irrevocable presence in the frailty and ephemeralness of the elements helps Merz to display the strength that thereby becomes transparent rather than defending itself from behind the shield of an idea or writing. The clay igloo with a neon sentence yields to *Untitled*, 1969, the igloo of plaster, twigs and broken glass, likewise shown at L'Attico:

When I made it [the igloo] of soil, I put a neon tube on it, but I added nothing to the glass igloo, because it was utterly clear, it is simply a problem of transparency: the fact that inside and outside are one and the same.[26]

In becoming transparent, the igloo became penetrable, revealing its availability and its courageous willingness to expose its interior, while maintaining its hazardous nature in the glass shards, which the artist sees as kindred energies: "Broken glass is like a friend for me, not an enemy or stranger."[27]

The exaltation of the transience of twigs and the opacity of glass, with jagged, broken outlines, speak of a time that wanes slowly, striving to make a way for itself, like light through glass:

The exhibition also included glass that I had found at a glazier's place. Those panes were covered with dust, and I coated them with plaster which made them very heavy, in contrast with the idea of glass, which is light and transparent. The light set up behind that group of panes was mellowed and, at the same time, it became very distant.... It had to make a tremendous effort to get out.[28]

Each element enhances the value of the existential and natural limit, rejecting the immense machine of industry with its metaphysical notion of progress.

Thus, there is no room for a concept of eternity and fixity; like the glass panes and fragments, the elements merely lean: leaning signifies rising and depositing with the notion of retaking. Those are the three irrevocable factors in Merz's oeuvre, which continually rises, deposits and reclaims its ensembles in order to install them elsewhere. It makes no difference if during this interesting and adventurous movement, the materials, such as glass, stucco, twigs, rocks

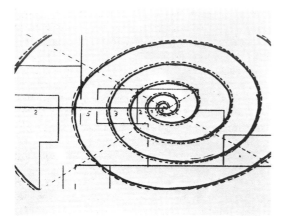

Drawing from Merz's book
Fibonacci 1202-Mario Merz 1970.
1970

*Fibonacci Progression on a Staircase
(Progressione di Fibonacci
su una scala).* 1971
Staircase and neon tubes
Private Collection, Turin

and so on, adapted to a specific moment and context, are dispersed or even destroyed – such is their fate. They will be replaced by others, equally precarious, which will be sacrificed to a new igloo, that is the same as or similar to the preceding one. For Merz, each construction is equivalent to another, because it lives the life of a branch, flowers and dries out, is lopped off, but is then reborn. Thus, it reemerges in a different form, with the same sap, and it can ultimately create a forest, like the forest made up of dozens of igloos at the Kunsthaus Zürich in 1985.

What's To Be Done?; also shown at L'Attico, Rome, in 1969, was a plaster sentence attached to the wall over an open faucet, from which water ran continuously. Those words come from "What's To Be Done?," a speech given by Lenin in 1912; however, their artistic import touches on their roots in the infinity of an unstoppable mutational process like the running of water:

This water faucet must have as its value the importance of the water, which runs out in relation to the sentence "What's to be done?," two things that are again in mutual suspension. For me, "What's to be done?" means: What is really to be done, in a meaning that is not directly significant, but probably that of the water. I did What's To Be Done? two times, once in Rome and once in Amsterdam, in March 1969, at the Stedelijk Museum, where, using a blend of earth and oil, I wrote out "WHAT'S TO BE DONE?" in gigantic letters. This piece was shown together with Unreal City, *1968, which was very close to* Never Has Stone Been Raised on Stone, *1968, which means: my unreal city, our cities are unreal, suspended in the void.* [29]

After Rome and Amsterdam, in the summer of 1969, Merz went to San Benedetto del Tronto, to execute *Traces (Tracce)*, a sequence of seagull footprints carved out in the inner wall of a building, leaving a trail from the floor to the window:

In San Benedetto del Tronto, I was walking along the beach when I saw the footprints left by gulls with three toes. I copied those footprints on the wall, using a hammer and chisel – a trail running up from the floor and going out the window. [30]

Merz continued his experiments with the infinity of a "walking towards"; the following year, when he first started using the

Fibonacci series, he did progessive numbers that could individuate an organic infinity. He still had to develop the animal subject, already present in *Horse Theater*, 1967, and then recurring during the 1970s. The use of animal symbolism involved the representation of a primitive and archaic mentality rooted in the depths of the unconscious. In *Traces*, it is purely a metaphor for the artist/painter, whose light tread across the sand or wall can leave indelible and almost countable traces, like the toes of a seagull.

The Organic Numbers

Primitive tribes do not have the concept of number, which is too abstract for them. Rather, a number is perceived – heard, seen, smelled – like a sound, a color, a smell; it is an aspect of matter. At most, such people have an awareness of quantity, based on aligning an image, so that the meaning of "forest" is communicated by a repetition of the tree figure, "crowd" by the repetition of the human figure, and so forth. [31] It is quite simply a matter of counting. *Traces* in San Benedetto del Tronto was a trail of footprints, scanning a quantity and an intensity. This rhythm was repeated in Bologna in 1970, on the occasion of the exhibition *Gennaio 70* at the Museo Civico, in the alignment piece *Propped (Appoggiati)*, 1970, a sequence of glass panes perforated by a line of neon tubes and leaning against a wall. Each unit is assigned a place in the natural series of groupings, whereby each pane becomes an ordinal number, which Merz writes in white on the glass; but, eschewing the normal sequence, 1,2,3,4, 5,6,7,8,9, he follows the Fibonacci series. Fibonacci was the nickname of the medieval Italian mathematician Leonardo da Pisa, who wrote *Liber abaci*, (1202, republished in 1228). The series he devised is both vegetable and biological, since the numbers virtually constitute sets of parents who give birth to the following children: 0,1,1,2,3, 5,8,13,21,34,55,89, 144.... This series can be used to calculate the offspring produced by a pair of rabbits within one year; the couples bear according to the Fibonacci series.

Merz's glass panes in Bologna add up to thirteen, and the sequence runs to 144; but their proliferation subsequently continues in New York, at the auxiliary space of the Sonnabend Gallery, and at the Kunstmu-

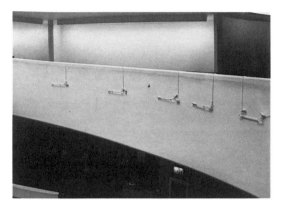

*Cat. no. 50, *Fibonacci Progression (Progressione di Fibonacci)*, detail. 1971

*Cat. no. 57, *Acceleration = Dream, Fibonacci Numbers in Neon and Motorcycle Phantom* (Accelerazione = sogno, numeri di Fibonacci al neon e motocicletta fantasma). 1972

Cat. no. 53, *Fibonacci Proliferation (Proliferazione di Fibonacci)*. 1973

seum in Lucerne, thereby becoming a sequence of sequences:

I did this work because it corresponds with the proliferations of the natural and corporal elements; for instance, we have a nose, two eyes, five fingers, etc. This series is biologically conceivable; hence, the work has a direction and real roots. This series is not a mere fantasy; it is used in computers, by mathematicians and architects; so I thought it would be possible to create relationships with it; I made continuously transportable signs that contain it and assume it.[32]

With the possibility of the Fibonacci numeric writing, Merz individuates the possible organic limit of an infinite voyage. He manages to give that limit a hardness and solidity akin to the lines or colors of his earliest paintings or the stratification in his Pisa painting. He presents "something" that is not a conceptual or theoretical abstraction. (Merz sympathizes with this conceptualism, but does not feel it, he assigns it a weight and a physical relationship, between vegetable and animal, with reality). For this reason, even the numbers, like Merz's panes of glass, lean on the ground, the wall or the ceiling; they are always anchored to the architecture. All they can do, as natural instruments, is to creep, like shrubs and leaves, along the solid surfaces of any edifice. They transform it into a trunk with thousands of branches and twigs, on which, quite naturally, we also find animals: in 1971, at the John Weber Gallery, New York, the sequence of numbers on the wall was led by an iguana.

In Merz's hands, the flexibility of creeping numbers offers a fiber for weaving and sewing together the fragments of the world. This thread infiltrates newspapers and glass, tables and walls, objects and paintings, rooms and stairways, galleries and museums. Tying them together, it integrates them in its warp and woof, an artistic texture. Like animal semen, it is a fecund sap, giving birth to new beings.

In relation to the history of art, it is a linear energy, similar to the Gothic and to Art Nouveau, which imposes its vegetable laws on buildings. Moreover, this fiber/sap/vine/number is the pivot of a naturalist cosmogony that contains references to Lucretius and Virgil, to Leonardo da Vinci and Caravaggio. The growth of numbers forms a net for capturing the landscape. We must

bear in mind that light is also a lance, and that the artist is a nomad warrior, for whom assault is consistent with their characteristics.

In 1972, Merz was given his first chance to do an installation at an American museum, the Walker Art Center in Minneapolis, which enabled him to approach the world by means of an assault, an attack, from the base of the museum.

The strategies of sensorial occupation took off from *The Key of the Fibonacci Series*, that is, the number sequence 1,1,2,3,5, and continued with that environment of *Function of Fibonacci from 8 to 28,657*. The numbers ran up the stairs, marking the doors and elevator shafts, forming the *Proliferation of Fibonacci Numbers from 1 to 377*, following an iguana on the wall, settling on a cloth igloo *1 + 1 = 2*, and accompanying a procession of newspaper bundles aligned on the floor and alternating with glass. The title of this last work is *Proliferation of the Positions of Newspapers on the Floor from 8 to 144*, because 8 was the next number in the sequence, and it followed the seventh and last step in the stairway.

No architecture succeeds in forming an incursion of numbers, creating an empty space around them in order to leave the central space to the igloo and the periphery to the iguana and the newspapers. Both signs, the igloos and the newspapers, interest Merz because of their extreme position in the communication system: one suggests a wordless motion devoted to hearing; the others are "reproductions of words and thoughts,"[33] recalling Merz's first drawing, which was published in 1949, in the Italian newspaper *L'Unità*. The time involved in a Fibonacci piece is the procession of the numbers, which, according to the medieval mathematician, are open. Change is constant; indeed, it is the very substance of their growth. With them, Merz reconciles continuation and heterogeneity, widening his radius and increasing his encounters with situations. His propping is characterized by a huge multiplicity and an indivisible pace. A contemporary chapter, involving the use of the Fibonacci numbers, is the recourse to the spiral, an evocative figure that can be seen in the vegetable kingdom (grapevines) and the animal kingdom (seashells and snails).

Cat. no. 66, *it is possible to have a space with tables for 88 people as it is possible to have a space with tables for no one.* 1973

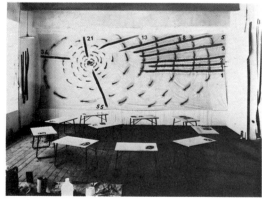

Up to 55 People (Fino a 55 persone). 1976
Mixed media on canvas, plaster, tables and spray paint on paper, variable dimensions
Collection of the artist

Merz used the spiral in an unrealized project for the Haus Lange, which was designed by Mies van der Rohe in Krefeld. It consisted of a drawing, published by Sperone in *Fibonacci 1202 – Mario Merz 1970*: this drawing, starting at the center, the crossroads of the lines uniting the four imaginary points of the house, developed in the form of a spiral for the inner rooms and outer spaces of the edifice, which was transformed into a museum. The artist's goal was to act upon this outline, intersecting the works with the walls – a threat to the traditional method of exhibitions. The plan did not work out. However, Merz did execute his New York threats, writing them on glass panes:

These writings were a series of threats. These threats were initiated in Krefeld when I found the Haus Lange by Mies van der Rohe and I thought of making an object that would relate directly and indirectly to the building; I wanted to make an object that would be inside and become the opposite of this so perfect edifice. That was when the spiral came into being, and together with the spiral, I began thinking of the threats to space. I did the threats in a space on the Bowery. The sentences are: "Does square space threaten round space?"; "Does round space threaten square space?"; "Is the plan thus round or square?"; "What is a house, is it a shadow on the ground or an unclear fraction of space?"...[34]

The helicoidal spiral differs from the flat spiral; symbolizing a labyrinth, it evolves from the center and then curls back into the center. In this way, it implies both directions of movement, birth and death, positive and negative. In nature, it is visible in the seashell; it also exists in man-made form as the Solomon R. Guggenheim Museum in New York, designed by Frank Lloyd Wright as an upside-down conch, with its belly towards the sky.

In 1971, on the occasion of the Guggenheim International Exhibition, a proliferation of neon numbers was assigned to the outer face of the ramp, stretching on into the hollow. It was visible, indeed legible, from the ground floor, from bottom to top. The effect was almost magical: the numbers ran along the balustrade, expanding organically. One had the impression that they would never end, because Wright's spiral suspended them aloft, projecting them to-wards the skylight, the outside, where the artificial neon light fuses with natural light. This was no threat, but an organic love relationship with Wright's organic architecture. Nevertheless, says Merz: "My goal was not to pay tribute to Frank Lloyd Wright. I wanted to reveal our ability to make contact with things. Europe is not conceived of as moving towards the American future. The fact is that we Europeans experience reality in a different way."[35] The proliferation thus demonstrated and allowed onlookers to visualize that Fibonacci was the inspiration for the architect of Taliesin and his museum discourse. This work

has the power to lighten walls and crush the numbers proliferating across the mural current and make random things of the photos, paintings, mirrors, works on paper, and all the other objects inside the building. These numbers made the entire building a bit silly – and that is their horrible secret.[36]

By placing the neon numbers along the inner balcony of the edifice, Merz revealed a precise reading of Wright's architecture, which, in the Guggenheim Museum, inverts the design procedure of the nineteenth century since it conceives and constructs from inside to outside.[37] Finally, for both Merz and Wright, the walls are a husk functioning as a natural defense – hence, unthinkable in terms of an abstract concept. As the architect said, his sense of the wall was not as the side of a box. It was a refuge against bad weather or heat, wherever necessary. But it was also the vehicle for bringing the outside inside and allowing the inside to project into the outside.

Today, Merz is still using the visual catalyst of the neon Fibonacci numbers for reading either the transfiguration of his architectural positioning, the construction of the igloo, or the rules and methods of architecture and hospitable landscapes. He has looked everywhere for opportunities, revealing a numerical repetition, which signifies an interpretational renewal of spaces.

The museums of Krefeld and New York were followed, as sites for installations by the Antiche Prigioni in Pescara in 1976, the dome of the Mole Antonelliana in Turin in 1984, and the project for the outside of the Guggenheim Museum, now, in 1989. In all these installations, the proliferation of numbers, sometimes accompanied by an object,

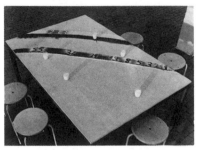

A Sum of People is a real sum a real sum is also a serial sum a serial sum is a form human beings have a serial function as history the serial extension of paintings gathers a serial sum of human beings the spiral forms of fruit are serial sums of quantity we invite you to come on (...), 1973, at (...) o'clock to a serial function of the art academy. 1973
Wood, spray paint and glasses of milk, variable dimensions
Courtesy Akademie der Künste, Berlin

such as a crocodile, shatters the silence of a facade or curved envelope, giving them a rhythm and scansion, occupying them and making them conquerable. Furthermore, this proliferation demonstrates that the numbers, like animals or shrubs, creep anywhere. They are agile and liable to take any position, like paintings, which "do not necessarily have to be hung on a wall, they can be placed on the floor or attached to the ceiling."[38] The circularity of languages and artistic media, of culture and painting, has become total; all frontiers and limits have fallen, so that objects and images, paintings and materials can follow all possible and imaginable trajectories. In 1979, a crocodile, always followed by neon numbers, crept across the ceiling of the Museum Folkwang, Essen. And in 1972, a motorcycle, that strange mechanical animal with horn-shaped handles, charged across the wall of the rotunda in the Museum Fridericianum, at *Documenta 5*; the title of Merz's installation was *Acceleration = Dream, Fibonacci Numbers in Neon and Motorcycle Phantom (Accelerazione = sogno, tubi di Fibonacci al neon e motocicletta fantasma).* The goal of the incursions is to keep the outlines of indefinable frontiers and limits alive in the system of art. No one can bank on a closed and protected perimeter or frame, because at times open spaces, crossings and streets, are the most interesting and problematical routes.

In this area, Merz, since the 1970s, has been finding accomplices in Joseph Beuys and Kounellis, in Daniel Buren and Maria Nordman, in Fabro and Michael Asher, all of whom have enlarged the horizons of our surroundings; they have thereby discovered widening paths and histories, opening up their visual possibilities and complexities. These artists have enabled us to witness a symbolic exegesis and structuring of the possible linguistic intersections of both the anthropological and architectural environment. Under the pressure of our surroundings, each artist particularizes an aspect in order to make it intelligible. The critical consciousness of this phenomenon varies from one society to the next, from Europe to America, sliding towards an inquiry into the primitive magic or perceptional and functional implication of architecture. That critical consciousness focuses on the histori-

cal and symbolical stratification as well as on the emptiness and the material, starting with natural light and with sound (issues raised by California artists).[39]

Merz favors material writing in and with the environment, exalting the mise-en-scène of a concrete event more than his own project and its analysis; he bases his method on a definition of common practices linked to vegetable growth, to human and animal physiology and biology. Rather than turning his back on vital reasons and issues, he takes them on. For deciphering his environment, he prefers using a naturalist symbolism of a global, indeed, universal character, so that the decoding proceeds on levels of primary exegesis. As we have already underscored: for Merz, the key to interpreting architecture comes from within it, from the elements surging and wallowing on the inside. We have already compared the igloo to a cup or bowl, a container for liquids and food, for which the problematics of food, as visual and architectural energy, should come as no surprise, partly because feeding oneself nourishes the élan vital, reconciling with the existential and artistic continuum.

Paintings with Paws

Working on the visual conversion of the numerical progression, after the objects and spaces, Merz began basing the Fibonacci sequence on the mobile quantity of human beings. In order to function as an act of quantitative homogeneity, the capacity for individuating any of their routes or contexts was anchored to feeding – an energy process that focuses on the consumption and enumeration of food (fruits and vegetables arranged according to the Fibonacci series were first used by Merz in Naples in 1976). The artist produced the concrete physical perception of such a quantity of human numbers – *A Real Sum Is a Sum of People*, 1972 – by inviting people to dinner at a Turin restaurant or drinks at a London pub: first one guest, then a second, then two, three, five, eight, thirteen and so on. Seated at the table or the bar, documented photographically, each group comprised a number in the Fibonacci series. The flow of people produced a collateral effect: the artist realized that while the human bodies multiplied, occupying a progressive space, the same was not true of the tables. The tables remained indifferent, never synchronizing

Cat. no. 81, *Prehistoric Wind from the Frozen Mountains (Vento preistorico dalle montagne gelate).* 1977

Cat. no. 80a, *Nature Is the Art of the Number (La natura è l'arte del numero).* 1976

with the number of guests, never adapting to and taking in the extent of their presence. Yet such a reception is psychologically important. According to Ronald Laing, the world can be synthesized "in the difference between a receptive environment and a nonreceptive environment, being welcome and not being welcome".[40] In other words, the environmental condition has a psychological impact, space acts upon the psyche,[41] triggering happiness and subjection, power and security, rejection and abandonment. Space is not merely homogenous and isotropic, conceptual and geometric; it is a material that protects and envelops; it is a physical extension of the self (yet another reference to organic architecture).

However, not all perceptible environments breathe with us, drawing in and out, changing because of us, altered by our bodies and our presences. Some are monolithic and one-dimensional, never moving or fluctuating. Now just what is a table and how is it to be represented? Merz chose to draw it as simply as possible: "I used the two-colour system, horizontal and vertical colour in which the horizontal is the plane or surface of the table and the vertical is its support."[42] The code is pictorial, recalling the medieval iconographies of Masaccio's and Giotto's frescoes, and it is therefore very primitive. Yet it brings the object or sculpture back to painting: a table is a painting with paws. The awareness of remaining within the precincts of art thus allows the artist to leave reality and step into the impossible and the fantastic. The tables began to grow, multiplying their support plane; they recall Duchamp's idea of making a Readymade in which a painting would function as an ironing board; it reminds us of the tradition of painting and its large formats, from Pollock until today. *I wanted to make the most objectivized table possible, without bringing in any abstract cultural games. The table is a basic discovery and instrument. It is a square or rectangle in which the spaces are determined by the quantity of space occupied by each person. I calculated 50 centimetres per person as a standard measure.... I didn't represent the people, but I represented the space that a person occupies, so the first table is 50 centimetres square and the sequence follows proportionally.... I was trying to create a relationship between the space of the canvas*

and real space. The space of the canvas is unreal, but the spatial measurement is real. The question is: Is it possible to make a canvas of this kind? In reality it is possible.[43]
In 1973, at the John Weber Gallery, New York, Merz constructed: *it is possible to have a space with tables for 88 people as it is possible to have a space with tables for no one.* This installation realized his plan for an organic growth of tables: in a spiral design, he arranged nine tables with progressively widening tops that bore the neon numbers 1 to 34. Thus, the total number of seated persons was eighty-eight. The progression ended because the gallery space was not large enough to hold more tables; if the sequence had gone on, it would have collapsed, like the Pisa painting in 1963.
In Berlin, at the Haus am Lützowplatz in 1973, the tables followed a physical growth, emphasized by the numerical presence of stools, but greatly exalting their pictorial aspect. The support surfaces were traversed by portions of the colored spiral, which was red, like the lance, the wine and the light of 1967, in which the Fibonacci numbers appear in the negative. And his tables were once again painted red in the large painting at the entrance to the Cascina Ova, in Tortona in 1974. The painting *Boards with Paws Become Tables (Tavole con le zampe diventano tavoli),* 1974, restores the breath of painting, which the artist had never fully abandoned, although he seldom practiced it from 1967 to 1974. Thus, because of the impossibility of controlling the concrete imaginary nature of the tables, whose growth was becoming unreal, Merz went back to representing the imaginary. He compensated for that impossible growth:
Then I felt I couldn't do any more because making those tables was a tremendous jolt with reality. So much so that in order to express the same thing quickly you can take a piece of paper and make a little drawing of it, precisely to avoid that jolt with reality....
Anyway, this jolt with reality was so terrible that I said to myself; art is really a phenomenon that absorbs the jolt, softens the blow. It's true: think for instance of a medieval town, built with such enormous effort on the part of a whole community. Then along comes a painter and reduces the whole thing onto a little panel; he gets everything onto a tiny piece of wood.... Since the real table

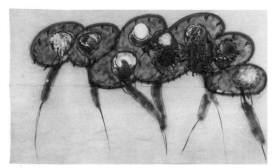

*Cat. no. 89, *Nine Vegetables
(Nove verdure).* 1978

Cat. no. 102, *Do the Houses Walk
Around Us or Do We Walk Around
Houses (Le case girano intorno a noi
o noi giriamo intorno alle case?).*
1979

exists, I can substitute the representation.[44]
During the period from 1974 to 1976, the paintings of tables were done in various media: oil on canvas in *Untitled*, 1974; verdigris or copper sulfate (green liquid pesticide applied to grape vines) in *Tables (Tavole)*, 1976, on the rough walls of the International Pavilion at the 1976 Venice Biennale. Ultimately, the game of alternating between green and red created a dynamic polarity. Green symbolizes the vegetable kindgom and, together with the alchemical red of the burning fire (the food, the people, the wine around the table), it reaffirms the regeneration of forms and energies. In 1985, Merz constructed his huge red paintings for public use at the enormous green meadow of Parc Lullin in Geneva.
The proliferation of tables created the proliferation of canvases. The numbers were regenerated on the canvases as well. In *Up to 55 People (Fino a 55 persone)*, 1976, ten small tables based on the Fibonacci series, the latter painted in the negative, were placed under a painting of centrifugal circles radiating lines and numerals up to 55. On the other hand, *Stopgap Leaves (Foglie tappabuchi)*, likewise 1976, offered the same sequence, but linked it to images of shrubs. The growth of numbers was tied to the expansion of languages as well as surfaces. The shrubs leaned against the walls and the canvases, electrifying their functions and vocations. This reacquisition of the intensity and freedom of painting was accompanied in volume by the formal explosion of the tables and the pictorial explosion of the igloos. The reciprocal confines jumped, and each influenced the other. The table took on a triangular form and entered the igloo in *On the Table Which Plunges into the Heart of the Igloo (Auf dem Tisch, der hineinstösst in das Herz des Iglu*, 1974. Or else the igloo turned black and tarry; or else the same black was used to draw the surfaces of tables, rendering them as wall drawings in Berlin. At times, the table stretched out in a spiral, with glass, rocks and twigs: *Untitled*, 1976. Or the interior of the igloo took in rocks, plaster and glass: *Igloo – Paving Stones and Broken Glass from the Destroyed House Reactivated by Art in a Gallery – in a Museum (Igloo – Pietre del selciato e vetri rotti della casa distrutta riativati per l'arte in una galleria/in un museo)*, 1977. Or else

it involved a wedge of broken glass, propped and transfixed by light, as in *Propped*, 1970.
As of 1975, Merz had more and more opportunities for shows, and the possibilities of propping his pieces in museums and galleries impelled him to travel more and more to new and diverse places. Trips from Berlin to Basel, from London to Milan, from Turin to Essen were marked by the igloo, which became the focal point of equilibrium and radiation in Merz's artistic precinct. He used the igloo like the Navaho wigwam or the Mongolian yurta[45] as a cultural value that provides a support for living and surviving. Referring to the societies and cultures that Merz experienced – German or Swiss, British or Italian – the igloo was charged with moods and impressions induced by whatever the artist discovered in situ. Thus, in the isolation of his Berlin studio, Merz darkened his igloo, covering it with black tar and blocking its relationship to the outside world. However, this relationship was soon restored by the presence of transparent panes when the igloo was presented as a social mechanism: at the Haus am Lützowplatz; or by including urban fragments, a car door, in *Evidence of 987 (Evidenza di 987)*, 1978, at the Galleria Antonio Tucci Russo in Turin. The linguistic capacity of the igloo is maximal, and the interrelationship between the internal and external factors helps to determine its environmental recognizability. Thus, the igloo becomes visible in order to take in a participatory process in regard to the city, the culture, the art system, which never ends. Igloos too form a proliferation. It is no use trying to fix the process of formation and information a priori: that process is continually found.[46] Although an objet trouvé, it has a mode of existence that is sometimes personified by way of the memories of experiences in the territory that has been traversed. It is a sign and a dream of encounter. Two poles fusing and confusing the creative function and the gnoseological function.
I claim that the igloo is inhabitable and that thus it is easy to arrive at the idea that the igloo has a close rapport with people. From my experience I have seen that people love it because they understand immediately its real and cosmological vocation.[47]
The artist wanders freely, and so objects

The Bridge (Il ponte). 1969
Bamboo, glass, plaster, twigs and metal tubes, 59 1/16" × 16' 4 7/8" (150 × 500 cm.)
Collection of the artist

Small Parcel (Il pacchetto). 1969
Metal tubes, glass, plaster and lamp, 11 13/16 × 51 3/16 × 51 3/16" (30 × 130 × 130 cm.)
Collection of the artist

travel, too: the iguana and the crocodile overcome the force of gravity as they crawl over walls and ceilings; the raincoat again signals halts and stages; the jutting forms of 1965 are reintegrated in topicality: *Prehistoric Wind from the Frozen Mountains,* 1978; the paintings link up with twigs, forming a simultaneous whole, in which every element depends on every other, circulating in all of them.

In the vast neoclassical room of the Museo Pignatelli, Naples, Merz installed *Nature Is the Art of the Number (La natura è l'arte del numero),* 1976, in which all his texts resonated in mutual interpenetration. An igloo made of glass, twigs and stone was at the center, radiating a curvilinear iron table in the shape of a spiral and tongs: leaning on the tabletop were neon numbers, twigs and glass, as well as fruits and vegetables, piled or arranged in a progressive order. Several table legs stood amid packets of the newspaper *Resto del Carlino* of Bologna, which bore neon numbers continuing the Fibonacci sequence.

There are many zones of interference in this piece: the igloo runs into the table, the table into the newspapers, the fruits into the twigs, the stones into the glass and so on. Each item, as in Dadaist and Surrealist transmutations, becomes "other than itself," whereby the individual perceptional codes intermingle, so that the totality is imbued with an overall synesthesia. However, the encounters, for the first time, give way to an operatic whole, which takes the form of a primitive village or a huge seventeenth-century set decoration. It is almost a translation of the fantastic paintings of Grünewald or Bosch into reality and architecture.

The reappearance of naturalistic subjects, such as fruits and vegetables, recalls a distant realism of Merz's paintings of the 1950s, claiming, as it does, to represent the world by means of the world, outside the common notions of painting and sculpture, including those of the Dadaist assemblage, which Merz takes up in an aggressive and polemical way. The inclusion of real produce in his oeuvre expands the possibility of testifying to the transience and ephemeralness of life. Produce does not resist time, it dries out or goes bad and is then replaced. Object "naturalism" from Duchamp to Rauschenberg is universal and ideal, while

Merz's is particular and concrete. The Italian artist identifies nature with history, but excludes the authority of its permanence: the object is historical because it does not remain, it is consumed and it perishes. Merz accepts the data of reality in its rawness; reality is that which is neither comely nor homely, nor interesting to interpret. All we should do is accept it and prop it inside ourselves. Fruits and vegetables, from lemons to tomatoes, from pumpkins to beans, have an offensive beauty: they seduce with their colors and shiny, delicate skins, with their fragrances; but then, when time consumes them, they repel us; squooshy and wrinkled, rotten and foul-smelling, they bear a resemblance to life and death. It is particular time that is narrated, the hic et nunc of a historical experience that brooks no distinctions or hierarchies of value, because it relies on the "truth" of a fruit or vegetable, which possesses a natural time. Merz has always been opposed to a descriptive painting "of history"; he has chosen the drama and tragedy of living "in history." Along these lines, one could state that the artist intends to refashion himself in terms of a realism whose positions are those of Caravaggio's. He thus makes a moral and political commitment as an artist, and also reveals his polemical and critical character in confronting formalist and classical art, from Minimalism to Neo-Expressionism. As a good observer of truth, Merz believes solely in the history of the factual given, whatever it may be, as in wall works like the painting *Nine Vegetables (Nove verdure),* 1978, or floor works; *The Island of Fruit (L'isola della frutta),* 1976, which comprise the entire process of maturity and aging, life and death.

The passage of time is cannibalistic; every minute devours the previous one, projecting itself into it and introjecting it, in a continuous feeding, just as the table devours the igloo and the newspapers devour the table: information eats forms, but the latter submerge in thought and news. *At the Villa Pignatelli, the newspapers actually represent the force of expansion, the twigs the force of cohesion, the igloo the concentrated weight of a dome. Nineteenth-century landscapes always have a powerful shadow that comes from the forest, a powerful light that comes from the plain, a powerful expansive panic that comes from*

Wood Shavings (Trucioli). 1967-69
Bale of hay and neon tube,
59 1/16 × 31 1/2 × 27 9/16"
(150 × 80 × 70 cm.)
Collection Musée Departemental
des Vosges, Epinal

Cat. no. 43, *Automobile Pierced by Neon
(Automobile trapassata dal neon).*
1969

the sky. These three powers together produce the landscape. This, we may say, is a real landscape, a true modern landscape, with electricity, newspapers, twigs, glass.[48]
The precise topography of a landscape or grove, a blend of woods and architecture, streets and gardens, demonstrates that Merz's work has no archeological value, this is no dig in the history of contemporary legend. The fruit island is an atoll in a huge archipelago, with flourishing gardens, like Pratolino and Bomarzo, and fairy-tale imagery. It is a reservoir of marvels and wonders, a *hortus conclusus* of medieval remembrance, where the tumultuous speed of Merz's imagination and his hand give breath to prodigious and unwonted apparitions. He thereby takes up the pre-Renaissance tradition[49] of visualizing prodigious places and creatures, associated with the labyrinth of the forest and with the underworld. The presence of such monsters (Latin *monstrum* means "marvel")[50] marks the history of art, recurring as an aesthetic and iconographic motif from Mannerism until the present, in Bosch and Giambologna, in Grünewald and Goya, in Arcimboldo (to whom Merz, in 1987, dedicated a large painting involving wicker, glass, fruit, and a silver crocodile) and Chagall, all the way to de Kooning.

The appearance of fruit became important for me, from an existential point of view: I am impressed by the tremendous reproductive capacity of nature.... Faced with the enormousness of a thing, such as a heap of fruit, you are bound to discover something similar to innocence. You have to rediscover an elementary imagination and a kind of innocence inside yourself, since emotion is something truly upsetting.... I can understand Leonardo da Vinci's problem: he had to comprehend nature and depict it as emotionally as possible.... When the painter's hand becomes nature, it represents the imagination.[51]

Not surprisingly, as of 1976, Merz moved from constructing an imaginary, indeed fantastic landscape to painting or depicting a fauna of portentous animals and extraordinary beasts, which henceforth roamed plains and mountains, vistas and cliff walls (in galleries and museums) during the artist's vagabondage. The inclusion of animals was part of the hunter's panorama. The fantastic zoology, going back to the

Late Paleolithic, from Altamira to Lascaux, was affirmed in relation to the voyages of the Phoenicians and the raids of the Celts; it was used by Dürer and metaphorized by Beuys. The sources are thus ancient, but the sensibility is contemporary. What makes these motifs attractive is the exaltation of the poetic nature of the elements, their mythical and mysterious character. Nevertheless, Merz does not indulge in any meticulous or controlled observation of his animal morphology; he is interested in the fantasy value, not the scientific meaning. His creatures are organic in terms of his notion of landscape and nature, forests and mountains, history and time. They come from far away to achieve a resemblance, participate in his portrait, in the line that began in 1945. The memory of their existence is topical and contemporary, because, at the time of their depiction, 1976, when art, with Neo-Expressionist painting and appropriation, Transavantgarde and Neo-Fauve, with the citation of history and the eclecticism of images that come from his past, Merz looked back to prehistoric times, to archetypes and primeval images. Rather than reworking, refiguring history, he returned to original exemplars, not in archeological or monumental terms, but from a critical vantage point: that of the artist living in his own time, in his contemporariness. Fundamental to grasping this direct and immediate coexistence of past and present, memory and topicality, is the painting *Prehistoric Wind from the Frozen Mountains*, 1977.

The "prehistoric wind" is something that removes the purely physical aspect of the wind, offering a sense of time that every man has inside himself: the sense of prehistoric time is that of a gigantic time which manifests itself as a kind of wind. The frozen mountains are a poetic expression for glaciations. My work is always linked to time, to the sense of time that occasionally contradicts the realism of current time, resembling, instead, a metaphysics of time. Time is the path on which humanity is bound to live and the history of being history.... The night of humanity is the animal, especially the most ancient kind.[52]

This canvas shows the image of a mountain or erupting volcano marked by the Fibonacci numbers and with a leaning forest of twigs. The impression is that of a landscape

35

Crocodilus Fibonacci. 1972
Stuffed crocodile and neon tubes;
crocodile 71 5/8 × 23 1/4 × 15 3/4''
(182 × 59 × 40 cm.); with neon 72' 2
1/4'' (2200 cm.)
Musée National d'Art Moderne,
Centre Georges Pompidou, Paris

Rhinoceros (Rinoceronte). 1980
Mixed media on canvas and neon tube,
118 1/8'' × 16' 4 7/8'' (300 × 500 cm.)
Private Collection, Turin

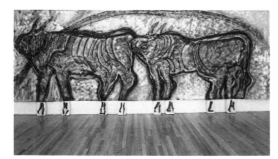

*Cat. no. 146, *Bison (Bisonti)*. 1982

with a mountain looming above the forest. Above all, the twigs

represent the woods, but they are also interesting in that they represent a totality, a numerical series. They are close together, thus creating an intensely emotional situation. If you take a tree and isolate it, you have something very poignant and fantastic.... Art is recognized more by imagination than by escape and scattering.... The vivacity of fantasy is fantasy itself: it is not subject to any normal process. It has sudden discharges that set up new image problems. Because some images seem to move more swiftly than others, which are stable.... For me, painting is velocity.[53]

The twigs return, together with the title, *Prehistoric Wind from the Frozen Mountains* in other works about time and the swift flow of images. In 1979, at the Museum Folkwang, Essen, they were inserted into the *Untitled* works of 1965, while *Crocodile (Coccodrillo)*, 1979, offered shrubbery to conceal the moving reptile. As of 1979, Merz's paintings of animals formed a fantastic herd, joining the parched, aggressive plain of the igloos and tables, covered with stone and glass, crawling over walls and through rooms containing terrestrial systems, mathematical writings and migrant natures. A legendary fauna and flora developed, actuating a spatial merry-go-round, two-dimensional, three-dimensional, subjecting fantasy to the banality of everyday life. In this circulation of nocturnal figures such as the owl, or portentous figures such as the lion and the tiger, the dream of a prehistoric wind becomes reality. *Old Bison on the Savannah (Vecchio bisonte nella savana*, 1979, *Rhinoceros (Rinoceronte)*, 1980, *Cervidi*, 1981--these creatures live in forests, plains, mountains, they seem to have come down to the threshold of the igloo: solitary and autobiographical evocations of a both archaic and current genesis. *Mountain Lion (Leone di montagna)*, 1981, can represent the fate of the artist, a loner on a mountain peak, gazing at his illuminating investigation, his organic thought: the Middle Ages claimed that the lion came into the world with his eyes open towards the sun.[54] Sharing the same bellicose attitude is *Tiger (Tigre)*, 1981, which has more powerful instinctual thrusts – sudden movements, which make him more aggressive and dangerous. However, these animals have a

diurnal vision, which is soon joined by the nocturnal vision of Merz's *Owl (Gufo)*, 1981, and *Nocturnal Animals (Animali notturni)*, 1981, which close the natural circle.

As animals, these paintings go around the architectural obstacles, crawling over walls, jumping and loping on ceilings, nervously passing through space, like the painting *Untitled*, 1981, which, at the ARC/Musée d'Art Moderne de la Ville de Paris, ventured up to the skylight, together with its twigs. Merz bends them and adapts them to all situations, because he wants to *shatter* the immobility and perceptional rigidity of painting.

Beyond tying them to the ground, I see my paintings crawl up the wall. They promptly turn into a creeping crocodile or lizard. They are the gecko with its perfect anatomical balance that hovers on the wall.

I very much want the canvas to creep rather than being on the wall in a decorative sense. And since for me, the crocodile is a mythically enlarged gecko, it can represent paintings. The canvas becomes a gecko and vice versa, and they both creep along the wall.[55]

And, like a gecko, Merz's paintings wind through all sinuosities, bending to the turns and accidents of architecture. His paintings stop where the wall stops – *Billiard Hall (Sala dei biliardi)*, 1981 – or replace the wall, thereby creating their own structure: *Sphinx and Chickenlike Predator (Sfinge e rapace gallinaceo)* and *Gecko (Geco)*, both 1983. The horizon of the twigs, with its memory of forests and savannahs, woods and fields, sees the moving twigs, imposing and rapid, with their blazing and explosive colors, swiftly sprayed or violently squeezed out of the tube and upon the canvas. These two techniques – swift spraying or direct application of pigment on the canvas, which is never mounted on a stretcher, join the artist's hand in sharing the risk of error and astonishment.

The decision to work in this way on the execution and the continuous surfaces, which can adapt or submit to the environment, ultimately demonstrates the naturalist and animal character of Merz's artistic project. Unlike Kiefer, Merz does not try to perfect the world, expanding his historic strokes, the dramas of his legends and massacres, because he has already analyzed

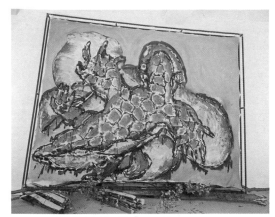

Cat. no. 159, *Gecko (Geco)*. 1983

Painter in Africa (Pittore in Africa). 1983
Wire mesh and neon tubes, 98
7/16 × 78 3/4" (250 × 200 cm.)
Courtesy Galleria Christian Stein,
Milan and Turin

and expiated them politically and ideologically. And unlike Baselitz, Merz does not attempt to confront the problem of verisimilitude in order to force it to a crisis by turning things upside down pictorially and visually. Rather, Merz prefers to reach the profound waters of the imagination, moving at high speed in order to avoid being shattered. Still and all, his attitude cannot be regarded as romantic. His *prestissimo* is that of the metropolis, where the individual moves in an evanescent and foreign manner; where memory is lightning, an instantaneous eruption of images. Certain images manage to get composed into figures: a landscape, a face, a leaf, an animal. Everyone lives in them, because, as Paul Valéry puts it, "we are enclosed in an eternal fragment of ourselves."[56]

Naturally, Merz is fully aware of the risk involved in his unreal existence; as a result, he sometimes violates its silent and circumspect shifts, immobilizing them by transfixing them with a neon arrow: *Crocodile in the Night (Coccodrillo nella notte)*, 1979, and *Rhinoceros*, 1980. He also proposes them anew as cognitional icons (neon, we recall, illuminates and also symbolizes the critical consciousness), for a painting that philosophizes about the beloved world. The luminous arrow is the index of a descent into the secret profundities of the unknown, the seat of the imagination's power. Indeed, neon is assigned the task of offering the poetic writing of the artist. It cools off the words written by a mysterious creature, a strange nomad who passes through *Places Without Streets (Luoghi senza strada)*, 1979, or *Arrives at Borders*, 1983. A warrior and a poet who identifies with Giap, the Vietnamese general, or with Ezra Pound: *If the hoarfrost grip thy tent thou wilt give thanks when night is spent*, 1978. Or else he defines utopia and creates a dream identity for the artist: *If the Form Vanishes, Its Root Is Eternal (se la forma scompare la sua radice è eterna)*, 1982, and *Painter in Africa (Pittore in Africa)*, 1983.

Water houses

Whether in the guise of a number or a line, neon, for Merz, represents union, the passages between materials, filling the gaps between them. Its illuminating presence in the body of the canvas or the beast, an object or an igloo, not only lacerates them,

but also reveals their secret underground centers; it makes them transparent and brings them up to the surface. It thus exposes their thickness, which is a bark or a skin, a glass or a pigment, a canvas or a net: any material captured by the artist's eye or by his history as a nomad.

Starting in 1979, after years of movement, the igloo turned up among Merz's captured images. *Double Igloo (Doppio igloo)* appeared, first in Essen, then in London, Eindhoven and Paris;[57] it consisted of a big glass igloo, which in turn contained a clay igloo, both of them transfixed by two or three lines of neon light. One igloo captures the other, housing it and superimposing itself. It simultaneously dreams it and blocks it within time. The superimposition alludes to the geological theme of sediments, adding something that it did not have originally: it places it in perspective and historicizes it. By establishing a before and after, an inside and outside around itself, it permits a self-generation, a capacity for initiative, which will allow it to be alone or together with other igloos, to appear delicate and light or robust and heavy, ultimately achieving a circumference of several yards in *The Drop of Water*, Bordeaux, 1987. When all is said and done, the double igloo is a snail or spiral that carries inside and around its own soft body, in clay; its sap and its sensory apparatuses, which, until 1979, were exposed, are now shielded by a second igloo.

What does that mean? During the 1970s, such artists as Georg Baselitz and A.R. Penck, Francesco Clemente and Enzo Cucchi, reacted to the cold Conceptualist analyses and the mythopoetic or dematerialized images created by poor and raw materials. The new focus of interest was the quest for an imagery that would restore the absolute value of the canvas, the painting, removing all ideology and utopia from its territory, all radicalism and love of the future, and exalting an exasperated subjectivism indifferent to the outside and concentrating solely on the individual and linguistic introjection, that of painting per se and painting for painting's sake. There was a passionate demand for a return to history as the history of art and for an expressionist painting that would confirm the ironical invention, as a process of the self.

Starting in 1980, the expansion of that

Cat. no. 106, *Double Igloo (Doppio Igloo)*. 1979

Cat. no. 151, Installation, Flow Ace Gallery, Venice, California, August 1982

"new" painting turned into an avalanche, powerfully impelled by a market that wanted to eliminate the "difficulties" of Conceptualism, Body Art and Land Art. Defense was necessary, and here the igloo repaired itself, its history and its nucleus of sensitivity, while the paintings of animals were not stable, but agitated, pierced by neon, labile and mobile, because they synchronized with the changing moods of the forest of twigs or the hardness of mountain stones.

The stratification of painting during the 1980s signifies more than just a mercantile invasion; it connotes the loss of a political sense and the renunciation of a critical ability. It also exalts a cynicism that permits itself no power of social depth and is intent solely on creating a personal and narcissistic myth: the artist as hero. Nevertheless, the impact on conceptual and bodily arabesques, which took shape during the late seventies with the mannerist involutions of Conceptual Art and Process Art, triggered a new interest in the painting of historical vanguards--the kind of painting that had not accepted the Dadaist emptying, a matrix for the reductivism and nonphysicality of the object in the 1960s. The focus shifted to Futurism and Italian metaphysics, from Boccioni to Giorgio de Chirico as well as Max Beckmann's renewal of Expressionism. And it was on this side of the reference to history that Merz's painting/sculpture differed from the works of the new painters. If Kiefer and Georg Baselitz believe in a common appeal for the solidification of a creative élan rooted in the tragedy and Dionysian spirit of Nietzsche, and if Cucchi and Clemente look back to the visionary and metaphysical paintings of Odilon Redon and Alberto Savinio, Mario Merz is a child of Futurism. He follows a tradition that links Boccioni to Fontana; he feels that the object is in perpetual motion, seeking a different space, exploding in light or crossing a threshold into a new dimension. Merz works on simultaneous situations and on a sequence of energy flows, so that, as in Boccioni, material and light enter the painting, or, as in Antonio Sant'Elia, the architectural totalities are generated by the joint presence of materials and forms, rhythms and diverse planes, which, however, flow into one another.

Evidence for this difference is to be found in *Dark Light Light Dark (Oscuro chiaro chiaro oscuro)*, presented in San Marino in 1983. This installation consisted of two tangentially intersecting igloos: one, made of twigs, was closed and dark; the other, made of glass, was light and transparent. Further evidence is offered by *Giant Woodsmen (I giganti boscaiuoli)*, 1981-82, and *Coniferous Gems (Gemma conifera)*, 1981-82, which brought back not only animals and mountains, but also the theme of the lance, a sign of speed and penetration, of racing and the internal/external relationship, as well as the cinematic multiplication of steps – typical Futurist subjects:

I wrote chiaro/oscuro (light/dark)*: dark and light are not opposites, they overlap and probably recognize one another. In that sort of condition, they recognize one another instead of declaring themselves to be in a formal antithesis.... The material is transformed.... It is truly a material that flows rather than covering.... I must say that certain of Sant'Elia's drawings of future cities were done according to the same system.*[58]

Giant Woodsmen, which sparked a series of large-format works shown at the Sperone Westwater Gallery, New York, and in *Bateau ivre*, 1983, shown at Leo Castelli, Greene Street, New York, in 1985, create the sensation of movement by reiterating the figure and its steps, just as Balla's *The Girl Running to the Balcony*, 1912, used the repetition of the gesture of walking. The figure was already present in Merz's *Running Legs (gambe che corrono)*, 1980, and in the repetition of the strange bodies in his *The Lombard Plane (Pianura Padana)*, 1981, where, however, it became monumental and obsessive. In *Giant Woodsmen*, it leans against the vertices of two lance wedges; while in *Bateau ivre*, it is accompanied by the sequence *Four Tables in the Shape of Magnolia Leaves (Quattro tavole in forma di foglie di magnolia)*, 1985.

In *Giant Woodsmen* the sequence, running from top to bottom, shows the mountain bearing the two lance cones on which their steps rest, two portions of the human figure. The metaphor can be deciphered: natural matter (the mountain with its soil, woods and twigs) bears on its peak the two lance cones, whose three-dimensionality recalls the triangle in space, a magical figure of movement and sensory initiation. Two human figures, whose bodies are not visi-

Cat. no. 179, Installation, Leo Castelli Gallery in collaboration with Sperone Westwater Gallery, New York, November 1985

Installation, Galleria Antonio Tucci Russo, Turin, November 1981, including from right to left: cat. no. 130, *The Musicians (I musicanti).* 1981 *Cat. no. 129, *Mountain Lion (Leone di montagna).* 1981

ble, prop their feet on their points. The double corporality represents the artist's dual being, the sum of one and one (again Fibonacci): the artist sees himself as separate, dispossessed of a process of self-producing that goes from inside to outside, existing as a shadow and radiation of himself. The human figure, with a twisting of its own center – attested to in *Bateau ivre*, by the canvas that twists inversely – turns into a shrub and a tree. The gliding of visual energy is thus framed in a perspective that is historical, in the sense of referring to the energy emitted by Futurism, and alchemical, in its thrust towards transforming the human being into an "other." A propos of Merz's earliest paintings, we spoke of their correspondence with Dubuffet's *Texturologies* – a bond that recurs in these paintings, but in a totally opposite pattern, in the use of colors – specifically, in their impasto and luminosity. Merz's pigments and spray techniques reject Dubuffet's altered perceptions of primitive and cursed culture, his connections with Art Brut. Rather, Merz's pigments are inspired by the chromatic and dazzling explosions of the modern city, by the speed and chaos that characterize them, by the pointless labyrinthine play of encounters amid factors contrasting with nature.

But what is a lance or an arrow if not a bar that separates the *gap* between things? And that is why Merz always confronts the problem and "the need to negate the assumption that painting was something self-contained... that its exact contents were the tables and objects surrounding it."[59] This is a better solution for filling the gap between sculpture and painting; they are combined by the canvas and the igloo. Hence, doing away with the antithesis between the soft, vertical body of the canvas and the sharp, rigid, closed, dome-shaped body of the igloo means legitimizing their dialectics, making it impossible to distinguish them in order to have them live on their mutual bewilderment. In *Architecture Built by Time, Architecture Demolished by Time (Architettura fondata dal tempo, architettura sfondata dal tempo)*, 1981, the duality of an osmotic existence linking the parts is affirmed to its maximum potential. Above all, the title speaks of a totality motivated by a twofold condition of construction and destruction. That is to say, it

constitutes a closed, sheltered covering that is then opened by way of windows and doors. The double-fronted use of a single definition establishes that the verbs, that is, the actions, hence the actors, can exchange roles (Artaud's *The Theater and Its Double* is often mentioned in connection with Merz). In *Architecture Built by Time, Architecture Demolished by Time*, the bodies of the painting and the igloo forfeit their autonomy and are framed inside one another, constructing themselves and being destroyed. The same may be said of the painting. For the first time, the edges of the broken glass are marked with pigments, as if demonstrating that painting must remain jagged and hazardous, just as the igloo can become frail and colored.

Khadafi's Tent (Tenda di Gheddafi), shown at the Musée d'Art Moderne, Centre Georges Pompidou, Paris, had the usual metal structure of Merz's other igloos, but for the first time its dome was covered with painted burlap and each segment contains the image of a lance. Finally, likewise for the first time, the igloo had an open side through which the public could enter. Both this piece and *Architecture Built by Time* speak of a simultaneously external and internal vision; both operate with ambiguity and on the threshold established by the dissociation and association of the oppositional dyads: painting/sculpture, inside/outside, transparent/opaque, rigid/soft.... Art is thus a union of extremes, existing at the extremes, connecting two opposite edges, as in *Stone Igloo (Igloo di pietra)*, 1982, shown at *Documenta 7*, Kassel, which straddled a small stream. It was virtually a gangplank, an overpass, a bridge, made of tie beams and wooden structures, as in *Une ouvrée, une mésure de terre qui donne un portrait bien terrestre*, 1987, exhibited at the Galleria Pietro Sparta in Chagny. In this installation, the beans of wood and the iron ramps bear numbers, which pass across an ocean of twigs and cement blocks. We see the image of water discharged in *What's To Be Done?*, 1968, except that the situation is now changed, the small spurt can become a stream, as in Kassel, or a river, as in *The River Appears (Il fiume appare)*, 1986, a title covering two different installations (a further duality and polarity). The version shown at Galleria Antonio Tucci Russo,

Cat. no. 152, *Stone Igloo*
(Igloo di pietra). 1982

Installation,
Museum of Contemporary Art,
Los Angeles, February 1989

Turin, had metal arches over a river of packets of newspapers; while the version presented at the Prato had a huge canvas with the image of a cone plus Fibonacci numbers in paint and neon and, on the inside, a stream of transparent glass, like water. Water also turned up in Bordeaux, in *The Drop of Water*, 1988, and in Nagoya, in *Pouring of Remote Times, Here, Now (Versamento di tempi lontani, qui, ora)*, 1988, in which water running from a faucet constituted an analogy with the growth of Japanese bamboo and mellowed the sharpness of the Bordeaux installation; in fact, it was placed on the sharp point of a large triangular table.

Water, writes Gaston Bachelard, "is the element most apt to illustrate the themes of combinations of powers. It assimilates so many substances. It gathers opposite materials with equal ease."[60] So far, our reading of Merz's work has focused on the dialectical and osmotic character of the elements. It lives on their blendings, on the way they cooperate to concretize a real imagery. Merz began with a fire water (a bottle of wine), which turned into neon light and recurred in a torrent of twigs and glass, as if the artist had managed to drive the materials crazy during his decades of travel, ultimately entrusting himself to his delirious, yet fantastic and astounding way of experiencing them and seeing them.

Or perhaps we should say that the artist himself is a torrent of water, which, in order to find or build a conduit, has been impelled by its own desires or by the historical and cultural situations to traverse valleys and plains, museums and galleries, flowing amid their stones and boulders, portals and columns, finally to achieve – albeit only for a split second – a continuous voyage, a "house of water." A huge lake with an archipelago of imaginary islands – imaginary because they are made up of twigs and stones, igloos and tables, glass and plaster, neon and wax, pigment and canvas, sculpture and painting. Such were the results during the past few years: at the Kunsthaus Zürich in 1985 or the Capc of Bordeaux in 1987, or the Chapelle Saint-Louis de la Salpêtrière in Paris, in 1987, or at the ICA of Nagoya in 1988, or the Los Angeles Museum of Contemporary Art in 1989. In all these spaces, Merz moved like water running or grass growing amid rocks.

Inspired by a love-hate attitude towards architecture, he tended to stake off a refuge independent of any given context: whether it was a modern edifice in Zürich, Nagoya or Los Angeles, or a historical one in Bordeaux or Paris. At those sites, he created a personal architecture capable of occupyng the absolute center of the environment and functioning as a sacral and ritual icon: a frail, sensual moss on which to delicately prop his writings and his igloos.

Naturally, given the diverse cultural territories of Europe, America and Asia, Merz had to adapt to varying situations. In Zürich, amid a Swiss silence, the artist loudly aimed at the totality, or quasi-totality, of his igloos. Rejecting the serene climate of Nordic contemplation, he insisted on a synesthesia of forms and media, materials and writings, which identified each single igloo. Merz constructed an arcane and primitive village, articulated in its paths and streets, with its own flora and fauna (paintings on walls). He managed to set up the entire body of a nomadic existence, a life of sulfur and fire, of hunts and lances, in the company of crocodiles and rhinoceroses.

On the other hand, in Nagoya and Los Angeles, he worked with spaces that lacked sulfur, he confronted hieratic spaces with an Oriental matrix. Merz thus attempted sudden swerves that broke the immunity and shattered the frozen and controlled climate of the given architecture. He produced a spiral table whose organic form contrasted utterly with the given composure and order. In order to intensify the disharmony, the artist covered the table with stones and lead, achieving a brutally decomposed image. Beyond the initial impact of aggression towards and energetic contortion of architecture, the table reveals a sensitive interior that harmonizes with the site. Thus, in Nagoya, in relation to the Zen gardens, the center of the spiral (or its end, depending on your standpoint – yet another duality) is marked by a bamboo cane and a waterfall. The water, flowing continuously, is linked to a red neon light, virtually signifying the integration of or osmosis between water and fire, Antiquity and Modernity, nature and technology – the vast flowerbed of recent Japanese civilization. Finally, we have the ensemble of works at the Chapelle Saint-Louis de la

Cat. no. 184, *Do We Walk Around Houses or Do Houses Walk Around Us? (Noi giriamo intorno alle case o le case girano intorno a noi?).* 1985. Also visible: *cat. no. 144, *If the Form Vanishes Its Root Is Eternal (Se la forma scompare la sua radice è eterna).* 1982

The River Appears (Il fiume appare). 1986 Newspapers, glass, neon tubes, iron plates and metal tubes, 19' 8 1/4'' × 91' 10 3/8'' (600 × 2800 cm.) Collection Ceat-Cavi, Turin

Salpêtrière. Suposedly, the chapel rose in this place, which was sanctified, because it yielded a precious material like saltpeter. Eventually, the building was turned into a powder storehouse, and then, during the late seventeenth century, under Louis XIV, it became an asylum for vagabonds and lunatics. Here, Jean Martin Charcot conducted his early neurological research on hysteria. At present, the chapel is part of the complex of the Salpêtrière Hospital.

The chapel per se is already a grand metaphor. It delineates a wavering between the joining and disjoining of historical aspects, the great oscillations of human affairs, the multiple sections of a building, its conversions and fundamental exoduses, from positive to negative, from vital to mortal. This grand metaphor also involves the memory of an immense flow of energy and blood, passion and death, religiosity and lay dereliction. Merz came here in autumn of 1987 and set up his alchemical repertoire, his flow of thoughts and materials, his writings and his igloos. He did so conscious of the energy imprisoned here. He touched neither the sacred decoration nor the walls; that is, rather than asking for an environmental purification, he agreed to integrate himself into the crumblings of architecture and history; and, rather than trying to re-release them, he pursued a brinkmanship along their abyss.

Facing the altar, Merz wrote an enigmatic sentence in neon on net, indicating a suspension that torments both art and life: *If the Form Vanishes, Its Root Is Eternal.* Around this, following the cross structure of the church, the artist placed, in the main transept and in its side chapels, the stratifications of stone and glass that produced the triple igloo *853*, 1985, *The River Appears*, 1986, *Homage to Arcimboldo (Omaggio ad Arcimboldo)*, 1987, and *Path Through Here (Sentiero per qui)*, 1986. The resulting landscape had a disfigured heaviness, as if the totality wanted to participate in the darkness of history and of the site. Everything seemed blackened, as if mindful of an image of putrefaction, but also imbued with the dust of time. It emanated a sacred presence and horror. The scene was charged with a profound truth, which recalled a fleeing thing.

Nevertheless, the stones of the igloo struggled against the suction of the floor stones; the cold neon light contrasted with the skylights and sunbeams; the igloos, with two and three domes, resisted the architectural whirlpool. And finally, the lay thought that believes in materials and human beings, in nature and animals, dialectically opposed the religions vision. As usual, it was important for Merz to enter the very belly of the situation and establish a bond between his own existence and the context. However, he passed amid the stones like water and grass. In this sacred perimeter, he staked off and constructed a smithy and a refuge. The artist was at their center, like the glass igloo *Places Without Streets*, 1987, which was isolated by a field of twigs; he surrounded himself with altars, confessionals and faldstools. It was here that Merz, after accepting the encounter or dialectics with sacred architecture and its tragic events, cut himself an inaccessible perimeter, soft and delicate, hard and granitic, transparent and dark; an intimacy shielded by those same twigs, but irrigated by the liquid fire of light, settled upon the igloo. What did this new environment represent? If the twigs are a forest, is the igloo in the middle the lair of a human being or an animal? Are good or bad forces, conscious or unconscious, rational or irrational forces channeled into this space? Is the central edifice a site of pleasure or pain, frailty or cruelty? Merz certainly worked with the mobility of the metaphors, with the simultaneous active/passive and positive/negative function of the meanings, which took in all the opposites; yet the place nevertheless presented something more. The continuous state of metamorphosis in his oeuvre assumes dramatic connotations. His creative research is transformed into a place where all the linearities and immobilities of the system of art crumble, because they result from a lucid madness, typical of a nomad who, like a vagabond and lunatic, lives on the limits of traditional art.

August 1989

1. Quoted in Germano Celant, "Mario Merz" [interview] in *Mario Merz,* exh. cat., San Marino, Palazzo Congressi ed Esposizione, 1983; published in this catalogue in English as "Interview with Mario Merz, Turin, 1983."

2. Mario Merz, *Biografia come sostentamento,* typewritten manuscript, ca. 1975, in Germano Celant Archive, Genoa; published in San Marino, 1983.

3. Quoted in Celant, "Interview, Turin, 1983," this catalogue.

4. Quoted in Ibid.

5. Quoted in Mila Pistoi, "Intervista a Mario Merz," *Marcatré* (Rome), no. 30-33, July 1967, p. 267.

6. Quoted in Ibid., p. 268.

7. Michelangelo Pistoletto, as taped by Mirella Bandini, "Il significato di Gallizio" in *Pinot Gallizio e il Laboratorio Sperimentale d'Alba,* exh. cat., Turin, Galleria Civica d'Arte Moderna, 1974, p. 28.

8. Quoted in Celant, "Interview, Turin, 1983" this catalogue.

9. Mirella Bandini, *L'estetico il politico,* Rome, Officina, 1977; Jean François Martos, *L'histoire de l'internationale situationiste,* Paris, Gerard Lebovici, 1989.

10. Antonin Artaud, *Heliogabale ou l'anarchiste couronné* in *Oeuvres complètes,* vol. 7, Paris, 1965-67, p. 22.

11. San Marino, 1983, figs. 19, 20, pp. 34, 35.

12. Quoted in Pistoi, *Marcatré,* 1967, p. 267.

13. Ibid.

14. Ibid., p. 268.

15. Severo Sarduy, *Baroque,* Paris, Editions du Seuil, 1975, p. 53.

16. For a detailed list of the exhibitions in which these artists participated in Turin from 1966 to 1984, see Giovanna Castagnoli, Ida Gianelli and Floriana Piqué, "A Torino 1966-1984" in Germano Celant, *coerenza in coerenza dall'arte povera al 1984,* Milan, Mondadori, 1984, pp. 134-169. For an international chronology of Arte Povera, see Ida Gianelli. "Chronology of Exhibitions" in *The Knot: Arte Povera at P.S. 1,* exh. cat., Long Island City, New York, Institute for Art and Urban Resources, P.S. 1, 1986, trans. Joachim Neugroschel, pp. 219-239.

17. Quoted in Pistoi, *Marcatré,* 1967, p. 267.

18. Quoted in Celant, "Interview, Turin, 1983," this catalogue.

19. Quoted in Germano Celant, "Interview with Mario Merz, Genoa, 1971, this catalogue.

20. Quoted in Celant, "Interview, Turin, 1983," this catalogue.

21. Brenda Richardson, *Bruce Nauman: Neons,* exh. cat., Baltimore Museum of Art, 1983; Coosje Van Bruggen, *Bruce Nauman,* New York, Rizzoli International, 1989.

22. Quoted in Celant, "Interview, Genoa, 1971, "this catalogue.

23. Some of these aspects of interpreting the igloo were discussed in Germano Celant, "Mario Merz: The Artist as Nomad," *Artforum,* vol. 18, December 1979. pp. 52-58.

24. Quoted in Germano Celant, "Mario Merz," Genoa, March 1981," unpublished interview.

25. Quoted in Germano Celant, "Mario Merz," *Domus,* no. 44, June 1971.

26. Quoted in Germano Celant, "Centauro sopravento" in San Marino, 1983.

27. Quoted in Caroline Tisdall, "Interview with Mario Merz: An Interview by Caroline Tisdall," *Studio International,* vol. 191, January-February 1976, pp. 11-17.

28. Quoted in Celant, *Domus,* 1971.

29. Quoted in Ibid.

30. Quoted in Ibid.

31. Georges Ifrah, *Storia universale dei numeri,* Milan, Mondadori, pp. 11-19.

32. Quoted in Celant, *Domus,* 1971.

33. Quoted in Richard Koshalek, "Interview with Mario Merz" in *Mario Merz,* exh. brochure, Minneapolis, Walker Art Center, 1972, p. 3.

34. Quoted in Celant, *Domus,* 1971.

35. Quoted in Giuseppe Risso, "Incontri con... Mario Merz e il numero," *Gazzetta del Popolo* (Turin), March 1, 1978.

36. Quoted in Celant, *Domus,* 1971.

37. Cesare Brandi, *Struttura ed architettura,* Turin, Einaudi, 1967.

38. Quoted in Pistoi, *Marcatré,* 1967.

39. Germano Celant, *Ambiente/arte, dal futurismo alla body art,* Venice, Edizioni Biennale di Venezia, 1976, pp. 118-131.

40. Ronald D. Laing, *The Facts of Life,* New York, Pantheon, 1976.

41. Tisdall, *Studio International,* 1976.

42. Quoted in Ibid.

43. Quoted in Ibid.

44. Quoted in Ibid.

45. Enrico Guidoni, *Architettura primitiva,* Milan, Electa, pp. 62-67.

46. Here I am returning to some of the concepts discussed in Celant, *Artforum,* 1979.

47. Quoted in Ibid.

48. Quoted in Jean Christophe Ammann and Suzanne Pagé "Entretien avec Mario Merz" in *Mario Merz,* exh. cat., ARC/Musée d'Art Moderne de la Ville de Paris and Kunsthalle Basel, 1981.

49. Eugenio Battisti, *L'antirinascimento,* Milan, Feltrinelli, 1962.

50. Baltusaitis, *Le Moyen Age fantastique: Antiquités et exotismes dans l'art occidental,* Paris, Klincksieck, 1973.

51. Quoted in Ammann and Pagé in Paris and Zürich, 1981.

52. Quoted in Ibid.

53. Quoted in Ibid.

54. Jean Chevalier and Alain Gheerbrandt, *Dictionnaire des symboles,* Paris, Laffont, 1969.

55. Quoted in Celant, "Interview, Turin, 1983," this catalogue.

56. Paul Valéry, *Cahiers,* ed. J. Robinson, Paris, Gallimard, 1973, vol. 1, p. 1334.

57. Merz constructed his first double igloo in 1979 for the Museum Folkwang, Essen; its materials were glass, clay and various neon lights. It was reexhibited that same year at the Sperone Westwater Gallery, New York; again in 1980 at the Whitechapel Art Gallery, London, and the Stedelijk Van Abbemuseum, Eindhoven; and in 1981 at the ARC/Musée d'Art Moderne de la Ville de Paris. As of 1981 the joining of a glass igloo and a clay igloo was enriched by the creation of igloos in various materials and with various writings.

58. Quoted in Germano Celant, "Mario Merz," Turin, 1987, unpublished interview.

59. Quoted in Celant, "Interview, Turin, 1983," this catalogue.

60. Gaston Bachelard, *L'Eau et les rêves: Essai sur l'imagination de la matière,* Paris, 1942.

Mario Merz
1952-1989

*Indicates work in the exhibition.
Dimensions are not given for room-
size and outdoor installations. As most
of the works are irregular, dimensions
are approximate.
Dating:
A hyphenated date, for example 1966-
67, indicates that the object was
worked on for the duration of time
cited; the appearance of a plus mark,
1966+67, indicates that the object was
altered at the later date; the use
of parentheses, 1966(85), indicates
that the object was refabricated
at the later date.

I would like to begin this interview by asking you about your earliest childhood memories. What images have you retained about your childhood, your home and your parents?

My strongest image is that of a chestnut tree that touched the windows of my room. Its branches, covered with chestnuts and leaves, knocked against my window panes, so that throughout my childhood, I spent hours and hours watching the changing colors and forms. The tree looked like an enormous mass next to our house, which stood on a hill. Our home wasn't very large, and during the war, my father, an engineer and inventor, added a shelter. This refuge was built at a right angle into the hill – almost two perpendicular parallelepipeds dug into the tufa. That was where we hid out, even from friends. Another memory I have of those years is the burned synagogue of Turin. It made a profound impact on me, and I can still see that image today.

How old were you?

Oh, let me see, I spent years upon years in that room, so I don't recall exactly how old I was. I have to add that I don't have much of a sense of time. For me, time continues and never stops, and when a past period of time comes back, it is the same time, even if it has become something different. This sense of not having a sense of time puts me physically, but not systematically or mentally, close to certain Eastern religions, or rather, not so much religions, but certain Eastern ways of thinking – mentalities that do not have a sense of time – that sense has expired. The Western mind thinks in terms of, say, your first girl friend, then finds the second one; while the sense of time as today, which binds up everything, is highly important for me. Without realizing it, I have always instuited that the advance of time allowed me to decipher a mode of existence: being and living with these images in front of me – this tree, which was that tree.

A very romantic memory.

I've always been very fond of Romanticism, both the German and the Italian kind, that of Giacomo Leopardi [1798, Recanati – 1837, Naples; Romantic poet], for that sense of scansion, and even Oriental Romanticism, because the sense of seasons is not so marked in human beings. A human being does not become aggressive or wicked according to passing time; rather, it is

passing time that is deciphered.

Actually, I suggested this reading in time because today it is impossible to determine that a branch struck your window . . . .

Certainly, but today I find that it is the same branch, it hasn't changed. When I read the newspaper and see the things that are happening in Lebanon, I tell myself: I have experienced these things. I don't know why, but I have experienced them, in periods when the positions were totally different.

Then you remember the bombings, the flights to shelters, the experiences of war . . . .

Yes, those are events that I have experienced, like the physical trauma of death, in the presence of something that strikes you mechanically from the outside. I have already experienced the sense of total indifference to such dramatic things, the ability to withdraw. But I have also experienced the sense of enjoying the seasons, the arrival of the marvelous summer, with its fruits, even amid bombings, as well as the fact that people always have both a physical and a physiological hope of survival. I have experienced that.

And the hillside house you were talking about – was it bombed when you and your family were inside?

We were underneath, in that famous shelter. When we emerged, part of the house had collapsed.

Did you and your family hear the bombs?

We kept hearing an intense noise. Further down the hill, our friend's house was on fire. The entire roof was already consumed, and so the house was destroyed in no time at all, the walls couldn't hold. In contrast, my father's house, where I lived with my mother and my sister, was still half erect. They put up a wooden staircase on the outside, and life went on. I remembered using that stairway for years. I attended school, and I always managed to use that outside wooden staircase. I had no problems with it.

That was 1943, wasn't it?

I'm not sure whether I want to get into exasperating political situations, but after those bombings of 1943, Pietro Badoglio [marshal during Fascist regime, subsequently Viceroy of Ethiopia and then made premier of Italy by King Vittorio Emanuele III on September 8, 1943, after Mussolini's

fall] and the armistice came in September, and then the Germans arrived.

You instantly joined a Partisan group?

Turin was extremely political, especially the bourgeoisie. There was Giustizia e Libertà [partisan group during Fascist regime] which I joined, and the Communists, who attracted Luciano Pistoi [who was to become director of the Galleria d'Arte Notizie, Turin, which first presented artists such as Paolini, Fabro and Melotti] together with a whole series of other people who were actually Communists. There was a slight difference between the Communists and Giustizia e Libertà. Today, when I read Giustizia e Libertà in the old bulletins, it's like reading current publications by the Autonomia and Democrazia Proletaria [left-wing political groups]. They were terrible . . . Marxism. The Liberals formed still another group.

Did you head for the mountains right away or . . .?

No, I didn't head for the mountains, I was too young, I was still in school.

You were eighteen?

I was going to school, but associating with people who distributed leaflets. I handed the leaflets out in school, and, naturally, one fine day, the last Fascists mounted an attack, they were so strange in those outfits, I always saw them as something strange. They were terrible Fascists, they would shoot on sight . . . so strange. It was a miracle that I wasn't killed. Yes, it was a miracle because Luciano Pistoi was more involved in the organization and he was defended, but I was not defended.

So they arrested you.

Yes, I was arrested and instantly interrogated. But they didn't beat me, because at that time, even they . . . .

Were afraid . . . .

Then they put me in that enormous dungeon, the Carceri Nuove of Turin. That was where I met Pistoi, because the prisoners kept going from cell to cell, even though it was prohibited. The cells were ten feet by sixteen, with bunks, and I lived there with thieves and such people.

You were able to exchange ideas and make contacts . . . .

A little, but we were waiting for the much-touted arrival of the liberators, we knew that the terrible war was coming to an end. But no sooner had I gotten out than

– you know what I did? The very next day, I took a small sheet of paper and a pencil, and I went into the countryside, far from home, far from everybody, and I started to draw, because I told myself: Art has to become the new message.

But before that time, 1943, had you already painted?

I ought to vay that I had already gotten to know Matti Moreni [b. 1920, Pavia; painter who worked in an expressionist, figurative mode].

In what sense: his work or the man himself?

As a painter and as a person. It was Moreni who told me: You have to make art.

Where did you meet him? In Turin?

Moreni was living in Turin. I met him when I went to a paint store. Then I joined the Galleria d'Arte La Bussola because Turin was a city where the art life was intense.

Aside from the world of art, were you interested in anything else, say, music or literature?

As a boy, I read Kafka, then I got to know Cesare Pavese [1908, Santo Stefano – 1950, Belbo; anti-Fascist writer] and Elio Vittorini [1908, Siracusa – 1966, Milan; anti-Fascist writer] – they were incredible.

Through politics?

No, always through art, even if Turin had a highly political side during the forties.

How did you get to meet those people?

I went to the bar frequented by Moreni and I listened to him, my mouth gaping. I heard a man who was older than I. So was Luigi Spazzapan [1889, Gradisca – 1958, Turin; painter who worked in an expressionist style combined with elements of realism, associated with the group I sei pittori di Torino]. That sense of art as intensity . . . . Then I remember that my mother got me to read Kafka. She said: This is a book you ought to read.

So your parents were, very educated and open-minded . . . .

Especially my mother. My father was educated in his profession. I recall that at most he had read D'Annunzio. He regurgitated his cultural background – not Nazi but Swiss German. I remember my father listening to Hitler's speeches on the radio and yelling back. When he listened to him, he was sure that Hitler was already dead, that Mussolini was already dead, that all of them were dead.

How come?

He was an Anglophile, he loved Anglo-American culture. He said that the Anglo-Americans were potentially stronger, so he was certain the Nazis and Fascists had lost. That was why he was on the opposite side, in the most technical sense of the term. In fact, when the first bombs were dropped on Turin, he said to me, "You see? I told you there was nothing we could do." My father was an engineer, an aeronautics designer, and he knew that the Anglo-American countries had a decisive technological superiority over the Nazis. The Nazis had the superiority of national emotions, but when the "nation" fell apart technologically, Germany and Italy could no longer hold out.

What about your mother?

She was against the Fascists, because she sided with culture. My mother was against D'Annunzio, while my father was for him. She was against D'Annunzio and for Kafka, and so she got me to read him. My mother isn't Jewish, but she got me to read Kafka, because in Turin, the cultural system was determined by the publisher, Libreria Einaudi, and I read all the books they published. I went to the seashore, to Rapallo, and there, one of my friends pointed out Ezra Pound; he was sitting in a café surrounded by women and men, an elderly gentleman with a white beard. Then I read Steinbeck's *Of Mice and Men*, Pavese's *Paesi tuoi*, and Montale's *Ossi di seppia* [Eugenio Montale, 1894, Genoa – 1981, Milan; anti-Fascist poet associated with the literary current Ermetismo].

So, as a boy . . . .

I was already familiar with world literature.

And you were deeply involved with it.

Yes, but I was very emotional, and like all emotional people, I was unable immediately to structure the thing logically and in terms of an overall education. Instead, I was simply fascinated.

But you associated with poets and artists, while your personal readings were extremely advanced compared with your school curricula . . . .

I also had a teacher of Italian and art history, a priest – he knew Giampiero Bona, he was a friend of the Bona family and Felice Casorati [1893, Novara – 1963, Turin; Magic Realist artist] and Morandi. His name was Fra Pontino. He was an extraordinary man, who had known Picasso

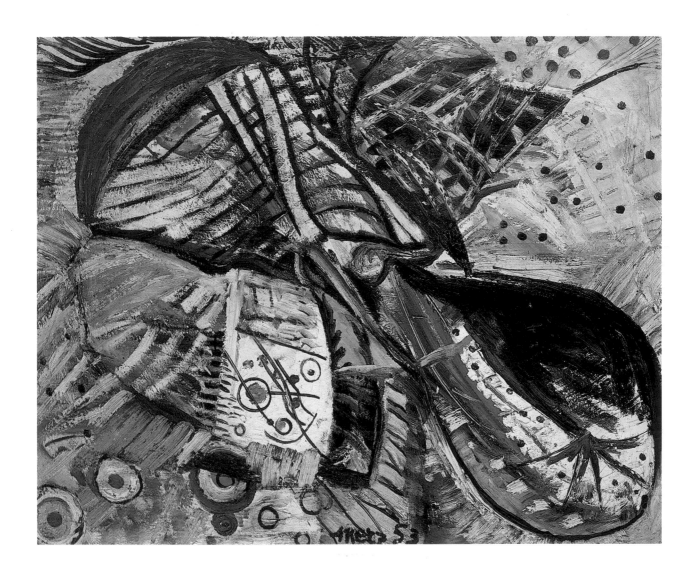

and Braque, and so he informed me about all sorts of cosmopolitan things.

Your education was incredible for that period.

And how! It was totally different from what came after. When the war got hold of me, and I was sent to prison for a year, I experienced the very opposite of my schooling. Instead of openness and free circulation, I experienced more violent methods.

Were you already painting?

I had begun painting at home. I had gotten to know Moreni and, above all, Fra Pontino. I liked him, and I thought I could become a painter. I was fascinated by the speed of painting as the idea of a possible attack on reality, rather than literature, which seemed far slower in its processes, including its linguistic processes.

Hence, it seemed more difficult to implement . . . .

It was like telling a boy: Painting can be done from one day to the next. And that's what it was all about. I did my first drawing. I tried to do a drawing in which the line would take over the entire surface rather than constituting a negative/positive relationship.

In what way?

The line taking over the entire surface is distantly related to my present-day igloos. The surface is worked by the line so that the line occupies it fully, like the moon. The drawing is a total fact, dictated by a need to exist rather than a need to represent – or else representing in such an exclusive sense as to become a mode of existence. That was why I headed for the countryside right after the war and began to draw with my pencil on wrinkled paper. Those drawings captured the idea of grass and leaves, the idea of the wind on grass and leaves, and the idea that they were a medley, an "impasto." They were exemplary drawings, inspired perhaps by my reading extremely emotional and new texts, like Kafka's writings. Since they came from a different and remote world, there was no problem of repeating his work here, but my drawings had to be as strong here as his work had been there. That was the lesson I learned from certain texts, and I believe that Moreni too had the same goals during that period. But his ambitions were frustrated because he felt he had to be informal, absolutely informal. It had to be the most perfectly informal

message, while that idea never even crossed my mind . . . .

How did you get to La Bussola, and what did you show there?

Luigi Carluccio [1911, Calimera – 1981, São Paulo; art historian and critic] was there, he was an extremely intelligent man with a very free mind, unshackled by rules. During the fifties, he suggested that La Bussola mount a show of young artists in Turin.

What did you show at La Bussola?

I had done *Gypsy Wagon (Carrozzone)* in 1953. Its side was the right or left side of a Gypsy wagon. That's why I titled it *Gypsy Wagon*.

Was it photographed or painted?

It was painted, but it looks like a photo. It's an odd painting.

When did you meet Pistoi?

We were in prison together, and when he got out, he joined *L'Unità* [daily of the Communist Party of Italy], he got into journalism. At that time, *L'Unità* was the largest newspaper, while *La Stampa* [Turin daily] was shut down. *La Stampa* appeared again several years later, with an image of Fiat and Vittorio Valletta [president of Fiat from the 1950s to the 1970s], with the image – let's say – of ultraconservatism and the capitalist reconstruction of Europe. That was the moment when Pistoi joined *L'Unità* as a journalist and published my drawings – I think, in 1949.

Have you always used very dense materials like the ones in Gypsy Wagon?

I did paintings that had elemental power and yet were thoroughly refined. I was against Art Informel. I recall a session with Ennio Morlotti [b. 1910, Lecco; painter who worked in naturalistic Informel style, in 1952 belonged to group Otto pittori italiani] and Moreni at a café on Piazza Castello [a central meeting place in Turin]. I came out as absolutely opposed to the Informel, because they thought they were exporting Milan's informalism and Moreni believed he was the bearer of Turin's informalism. They were the "Parisians" of Informel.

Yet your themes were naturalistic, for instance, leaves and trees . . . .

No. The leaf had become a symbol, the symbol of the organic whole. In line with that, *Gypsy Wagon* symbolized a form of anarchism.

Did you hear a great deal about anarchism and Existentialism? Were you acquainted with Sartre's world?

I don't know, because Sartre's world was considered a world of societal relations. My relations were with individuals, which I now see in terms of the Veda. The igloo brought out the Buddhist side of Giap [Vo Nguyen Giap, 1912-1975; North Vietnamese military strategist and political leader], not the militaristic side.

Sitting in the field . . . .

Yes, but with a weapon in hand, not just contemplating.

Let's talk about time again. Is it true that you did your paintings over and over again?

It's just as true today, because you can never be sure . . . .

The work can always evolve or be integrated in the present moment, like the yellow-brown angular structure, the bundles of twigs and the Fibonacci series.

I believe that we can put literature into painting just as the Byzantines did. The ancient Arabs succeeded in doing so – writing became painting. This has been repeated today in American graffiti. For me, drawing is writing, and this phenomenon of painting-writing was something that I felt very deeply.

Are you talking about the years 1953 through 1957, when your writing was filled with color and figures?

It is writing – naturally without an extreme awareness of that term. It is a light interweaving of dreams and material, yet this blending of things created the beauty of those paintings rather than ugliness. If you see Morlotti's paintings today, they look dusty and dated; they are period pieces, while the *Gypsy Wagon* painting is not trapped in any era. In 1953, I suddenly began doing paintings like *The Welder (Il saldatore)*, because I was always going out at night, and I was struck by the blowtorches of the rail welders. I told myself: Why not paint them? Instead of flowers, I'll paint a welder holding a blowtorch. So I did about ten paintings, but then I grew tired of the theme – I don't remember why.

Were you still in Turin in the late sixties, or somewhere else?

I traveled very often. I went on long bicycle trips, and I was always preoccupied with art. During those tours, I painted a mill in Lanzo. Around that time, I met a lung

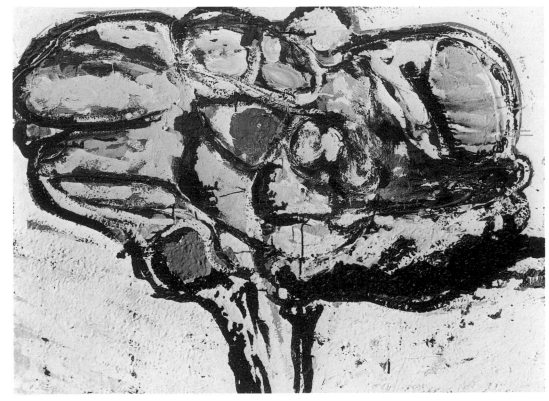

patient who was locked up in a kind of hospital for the criminally insane, and he introduced me to Ezra Pound. Turin was a strange world, and I must say that Ezra Pound is poetically involved in my work to a high degree. Lots of my ideas come from him.

Was it Pinot Gallizio [1902, Alba – 1964, Alba; painter involved with Situationist group and Bauhaus Imagistes with Jorn and Constant] who introduced you to the Cobra group, to Appel and Jorn?

Not really. Gallizio was very possessive – that was his big failing. He was so possessive that he remained alone. He was very generous, but also very possessive. Actually, I got more information through the international magazines on Pollock. I found him very powerful and more important because he was less overblown.

That's clear!

It's clear now, but it wasn't clear at the time. The Situationists said: "We're the ones who are making things advance." They went to Paris, they went here and there. If you see Pollock, it's Boccioni, whereas if you see Appel, you see a degeneration from the late Picasso, a surface existentialism.

How did you get to know Marisa?

I met her in the late fifties. Then we went to Switzerland.

In 1962, Carla Lonzi [1931, Florence – 1982, Milan; art historian and critic, author of Autoritratta, *1969, the first collection of dialogues with such artists as Paolini, Fabro, Pascali, Kounellis and Twombly], in the introduction to the catalogue for your show at Le Notizie, talks about the way you stand out and about your solitude, and she also writes that many of your works have been destroyed.*

Well, she talks about it in a grandiloquent way, whereas for me, it was something very concrete, and not at all grandiloquent. If I see the painting that my mother owns, it is a very strange painting, it has a sense of electronics and pulsation, not of the figure, but rather of a flux.

So then you worked in Switzerland for a while?

I went to Switzerland and I did paintings that involved very natural drawing. That is where the twigs come from.

They have the same rugged, graphic qualities. Moreover, you didn't use much color, and if you did use any, it was never loud.

Then it became more Baroque, as in your 1962 show in Turin.

In that show, the sense of isolation was transformed into pleasure.

In the early sixties, Turin was a city on the move. I remember that in 1963 La Galatea showed Bacon and Max Ernst – all its artists were big names, with great economic importance. It was a jewelry shop – you had to ring the buzzer to be let in and received. Next to it, there was Il Punto with Gian Enzo Sperone [director of a gallery located first in Turin, then in Rome and New York] and Pastori.

The latter were already established. Pistoletto was already in a solid position, and they were all very suspicious of one another, partly because Gian Maria Persano had bought one of my paintings, and Pistoletto had criticized him. He was doing his mirrors, and his dealer was Ileana Sonnabend. That was the period in which Turin was moving towards internationalism.

When did you first get your studio on Via Santa Giulia in Turin?

It was after I moved to Switzerland with Marisa. Next, we rented a house in Pisa – it was infested with mosquitoes – a big house, where I could paint; and that was where I did the painting that I put on top of my car – I drove it to La Promotrice [Società Promotrice delle Belli Arti di Torino, active since the second half of the nineteenth century], I showed there with Pistoi, Lucio Fontana [1899, Rosario di Santa Fé – 1968, Comabbio; painter who made space his subject matter and executed slashed canvases] and Gallizio, but my piece wasn't accepted by the others. I couldn't get it off the car roof, so I told myself: "This is no way to transport a painting!"

Did you use pigments or impastos of material?

No. It was the spiral.

The vertical spiral?

The spiraling of color, the one I executed afterwards with numbers. It was done with pigments, very dense, enormous – gigantic. I had bought up all the tubes of paint in Pisa and Viareggio, and I put all the pigments on the canvas. It was totally crazy.

I recall that in the Santa Giulia studio, there was a room with the jutting paintings, burned wicker and neon light, and there was another room – my memory's hazy on this point . . . . There were objects by either you

*5 *Gypsy Wagon (Carrozzone)*. 1953
Oil on canvas, 70 7/8 × 79 1/8''
(180 × 201 cm.)
Collection Udo and Anette Brandhorst

50

or Marisa. They were made of bamboo and fishnets. Were those your works?
Yes. They were done in a studio that I had near the Porta Nuova [main railroad station in Turin].
So that was a transition between the canvases and the jutting pictures?
In 1963-64 Sperone had very powerful international connections; Lichtenstein and Warhol had come with him from America. As for me, in 1965-66, I invented neon – that is to say, it was an invention for me.
Speaking of the jutting paintings traversed by neon, I see them today as tents that, if brought from the wall to the ground, become triangular igloos. At the same time, I associate the neon fire with the welder's blow-torch – it's a highly potent image, which perforates the material, just as the neon perforates the canvas and then the objects.
I have always looked for a passage through painting, and I am still looking for it today. It is a transverse passage, like an airplane charging into a cloud and then flying through another and yet another. Next it crosses a space above America, a space above Greenland, a space above South America, and finally it lands in Australia. That is painting. For me, a painting is not as Carlo Maria Mariani [painter who uses Neoclassical iconograph, associated with Citazionista group] sees it: he wants to take on the whole human condition in an all-encompassing manner. And I'm not like Sandro Chia, who perceives painting as if it were something secure, to be done. I have always regarded painting as total insecurity, and not at all as a type of secure or accepted language. But as a form of insecurity that a person traverses. On the other hand, it's not like the overblown painting of the Americans or the facile historicism of the Italians.
Do you think that this security, which is tied to faith by a truth, depends on historical legacy or on the culture of the ruling class?
I have not really taken on the historical legacy of the Italians, because, basically, I'm not one hundred percent Italian. I was fascinated by that legacy, but not overwhelmed, I did not believe that the idea of painting is that of history. Even today, when I go to museums, I enjoy seeing de Chirico make fun of painting, just as Ensor and Rembrandt make fun of it. I actually

stop before gigantic obstacles like the Raphaels and Titians, and the paintings they did. In my opinion, they did those paintings after challenging everything else. Picasso and Matisse did both painting and nonpainting.
Are you saying that all avant-garde movements are a struggle with painting?
A never-ending struggle, an effort to get through it. Once you succeed in getting across, then you invent the igloo. You enter the cloud, you pass through it, and then the possibility of making the igloo explodes, and then you enter another cloud, and so on and so forth.
I find the same analogy in the bamboo works: a flux of framed elements.
I see all my output of 1950 almost like premedieval painting, from an era in which painting, for the medieval world, meant entering a cloud, entering religion, at any price – painting was forgotten. Today, I'm not after big painting. An artist can go back to Art Informel or the eighteenth century, like Mariani. But it's all nonsense, because actually, you're entering a cloud that doesn't exist.
It's an artificial problem.
Completely artificial. It gives you a feeling of artifice, which the Americans absorbed in their formalistic culture. Nonetheless, when I visited the Tate Gallery, I saw those facile graffiti artists, who immediately condemned Schnabel to becoming a master after a year or two. It's ridiculous: a man is condemned to being a master when he's really looking for something entirely different.
They bury him immediately.
They destroy you. Keith Haring and his ilk are laughable, they derive from Klee . . . . Yet they bury any desire to create, they bury Schnabel's desire to redo the great French sculpture . . . .
And Gaudí . . . .
By going back, Jasper Johns tried to reach Seurat. He's an American Seurat – that's his idea.
Are you saying that such speed destroys them?
Only twenty paintings are left, but you can't hold out. Works survive only as a desire for a transition and as an ability to get through those hazy clouds. You remain freer there, and you can do your work.
You can't be branded, which is what the

informational structure aims at. We said before that the anarchistic attitude allows us to move.
I had a lot of experiences like that. Not for private reasons, but for art's sake. In my opinion art is the only thing that allows us to get through things and to be a process of traversing rather than an arrival.
Otherwise, people remain frozen and rigid.
From time to time, you may reach a shore, but the voyage continues, and it's wonderful. You arrive here, then there. . . . It's fantastic. It takes a long time, but that's the way it is. We may not have the keys to all the doors, like the seventeenth-century organists in Germany, or the Italian singers and the great Catholicism of that same era.
Let's go back to 1967. How did you get from the jutting paintings to the igloo?
I was bored to death by the angles of those jutting paintings – and then the Giap idea came to me. It had no angles. Giap writing had no angles, and the igloo came out of it. The igloo as the idea of nonangularity. The angle was gone.
There were also rigid objects: the igloo is not rigid, it is circular, like the earth. But I remember the chamber pot and the drinking glass crossed by neon. There was a feeling of being unable to stop on anything. That's it.
Everything was slightly elusive. The neon threaded, sewed, cut, served to clean the studio, to burn it, to melt everything together. It was not very different from the paintings in which all the colors melted together – it was the same approach. A large fishing rod with all the elements inside one another. The bamboo keeps returning . . . and the igloo becomes . . . .
A perfection of that way of perceiving and thinking.
Everything moves along with the work. It is neither rough nor dry. It has an incredibly intense sensuality.
After the igloo, I began to think that I could do paintings again, because I needed to return to a self-willed possession not only of the intensity, but also of something acute.
This is the moment of returning and resuming . . . .
Yes. All those people coming from New York and demanding representation – it sort of reminds me of the representation in Baroque music, when the stories of Eurydice or the Barber of Seville turned into

completely musical stories. You don't know whether it's one music or another.

You can cover the whole range. During the return, anything can happen.

That's why it's dangerous. So as a reaction, I thought of numbers and tables. Something tragic – a person caught in a tragedy.

With regard to the objects that were in your studio during that period – did you find them in the street?

I actually found them by means of a sort of selection. Every so often, I made a big find – for instance, the empty wine bottle traversed by neon. It was something of an invention – that emerging spurt of wine represented by light instead of painting. Rather than painting that spurt, I emphasized the effect of explosion and flight. It became very sensual, but also non sensual, because it was reduced to a line.

Was that why you painted your red objects, like the lance and the neon?

Yes, I painted the lance. What the bottle now lacks is persuasiveness. I ought to find a second chapter – from sculpture to painting. I was very tempted to turn the igloos and those objects into paintings. I felt they could be reduced to paintings.

Like the tables?

Exactly. But it's very difficult, because you're again faced with the problem of painting, and thereby with representation with the problem of a fixed image. That was why I produced the works with real fruit. The invention of the discarded thing that is nevertheless there and has a smell. There is something anguishing and extremely sensual. The anguish of discovery and the sense of uselessness, the sense of both well-being and malaise. It may have been the most philosophical stage of my work, but it was useless for art because when I did the show at Sperone in New York in 1982 – Sperone only likes paintings and nothing else – he said: "Great, wonderful. But two days later, there's nothing left."

Throughout the 1970s, along with your tables and igloos, which occupy large architectural volumes, you started painting again. You used enormous masses of colors in spiral shapes as well as progressions of objects or natural elements. What was the source of that need to pass into a two-dimensional plane or to recover an image from the color of the natural object? Was it perhaps an urge to render the table surfaces in color? If

memory serves me, your first use of color on your objects, aside from the early lances and several neons, was in Berlin. It was on the progression of tables exhibited at the Haus am Lützowplatz in 1973.

I used bandages for the Berlin tables. My idea was to employ the elastic bands used for bandages. They were about four inches high, and the numbers were sprayed on them in colors. I constructed the space for 1, for 1, for 2, for 3, for 5, and so on, and they became very long. They served to represent the dimension of the development of the numbers – those applied to the tables as well as those shown on the walls. I did the same thing in Minneapolis in 1972.

So those were gauze paintings, long horizontal pictures?

That's right, and I use that same format even today, but I increase the height. The work was done on tables, across the table-tops. The first paintings were done like that, on and with the table. Since a table is a specific size for one person, two by two feet, I decided to paint a red square, two by two feet for one person or two by two for two people, for three, for five. There was no room for the surface of the object; so I painted the surface, making it become a table for fifty-five people. It was a huge, colored surface, and the development of the mass of color made it real.

Let's focus on the theme of color. At a certain point during an earlier interview, you spoke to me about red as a sign linked to wine. Not coincidentally, you painted a sequence of drinking glasses on a table. Is red linked to a natural entity, aside from fire and lightning? Is it also wine?

I would say that red contains them all, because it is an intense, yet symbolic color, which is so energetic that a red table on a white canvas is extremely aggressive. It holds together the content of the size and the content of the expansion of the tables, while assuming and defining the energy charge. Next, I thought of painting the cups for one person, the cups for two people, three, five, eight, etc., and little by little, the work took shape not only symbolically by way of the red and its expansion, but also as a thingly vision of a concrete event. Naturally, I even thought of the pictorial table in Antiquity: the table where they consumed the sacred meal was a place for a qualification of an event. The soup plate

was more than a still life, it was the basin for creating the ritual meal. My paintings have a wine red background, so that the passage from the soup plate to the table is a ritual rather than a still life.

Does the passage from the rigid and thingly table to the painting-table also involve the problem of keeping open the natural growth of the surfaces? In Arte ambiente *[at the XXXVII Biennale di Venezia, 1976, organized by Germano Celant], they were kneaded into a brick wall and became the wall by means of the painterly and "naturalist" elements of sulfur and verdigris.*

The work in the Venice pavilion, reduced to its architectural essence – the raw surface of the bricks – was phantasmagorical. The color of the sulfur and the verdigris, sprayed directly on the red clay of the bricks, had become almost an atomic imprint – sprayed and not painted. During that period, I liked using this technique of spraying enamel or pigment on surfaces, because this procedure made for a faster execution, and the greater speed turned the imprint into more of a phantasm – as in graffiti – more phantasmagorical, rather than being a painting in the traditional sense.

In the paintings of the fifties and sixties, the color was built up vertically, in layers of material that weighed down on the surface. In contrast, you moved on to a surface quality that emerged from the lighter and airier material of the spray paint.

The spraying creates a lightness and also an intense expansion of the painting rather than delicate shadings of sfumato. In Venice, it became an almost fantastic imprint.

That is the reason why you include fragile materials, like leaves or snail snells, scotch tape or mud, in drawings and paintings. The entire painted surface became fragile in the paintings you started doing around 1977.

I felt the need to negate the assumption that painting was something self-contained, I had to emphasize that its exact contents were the tables and objects surrounding it. For instance, the leaf applied to the spiral had the fragile look of a seed inserted into a spiral, which is stronger than the seed itself, so that the spiral closes and extends the leaf. It is very easy to crush a leaf on paper or canvas with scotch tape and not waste any time on overly abstract topics. The leaf becomes mentally lucid again. The other day, when I was strolling through a

garden, I saw leaves on the ground, and instead of forming a landscape, they became mounted stones. They attained a brightness in their isolation and a meaning in their transience. Ultimately, the outlines of the leaves had the superb qualities of cut-out silhouettes.

That's where your paintings become animals with their paws on the ground. They are figures that expand below, at the front, and on the sides. They emit sticks or pieces of wood; hence, they walk in reality, in architecture and in space.

Beyond tying them to the ground, I see my paintings crawl up the wall. They promptly turn into a creeping crocodile or lizard. They are the gecko that hovers on the wall, the gecko with its perfect anatomical equilibrium. I very much want the canvas to creep about, rather than being placed on the wall in a decorative sense. And since, for me, the crocodile is a mythically enlarged gecko, it can represent painting. The canvas becomes a gecko, and vice versa, and they both creep along the wall.

In some cases, however, it becomes a real animal with several paws, like at the Moderna Museet in Stockholm, where one of your paintings has a body with a metallic structure and wooden paws. What does this intensification of the vitality and movement of painting signify?

I feel that we once again have to see paintings in their context. When we see a Titian painting reproduced in a book, it is never presented in its original context. Then, when we see the real painting, we find it inside an architectural space, with a piece of furniture or in an arch. It is superbly inserted into a definite and concrete space. Now, my paintings and sculpture try to carry within themselves something of the environment in which I made them: for example, for the igloo at the Moderna Museet in Stockholm in 1983, I used from the port in Stockholm bundles of sticks, a metal parallelepiped – they are all elements that recall the feeling of that city. Furthermore, the inclusion of cords or stucco, trees or trunks, which are tied to the painting, reminds us that painting is a thingly process, not subject to photographic consumption. It requires a space, and that is why I often mount paintings inside my igloos. They are very large walls, extended with very swift pictorial formulas, like spray

paint or vast stretches of color that soak into the canvas, making it thick and intensely autonomous. I almost never prepare the canvas, I let it soak up the paint, so that the canvas absorbs the priming rather than being its support.

Your paintings can be very long, measuring as much as dozens of yards. Do you think of them as walls, even attaching objects and elements such as a raincoat or an oar to them?

In a certain sense, yes. In fact, the canvas that is a crocodile is penetrated by a neon lance, as if a luminous projectile were entering its body. The light transfixing it becomes either a symbolic fact (death) or a symbolic indication of the quality of the canvas, whose transparency is nourished by the light. A light meant as color and painting.

The same use of color recently appeared on the igloo, which used to be colorless and admitted only the tautological color of the elements employed, such as stucco, glass, cloth, clay, the blue of the fluorescent tube . . . the igloo never used to be painted.

The igloo functions as a moldable hemisphere, transparent and luminous. It may contain another igloo (the most recent one is the Cologne igloo, which is covered with phosphorus). This creates a highly luminous intermediary space, becoming a study of transparency and light, like a gorgeous ampule from Murano or certain ancient glass vessels. If you think of the ice igloo, it is not only a masterpiece of architecture, it is also a masterpiece of extraordinary luminosity. Moreover, for me, the igloo is an object contrasting with the cut of the right angle, which always creates shadows and is extremely violent. In the igloo, the shadows vanish with the darkness, and we see a color reflection hundreds of degrees wide.

Your igloo at the Centre Pompidou in Paris was neither transparent nor luminous, it was completely painted over, it could be entered and it was accessible to the public.

Yes, because I had painted it in terms of a tent. I wanted it to be a tent and remain a hemisphere, while evoking the model of a mythical tent. That was why I painted it. I covered it with cones, their tips pointing down, and with a figure that was in between an object in space and an object that cuts into it, between the tree and the soul of the

*8 *Spiral Leaf (Foglia spirale)*. 1955
Enamel, oil and dirt on canvas,
43 3/8 × 49 1/4'' (110.5 × 125 cm.)
Collection of the artist

tree, its gist. A spatial object, which, I feel, can stand in the air without any support, and that is how these objects become mysterious. They don't need to keep remembering that man, who stands with his feet on the ground and his head in the air, can also do the opposite. This is the symbolism of spatial positions, which today are basically natural. We know very well that we have our antipodes elsewhere, they have their feet upside down. We know that there are men who have been able to circumnavigate the earth . . . . This absence of weight is a goal of my representation.

What about animals like the crocodile, the tiger, the bison, the stag, bodies present in some of your Fibonacci works – why do they have a personal rather than a natural coloration? They almost become the transposition of your personal participation or of a reinvention that, since it doesn't have the weight of color, can therefore give a different weight to these images.

These figures are mythical, not domestic. But I was interested in having a crocodile at home, and not just a crocodile skin. I wanted a painted crocodile, a slightly unsettling image and presence: the presence of a ghost rather than of a skin. These animals made me feel light in life, because they have something ancient about them, a sense of the unknown, of unavailability as far as I am concerned. They are absolutely solitary creatures, they do not participate in the collective life of the street. The animals are all those things combined.

Hence their association with branches and dried trees. In fact, they always depend on this extremely harsh, arid, desiccated nature as if there were a sensory coherence between the animal and these parts of nature. What is the reason behind these adjacencies?

The twigs represent our everyday life. Several bundles of twigs together achieve a furious shadow: sometimes I've put them in the mountains – those desiccated woods, and together they almost seem to be waiting. They are extraordinarily evocative of an astronomical voyage, and even if they derive their meditative quality from an agricultural landscape, the mountains – they become more astral in the work, they turn into sculpture, between the living and the dead, they are neither sculpture nor nonsculpture. They are both living and dead at once, they are exceedingly bizarre.

Among your animals and your creatures with rigid bodies, you frequently include a rhinoceros.

The rhinoceros is an animal that is a drama in itself, it wears a shell, an armor, yet it can move rapidly. It's both a robot and an animal at the same time. I once saw a rhinoceros, and it looked strange, as if mud were attached to its shell. I couldn't tell whether its shell was shiny or muddy; it looked as if it were both at once, it was both shiny and muddy. It seemed to be of both the earth and the water, and it had a sense of bones, in that a bone is a bone emerging from the mud. I did paintings of this strange animal, using clods of earth as color.

Why did you penetrate them with neon, that is, an arrow of light?

The arrow is a very luminous element, and light can cross through anything. If you read a book on physics, you know that all bodies are traversed by other bodies. So, for me, neon crossing through a canvas or an image is always referring to that scientific situation of which we are fundamentally carriers: we know that all bodies are traversed by other bodies.

And that's why you put certain materials on the canvases? I remember stucco, palm trees, numbers, leaves, chestnuts, pinecones . . . .

Rather than stucco, I always put mud or earth or things with which I could revitalize an image on the canvases. In this sense, the clumps of earth can be thought of in musical terms and not just visual terms.

Are these elements musical notations?

They are groups of notes, and the image is revitalized from one to the other. Often, my starting a canvas depends on the possibility of rendering ensembles, sort of like building walls with lots of bricks. You can conceive of putting bricks in the air, so that they can stay up by themselves.

And how did the faces of leaves or pinecones get into the picture?

The faces are levels. There is the level of the eyes. There is the elevator of the nose, there is the cavity of the mouth . . . . This is a building with its floors, roof and stairs.

Architecture is always contaminated by the mutual penetration of objects. Does the same thing happen in your paintings with tables and the hamper?

Not only in my paintings, but also in my igloos. The fact that I have put one igloo on top of another is also a painterly image.

*9 Red and Green Face (Faccia rossa e verde). 1955
Enamel and oil on wood, 46 7/16 × 48" (118 × 122 cm.)
Collection of the artist

You feel that the human brain rolls up inside a skull, you can therefore glimpse it and assess it, like the intestines. If you could X-ray the human body mythically rather than scientifically, it would be extremely complex and have an extreme psychological weight. Such is the igloo in painting.

The subject of Anatomy Lesson (Lezione di anatomia), *with its interlacing of tables, twigs and the painting of a body, thus constitutes an oblique cut between painting and sculpture?*

In my work, the cut acquires a theatrical and cinematic meaning, it becomes a drama. That is why I sometimes indulge in the luxury of speed, so that I can be very fantastic in the cut itself. Thus, if you see bundles of twigs in a group, they become people, a crowd, they become presences that could not otherwise be re-created. Or at least, I aimed at re-creating them with this powerfully dramatic system.

Then you're interested in presenting the crowd of paintings at the same time as the crowd of materials . . . .

If you want to talk about crowds, I can go back to the igloo. When you see broken glass by itself, it is a strange element, inert and a bit annoying, because it recalls destruction. But if shards of broken glass start running one after another across the surface of the igloo, they acquire a strange lightness and strange obsessiveness. They lose the sense of the fallen, the falling and the broken. Instead, they acquire a meaning of strange forms that are always very bizarre, because they take on the form of brokenness. The form of brokenness put together with other forms of brokenness creates this surface, which is shiny rather than chaotic. It's like seeing the earth from very high up. Its chaos becomes more intense and takes on the meaning of its surface.

In your latest shows at the Galleria Stein in Turin and the Israel Museum, the igloos of cloth or mud had spatial forms on their surfaces, coming from a different dimension. They were in fact cut out of metal and painted. What did their presence mean?

Recently, I became intrigued by certain elementary themes of contemporary music. I would say that I am interested in an almost nonexistent music, somewhere between rock and electronic music. However, it exists in my mind. These forms are variations on that theme. They are cut out and painted as if they were flying pianos with white and black keys, which brings the sense of rhythm into the igloo.

Does the surface of the igloo become a musical score?

Yes, one that's visual. But more than anything, it evokes musicality, like a plumage of white and black. It's as if a piano had feathers instead of keys, as if a bird were a kind of mythical piano, so that music gets involved in painting in a nontraditional way. Instead of being all music, it becomes a painted music, and instead of being painting, it becomes a painting that is also musical.

55

10 *Composition (Composizione)*. 1954
Oil on canvas, 40 1/8 × 30 15/16''
(102 × 77 cm.)
Collection Valla, Turin

*11 *Untitled*. 1952
Enamel and oil on canvas,
51 × 35 1/2'' (129.5 × 90.1 cm.)
Collection of the artist

*12 *Untitled.* 1958
Mixed media on canvas, 63 × 35
7/16'' (160 × 90 cm.)
Collection of the artist; Courtesy
Galleria Antonio Tucci Russo, Turin

*13 *The Stone (Il sasso).* 1959
Oil on canvas, 78 1/2 × 59 1/4''
(199.4 × 150.5 cm.)
Collection Liliane and Michel
Durand-Dessert, Paris

14 *Untitled.* 1959-60
Oil on wood, 39 3/8 × 50 3/8''
(100 × 128 cm.)
Collection Ezio Gribaudo, Turin

15 *Untitled.* 1960
Oil on wood, 39 3/8 × 27 9/16''
(100 × 70 cm.)
Collection Renata Novarese, Turin

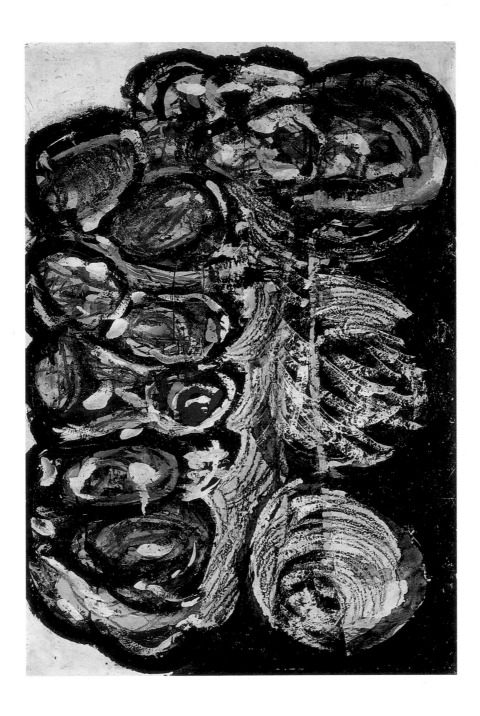

16 *Untitled.* 1963
Mixed media and watercolor on paper,
39 3/8 × 27 9/16'' (100 × 70 cm.)
Private Collection

17 *Untitled*. 1965
Mixed media on wood, 44 7/8 × 41
3/4'' (114 × 106 cm.)
Collection Giampaolo Prearo, Milan

18 *Untitled.* 1966
Wood, burned wicker and nylon
netting, 53 1/8 × 78 3/4 × 29 1/2''
(135 × 200 × 75 cm.)
Collection of the artist; Courtesy
Gian Enzo Sperone, Turin

A very long Sunday
has been going on
approximately since 1966
and this is 1976

We are reaching the end of the afternoon of a very long Sunday. We have never worked! For almost ten years, all we have done is think about spending a very long Sunday between two immense and gray work weeks that weigh us down before and perhaps after. Before 1966 did it seem to us that we all worked more or less and after? Afterwards, it appears to us that we have to work. (According to the rules of living in our century.)

We feel (on Sundays how we feel!) that we are not working. This consciousness makes us become slightly demonic, while we are such men during this very long Sunday.

Throughout our very long years of Sunday, they appear to our slow but solemn memories, they can appear to us; and, inadequately and a bit angrily, the faces and discourses of those who watched us work appear to our slow but solemn memories. The critics, the art dealers and, secondarily, the people who pay a little something, the collectors – they appear to and disappear from our slow but slightly angry gestures of boredom. We were not working, while when they appear (rarely), we think that they think that we are working, for culture, and hence for ourselves for them and for that which culture slowly reveals. Instead, we are stripping culture in order to see what it is made of. But this stripping takes forever, and this makes us remain in this very long Sunday, precisely to strip culture in order to see what it is made of. However, this stripping never ends!... And this stripping is truly ridiculous, although truly (let us say so) necessary.

Around 1968 (we barely remember during this never ending Sunday), we made an igloo with soil upon it and the soil was carved – or rather, not so much carved with a headstone as illuminated! The victorious political invective for the people of Viet – if the enemy masses his forces, he loses ground; if he scatters, he loses strength – we contemplated this irreversible dynamic idea, and we ignited it (with neon!), so that it wouldn't slip from our memory during our long Sunday. They won.

We discovered that culture is stripped and makes us see the war of liberation of an intelligent general

who says: If the enemy masses his forces, he loses ground, if he scatters, he loses strength. But it is the common people who say why it is the common people who dip their dirty fingers into the rice paddy and into the space that they are given to live in, an immense space! A country! They call it "their" country.

Down there in 1968, the sentence that was illuminated because it was irreversible was ignited. What a long Sunday! At dawn the announcement of war and its subsequent verification, but what a verification! For us, it is Sunday. We have had the pleasure of selling this product to our collector friend.

We are here to strip culture and every so often culture gives us its current themes by way of wars, and focuses on numbers to make sure they are truly alive and swift, how many kilometers have we covered on this terrible Sunday without work! Because we have never worked and are never conscious – we have always and only continued to exist in order to announce that no one could work very well in this eternal joy of war and of general work. The accumulation of newspapers! And of numbers!

We toured foreign countries a bit, smoking a few stubs which were shameful here and not proper there (but almost even there for those who work). Naturally we brought our Communist ideas there too, but no one there gave a damn about them, because there many people do not work on a workday. And this demonstrates that our Sunday is very long even in space. We abandoned our very long Sunday hands, our space/time drowsiness over New York, etc., etc.

Now antipathy is universal. Many artists tremble when throwing their colors on the canvas and we do not, we think we do not, but culture appears to us in light and stripped or clad in light the way the archangels appeared to Dante. We can therefore construct works in which culture appears and then disappears. This is our desperation.

It appears to us and then disappears and we barely have time (speedily) to have a work constructed or to construct it ourselves. (During our Sunday!) it appears and then disappears. Does it leave traces? In our opinion, yes, it leaves dreadful traces, like a fiery angel, it burns.

But a Sunday!
What a burning there can be on

Sunday if not a misfortune!

The angel who works burns the product on workdays, not on Sundays. Sundays bring misfortunes like wars and the accumulation of ludicrous products.

What antipathy for us poor people who endure such a long Sunday!

Our super-labor is rewarded in symbols.

When we immerse our hands in a unique and encompassing work, to strip a culture it is made up only of excesses and sediments, therefore to the sight and touch, chaos! To the real touch something exceeds something does not reveal itself. But this is filth! What exceeds and cedes here on a Sunday: to construct as is done.

We have worked with the products of other men. That is why we have worked with diverse cultures. That is why we have continued to live on Sunday.

Because, they say, cultures are, we say that cultures exceed and disappear that is why they are not eternal, except in memory, or in the energy of meanings whether before or after. During is the meaning. And therefore Sunday.

On Sunday culture strips off cultures of work and appears solemnly immersed in the filth of its inertia.

And we strip it (an attempt) while it returns to the filth real chaos of detritus of so many values – a culture of workaday works. Were we frank with one another?

First came chaos, then work, then the chaos of work, then chaos was stripped of work!

We are almost all Marxists because of the attitude that says: Marx saw this elementary process – chaos being stripped of work.

This is not a symbolic stripping.

We witnessed all this on Sunday – culture is a Sunday thing for people who work.

We witnessed all this. Symbols are nothing but filth.

Try with the seashell or earthshell, it seems symbolic to the culture on the nonexistent (to history!), but it is not a symbol of filth. It is filth.

Therefore with us, symbols can be tranquil in terms of their reality and identity, symbols are always made of filth or they quickly return to filth even when they raise their crest.

We know that a house is filth unless it is workaday culture, our Sunday continues to lull cultures in their sad but real identity with the earth. This is what art has always tried to do and has done (on Sunday) for those who view a symbol as a pretext that will drag them outside of this.

What is this? Filth, naturally on a Sunday. On a workday, filth becomes an object. Consumption has its job to do.

pp. 94-99

*19 *Small Salame. (Salamino).* 1966-67
Blanket and neon tube, 37 7/16
× 100" (90 × 254 cm.)
Private Collection, Turin

All writings can be found in Italian and German in Kunsthaus Zürich, *Mario Merz: Voglio fare subito un libro / Sofort will Ich ein Buch machen*, 1985. Page numbers listed after each text refer to this publication.

20 *Horse Theater (Teatro cavallo).*
1967
Plastic tubes, neon tubes and pillow,
98 7/16 × 118 1/8 × 19 11/16''
(250 × 300 × 50 cm.)

*21 *Horse Theater (Teatro cavallo)*.
1967
Plastic tubes and neon tubes,
98 7/16 × 118 1/8 × 19 11/16''
(250 × 300 × 50 cm.)
Sonnabend Collection, New York

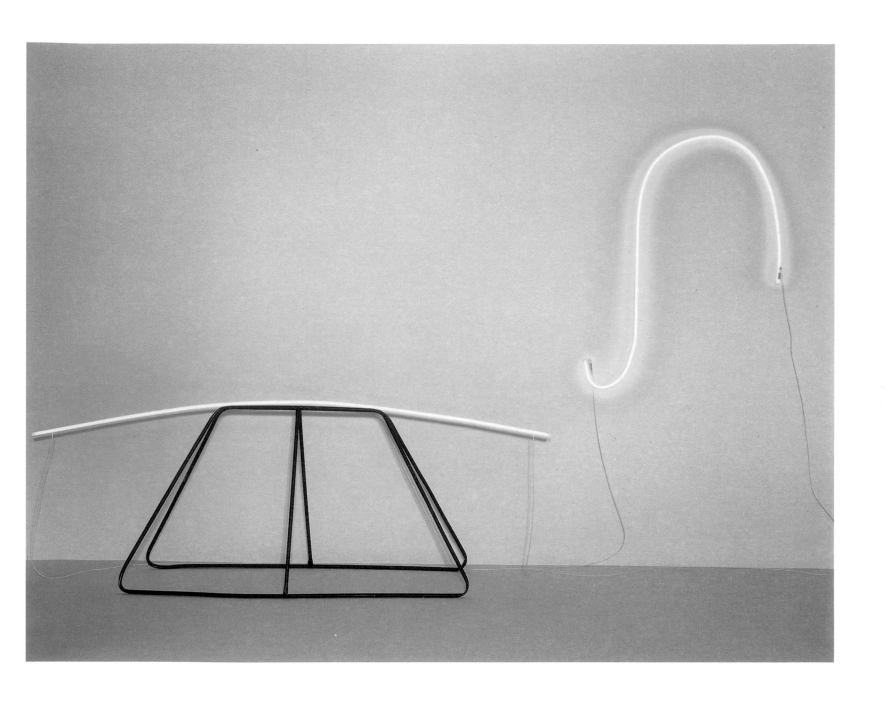

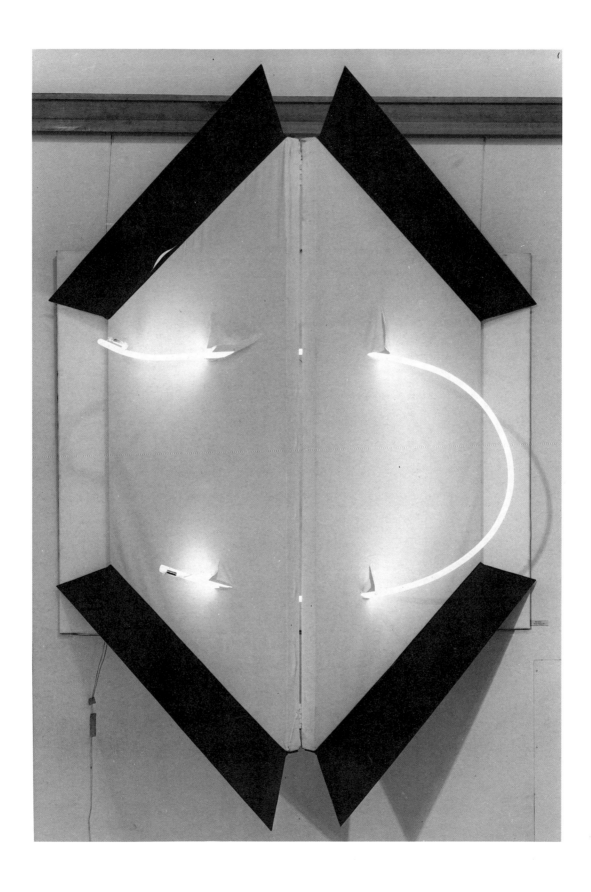

*22 *On the Street (Nella strada).* 1967
Wood, canvas and neon tube,
94 1/2 × 78 3/4 × 31 1/2''
(240 × 200 × 80 cm.)
Collection Galleria Civica d'Arte
Moderna, Turin

*23 *Untitled.* 1966-67
Murano bottle, glasses, spray paint
and neon tube, 40 1/2 × 13 3/8
× 27 9/16'' (103 × 35 × 70 cm.)
Collection Marcello Levi, Turin

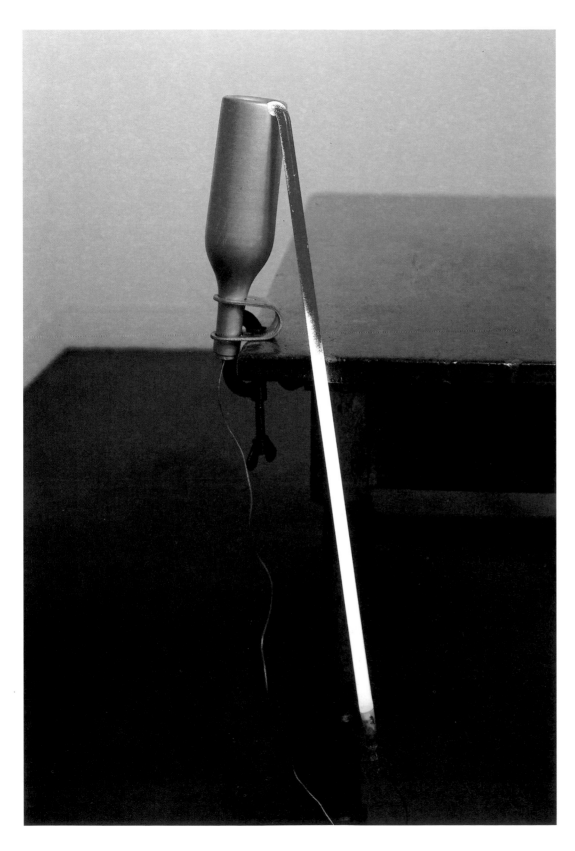

The brief bottle empty and full only
   in itself

The bottle is lifted up, the starry sky
The incomplete invisible star, which
   sheds clear light
From what expels the vapor from
   the bottle, from what has no
   memory
Because it does not adhere, nothing
   adheres.
The bottle has sunk towards the
   earth from what it can no longer
Expel, from what is the dust of my
   species
From the deposit, dust and soil
   intermingled
Dust and soils inhaled under the
   deposit, together
Between star and bottle
         THE BOTTLE EXPELLING THE
                  LIGHT.

pp.150-151

*26 *Hamper (Cestone).* 1967
Wicker basket, 53 1/8 × 78 3/4
× 29 1/2'' (135 × 200 × 75 cm.)
Courtesy Galerie Liliane et Michel
Durand-Dessert, Paris

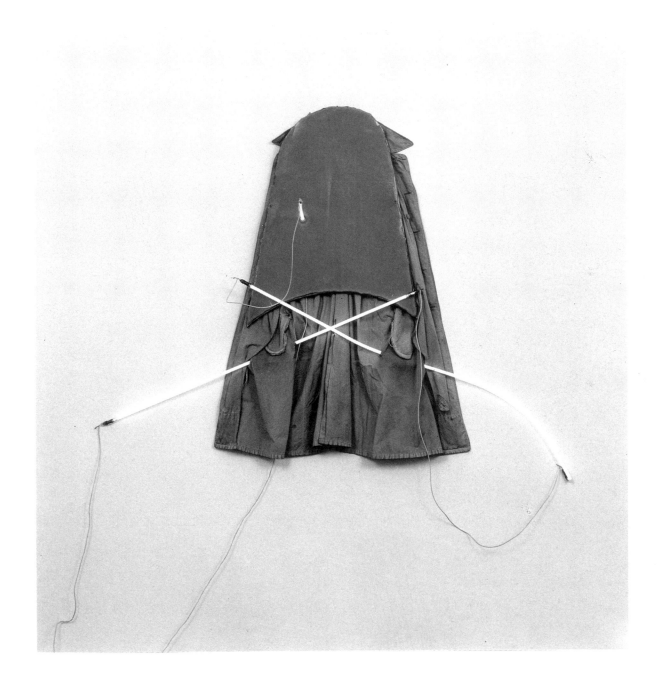

*28 *Umbrella (Ombrello).* 1967 (77)
Umbrella, neon tube and spray paint,
24 × 78 × 28'' (61 × 198.1 × 71.1 cm.)
Collection Giuliana and Tommaso
Setari, Rome

30 Installation, Galleria Gian Enzo
Sperone, Turin, January 1968,
including:
* *Lance (Lancia)*. 1967
Plexiglass and painted wood,
112 3/16 × 25 9/16 × 9 13/16"
(285 × 65 × 25 cm.)
Private Collection, Genoa

Untitled. 1966-67
Plexiglass, Murano bottle, glasses
and neon tubes

I worked on my first igloo during
the year 1967. The diameter of the
igloo was two meters [six and
a half feet] long.
Next, the diameter of the igloo was
lengthened to three meters [ten feet].
Then, in the following years, the
diameter grew to four meters
[thirteen and a half feet] and
six meters [twenty feet].
This igloo is five meters [sixteen and
a half feet] in diameter; it is made
of aluminum pipes, so that it can
easily be flown out of Italy.
The size of the diameters reveals
form structure dimension and
measure, a humanly correct measure.
In the man sitting in the interior
of this capsule as if to experience
thought, the diameter size – although
initially correct – of two meters
indicates the way in which art, or
the work that it aims at, has its sole
support in itself. The work and
the measure are second nature; hence,
they are structure and support.
Structure is its own support. The
small building, the master of space,
an atom of space, supports itself in
space, creates its own interior out
of itself by being a measure of human
space, and creates the exterior out
of itself: it creates external space by
being the measure of an internal
space.

IGLOO = HOUSE

The "optimum" of the "residence"
of the object is man's house. The
thermometer for measuring the
behavior of the object in regard to
itself is whether the object resides in
the house, or whether it is rejected
from there, partly or completely
rejected.

In that case, the object lives outside
the house, remaining in the
circulation of abandoned objects.
Unsold newspapers are objects that
are immediately rejected, for
economic reasons. Meaningful objects
that shoot from the hour of the new
edition of the bequest.
The object rejected by society,
the outdated object, the unsold
newspaper – it becomes art.
Art boasts that it can absorb rejected
bodies into its own body. Because of
enigma, because of history, because
of the nature of the body, because
of alchemy, the bodily grandeur
of rejected bodies is the desire
to harvest and to cause to grow
– a desire that is art.
Art grows the way rejected bodies,
rejected things, rejected objects grow.
To the point of exhaustion of the
process of making a body with art,
many newspapers have to come and
live in art, as many newspapers
as possible. The mathematical series
harvests countability, the greatness of
the increase of the number following
the mass social rejection of the
object.
The Fibonacci numbers, the series
that is complete unto itself from the
very start and runs towards infinity
in a nonstop process liberates the
mortified weight of the abandoned
object.
Thus, it is possible to recognize in
the words "OBJET CACHE-TOI!"
[OBJECT, CONCEAL YOURSELF!] the
twofold value of the very BEING and
NONBEING of objects. The object is.
The object conceals itself beneath the
lines of numbers, it changes value,
changes sign, liberates its own
defenselessness.

pp. 270-271

31 *Giap Igloo – If the Enemy Masses*
His Forces, He Loses Ground; If He
Scatters, He Loses Strength (Igloo di
Giap – Se il nemico si concentra perde
terreno se si disperde perde forza).
1968
Metal tubes, wire mesh, neon tubes
and dirt, 118 1/8'' d. (300 cm.)
Collection of the artist

*32 *Giap Igloo – If the Enemy Masses His Forces, He Loses Ground; If He Scatters, He Loses Strength (Igloo di Giap – Se il nemico si concentra perde terreno se si disperde perde forza).* 1968 (82)

Metal tubes, wire mesh, wax, plaster and neon tubes, 47 1/4 h. × 78 3/4" d. (120 × 200 cm.)
Musée National d'Art Moderne, Centre Georges Pompidou, Paris

*33 *Sitin.* 1968 (71)
Metal tubes, wire mesh, wax, neon
tubes and glass, 11 13/16 × 35 7/16
× 28 1/2" (30 × 90 × 72.4 cm.)
Collection Marisa Lombardi, Milan

*34 *What's To Be Done? (Che fare?).*
1968
Metal pot, wax and neon tubes,
5 7/8 × 17 11/16 × 7 1/16''
(15 × 45 × 18 cm.)
Collection Giulio Einaudi Editore
SpA, A.S., Turin

35 *Solitary Solidarity (Solitario solidale)*. 1968
Terra-cotta pot, wax and neon tubes,
5 7/8 × 19 11/16 × 7 7/8"
(15 × 50 × 20 cm.)
Collection Museum Haus Lange,
Krefeld

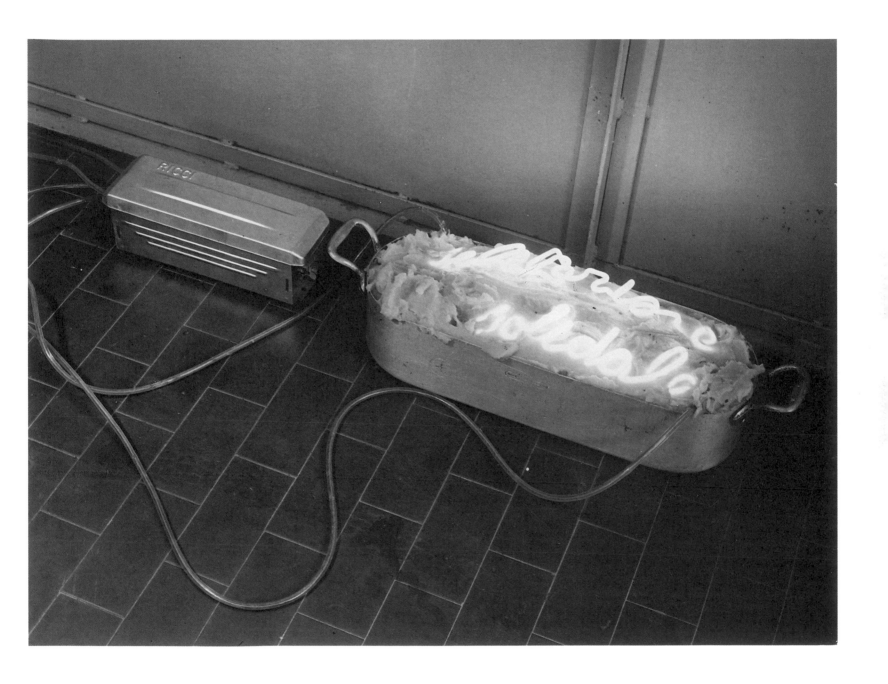

*36 *Never Has Stone Been Raised*
on Stone (Mai alzato pietra su pietra).
1968 (82)
Metal tubes, wire mesh, cloth and
neon tubes, 39 3/8 h. × 78 3/4'' d.
(100 × 200 cm.)
Collection Udo and Anette Brandhorst

*37 *Objet cache-toi.* 1968 (86)
Metal, wire mesh, cloth and neon
tubes, 43 5/16 h. × 82 3/4" d.
(110 × 210 cm.)
Sonnabend Collection, New York

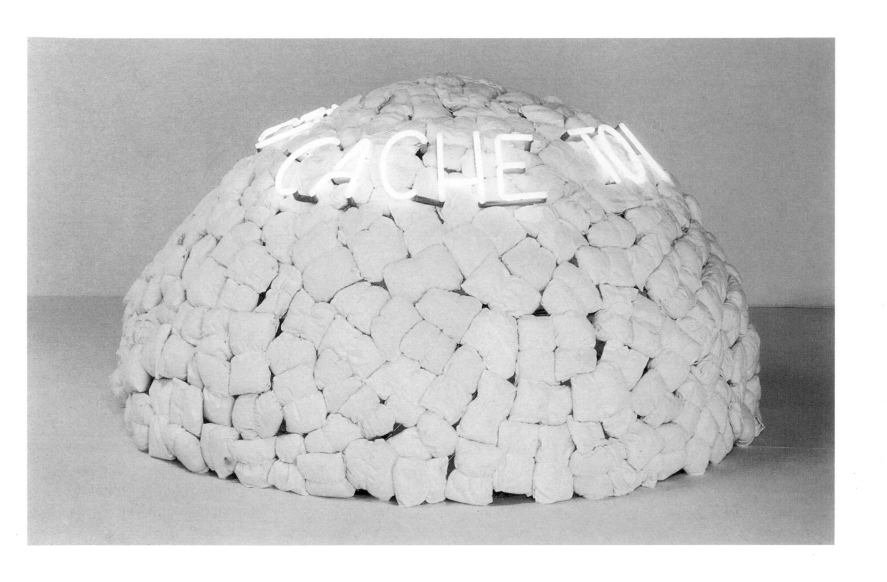

*38 *Wax and Rubber (Cera e gomma)*.
1968
Metal, rubber, incandescent lamp
and wax, 27 1/2 × 53 × 86 1/2"
(69.9 × 134.6 × 219.7 cm.)
Sonnabend Collection, New York

*39 *Hagoromo*. 1968
Metal tubes, wire mesh, wax and neon
tubes, 11 × 78 3/4 × 18 1/4"
(27.9 × 200 × 46.4 cm.)
Courtesy Sonnabend Gallery,
New York

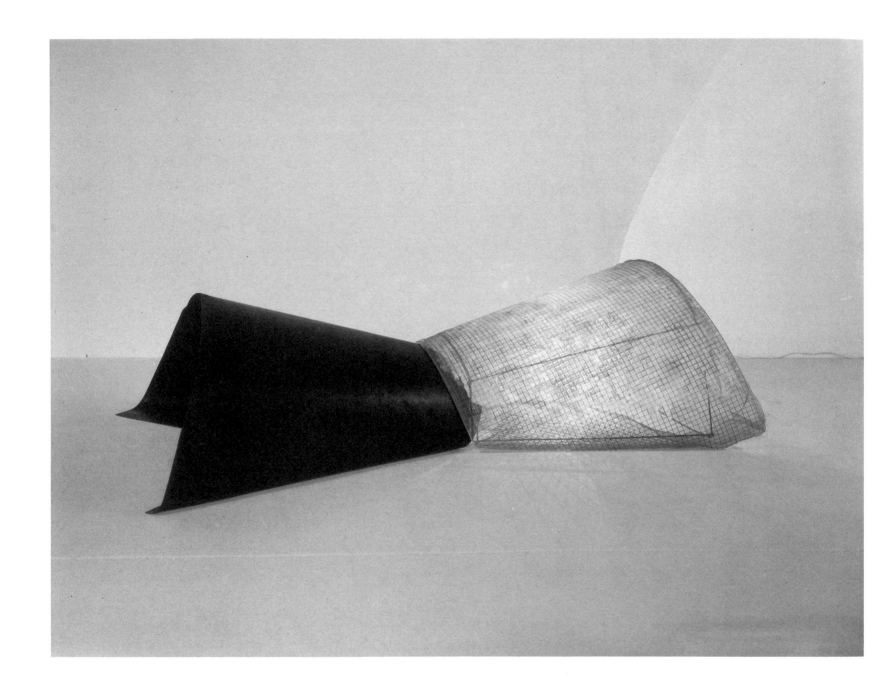

*40 *Unreal City (Città irreale)*. 1968
Metal tubes, wire mesh, wax and neon
tubes, 78 3/4 × 66 1/8 × 9 7/16''
(200 × 168 × 24 cm.)
Collection Stedelijk Museum,
Amsterdam

If nature is nature
what are we, what is art?
Is nature perhaps the GROWTH
of cells in sophisticated
complicated antinomies,
like incredibly complicated
drawings?
So where can art be if nature already
coincides with
complication, complications
incredibly more provocative
than any complications organized
by artistic expression?
I try to simplify – I keep
complication on the margins
complication is present in any case
in nature itself –
COURAGE is a simplification
of nature.
Courage in Romanticism is the
antithesis that opposes the
thesis that is nature and its terrible
complication, and
courage is its antithesis.
The waterfall reminds me of birth,
eternal snow, the silence of apparent
immobility.
But aesthetic theories that respond to
the demand for simplification taking
into account the actual impossibility
of simplifying and therefore giving
free rein to the taste for symbolism
are romantic theories. They are the
symbols (which are always
simplifications) of that which is
romantically simple and that which
is romantically complicated.
An example of the former: the egg;
of the latter: the tempest; and, in art
history, an example of the former:
painting; of the latter; music; and
if we could only pass through the
entire history of Romanticism from
Plato for the former to tragedy
for the latter.

pp. 46-47

*41 *Nugget (Lingotto)*. 1969(81)
Metal tubes, wood, wax and twigs,
structure 80 × 72 × 15 1/2''
(203 × 183 × 39.4 cm.); twigs 98'' h.
(249 cm.)
Courtesy Anthony d'Offay Gallery,
London

42 *Nugget (Lingotto)*. 1969
Metal tubes, wood, wax and twigs,
structure 80 × 72 × 15 1/2''
(203 × 183 ×39.4 cm.); twigs 98'' h.
(249 cm.)
Courtesy Galerie Liliane et Michel
Durand-Dessert, Paris

43 Installation, Galleria L'Attico,
Rome 1969, including from right
to left:
Igloo with Tree (Igloo con albcro).
1969
Metal tubes, glass, plaster and branch,
59 1/16 h. × 98 7/16'' d. (150 ×
250 cm.); with branch 10' 6'' h.
(320 cm.)

Collection of the artist; Courtesy
Galleria Christian Stein, Milan
and Turin
*Automobile Pierced by Neon
(Automobile trapassata dal neon)*. 1969
Simca 1,000 and neon tubes,
14' 9 3/16'' × 59 1/16'' × 78 3/4''
(450 × 150 × 200 cm.)
Collection of the artist

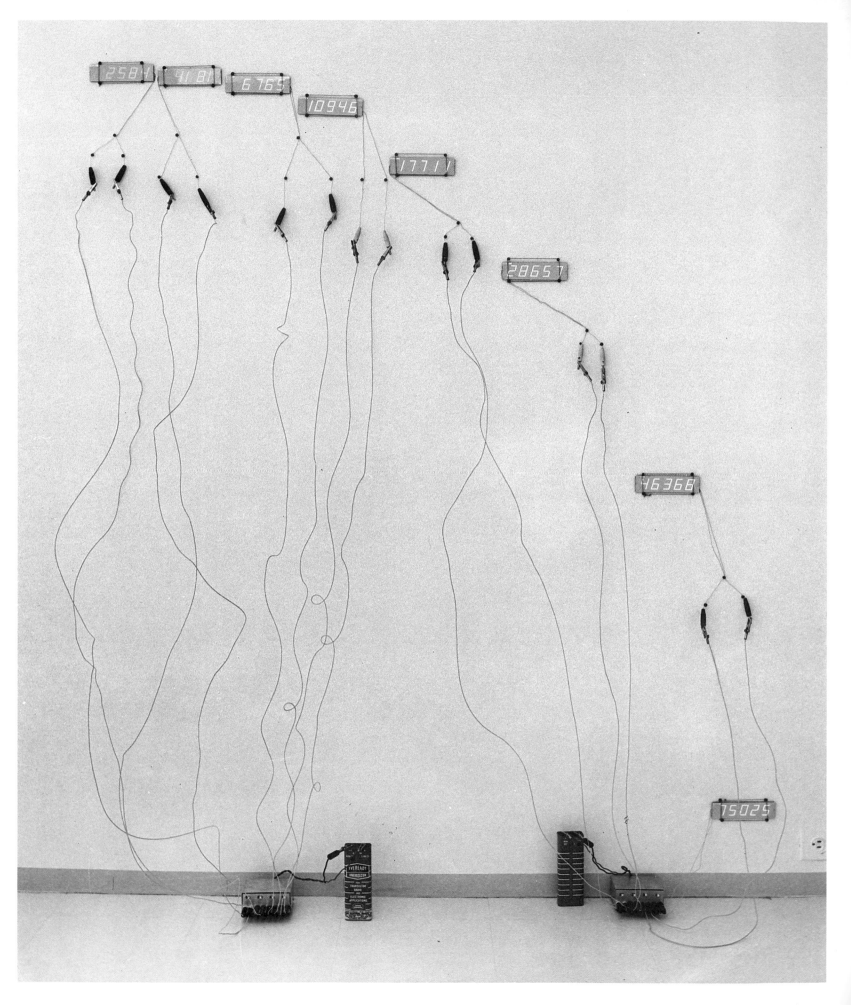

90

44 *Relationships of growth within
the development of a tree outlined
in an unbroken line according
to the Fibonacci series*. 1970
Neon tubes and wire, variable
dimensions
Courtesy Sonnabend Gallery,
New York

45 *Propped (Appoggiati)*. 1970
Glass, plaster and neon tubes
Courtesy Galleria Civica d'Arte
Moderna, Bologna

91

46 *Objet cache-toi.* 1968 (77)
Metal tubes, glass, clamps, wire mesh,
bottles and neon tubes, 157 1/2'' d.
(400 cm.)
Collection of the artist

47 *Untitled.* 1969 (78)
Bales of hay and neon tube, 47 1/4 ×
15 3/4 × 15 3/4'' (120 × 40 × 40 cm.)
Collection Lia Rumma, Naples
Refabricated for present exhibition

48 Installation, Sonnabend Auxilliary
Space, New York, 1970, including
from right to left:
*Igloo-Cancelled Numbers (Igloo-numeri
cancellati)*. 1970
Metal tubes, wire mesh, wax, Perspex
containers and neon tubes, 118 1/8"
d. (300 cm.)
Cat. no. 45 *Propped (Appoggiati)*. 1970

Following pages:
*50 *Fibonacci Progression
(Progressione di Fibonacci).* 1971
Neon tubes arranged along the inner
spiral of the Guggenheim Museum,
New York
Refabricated for present exhibition

*51 *Untitled.* 1971
Raincoat, neon tubes, spray paint,
wood and snail shell, 86 5/8 × 63
× 15 3/4'' (220 × 160 × 40 cm.)
The Arthur and Carol Goldberg
Collection

52 Installation at Sonnabend Gallery, New York, 1971, including from right to left:
*Aprons = Natural Numbers (Grembiali = numeri naturali). 1971
Metal tubes, wire mesh, neon tubes and plastic, variable dimensions
Sonnabend Collection, New York
1+1=2. 1971
Metal tubes, neon tubes and wire mesh, 39 3/8 × 78 3/4''
(100 × 200 cm.)
Courtesy Galleria Mario Pieroni, Rome

53 *Fibonacci Proliferation*
(Proliferazione di Fibonacci). 1973
Wire, neon tubes and plants, variable
dimensions
Collection of the artist; Courtesy
Galleria Gian Enzo Sperone, Turin

*54 *610 Function of 15 (610 funzione di 15).* 1971
Glass, newspapers and neon tubes,
11' 5 13/16'' × 63 × 26 3/4''
(350 × 160 × 68 cm.)
Refabricated for present exhibition

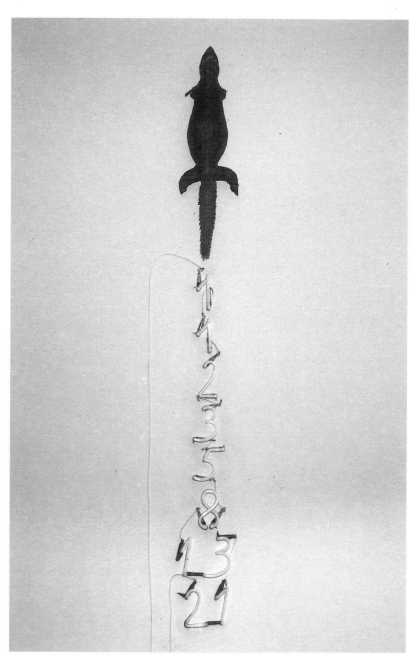

The Fibonacci numbers expand in an accelerated manner, they inspired my idea that it was possible to represent with new faculties all the examples that occur in the world of expanding materials viewed also as vital living lives.
Hence living materials that exhibit rapid and controllable expansion. The numbers are thus joined to reality; neither the numbers nor reality is dominant in that in the idea of this representative art two things have to be independent even if superimposed.
A fabulous example of independence and superimposition is to be found in the Fibonacci study of the birth of rabbits according to the Fibonacci series, or, of Fibonacci numbers superimposed as on a fantastic and realistic screen to the growth of rabbits.
Numbers are a relative extension of the body through the five fingers. Relative in that they exclude the psychological but not the physiological extension.
A wall is a load (bricks, stones, lime, historical anxieties, psychological anxieties) the numbers unload it the way music unloads the chemical density of the atmosphere. Music too has mathematical or numerical equivalences.
Time is a tap root immersed in the ground (the date of birth) time then develops in an objective and relatively free reality the way the tree develops from the tap root into the atmosphere. Time too is

an anxiety that develops in only one direction, but it can logically double back with the sign – the way numbers can double back with the sign.
The passage of light through certain holes and only through them is numerological.
Ancient architecture was not left to chance, because it was not only a covering of space.
What numerology lacks is narrative, but narrative is simply reality. Reality cannot be deformed.

pp. 202-203

The Fibonacci series published in Pisa in 1202 is based on a very simple idea. Each number adds up or involves the preceding number in the formation of the following one. One plus zero 1 + 0 = 1, hence: 1,1. Then one adds up with one to form two. And two adds up with one to form three.
Written in sequence, this makes 1 1 2 3. Then three adds up with two to form five. Five with three to form the number eight. Thus, the sequence extends, while rapidly widening like the growth of a living organism.
1 1 2 3 5 8 13 21 34 55 . . . .
the end of this operation obviously does not exist . . . .
but the microscopy of the dilation renews the organic ferment of development as proliferation.
They pour space into a larger space, which is infinite space.

pp. 116-117

*57 *Acceleration = Dream. Fibonacci Numbers in Neon and Motorcycle Phantom (Accelerazione = sogno, tubi di Fibonacci al neon e motocicletta fantasma).* 1972
Motorcycle, waterbuck horns and neon tubes
Collection of the artist
Refabricated for present exhibition

58 Merz during installation of *Fibonacci Unit* at Sonnabend Gallery, New York, April 1970

When I think back to our first meeting, in Turin in 1966, I recall the violent impact of the neon light ripping and burning the canvases, the bamboo and the objects. Those were the days of Pop painting and Minimalist structures, everything seemed controlled and perfect – almost a monolith without wounds or corners. The emergence of your works with that cold but irregular flash of lightning – the neon tube – created a destructive gash in the monumentality of the art object. Was your aim critical or destructive?

The neon work came into being as light or a bar of light or flow of light passing through the objects and destroying them in terms of the very idea of the object. I used neon to traverse the bottle in order to destroy the bottle, to turn the bottle into something else, which nevertheless remains a bottle and light. Prior to the bottle, I did canvases, which, in order to be seen, had to jut out from the wall. The neon, by traversing and piercing them, triggered a separation between the canvas and the light – that is, a concrete destruction of the canvas as the space of painting.

Nevertheless, the jutting structures of 1964-65 are not primary, nor do they tend to destroy structure per se; they are painted jutting structures. Since they were painted, they had a meaning; they remained paintings, they were painting/sculptures, something halfway between sculpture and painting. Then I felt an urge to create a vertigo by means of painting. Something that came to me with drawings – that is, spaces that are closed and painted in a manner that is closed and yet open. For instance, if we look at color, the jutting structures were painted in terms of stripes or bands. The color escaped from or slipped out of a band and moved towards and across the next band, creating a rainlike form. In a rainfall, the water glides over a thing and then escapes to the next one.

I now realized that by taking the structure itself, stretching the canvas and leaving it flat, without a painting, and piercing it with a neon tube, I produced the same form of vertigo, but in a different way, because the canvas was still pierced, although by light instead of color. The result was an intersection of objects, with the goal of destroying the preceding object rather than creating a different one.

Within these neon works, serial images were created – that is, a structure next to another structure produced a double painting, which was unified by the single neon light. The neon light pierced the canvas, emerging from it and then reentering it, coming out again, crossing the empty space between the two paintings, entering the second one – and my idea was that this could continue.

This was an idea that I then developed with the glass panes leaning against walls. In some of my exhibitions, I had as many as fifteen or twenty panes, if not more. The neon light leaned against the back of the glass; and here there was no more destruction, because glass is a transparent structure – it does not exist, and it is even canceled out by repetition. All that remains is a sequence of light, created by the neon. That led to the number, that is, the Fibonacci series.

The Fibonacci [Leonardo da Pisa, known as Fibonacci, ca. 1170 – after 1240; monk and mathematician] idea was the idea of a numerical series that involved proliferation rather than a purely mathematical meaning: each succeeding number is always the sum of the two previous numbers.

After the series of jutting paintings pierced by neon light, I put together bottles and other objects traversed by neon light. They represented a well-known physical reality: the bottle and – in the exhibition at L'Attico in Rome in 1969 – the car, the tree and other forms that are both familiar and unfamiliar at once. There were two panels in my studio, which you visited in 1967. One panel had wicker, a steel structure, a pillow and neon – and that same neon tube ultimately entered the objects, like the bottle, the chamber pot, the glass, the grape vine and the plants. My plan was to create a kind of thunderbolt that would enter objects.

Another idea of transfixing involves the lance, which I executed in wood, painting it wine red. The "wine" theme is very important, it involves glasses and then tables; moreover, this too is a theme of transfixing. This is because wine represents energy that passes through the body and alters feelings and perceptions. Through these images of transfixing or piercing with various elements I arrived at the work in which I put together a plant in water with a neon tube passing through the water. The meaning I achieved was that of luminescent electric current, visible, perceptible to the eye – a lance of light plunging through the water, the plant and the roots. Thus, the lance which, in my earliest objects, is painted wine red, becomes the image of the neon light – you can see the bottle in the clamp. Later the neon passes through the car, the glass, the bottle, and this entire transfixing is not an object – it is the power to say: "I think that in nature, the elements all crisscross one another." It was a kind of distance and, at the same time, a kind of proximity, rendering my idea of science. Science tells us that, in nature, the elements all pass into one another; the meaning of nature is transformation. This led to the idea of creating a sculpture that was not fixed, that was not geometric – a construction that would be a transformation rather than a construction. Since neon light actually has electric power as one of its own object qualities, it turns into light when it fully and perceptibly transfixes the glass object, that is, the tube. Piercing the car, the bottle, the glass, the water, or the plant with the neon tube meant physically carrying the action of transformation from one element to another.

You've spoken to me about nonobjects, a term you even apply to recognizable objects such as a bottle, an engine part, a glass, and so on. Yet they are all negated as recognizable entities – they are interwoven with one another and the neon light, they do not exist in reality. Hence, they are "abstract." Why, then, do you paint them with unreal colors like that cold red?

Precisely in order to eliminate the idea of the object-object, even if its color is that of wine, which makes you think of it as ultranatural.

Do you mean so natural as to become illogical?

Yes, indeed. Completely illogical and nonfunctional, so that, say, the raincoat I've worn that becomes a part of one of my works, no longer exists as a raincoat. A piece of wood is inserted into the two pockets of the raincoat, and the piece of wood is struck by neon light that is like an arrow.

It was after the jutting paintings. One day (I think it was in 1966-67), I decided to have the same shape redone by a workman

– not in wood, though, but in some kind of woven material. I exaggerated things, and I even had a handle done, because originally, I had told myself: the handle shouldn't be there, this has to be like a painting. Instead, I was now intent on exaggerating, and so I had the handle done, and it became an enormous basket hanging from the wall. After the huge basket, I did the cone – or rather had it done by a workman, as an immense osier trunk. Then came the work made of grass, a very precise work, which I am now taking up again in certain drawings. This is not a reprise, however; it is really a continuation. In 1945, at the end of the war, I was in prison for political reasons, and I did a portrait of another prisoner, a man with a huge red beard. I succeeded in doing the portrait in terms of hieroglyphics passing across his entire face – that was what enabled me to do it. At the time, the drawing had that significance. But now, in speaking about it, I describe it as a highly precise work, because I never once lifted the pencil from the paper. Today, I am doing the same kind of work in certain drawings. But, as I have said, they are not a reprise, they are a continuation.

When I left prison, I went straight to the countryside to do some drawings of grass, the same way I did the portrait. But this time, I went outdoors in the morning and headed for the field. The period of drawing in the field was the period of marking, which continued from dawn to dusk, and with the same method: I never once removed the pencil from the paper. I stopped towards sundown, and the fact that I had spent all day drawing that endlessly convoluted line, like a tangle of intestines, and never lifted the pencil, allowed me to think. I had spent the whole day thinking, following my thoughts and everything happening around me – for example, the twittering birds, the falling leaves, the distant rumble of a van. All these things entered the drawing, not in a natural way, of course, but as time, as a recording, as if the pencil lead were the point of certain instruments registering on a sheet of paper: the point keeps rotating, it records the humidity, the temperature, the noises, the sounds. Actually, it is never seen, but everything is in that point. Even if it isn't visible, it is entirely a passage of time. The significance for me

was that I was able to continue doing those things for months on end. The fact that it eventually was impossible to go on is meaningless; for anything that is done can also come to a halt. The important thing is that it was done once; and for me, that was very important. I kept it up for perhaps a year or two, but chiefly during the summer months. I couldn't do it in the winter months, that is, during the bad weather, because it would have been meaningless, non-naturalistic. The crux of it was the physical and mental possibility of being in a place, the place of that grass. That interested me, because it was probably the same thing that was done afterwards.

Then, my life became highly dynamic in that I had choices to make – these choices were very important in practical terms, because my father kept urging me to attend the university and decide on a career. I fled to Paris several times, out of my usual environment, and naturally these escapes interfered with my work. My choices were political – the act of going to Rome, for example, and doing things that had nothing to do with my previous work. It was all part of a social and political situation in my life at that time, and for years and years, I did no work. The recollection of that period would lead us far afield. So it makes no sense to talk about it.

Are there any works from that period that you feel are connected with the present? It seems to me that your work has taken a unique direction – a kind of pencil meshing that contains and heats up all your activity.

That's right. One summer during the 1940s, when I returned to Turin, I did poetry of a geometric nature, practically visual poetry. It consisted of typewritten words at angles, which created a form of poetry, a very old work, done before the war, and now lost. When I did the igloo with Giap's phrases, I remembered that it was the same thing: writing Giap's sentences in neon was a commitment, but at the same time, it was like doing visual poetry. When a person is bored by too many words, he says: I'll write two words, on a typewriter, so they'll be comprehensible, very legible. It's no longer my handwriting, I write them in a very precise spatial dimension, which in the igloo is roundness, and in poetry – to the extent that they are on the same plane – means writing two words in one direction and two in the other. The word imposed itself almost of its own accord, with the magnum force it could have in the social context, the context in which words are exchanged. All this is very important for my work: when language becomes a weight, when it becomes a number.

I made the igloo for three overlapping reasons. First, in order to discard the jutting plane or the wall plane and create a space independent of the process of hanging things on the wall or nailing them to the wall and putting them on a table. Hence, the idea of the igloo as the idea of absolute and self-contained space: it is not modeled; it is a hemisphere placed on the ground. I wanted the hemisphere to be nongeometrical, so the hemispherical shape created by a metallic structure was covered with sacks or with shapeless pieces of material such as soil, clay or glass. Then I began the work of writing on this structure. I felt it was so important to be able to write in an absolutely static form like neon. Originally, it was the idea of a hemisphere covered with a natural weight like soil; then, a sentence of the same quality as the sentence written by Giap was written on the soil. "*Se il nemico si concentra perde terreno se si disperde perde forza*" (If the enemy masses his forces, he loses ground; if he scatters, he loses strength). When I read that sentence, it dawned on me that it was talking about something essentially absolute, like war. In fact, it contained the word *enemy*, but in absolutely calculable terms, as a position. It was not the idea of the enemy as somebody whom one must move against; rather, the idea of the enemy in a dialectical situation that involves the person reading the words. This was very important for me; the idea of strength in an absolute sense was removed from strength itself. Strength became a dialectical quality in relation to the individual himself: this way of thinking is employed by Orientals, for whom physical meaning is absorbed by a mental idea, retained and maintained or, at times, abandoned altogether.

Is this the same situation as that involved in amalgamating the moving pencil with the landscape or grass, where the elements seem to fluctuate, suspended in space as they are, one inside the other?

The result was a situation of suspension, in which I made the igloo, because the igloo itself is a situation in suspension, in that it is suspended as an object, and the materials themelves are suspended. Starting with the Giap igloo "*Se il nemico si concentra . . . ,*" it was a moment of interest in what could be the meaning not of a word, but of a sentence: the specific meaning of the very gist of a thing. Then, during the May upheavals in Paris, some anonymous person wrote "*solitaire solidaire*" (solitary solidarity) on a wall. I was interested in the existential meaning of those two French adjectives placed side by side – they were important and, at the same time, they were suspended. I put them inside a material that would absorb a sentence. I went to buy some wax, I put the wax in a net, and on it I put that sentence, which did and did not melt in the wax, thereby remaining suspended. That is the meaning of this work. I did *Sit-In* because I had seen sit-ins both in photographs and in real life: people sitting on the ground within a given space. I planned to reproduce this image as an idea. In fact, this small iron structure with "sit-in" written in the wax had a meaning that had to do with the center of a space, which was the space in which the sit-in took place. The analogy was repeated when I wrote "*albero fiorito*" (flowering tree), mounting an idea in a precise space. The sit-in has to be very small, because it is a central point in which an event that is almost a calamity takes place. Next, in 1968, I did the *Hagoromo*.

But I'd like to talk about something else. At a certain point, I said: so much for that. I thought of concealing the object in an idea. The idea could counteract the object. We can say: we are against the objects we create. So then I covered the hemispherical object with soil and I made something that was somewhere between a cabin and the idea of the hemisphere. And over it, I wrote: "*objet cache-toi*" (object, conceal yourself). It derives directly from a graffito written on the walls in Paris in May 1968. This is a second work based on the structure of the igloo. Then I did another igloo, at the *Prospect* exhibition in 1968. It's a very bizarre thing, because the idea came from a piece by my wife, Marisa. Marisa had made small lumps of cloth – cloth folded into itself in such a way as to become like a loaf of bread. We placed a large number of those small loaves on the hemisphere, and on it we wrote in neon "*mai alzato pietra su pietra*" (never has stone been raised on stone). This is a sort of admonition to myself: bricklayers build houses, but I have never done so. I pretend to do some such thing by constructing those spheres with soil; however, I must say that this is a pretense, and that this was my statement about it.

In 1968 you embarked on your existence as a nomadic artist seeking to construct his creative core in relation to the spaces and environments that are offered to you or that you manage to occupy. Could you talk about this continual precarious journey?

In Amsterdam, for the *Op Losse Schroeven* show in 1969 I did a piece very close to the bread piece. The words "*città irreale*" (unreal city) were written on it. It means that the city is unreal, our cities are unreal and suspended in a vacuum. It is a huge triangle, each side of which is different from the others. Within this triangle, we see a filthy wax net with the words "*città irreale*" written on it in neon. At that same show in Amsterdam, there were leaning panes of glass on which I had drawn "*che fare?*" (what's to be done) in gigantic letters, using a blend of earth and oil. I did *Che fare?* twice: once in Amsterdam and once at L'Attico, in Rome, where I wrote it on a wall, again using that same blend of earth and oil. There was a water faucet on the wall of the gallery, and I turned it on. The faucet, which emitted running water, was supposed to emphasize the significance of the water that escapes in relation to the phrase "*che fare?*." The work consisted of the relationship between the escaping water and the phrase "*che fare?*" – it was still another example of suspension. For me, "*che fare?*" was to be taken literally, not in its direct political thrust. Rather, it meant: what was to be done with the water; and hence, it was a question I was asking myself.

The pieces in Rome and Amsterdam were done the same year that I did the works involving stucco and leaning panes of glass. In the leaning panes, the stucco raised the glass from the ground; at the same time, since the glass was leaning on the wall, the stucco created a soft organism between the glass resting on the ground and the glass leaning on the wall; hence, the glass was suspended in a shapeless material – the

stucco. I used an abundant quantity of stucco, so that the glass remained inside an ideal protective material. I began to do the series of leaning panes at L'Attico. Then I used bundles of firewood, panes of glass and stucco – three materials contrasting absolutely with one another: for instance, if dry branches and glass are joined, they scrape against one another. The structure is supposed to create a possible space between these contrasting materials; stucco, glass, dry wood inspire me even today . . . . Those are three words that have nothing to do with one another. There were also panes of dusty glass, found at a glazier's; I framed them with stucco. Inside the stucco, they became a very heavy material, contrasting with the idea of glass, which is light and transparent. The light placed behind this set of panes softened the glass, and the light also seemed very distant. This created the sense of the distance that actually existed between the panes – a sequence of about fifteen, placed against one another with the stucco. In order to emerge, the light had to make an enormous effort. It was filtered by the panes, which were separated by dusty gaps as well as by stucco, so that they had a very heavy material in the interstices.

In Rome I also took a box, and I poured wax inside it. Then I suspended the wax from a high structure. The meaning was the same as that of a nest in a tree – something incomprehensible, a piece of material abandoned aloft.

One of the works I did in Rome was a well made of glass panes and stucco, into which I had poured plaster. The plaster was then released into a triangular structure. I took it and propped it against a triangular iron structure. That was how I made the work consisting of the net with soil. In all the works of that period, the idea of "leaning" is very important. Everything leans on something else – that was a constant idea of mine. For me, writing leans on paper – that is to say, the paper is not intrinsic to the writing. Rather, the writing is propped against the paper, and that's why I am now doing proliferations of numbers. I feel that a number is propped against something, as if against a continuous wall. And if the number is propped, the wall is completely independent of what is propped against it. Intersection leaves one object on another without tying them together. In

sculpture, for instance, when one object is placed inside another, the sculpture itself becomes a desire to construct and insert. But my sculptures are the exact opposite: they are made in order to affirm that a thing leans against another, even in an irrational manner. For example, in the plaster triangle, there's a piece of crude iron, which was made by a blacksmith, and there's a plaster sculpture leaning against it. And, like something leaning against an arm, it is not an absolute object, it is a relative object, in that the piece of plaster, which I took from another sculpture (the glass well), is propped against that thing. One feels the action of somebody who has brought this here, propped it against the other thing, and left it. It is propped, not abandoned. That was why I called the panes of glass against the wall *Propped (Appoggiati)*. The word "propped" is very important.

There is darkness and light in the piece entitled *Wax and Rubber (Cera e gomma)*. The rubber was highly opaque. It created an embrasure, and from that embrasure another emerged, which was brightly lit by a lamp that was placed underneath. And then there was the wax. *Wax and Rubber* is: dark with the goal of darkness, which is the rubber; dark with the goal of light, which is the passage from rubber to light; light with the goal of darkness, which is the passage from light to rubber; light with the goal of light, which is light per se. It is a curriculum vitae and at the same time a thing that returns to itself and does not emerge from itself.

When I was in San Benedetto del Tronto, I went to the beach and I saw the footprints left by seagulls with three toes. I redid those imprints on a wall, carving them in with a hammer and chisel. I moved from the bottom to the top, making the imprints emerge from the window. This approach signified a passage of the environment into itself. I even added a small piece of paper with writing on it.

It seems to me that in San Benedetto del Tronto you shifted your attention to "natural traces," as if the unreality of the city had pushed you towards the countryside to look for motifs that are linked more closely to the earth and its irregular growth.

That's true. That was the period of my works involving poured wax. I was in the garden of a house and I noticed the space

*60 *Untitled (A Real Sum Is a Sum of People).* 1972
Black and white photographs and argon tubes, 24" × 16' 7 1/4" × 5 1/8" (61 × 506.1 × 13 cm.)
Collection The Museum of Modern Art, New York, Mrs. Armand P. Bartos Fund, 1974

A series of persons in a restaurant is more elementary than a series of numbers (the series is elementary but people gathered for a common function constitute something more elementary).

Numbers in the restaurant
persons in the restaurant
numbers like persons
in the restaurant

one person plus another person
makes two persons
two persons plus one arriving person
makes three persons
a real sum and a sum of people.
Fibonacci-Naples
an artistic choice that describes not free   time
but real (collective) time.

pp. 186-187

between tree branches. It was absolutely immense compared with my normal idea of space. We're used to measuring space in meters or kilometers, according to our material situation. If we have to move from one room to another, we think of space in terms of meters. If we have to move from one city to another, we think of space in terms of kilometers. Hence, we possess a pre-fixed space. But in that garden, I found myself dealing with a space that was not pre-fixed, in that the interval between two branches seemed absolutely nonmeasurable. I was unable to perceive it in metric terms. I then decided to calculate that space, and I measured it by making a calculation. I set up a canvas between two branches, and I poured liquid wax on it. The next day, the wax had hardened, so that when the canvas was removed and the branches were spread apart, this measurement of wax and space remained. Here too, we have the idea of leaning as the idea of the space between one thing and another thing leaning against it. It almost looks unreal, but actually, it is very real, because it can be physicalized, not calculated. The "casting" of the material re-creates that space in slightly absurd terms.

My use of the Fibonacci series began with the idea that it was impossible to stop inside any of those spaces. I put myself inside a contradiction between opposites – between empty and full, between life and death, which is, I believe, the contradiction between Mohammed and Buddha – the contradiction of man per se as a fact of life. These numbers do not so much cultivate the contradiction, as they absorb the *idea* of the contradiction; insofar as the numbers 5 in 5 are repeated, they are vegetative and biologically natural, considering that they have a sort of father and mother who precede them and produce the subsequent offspring. Thus, these numbers often correspond to the proliferations of natural elements and human elements: for instance, we have 5 fingers, 2 eyes, 1 nose – that is to say, we have, 1, 2, 5, and can easily recognize this number, which transcends itself in a divaricating sense. I did this series because it is biologically conceivable, because it has a direction and, above all, roots, but it has roots, because it has a biological meaning, even if the meaning is not directly scientific. This series is not purely imagi-

nary, but is used in computers, which was why I thought one could always create relationships with it. I derived drawings from it, which can be transposed from one thing to another within the same series. And that was why I made the Fibonacci igloo. I took pieces of iron, tied them together with joints; and, calculating the spaces with numbers, I constructed an igloo, the one in New York. Next, by using two leaning panes of glass, I enlarged the work. First, I took a pinecone and counted the circles down from the widest: the cone has 21 pineseeds, two circles further down 13, two circles further down 8, two circles further down 5, two circles further down 3, two circles further down 2, and it ends with 1. It was like the series of Fibonacci numbers: 21, 13, 8, 5, 3, 2, 1.

At a certain point, the Fibonacci series entered architecture. When was that?
That was at Konrad Fischer, in Düsseldorf, in 1970. I did a proliferation of the Fibonacci numbers on the wall, and it was absolutely arbitrary as a determination of spaces, but absolutely precise as a determination of distances and relationships. I was using the wall in a practical way to show something that can come to an end.
Next, I did the installation at Lambert in Milan. On the wall, some sort of module begins, and then we can see where it ends; and the wall is always an instrument to be leaned on. The written words *"sciopero generale, azione politica relativa proclamata relativamente all'arte"* (general strike, relative political action proclaimed in relation to art) were a secondary work. They interested me because I wanted to put them in the bedroom of a person who would thus have a graffito that had nothing to do with his life. It was like a newspaper, the idea of a newspaper was overturned. When you read the newspaper in the morning, you see and you read what has happened in the world; thus, you have an overturned writing. It is a work that I still have. I wanted to sell it only to a private individual, so that he could put it in his bedroom. Placing it in a bedroom has a significance for me, it strikes the nervous system as well as the mental system. During the 1970s, I did videotapes. The one I presented in Bologna was a work involving music. I hired a violinist, who played a violin, regulating his strokes and intervals according to the

Fibonacci series: ping, a pause, ping, a pause, ping-ping, two pauses, and so forth. The second tape, which I did with Gerry Schum, involved a snail shell. It came about because I had once gotten hold of a snail, and, using a magnifying glass, I scrutinized the spaces in the spiral of the shell. Between the two tapes, I did the spiral in Krefeld. When I went to the Museum Haus Lange in Krefeld, I found myself in front of a marvelous building designed by Mies van der Rohe. I then thought about the possibility of making an object relating directly and indirectly to that edifice. I didn't want to put an object inside, I wanted to make an object that would be entirely integrated with the building, yet would be the complete opposite of that building. However, the exhibition never came about. I only had the designs and plans, which then took shape in the book I did with Sperone.
This project seemed to emerge from a love-hate relationship with spaces, a sort of intense relationship with the environment, which may be extremely congenial as in Krefeld, or unpleasant, as in New York.
The New York panes, done on the Bowery, were actually about the intrinsic worth of the city. They contained writings – a series of threats. I can't remember all of them. Only the first four: *"L'espace carré menace l'espace ronde?"* (Does square space threaten round space?), *"L'espace ronde menace l'espace carré?"* (Does round space threaten square space?), *"On préfère voir la courbe ou l'imaginer?"* (Do people prefer to see a curve or imagine it?) *"Le projet alors est rond ou droit?"* (Is the project then round or straight?). They were written sequentially on the panes of glass, and the sequence went on to include statements against space, the space of the city, which I had perceived as violent. I had begun to think of these writings in Krefeld, where I had done a piece, which is documented, starting with those threats. And maybe that was the reason they sent me packing. *"Che cos'è una casa, è un'ombra sulla terra o una poco chiara frazione dello spazio?"* (What is a house, is it a shadow on the ground or a not very bright fraction of space?). That was a threat against space.
Where in architecture is there an infinite spiral that coincides with your work?
Why, in New York, of course, at the Guggenheim in 1971. While the structure

was originally extremely heavy, it became very light, almost magical. The numbers leaning against the walls eventually expand, giving the impression that they are unending. The spiral seems to suck away the interior of the museum. In fact, I say, "I think of numbers in a proliferating dilation; they are real, with the absurdity and lightness of idiocy." "This gives birth to the power of making walls light and crushing the proliferating numbers across the entire stream of the wall, so as to make the photos, paintings, mirrors, papers random. These numbers make the entire construction slightly idiotic; that is their horrible secret." In the Bowery piece, it is like a tale by Poe when I say: "This idea is equivalent to pouring water from a glass into the water of a river." "For my own security, I like to reduce to zero all the trouble caused by the objects and ideas that concern you using a maximum dilation." "Reading the num bers and understanding how they dilate is a pleasure never to be stopped, and destroying a space that empties into a larger space is a pleasure to be repeated forever." "Thought is expressed in spirals, in constrictions and dilations, thought is certainly an unknown nucleus charged with opposite polarities that cannot be taken for anything but calculus." "Is it a place to amass things or is it a place to conceal weapons or is it a place to receive elementary advice not to move?" These utterances were written in such a way that they started out feebly and eventually clashed with space. "Space is impracticable," "Space is round," "Space is intrinsically dynamic," "Space is against man today because man continues to turn space into a commodity," "Space doesn't give a shit about man, so long as man doesn't give a shit about space." That was written on the final pane. The statements were in French and English.
As I told you, this work began in Krefeld, not with a series of threats, but with a visual threat. For me, the house was a marvelous object; so I made an ideal center of the house, and then, using a progression, I made a spiral – or rather, I wanted to make one. The spiral, meeting the walls, would have had to pass through them, ideally breaking them. I was unable to execute this project. But then, I developed it in a book and in a series of drawings.
The snail work is the same thing, it is unthreatening, in that the snail is free, it is very tiny, and it has a little house with a spiral of the same size. I merely continued it on glass and I did the work for a videotape.
On the other hand, in Tokyo, I did the proliferation with a plant. I went to a gardener and obtained a dwarf pine, which I brought to my space. Starting with the joints of the small branches of the dwarf pine, I constructed, with the same module, the Fibonacci proliferation on the wall, using the four sides of the room and referring back to the pine tree. The module corresponded to the module of the small plant as a space, and then there was a module in the wall in that the wall was covered with sheets of cement with holes in them. If there was enough space inside a hole, I inserted a small cylinder of wood on which I had twisted a rubber band that led to another space.

It is certainly a highly Oriental piece, which seems to forget the concentration of the Giap igloo.

I disagree. In fact, in New York, I wrote a sentence in English, which said: "The calculation-thought of Giap is an Oriental calculation-thought." It serves to cleanse the mind of the fears of inexperience. It makes man an expert, so that, in the depths of his brain, he can foresee the forces unleashed in macroscopic space. The Giap igloo serves to stabilize relations between forces. Then I go on to say: "The power of calculation is the cleansing of calculation, as, in the Fibonacci calculation-thought, the trail of its passage is exclusively its cleansing, its inconsistency with itself in that it is elementary." After the writing came the series. I also wanted to do a proliferation of these numbers in a space that was not empty, but filled with objects, so that there would be both the proliferation and the objects, the objects would remain in proliferation to the extent that proliferation existed.
I wanted to implement this project in an office, so that the proliferation would have a meaning of both taking and abandoning, catalyzing all the objects inside.
In fact, I say: "The object encountered by the progression halts in space without proliferating, only the progression proliferates, the numbers proceed, their growth towards space and the object stops, innocu-
ous, folded by the force of an elementary but infinite calculation."
The thought is without images, the idea of these numbers is an intention without images; yet they succeed in becoming images – an image of thought and not an image per se. Actually, it is not an image, in that they are propped against a preexisting image – the walls. Finally, I say: "In 1968, in Rome, I showed the calculation-thought of Giap in the form of an igloo, in which the calculation-thought referred to three-dimensional space. The dilating numbers and Giap's thought are experiences of relations." "This plant grows, the space of its growth flows into infinite time."

61 *it is possible to have a space with*
tables for 88 people as it is possible
to have a space with tables for no one.
1973
Wood tables and neon tubes; modular
tables from 39 3/8'' × 39 3/8''
to 16' 4 7/8'' × 16' 4 7/8''
(100 × 100 - 500 × 500 cm.)
Courtesy John Weber Gallery,
New York

63 *Progressive Closet (Armadio progressivo)*. 1974
Wood, glass and neon tubes
Courtesy DAAD, Berlin

*64 *Zebra and Fibonacci (Zebra e Fibonacci).* 1973
Stuffed zebra head and neon tubes,
110 1/4'' × 12' 1 11/16''
(280 × 370 cm.)
Collection Museo d'Arte
Contemporanea, Palazzo Reale, Milan

*65 Boards with Paws Become Tables
(Tavole con le zampe diventano tavoli).
1974
Ink on canvas, two parts, total 17'
3/4'' × 50' 2 3/8'' (520 × 1530 cm.)
Collection Rijksmuseum Kröller-
Müller, Otterlo

*66 *For the Tables (Per i tavoli)*.
1974
Mixed media on canvas, 110 1/4''
× 12' 1 11/16'' (280 × 370 cm.)
Collection Angelo Baldesarre, Bari

The presence of numbers is irremediable. The number itself is already in transformation through concepts of positive and negative that acquire the values of time and space. As a result, the number, given its striation which is sensitive to all innovations and transfers, acquires new fields of observations and strange metamorphoses. The quantity and the velocity of thought, the quantity of images superimposed without a mathematical rule but with a purely practical rule, that is, quantity as a natural number, is an arrival point of the avant-garde tradition to the extreme offshoots of body art.

A quantity that uses itself as in terms of speed, that is speed in a progressive proportion, acquires from the very quantity of cases that qualify themselves, they do not lie down supine in quantity itself.

An example of this technique of quantity is the photographing of people in a restaurant as a place for performing the action of satisfying alimentary needs in a numerical progression.

pp. 188-189

68 *The Number Grows [Like] the*
Fruits of Summer and the Abundant
Leaves 1, 1, 2, 3... (Il numero ingrassa
[come] i Frutti d'estate e le foglie
abbondanti 1, 1, 2, 3...). 1974(85)
Painted wood
Courtesy Promenades, Parc Lullin,
Geneva

69 *When the Plants Invade the World*
(Quando le piante invaderanno
il mondo). 1975
Mixed media on canvas, neon tube
and terra-cotta vase
Courtesy Gian Enzo Sperone, Turin

Watching the yellow river swollen with rain, watching it carry trunks and refuse, I saw books words impudent things drifting by, incredible baseless quarrels – in short, the things of life, gazes, irresponsibility, maniacalness; the things I did not see drift by, strangely enough, were paintings and sculptures. Yet I could also have seen other things carried on the river: tickets by Lawrence Weiner, empty bottles floating with their bottoms towards the sky, horses with bloated bellies, I did not see art drifting by, not even the ultimate art, certainly no upside-down Titians, I saw no upside-down Titians, nor any horses or empty bottles or tickets. Since all these "things" represented art and were therefore berthed in a safe place and were not only chimerically but also realistically, sociologically safe in a given place: the port of chimerical and real art. It is a place inside us. From there, I got the emotional but real contrast between art and literature. Literature is an object, the book, words, dispersing consciousness and reabsorbing it continually in the mind just as the mind contains the river and whatever the river carries.

Art, on the other hand, contains the chimerical and tranquil place of calm, limpid waters, a state of grace. Art is the chimera, of the forward flight and the scattering flights of the hunt of fear of everything that goes and never returns, literature is born. Art uses things that go irresistibly, and it renews them with visible strings in sculptures works paintings in which we can find ourselves in the safe place of the chimera known as art. I mean, the shriek on the bridge is not emitted beyond the bridge and it goes with the river, but this remains present in a place that is there, I don't know where, but the object, the drawing has stopped it. This stop in a chimerical yet real place is the sole conquest of art. It is the sole and irreversible conquest of man: if man is chimerical, then in art he assumes the real aspect of the chimerical, he joins the chimerical, he dwells in it, even if his dwelling in it means having to submit to exhibiting in a museum, a palace or a garret. The place is not chimerical, it is literary, art is chimerical; placed anywhere, it can be left out. This is a declaration against the death of art. The death of literature sociologically involves the very form of literature. The weights of contemporary art are already employed at the place of the chimera, while the tempest enrages, literature is twisted and almost has no face, while the tempest enrages, the face of the twisting is methodically and irresistibly recomposed in the showcase of its support. Christ remained in the eyes not because of his literary quality but because of his ironic quality. He is present, from the confusion of death he too has taken distances across his iconographies.

pp. 12-13

70 *Untitled.* 1976
Metal tubes, stone, fruit, vegetables,
glass and branches
Courtesy Galleria Mario Pieroni,
Rome

71 *Untitled.* 1976
Neon tubes arranged on the facade
of the Antiche Prigioni in Pescara
Courtesy Galleria Mario Pieroni,
Rome

*72 *Stopgap Leaves (Foglie tappabuchi)*. 1976
Mixed media on canvas, 59 1/16''
× 12' 9 9/16'' (150 × 390 cm.)
Courtesy Galleria Antonio Tucci
Russo, Turin

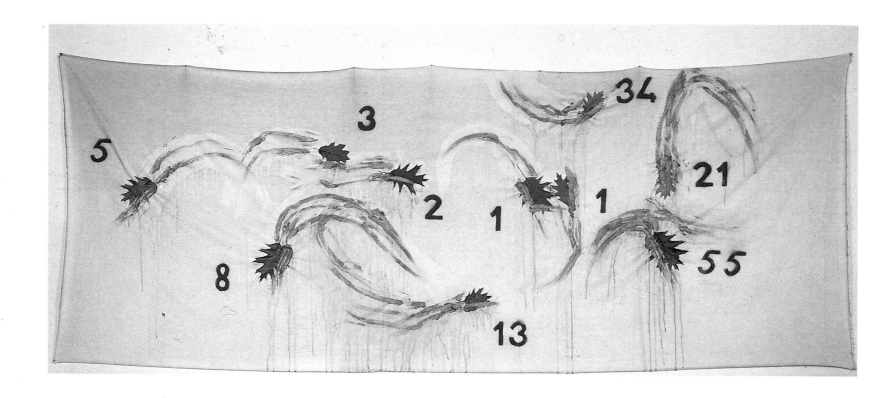

73 *Spiral Table for Banquet of Newspapers Dated the Day of the Banquet (Tavolo a spirale per festino di giornali datati il giorno del festino).* 1976

Metal tubes, glass, fruit, vegetables, twigs, crystal, stone, newspapers and neon tubes; spiral table maximum 26' 3'' d. (800 cm.) Courtesy Galleria Antonio Tucci Russo, Turin

74 *Fibonacci, 1975.* 1975
Stuffed ibex head and neon tubes,
variable dimensions
Collection Peppino Di Bernardo,
Naples

*75 *The Island of Fruit (L'isola della frutta).* 1975
Color photographs and neon tubes,
118 1/8 × 196 7/8'' (300 × 500 cm.)
Collection Galleria Mario Pieroni,
Rome

76 *Tables (Tavoli)*. 1976
Painting in copper sulfate and sulfur,
and dirt
Collection of the artist

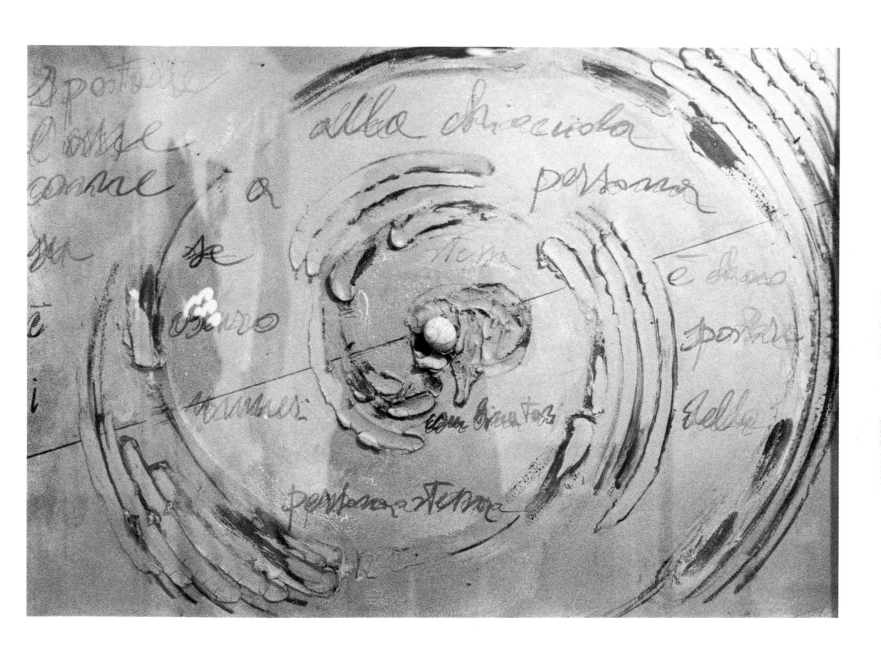

The race for life (in art) is galloping across a heavy terrain. Everything has been done so that artists can be more or less pursued in acts of idiotic consumption of calculations by collectors. All the galleries without exception are consuming useless energy in this race towards artistic consumption, to cretinizing power.

Art defends itself against forms with ideology the way life defends itself against repression with ideas.
In the history of art I feel ridiculous I cannot exhibit my ridiculous works . . . .

My opinion is to mediate on this ancient and present truth.
The art galleries have little likelihood of representing the artist, just as the artist has little likelihood of representing reality.
The asocial is the present situation of art, the asocial represents the unconscious for everyone the commercial representations do not maintain the asocial on the level of possible individuation so that I do not feel tied to any steady commercial representation.

pp. 64-65

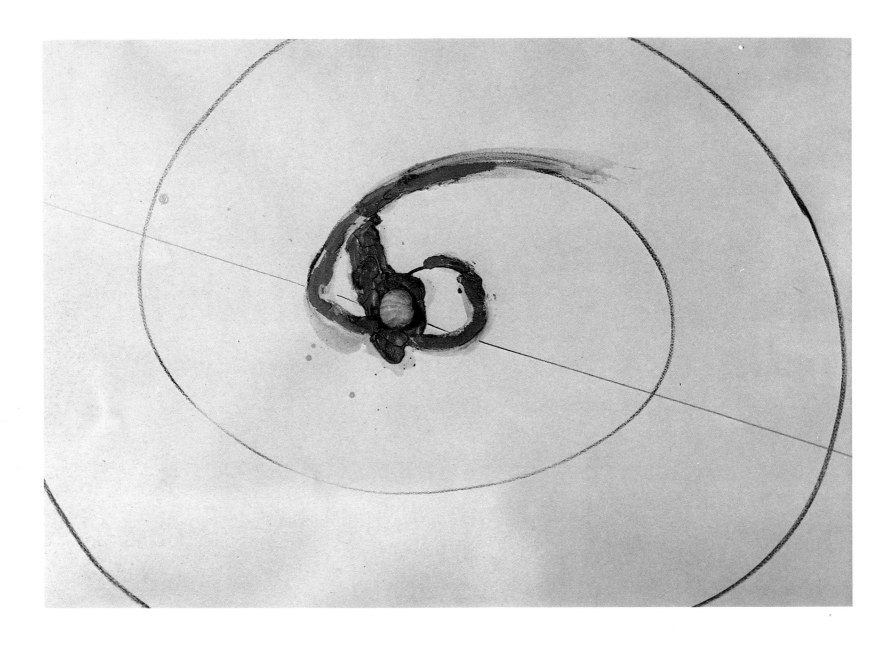

79 *Untitled.* 1976
Mixed media on canvas and snail
shell, 28 3/8 × 40 13/16''
(72 × 102 cm.)
Collection Jean-Paul Jungo, Morges

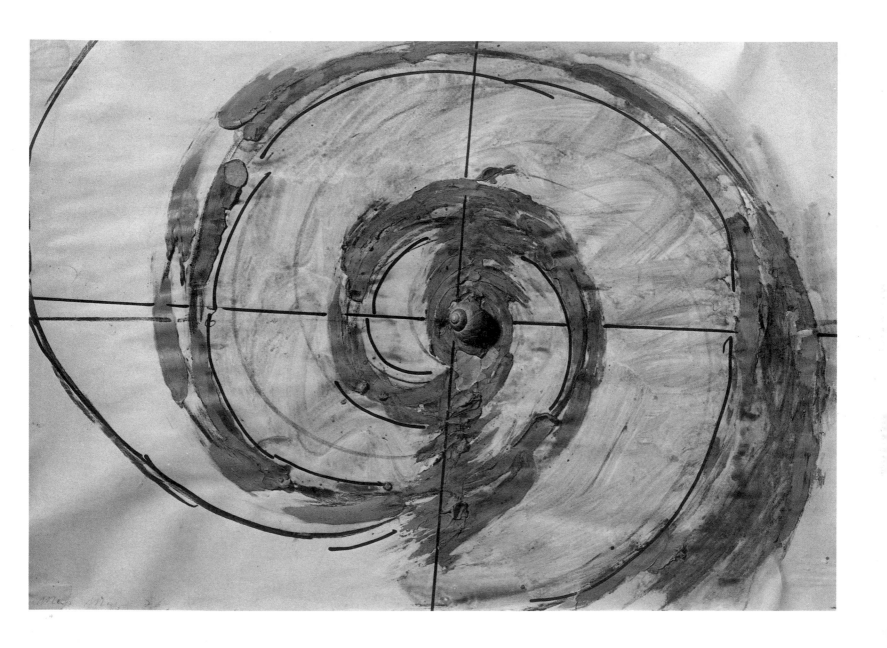

The fruit is here!
We do not genuflect and say:
Thank the Lord!
God has given this to us!
Our ancestors said it.
We say:
The fruit is here!
But we do not know
where it comes from,
where it comes from,
the fruit.
We do not know
why the fruit is here!
We think that the fruit
is our property,
then we get very suspicious.
Perhaps the property
of eating fruit
is properly ours.
But we do not know
whether the fruit
is ours.

The fruit counters
are grand
then truckloads of fruit
are dumped upon them.
We suspect
that the fruit is not in our hands,
if the fruit counters
became palaces
we would suspect
that the palaces are ours!
But we have deep suspicions
about the ownership
of the fruit.
If the fruit spoils
quickly in time,
then we too will spoil
in the long run;
do we harbor suspicions
about ourselves too?
We are not properly
fruit!
Our palaces

are ours!
But the fruit
is not ours!
How can we suspect that something
in the world
is not ours?
However, the fruit sellers
seem to harbor
deep suspicions
about the ownership of the fruit.
The passage of ownership
is very speedy.
Then we suddenly
know something
from which
our suspicions
are suddenly
remote.
The fruit is
very beautiful.

pp. 162-165

80a *Nature Is the Art of the Number*
(La natura è l'arte del numero). 1976
Metal tubes, glass, clamps, plaster,
crystal, stone, neon tubes, fruit,
vegetables, twigs and newspapers,
variable dimensions
Courtesy Museo Aragona Pignatelli,
Naples

A set of numbers is a house

A tree occupies chiefly time.
Two trees occupy the same time but a larger space.
A forest occupies the same time and a large space.
Space is time that can be eaten.
The time of the falling of a fruit is proportional to the size that the fruit has taken time to attain.
In moments of reproduction animals are independent of animals of other species. Numbers in reproduction are independent of numbers in other classes. Numbers take on a proliferation force from distinct but connected unities like animals.
One is one, one is one.
Two is one encounter, a front.
Three is an ensemble of the preceding encounter plus the solitary recovery of a distinct unity.
Five is the front of the two unities plus the moment of recovery, and all this in a new ensemble.
Thus this means that one, one, two, three, five, are in proliferation, they are alive, they are not an inert procession of unities. Following the process of proliferation leads to an antiparodistic vision of things, and hence to constructing houses.
Becoming large (growing) is antiparodistic.
A house is a grown product.
MAKING a house is taking into account the proportion of growth.
Making a house to meet the

requirement of applying a limited order in the face of an unlimited disorder.
Making a house in order to follow the will to survive.
Making a house by negating natural space (it is in its requirement for growth). In everyday life a portion of the unknown is uncommunicable it is inside the house.
Making a house is a proportion between a man and a squandering of nature. Do the numbers of the house relate to economic processes or to the space occupied by bodies and the years that lives occupy in time?
Is a set of houses a moving chorale of detached pieces or does it in itself represent a totality?
Are houses a sum of spaces or a living proliferation?
The Fibonacci house is deliberately constructed on the numerical series of that name.
The fact that it is deliberately constructed can be a merit or a defect according to architectural tradition.
My intention is to apply the Fibonacci series as the succession of elementary numbers is applied with the linear measure.
Art exists because of the need to apply a limited order in the face of an unlimited disorder.
Architecture is the application of construction material in a place where it is appropriate for a group of people to live.

The proportions of reality the mental disproportions occupy like drawings.
Constructing a house is abandoning the idealistic disproportion of pure thought and accepting construction with the proportion from reality.
Reality contains everything
with the will to survive
and
the consciousness of negating
the consciousness of the positive
and the unknown which then acts like
a product of the contemporary.
Constructing is knowing the proportion between man and the squandering of material used by man. Using solar material.
All space/time proportions are correlated with the space occupied by the body and the years occupied by life in time.
The house is a relationship between space and time.
Time is a creator and destroyer of space.
Space is not autonomous or static.
Space is controlled by time.
A tree occupies chiefly time.
The fragrance of pines is a derivate of time.
Eating a piece of fruit is eating time in a space.
The time of the falling of a pinecone is proportional to the size that the pinecone has taken time to attain.
Becoming large (growing) is the house, making the house is taking

into account the proportions of growth in biological time.
The artwork is the only source of money that I have for acquiring a sufficient amount for starting construction work.
I construct in order to limit the automatic disorder of our way of life.
To get to know less approximately my present real dissatisfactions.
Constructing is above all an alert recognition of everyday life.
It is different from the hedonistic material intrinsic to art, this real concrete and grossly differentiated material intrinsic to the construction of installation. In art the material comes from tradition.
In order to construct one must frequently change the materials.
Wood is the material of forests.
Forests no longer exist.
Wood must be canceled as a material.
Glass is the laboratory material closest to the conditioned separation of spaces.
Head and sight separated and united by glass.
Only constructing today has the attraction of making art grow rather than reducing it to a symbol.

pp. 248-252

81 *Prehistoric Wind from the Frozen
Mountains (Vento preistorico dalle
montagne gelate).* 1977
Mixed media on canvas and twigs,
98 7/16 × 70 7/8'' (250 × 180 cm.)
Collection F.E. Rentschler, Laupheim

*82 *The Bridge of the Big Mother Round Trip (Il Ponte della Gran Madre Andata e Ritorno).* 1977
Mixed media on canvas, 56 1/16''
× 16' 1/2'' (150 × 489 cm.)
Collection Guido Accornero; Courtesy
Galleria Antonio Tucci Russo, Turin

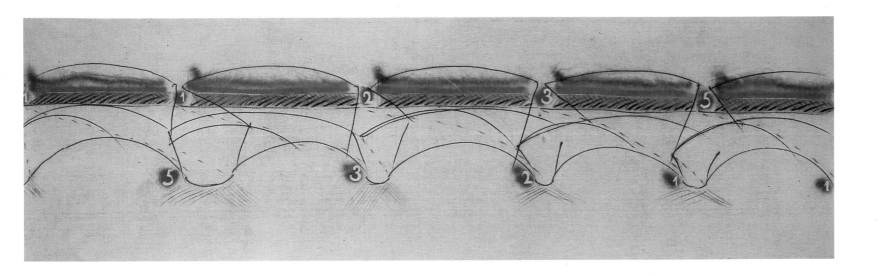

Today in the glorious park of fog
Next to the nameless walls
Cracked by insult
And covered with the cover of light
  and fog
The incandescent snail lives enclosed
  in its spiral!
Violet lamp of nature my foot in
  space
Covered with fog walks swiftly
The solitary pinecone squeezes its
  pine seeds
Into its tiny and perfect space!
My walking foot squeezes its bones
The way the solitary pinecone
  squeezes its pine seeds
Into its tiny and perfect space
In the inadmissible park attached to
  the ruins
A glorious globe of fog
The park squeezes the solitary
  pinecone
In the park my solitary and human
  foot crunches
It is a numbered ossuary of small
  things of bones
Numbered and living

Squeezed, the way a pinecone
  squeezes its strange pine seeds
Thus, inside my foot my pine seeds
  of bone coexist
In the glorious park of ruins and fog
With the squeezed pine seeds of the
  solitary pinecone
Here the crunching foot, there the
  silent pinecone
I go back always to the snail, the
  incandescent snail of my brain
Having made its spiral with a single
  total bone
An ossified spiral shell, in order to
  be small and precise
In the glorious globe of fog
In the park the hidden incandescent
  snail of the brain
Squeezes into the ossified spiral shell
In order to be small and precise
My human foot crunches in the park
It is a numbered ossuary of small
  things of bones, squeezed into the
  foot.

pp.132-133

83 *Fibonacci Drawing.* 1977
Drawing in chalk on Louis Sullivan's
Chicago Stock Exehange Quotation
Board at The Art Institute of Chicago,
each board 11' 3'' × 16' 9'' (342.9
× 510.5 cm.); total 35' 6'' × 16' 9''
(1082 × 510.5 cm.)
Destroyed
Courtesy The Art Institute of Chicago

84 *Igloo – Paving Stones and Broken Glass from the Destroyed House Reactivated by Art in a Gallery/ in a Museum (Igloo – pietre del selciato e vetri rotti della casa distrutta riattivati per l'arte in una galleria/in un museo).* 1977

Metal tubes, glass, clamps, stone, plaster and lamp, 22' 11 5/8'' × 165 3/8'' × 82 11/16'' (700 × 420 × 210 cm.)

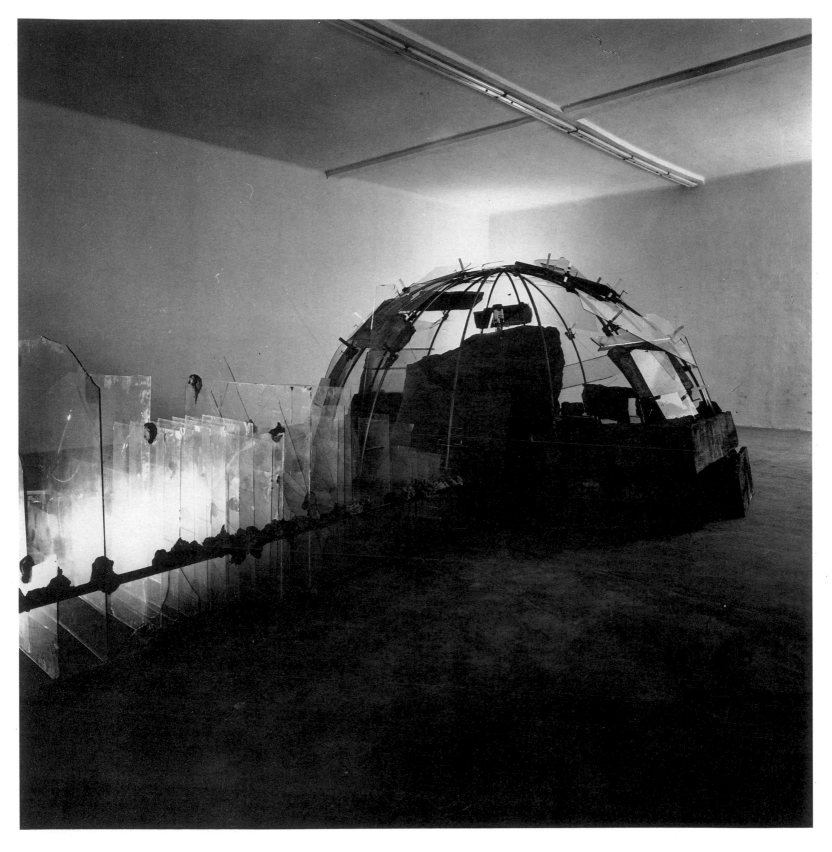

*85 *Fountain (Fontana)*. 1978
Neon tubes, metal can, metal tubes
and fountain pump, 92 × 32 × 6''
(233.7 × 81.3 × 15.2 cm.)
The Arthur and Carol Goldberg
Collection

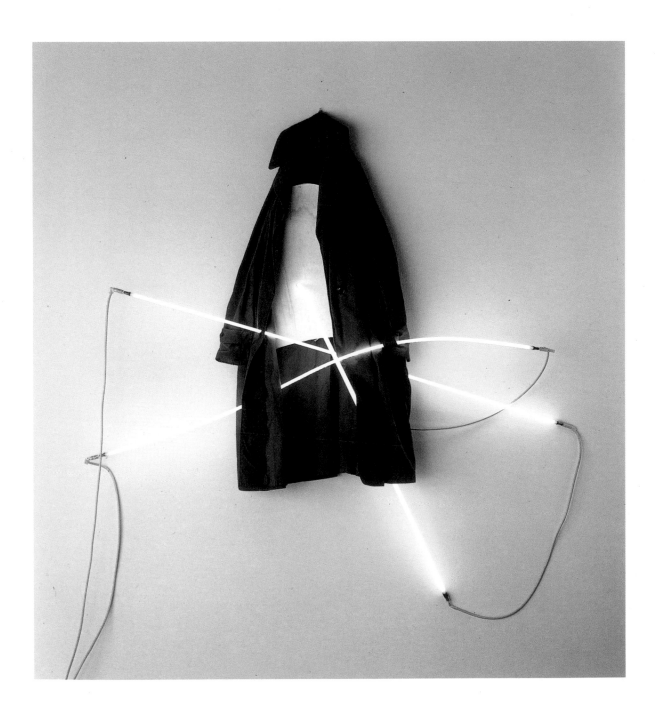

87 *Untitled.* 1978
Mixed media on canvas, 31 1/8 × 55 1/8''
(79 × 140 cm.)
Collection Ippolito Simonis, Turin

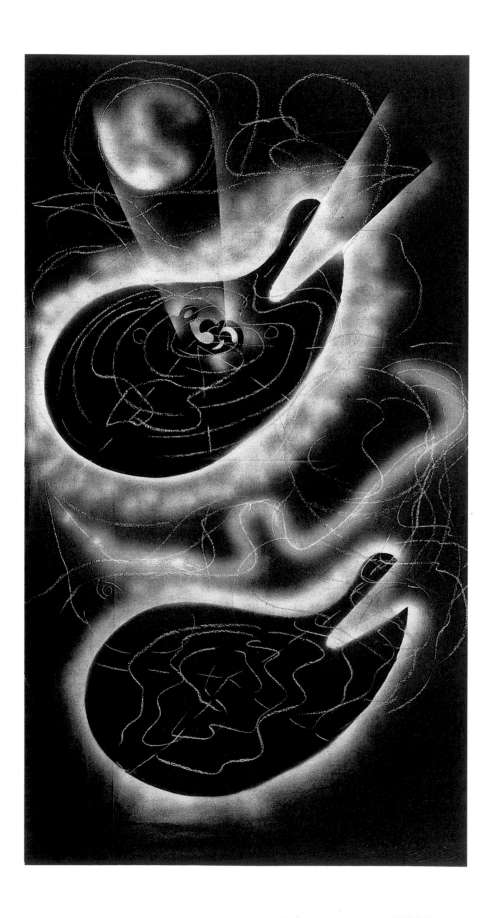

*88 *Panther on Cone (Pantere sul cono)*. 1978
Mixed media on canvas, two parts,
each 78 3/4'' × 13' 1 1/2''
(200 × 400 cm.)
Courtesy Konrad Fischer, Düsseldorf

*89 *Nine Vegetables (Nove verdure).*
1978
Mixed media on canvas and
vegetables, 70 7/8 × 118 1/8''
(180 × 300 cm.)
Metzeler Collection, Düsseldorf

90 *Prehistoric Wind from the Frozen
Mountains (Vento preistorico dalle
montagne gelate).* 1965+78
Wood, oil on canvas, neon tubes and
twigs, 79 1/8 × 78 3/4 × 23 1/4''
(201 × 200 × 59 cm.); neon 10' 2 3/4''
× 1'' (312 × 2.5 cm.)
Collection Rijksmuseum Kröller-
Müller, Otterlo

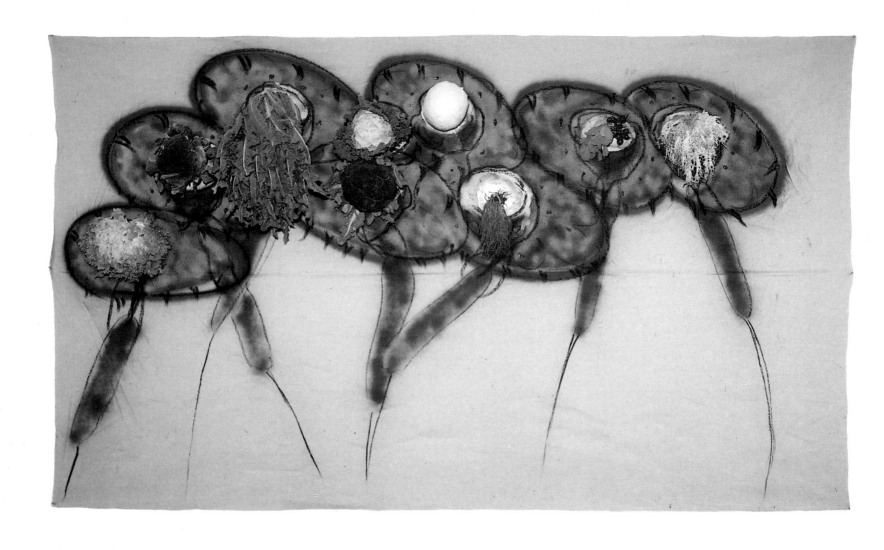

91 *If the hoarfrost grip thy tent thou wilt give thanks when night is spent.*
1978
Metal tubes, wire mesh and neon tubes, 13' 1 1/2'' d. (400 cm.)
Collection Annick and Anton Herbert, Ghent

92 *Evidence of 987 (Evidenza di 987)*.
1978
Metal tubes, glass, clamps, car door,
metal objects, canvas, branches,
painted canvas, burned branches and
neon tubes, 19' 8 1/4'' d. (600 cm.)
Courtesy Galleria Antonio Tucci
Russo, Turin

*93 *Old Bison on the Savannah*
(Vecchio bisonte nella savana). 1979
Mixed media on canvas, neon tube,
branches and bottles; canvas 12'
× 13' 6'' (304.8 × 411.5 cm.);
branches 53 × 90 × 110''
(134.6 × 228.6 × 279.4 cm.)
Private Collection, Sydney

94 *Rhinoceros (Rinoceronte)*. 1979
Mixed media on canvas and neon
tube, 114 9/16'' × 14' 1 5/16''
(291 × 430 cm.)
Private Collection; Courtesy Galleria
Christian Stein, Milan and Turin

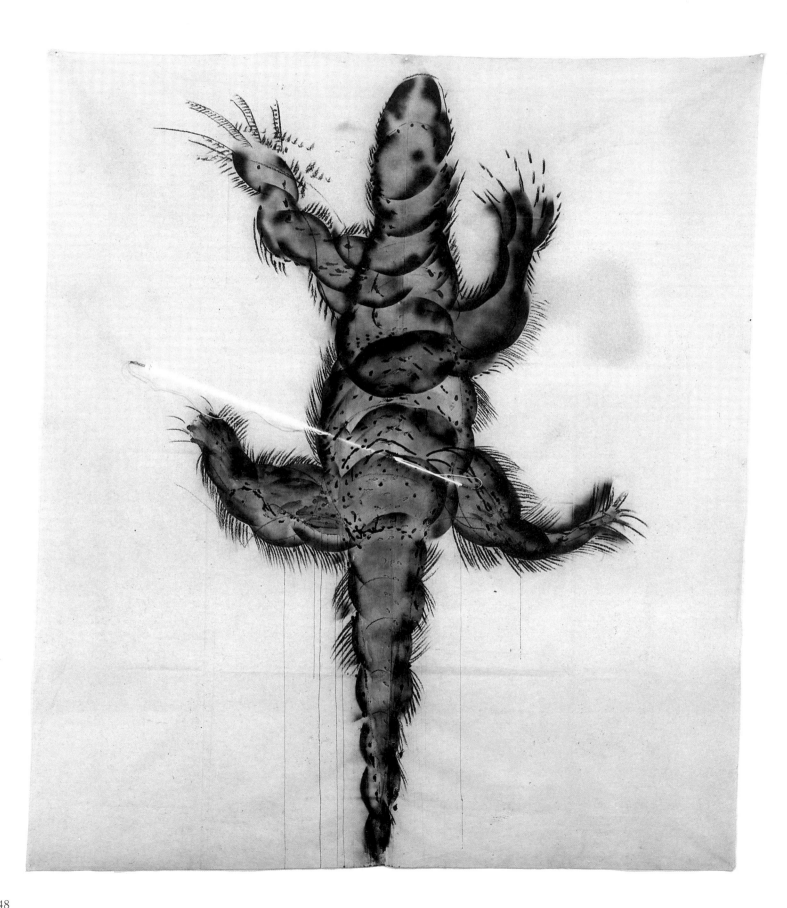

96 *Round Legs (Gambe rotonde).* 1979
Oil on canvas, metal tubes and
branches, 98 7/16'' d. (250 cm.);
canvas 57 1/16'' × 12' 9 1/2''
(145 × 390 cm.)
Collection Egidio Marzona, Düsseldorf

*97 *Untitled.* 1976+79
Leather jacket, painted plexiglass, neon
tube and twigs, 39 3/8 × 47 1/4 ×
11 13/16'' (100 × 120 × 30 cm.)
Collection Udo and Anette Brandhorst

*98 *The Sum in Your Pocket*
(La cifra in tasca). 1974
Jacket, wood, spray paint and neon
tubes, 39 3/8 × 59 1/16 × 9 3/16"
(100 × 150 × 25 cm.)
Collection Elisabeth and Ealan
Wingate, New York

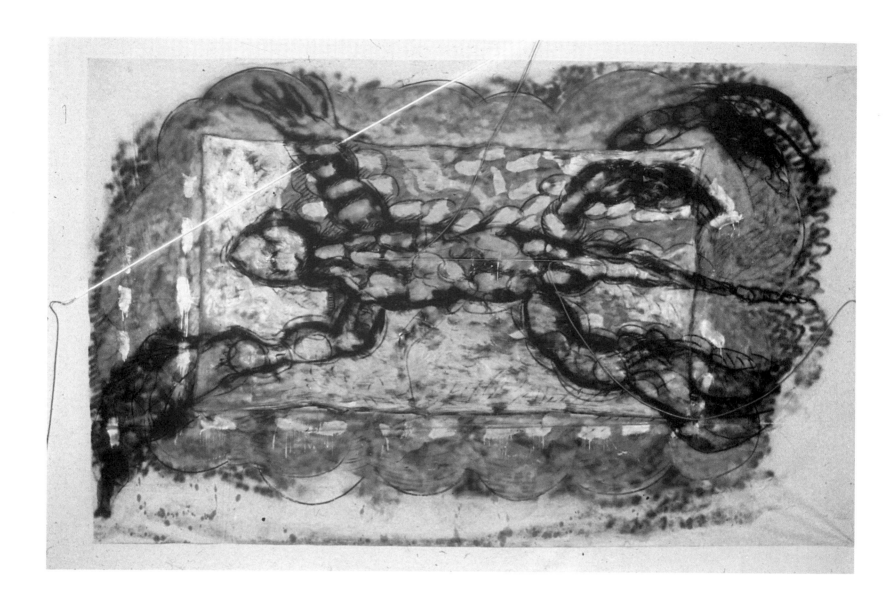

100 *Irritable Irritated (Irritabile irritato).* 1979
Mixed media on canvas, plaster and
neon tube, 110 1/4'' × 17' 4 11/16''
(280 × 530 cm.)
Courtesy Annemarie Verna Galerie,
Zürich

102 *Do Houses Walk Around Us
or Do We Walk Around Houses?
(Le case girano intorno a noi o noi
giriamo intorno alle case?).* 1979
Bamboo, glass, plaster, lamp and paint
on tracing paper, 11' 3 13/16'' × 12'
11/16'' × 13' 1 1/2'' (360 × 370 × 400
cm.)
Collection Museum Van Hadendaagse
Kunst, Ghent

103 Installation, Museum Folkwang, Essen, January 1979, including from right to left:
Raincoat (Impemeabile). 1979
Spiral with Bottle (Spirale con bottiglia). 1979
Metal tubes, wire mesh, bottle, neon tubes and basins of sand, variable dimensions
Collection of the artist
Cat. no. 109 *Prehistoric Wind from the Frozen Mountains (Vento preistorico dalle montagne gelate).* 1966+79

104 *Places Without Streets (Luoghi senza strada).* 1979
Metal tubes, wire mesh, bitumen and neon tubes, 78 3/4" d. (200 cm.)
Collection Stedelijk Van Abbemuseum, Eindhoven

105 Installation, Galleria Franco Toselli, Milan, October 1979, including from right to left:
Untitled. 1979
Mixed media on canvas and neon tube, 98 7/16'' × 12' 5 5/8'' (250 × 380 cm.)

Courtesy Galleria Franco Toselli, Milan
Three (Tre). 1979
Metal tubes, mixed media on canvas, neon tubes, twigs and bottle, 78 3/4 × 78 3/4 × 46 5/16'' (200 × 200 × 25 cm.)
Courtesy Konrad Fisher, Düsseldorf

Silver Crocodile (Coccodrillo d'argento). 1980
Mixed media on canvas and neon tube, 13' 9 3/8'' × 78 3/4'' (420 × 200 cm.)
Private Collection, Courtesy Stedelijk Van Abbemuseum, Eindhoven

106 *Double Igloo (Doppio igloo).* 1979
Outer structure: metal tubes, clamps,
glass and hat; inner structure: metal
tubes, wire mesh, dried mud and neon
tubes, 118 1/8'' h. × 19' 8 1/4'' d.
(300 × 600 cm.)
Courtesy Museum Folkwang, Essen

108 *The refuse of newpapers or the*
refuse of nature or the refuse of body
of the snail have in themselves
the spiral or the continuity in time
of power of space. 1979
Mixed media on canvas, newspapers,
glass, neon tubes, bottle, branches
and pinecones

Collection Gino di Maggio, Milan;
Courtesy National Gallery of Victoria,
Melbourne

109 *Prehistoric Wind from the Frozen Mountains (Vento preistorico dalle montagne gelate)*. 1966+79
Canvas, neon tube and twigs,
118 1/8 × 98 7/16 × 31 1/2''
(300 × 250 × 80 cm.)
Courtesy Museum Folkwang, Essen

110 *Untitled.* 1979
Metal tubes, mixed media on canvas
and neon tubes, 11' 5 13/16'' d.
(350 cm.)
Collection U. Hodel, Zürich

111 Installation, Castello Colonna,
Genazzano, November 1979, including
from front to back:
Untitled. 1979
Metal tubes, clamps, stone and neon
tubes, igloo 118 1/8'' h. × 19' 8 1/4''
d. (300 × 600 cm.); circular structure
11' 5 13/16'' d. (350 cm.)
Collection of the artist
Cat. no. 110 *Untitled.* 1979

Arte Povera, they say, has made it possible for commercial, technological and manufacturing materials to represent an artistic idea; it has destroyed or simply obfuscated a certain reduced quantity of artistic surface materials in order to restore to the surface the meaningfulness of destiny in a broad sense. For instance, *Arte Povera* has done away with the frame as a support in order to give value to the more elementary, but also more complex support of the immobility of the floor, of the field, or the vertical immobility of the wall made of bricks, stones or concrete. *Arte Povera* has taken hold of beams or trees. These alternative supports have liberated art from fixed programs, not in order to create new iconographies, but in order to

free the feeling of art to probe between diverse and opposite realities rather than to close art or to enclose it in traditional supports, thereby reacquiring it; art has relationships with iconographies or amid iconographies. We cannot speak of relationships between Expressionisms, Goya, Pre-Raphaelite iconographies, Fauve iconographies, etc., etc. This marked sense of innovation does not protect art, it does not open it and fan it out, but it enables it every so often to probe amid realities, objects and languages destined for other values or other types of readings; for instance, Conceptual art is a probe amid printed words, luminous writing or notes written in a swift instinctive nervous calligraphy.

Objects or natures very remote from being art, or artistic supports, gather together in the new art.
A parallelepiped of iron pipe can become a frame for stretching a portable canvas, a heap of twigs brings into art the irremediable opacity of a product of the earth, because, in art, it is united with the irremediable luminosity of electric power. A canvas is an image swiftly sprayed in ten minutes of craftsmanship and not painting, it reveals the possibility of immersing this image, derived in whatever manner, in the probe that unites it with twigs and electric power, and views it as stages of fleeting or permanent places to speak, stand, actors those images by alternate or concatenated musical scores.

That is the art of today.
This art is never a relationship between opposing iconographies, between oppositions like "turning a page" and "iconographic stabilities." The rapid images have entered the dimension of this art in order to bring in the image and not the "painting" dedicated by other, more stable iconographies.
It would be absurd to go through static and pictorial iconography with a lamp, but it is possible to carry a lamp through the very rapid image and yet "as it comes, it comes," with a few seconds of making, because this is already part of the intuition of the passage across.
This is what it is.

pp. 68-69

112 *Reflections on the Table
in December 1979 (Riflessi sul tavolo
nel dicembre 1979).* 1979
Spray-painted tables, poles covered
with metal shavings attached to lumps
of plaster, neon tubes and cups,
variable dimensions
Collection Salvatore Ala, New York;
Courtesy Galleria Salvatore Ala, Milan

113 Installation, Galerie Albert
Baronian, Brussels, 1980, including:
Près de la table. 1980
Spray-painted tables, poles covered
with metal shavings attached to lumps
of plaster, neon tubes, cup, branches
and canvas, variable dimensions
Collection Arnold Forde, Los Angeles

114 *Billiards (Biliardo).* 1981
Mixed media on canvas and neon
tube, 78 3/4'' × 19' 8 1/4''
(200 × 600 cm.)
Collection Christian Stein, Turin

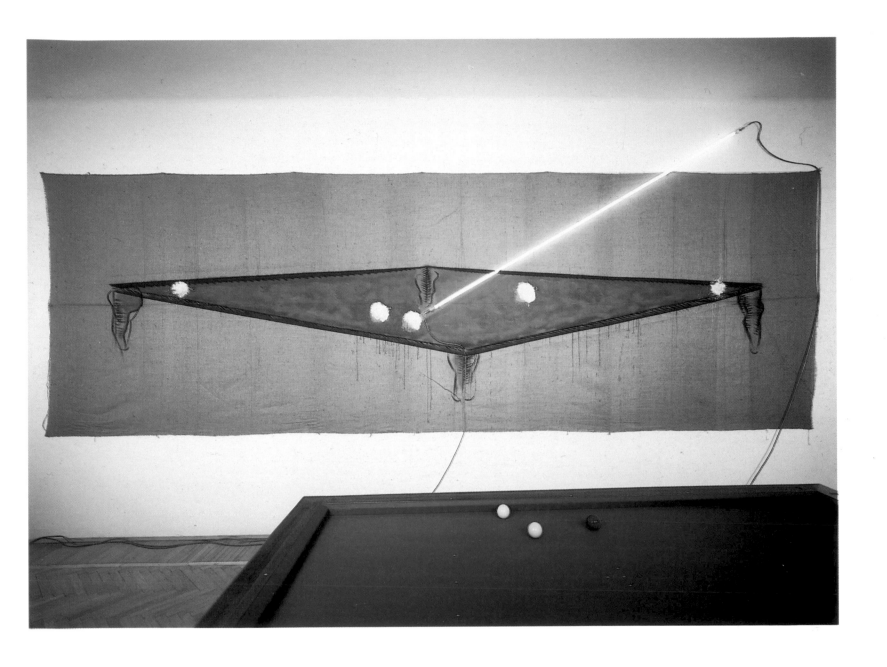

115 *Tincta purpura tegit fuco roseo
conchyli.* 1980
Metal tubes, wire mesh, stone
and neon tubes
Courtesy Kunsthalle Basel

116 Installation, Stedelijk Van Abbemuseum. Eindhoven, April 1980, including from front to back: Cat. no. 120 *Untitled.* 1980 **Anatomy Lesson (Lezione di anatomia).* 1979 Oil and crayon on canvas mounted on steel frame, metal tables and neon tube: canvas and metal frame 102 3/8 × 16' 5 1/2'' × 13'' (260 × 500 × 33 cm.); tables, each 35 × 55 × 98 1/2'' (89 × 139.7 × 250.2 cm.) Collection Bonnefantenmuseum, Maastricht, The Netherlands

117 *From the Overturned Bottle*
(Dalla bottiglia rovesciata). 1980
Metal tubes, neon tubes, bottle,
spray-painted crystal and soup plate
Collection of the artist

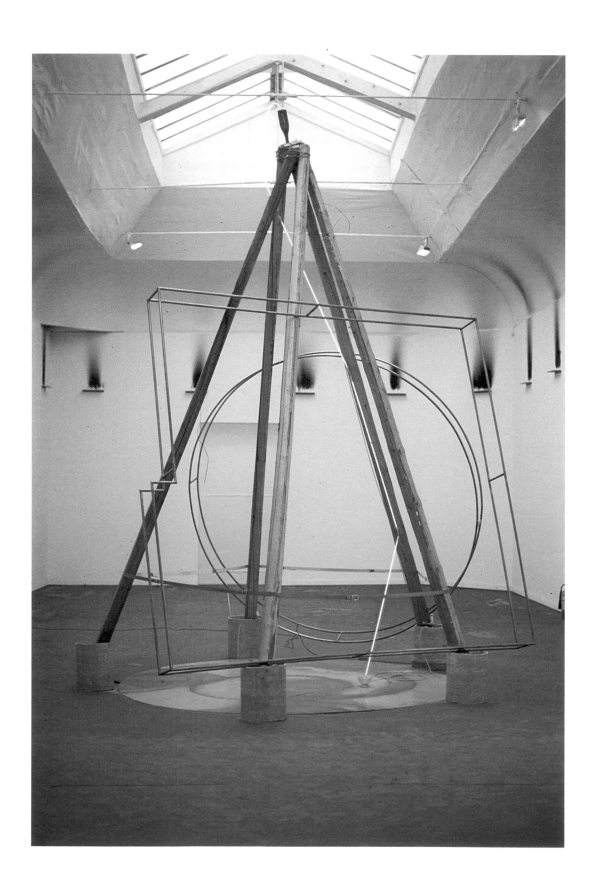

118 *Traveling Animal (Animale in viaggio)*. 1980+83
Mixed media on canvas and metal tubes, 98 7/16'' × 16' 5 5/8''
(250 × 502 cm.)
Collection Berjer, Stockholm

119 *Running Legs (Gambe che corrono).* 1967+80
Mixed media on canvas, neon tubes,
twigs and wicker hamper
Private Collection, Hamburg;
Courtesy Konrad Fischer, Düsseldorf

172

120 *Untitled.* 1980
Metal tubes, twigs, stone, bottle,
neon tube and wicker cone

121 *Cervidi.* 1980
Mixed media on canvas and twigs,
12' × 3 5/8'' × 13' 1 1/2''
(375 × 9 × 400 cm.)
Courtesy ARC/Musée d'Art Moderne
de la Ville de Paris

122 *Untitled.* 1980
Wood, clay, terra-cotta, rubber,
leather, bottle, glass and neon tube,
10' 10'' × 55'' × 55'' (330.2 × 139.7
× 139.7 cm.)
Courtesy Barbara Gladstone Gallery,
New York

123 *The Painting Is Long and Swift*
(La pittura è lunga e veloce). 1980
Canvas, metal tubes, stone, twigs,
glass and clamps; canvases 78
3/4'' × 26' 3''; 78 3/4 × 118 1/8'';
78 3/4'' × 13' 1 1/2'' (200 × 800;
200 × 300; 200 × 400 cm.)
Collection Salvatore Ala, New York

124 *The Painting Is Long and Swift*
(La pittura è lunga e veloce). 1980+82
Oil on canvas; canvases 78 3/4'' ×
26' 3''; 78 3/4 × 118 1/8''; 78 3/4''
× 13' 1 1/2'' (200 × 800; 200 × 300;
200 × 400 cm.)
Collection Salvatore Ala, New York

125 *Double Igloo (Doppio igloo).*
1979+81
External structure: metal tubes, glass,
clamps and hat; internal structure:
metal tubes, wire mesh, dirt and neon
tubes, 19' 8 1/4'' d. (600 cm.)
Collection Staatsgalerie, Stuttgart

In the course of our dialogues, I have always thought of your igloo as the result of a linguistic nomadism, in which the shape of the hemisphere is posited as an artistic edifice to store the materials coming from the territory through which you have happened to pass. For example, after your Zürich show, which included all your igloos, I felt I could perceive this form in various ways. It seems like a planet, located near other planets; and with its energy, it appears to attract all the linguistic meteors that orbit around it – both painting and sculpture, as well as opacity and transparency, calm and speed, artifice and nature. Thus, the form of the igloo is a terrestrial archetype that circles within your work and is capable of creating a fantastic and infinite constellation, in which the planets are made of sticks and glass, stucco and earth, cloth and wax. If the igloo is taken as a gravitational space, then I also see it as a constrained form – that is to say: once it becomes part of your work, it involves all possible sensations. It is also a stimulus for you, so that you can test yourself and explore the wealth of its chances of survival. It is as if you had invented it in order to confront yourself with your own eyes, which always have to see new and different images. Is the igloo a place of reflection in both senses: thinking and mirroring? Is it a place where you project images that come back to you as particular igloos, whose reproduction creates a galactic system or – as in Zürich – the Merz "village"?

The thing that shapes it, the specific form of the sphere, inherently holds continuation. I tried to incorporate planes, and at a certain point, these planes called for a sphere. I also tried to include things that seemingly contrasted with the sphere, for instance, the famous clamps, which are bases, systems – they are not only connection systems, but also propulsion systems. These thrusts ultimately wind up in the sphere itself. Hence, it is a system in motion rather than a fixed system. Just as the vertical and the horizontal – that is, the cube – tend exclusively towards self-reproduction, so too the dome ultimately becomes a formula. It is a formula, but one that reflects light in a different way. Yet each light ray has a different incidence. Every centimeter of the light ray falling here is ultimately reflected in a different way from

that of the preceding one. Thus, not only the preceding one on the vertical, but also the preceding one on the horizontal. It is sort of like saying that you get to New York via the North Pole, because the polar route is easier, faster, and not because of the mere idea of the pole itself. Speed is of the essence. As a result of this meaning of speed, which is inserted into this type of work on the hemisphere, the materials are ultimately magnetized by the surface; and, being magnetized by the surface, they are not only taken by the surface, but virtually readjusted, so that they can act from the surface itself. The surface becomes a theatrical stage. I have seen extremely crude, really very crude lumps of soil on this hemisphere, and they looked like highly sophisticated things. They seemed intentional, elegant. The elegance derives from the speed that the lump of soil gets from its position – it's the position that creates the movement. This position is extremely ancient. But while it may be a product of Antiquity, it is also a product of the modern era. Oddly enough, in this area ancient and modern converge, but I have found that certain surfaces – always the vertical or horizontal – need a historical definition, in architecture. Actually, the hemisphere requires no historical definition, so that when we used tar on surfaces in the Berlin installation, it was almost natural. It's not like saying: Now I'm putting tar on this wall. The tar on this wall means that the wall has to support something else, which may even be antithetical to the wall itself.

But there's no antithesis here. . . .

There's no antithesis because the tar adapts almost voluntarily to this hemisphere. It undergoes strange contortions, but eventually it becomes normal, reproducing itself in a similar movement. We proved this with the lumps of cloth made by Marisa, with the pieces of clay for the *Giap Igloo*, with the Berlin tar, with the Düsseldorf lead, with wax, with painting.

It is this pure form that puts the malleable and external disorder in order, giving it a way of circulating. . . .

It is the incidence of light on the surface. The surface is immediately animated on its rotundity, it is instantly animated in that the incidence of light, even the dimmest light, is immediately palpable.

In an igloo, you take a pure form and start

126 *Prehistoric Wind (Vento preistorico).* 1981
Mixed media on canvas, 94 1/2'' × 16'
4 7/8'' (240 × 500 cm.)
Courtesy Galleria Buchmann,
Saint-Gallen

127 Installation, Kunsthalle Basel, July 1981, including from right to left:
Prehistoric Wind (Vento preistorico).
1981
Mixed media on canvas, 98 7/16''
× 19' 8 1/4'' (250 × 600 cm.)
Courtesy Kunsthalle Basel
Far-Seeing Igloo (Igloo lungimirante).
1981
Metal tubes, clamps and stone, 118 1/8''-
19' 8 1/4'' d. (300-600 cm.)
Courtesy Kunsthalle Basel

128 Installation, *Mario Merz-Morgen*, Studio ORF, Salzburg, 1981, including:
Igloo. 1981
Metal tubes, glass and twigs
The process of creating the igloo was videotaped by Austrian radio-television.

to accumulate a series of energy data, light data. But in Zürich there were a lot of spheres. How did you see that accumulation of igloos, all together? You suddenly saw that there were various densities of material and various speeds. How did you see this phenomenon, which you yourself produced?
I saw that, for instance, in the hemisphere of twigs – the twigs were no longer those of a farmer's barn. This is an igloo made of twigs, but we are impressed by the fact that it instantly becomes like a house that transcends a house, because it is a spherical house. Hence the tension of the twigs and branches on the top, which then supports more, which in turn supports more. We end up with a series of arches that create the entire spherical tension, which is the tension in a drop of water. We know that when a drop of water is struck by a far more powerful force, like perhaps that of a teaspoon, the drop escapes from the spoon, reforming as a hemisphere because of the surface tension. The surface tension of the molecule causes the drop to assume a specific form, rather than becoming a shapeless entity, and the ideal form is the spherical form. The same thing happens here. In Zürich, I saw this awesome igloo of twigs, that is, wood, trees, precisely because it was put into this form – which, however, is a form that the eye always reveals. The eye is never mistaken, it has an extremely powerful perception of this form, because it is a form that is flexible, crazy or meager, crazy or reductive, Baroque or reductive. In other words, it's intrinsically a highly classical measure. The measure is classical, and the eye perceives it; the material is anticlassical, the eye perceives the fusion of anticlassical material and a form that is not classical in the sense of classical architecture – but rather, it is classical in the sense of the human mentality. The human mind is very close to the form of the sphere. Man has an intuitive consciousness of the sphere – a piece of fruit, a ball. It is an age-old intuitive form. Actually, it supports. I could make a gold igloo that supports. The gold igloo would support itself very well next to the wax igloo or the broken-glass igloo or the forest igloo. No two things seem more staggeringly different than a sheet of gold and a surface of wood. Yet if the sheet of gold is placed in a position of tension on the hemisphere

and if the wood is placed in a position of tension on the hemisphere, they have something in common, which transcends the fact that the two materials are so distant from one another.
Hence, the igloo maintains the classical form – which I would define as archetypal – and the material chaos, although in an equilibrium; but where does this fluid whole originate? In an atmospheric bombardment, perhaps, due to the place and the sensations of the moment? Where do your material meteorites come from? At the same time, there is a difference in scale, so that the New York igloo, which seemed enormous, has gradually gone down in size, and now it is shrunken compared with the twenty-foot igloo in Stuttgart or the forty-foot igloo in Bordeaux. What has changed in your atmospheric and territorial conditions?
The atmospheric relationship is very powerful to the extent that it is allowed to exist. That kind of circumstance allows the atmospheric condition to exist rather than letting it remain purely a tension as an alternative to something that can be a form. Intrinsically, it is a tension that allows even the most fragile thing to exist. The broken-glass piece is typical . . . .
Or the soil of Jericho – it's something almost impalpable because it's dust. . . .
Those are things that have no power in themselves. On the other hand, I saw that as this igloo took shape with pieces of cracked and broken glass, with horrible jags, with sheets, streaks, hubbub – I would even say howls – those howls come to a stop, as if you were watching the ocean from up high, the howling ocean. If you see it all around, then, at a certain point, it stops howling, it calms down into a mythical form, which is actually that of the earth.
Do you then think that there is a dialogue between fragile and rigid?
There is a dialogue between the extremely fragile and the archetype, which has tirelessly permitted this flow of materials, for this is really a flow of materials.
You feel it as a flow?
Actually, rather than choosing the material, I find it, in a natural condition. At a certain point, the material itself wants to get up on that stage, that platform, that spherical form, for we have even thought that materials per se, opaque material and transparent material, are two extremes of a single

concept. That was why I wrote *"chiaro/scuro"* (light/dark), which is also found in the Buddhist canon: light and dark are not opposites, they intersect and probably recognize one another. In such a condition, they recognize each other rather than declaring that they exist in a formal antithesis. I have the feeling that the true meaning of material is transformed the instant it is put in this condition. It is actually a material that flows rather than a material that fixedly covers.

Your works also depend on being traversed by energy. Your igloo and your tables are always penetrated by other elements, which graze and disrupt their compactness and uniqueness. For instance, the hemisphere can be traversed by a painting or another igloo, by an automobile or a found object. It's as if the light rays solidified, taking on the shape and consistency of reality – an everyday reality or an artistic one. At times you create an incredible bond between an object and an animal, an edifice and a fragile form. Ultimately it all becomes a drop of water, through which all reflections pass without disrupting the surface or the shape. Everything lives in a highly sensitive equilibrium.

You know, when you see it, I have to say that certain futuristic city designs by Sant'Elia were done according to the same system. There was a train in, let's call it, an aerodynamic form, which, at the level of, say, the third floor, passed through architectural forms. And this train, charging through architectural forms, was actually a dream – but it was a lucid dream. The design had this rational form traversed by a kind of luminous train, which was rendered by luminous numbers, but also by opaque rocks, and it was interrupted by things. The spectator's eye seemed to sense that the traversing would continue. Hence, the traversing of this "drop of water" made of glass ultimately became an almost virtually mythical penetration.

Then you don't see an extension of the energy of the sphere; instead you see a visual arrow, which penetrates.

Yes. In this case the important thing was the dimension of the street that traverses, the arrow that traverses, the ray, the laser beam, that traverses. I remember that in the famous church of Milan, which is no longer used as a church – it had four inches of dust on the floor – and we put up a glass igloo, in the dark, of course. Then we brought in a laser, and the laser beam went through that layer of dusty material, which was the church itself, and it went through that drop of water, which was the tarpaulin and the broken glass, in a truly mysterious way, because the traversing was not a traversing of, say, the laboratory, it was more the traversing of a thing that came before the laboratory, after the laboratory, during a remote catastrophe. Or else it seemed like something that could exist there, but that could also exist behind it, around it, it could be seen from different points of view. Hence, in its simplicity, it permitted both visual and mental reasoning – they were united. I find that this is the condition that allows these works to exist even ephemerally – for we had to leave that church. We had the sense of the ephemeral, because the thing was truly ephemeral. But the power of vision was not ephemeral. It remains.

At times the igloo and the table enter into a dialogue with very powerful architectural obstacles. I am referring to Tucci Russo's columns in Turin or the Palacio de Cristal in Madrid, and now Bordeaux. How do you see this traversing, which you often produce subsequently, by intersecting the igloo with another object, such as the painting, which traditionally is hung vertically and never covered or integrated with anything else?

In the case of the painted igloo in Turin, the painting placed across it functions as a challenge to painting per se, and, at the same time, as a challenge to painting as an object. Thus, there are two reciprocal challenges to be maintained in the same work. One is a real challenge, because it seems impossible for the painting to be related to a hemisphere, precisely because it is created on a flat surface. At the same time, the hemisphere is a challenge to painting because, at a certain point, it actually requires an atmosphere that can enclose a painting and keep it in vitro – in the glass. As a result, these are two challenges that, instead of canceling one another out, have remained in contact as challenges and have maintained the possibility of being seen as two highly emotional elements. The painting, rather than being suspended from a nail on the wall, ultimately became part of an atmosphere that was very different from the one that the art of painting normally has and wants to have. *Yet by using these highly fragile elements, you also need to anchor, or else to challenge, the architecture in which you place these elements. In Spain you confronted it with the column, which means that the igloo accepts the violence of the column.*

I would say that one can embrace a column. I would say that one can again take up the image of the ocean, because the image of the ocean seen from a mythical height, above the earth, embraces a large amount of space in its curve. I realized that the object forming this hemisphere is voracious, rather than being an object that repels material, just as a wall normally repels material. In order to be able to avoid repelling material, the wall has to become almost a decoration. I would say that it has to become like an absorbent skin. In the case of the igloo, in the case of the hemisphere, the material usually placed on the hemisphere is involved in a movement of light and/or space, and hence modes of existence . . . .

Which supports everything . . . .

Which supports being at the mercy of this object. Instead of remaining virtually impaled, crucified, it remains spread out on a bed, it remains propped, it remains in a more organic state. The thing I've always found awfully troublesome in the art of painting is the impalement of a painting. . . . Only the greatest paintings manage to transcend this feeling . . . .

Of rigidity.

Practically rigidity, crucifixion, which is part of every painting. In contrast, the meaning of a painting that traverses the igloo – or, in certain cases, a painting that is merely left to its own devices on the igloo – ultimately reaches a more organic state, hence a state that is less ill, less tense, less that of a sacrificial victim. Thus, there is less of a sacrifice here, less of a sense of sacrifice.

Less of a rigor mortis . . . .

One of the things that are absolutely necessary for me, I even would say vital, is this. I have always noted this terrible problem: art has a very high moral tension, yet it is this feeling of impiety in the very situation that provides a notable lag – I would say that it's kind of like reading poetry. Perhaps a poetry of the past, one that was sung – it had to be more organic . . . .

More magical.

More magical, hence . . . .

Hence, it has a mellow feeling, something ancient . . . .

Ancient, yes, something that reading, for instance, always gives you the sense of. Even reading, precisely because it's a construction . . . . Look, these are sort of the conditions that have always attracted me. Instead of abandoning a certain culture in the form of the igloo, I have always been attracted, and in my attraction, I have always come to use intrinsic materials. Perhaps there was no need to make the gold sheet, because in reality, the light coat of tar ultimately becomes a sheet of gold. The broken glass ultimately becomes a sheet of gold.

Yet in the course of time the form of your igloos has expanded. Originally you restrained it, but now it contains more and more, to the point of dominating us.

Yes. I would say that there are two tactical approaches. One involves reappropriating the most geometrically felt form, and the other involves sentiment – I am again referring to the idea of the earth viewed from far away, which ultimately imparts a sense of organic spaces. What we experience in the hardness of our earthly position has a certain distance, and the eye no longer perceives – instead it perceives the sense of the organic . . . .

Yet how do you see the change, say, in the size of your igloos, your tables? Do you see that change as a natural process relating to spaces; or do you see it as a surface – let's call it pictorial – an increasingly large, increasingly soft surface?

I have the impression that by means of the hemispheres I am defending myself against largeness (because largeness per se is a terrifying thing) or smallness.

Largeness or smallness – the tension towards the largest or the tension towards the smallest – those are two intrinsically terrifying phenomena.

But when they are put in that condition, largeness loses its expansion pure and simple, becoming an expansion in itself. To value the small and the large – perhaps you put it most effectively today, saying that to value the small and the large becomes difficult because something that seemed large becomes smaller, something that seemed too large would become normal.

Now, in Bordeaux, we see what will happen, because this will be a very large affair; and even as I hope to succeed in making this object, I have an intuition, I have the impression that I have to do it in such a way that it becomes a road – not veering across at a diagonal, but crossing the surface, a highway that runs across the surface, because, by crossing the surface, perhaps too large a surface, it ultimately reaches the verge of existence.

How do you mean that? The road of material or . . . .

No, the road of objects, because I planned to use glass panes, drinking glasses, rather than making rays that come from a sun, as is done in depictions of the sun. In lieu of rays, you can imagine drinking glasses. Naturally, if used in a certain way, they can form an organic road. If misused, they may remain simply an expedient – say, a Dada device. But if they are used well, they could become the famous spring pouring into the other, the famous spring that keeps pouring and pouring ever afterwards.

In other words, it would have to become a continuous movement.

That's right, a continuous movement.

What do you plan to do with regard to space?

With regard to space, there are fannings-out. It will become a kind of orange. Imagine an orange that has very large sections and very tiny sections. This is a link with an internal architecture, which is different from spherical architecture. A link with internal architecture – I'm thinking of painting certain elements on the inside, so as to create a reading of the nucleus, too. Otherwise, the largeness would be slightly exasperating. You know, this problem is inherent not only in the sculptural or painterly object, but also in the architectural object – it's really a problem. I once talked about it with you, about what the architectural object is today – it has become merely an object of signification pure and simple, an indication of space, instead of an indication of an internal space that can ultimately be seen on the outside.

If I understand you correctly, you intend to create a wood or a forest of forms and elements in which the boundary is not defined, in which the end cannot be seen. Everything is to be closed and interwoven, yet open and transparent – almost a dialectics of finite and infinite. This visual magma,

traversed by swift forms and objects, by animal figures and igloos – what will it live on?

Perhaps the thing that was the clearest in this sense was when there were elements inside one another, which is once again an appeal to the nonfinite. By making the finite an appeal to the nonfinite, in that man realizes what materials are inside his natural "habitus," which is actually the geological formation of the earth, he would be infinitely more content to live on a crust, because the mere fact of living on a crust is always an over-simplistic fact, while even a da Vinci vision of things, that idea of the interior of the body, is always something that creates a sense of the nonfinite, and thereby a sense of further possibilities. . . .

The object takes the spectator in hand rather than being taken in hand by the spectator. It is the object itself that takes him in hand, because it makes him see it on the inside. By making him see it on the inside, it creates a model of open culture, which is superior to the fact of the surface, of the impact on the surface, when you don't know the interior. This is the phenomenon that I want to keep looking for, and naturally, here, on a large scale, it will be a moment of tension. At a certain moment, the tension between small and large will emerge. The issue remains open.

*129 *Mountain Lion (Leone di montagna).* 1981
Mixed media on canvas and neon tubes, 98 7/16'' × 18' 8 7/16'' (250 × 570 cm.)
Courtesy Galleria Antonio Tucci Russo, Turin

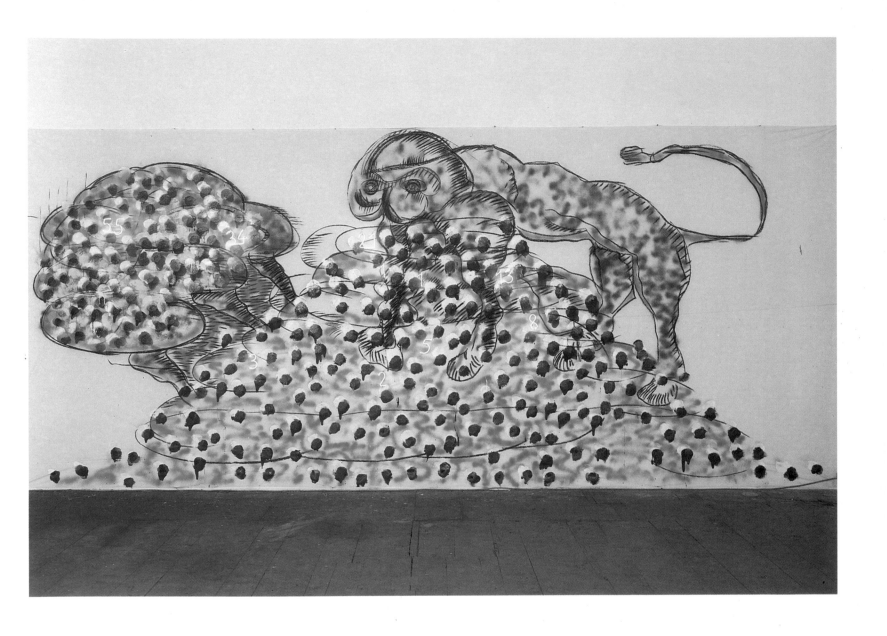

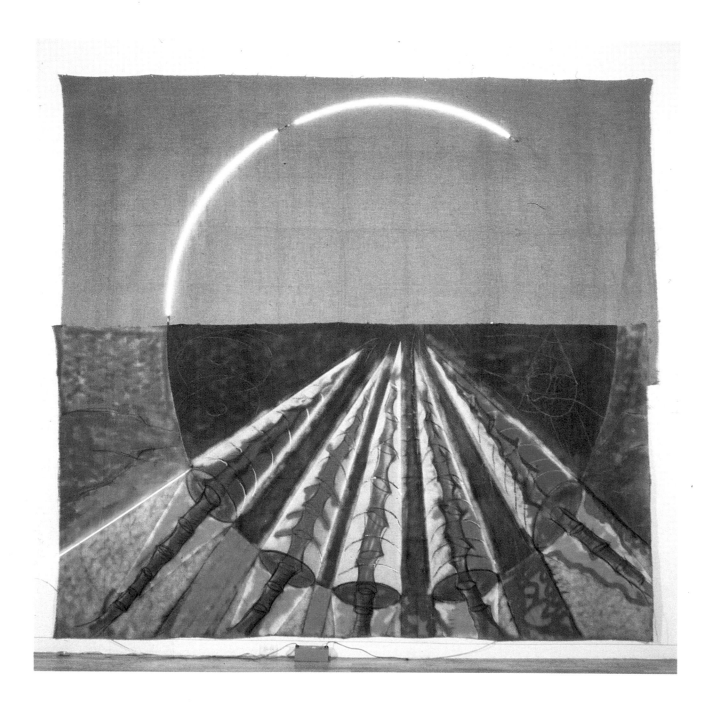

*132 *Khadafi's Tent (Tenda di Gheddafi).* 1981
Metal tubes and acrylic on burlap,
98 7/16'' h. × 16' 4 7/8'' d.
(250 × 500 cm.)
Collection Castello di Rivoli, Museo
d'arte Contemporanea, Rivoli (Turin)

133 *Untitled.* 1981
Mixed media on canvas, neon tubes,
spray-painted bottle and glass,
94 1/2 × 102 3/8'' (240 × 260 cm.)
Collection Museum Ludwig, Cologne

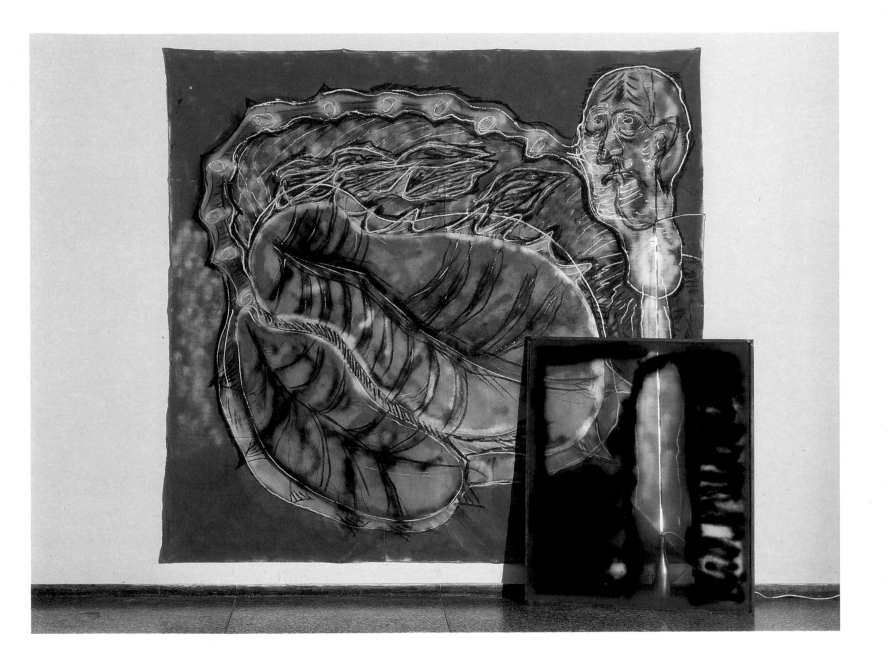

Following pages
*134 *Architecture Built by Time,*
Architecture Demolished by Time
(Architettura fondata dal tempo,
architettura sfondata dal tempo). 1981
Metal tubes, painted glass, canvas,
mixed-media on canvas, neon tubes
and twigs; igloo 118 1/8' h. ×
19' 8 1/4'' d. (300 × 600 cm.); canvas
on metal frame 102 3/8'' × 15' 6
1/4'' × 7/8'' (200 × 473 × 20 cm.);
table 13 3/4 × 116'' d. (35 × 295 cm.)
Collection The Rivetti Art Foundation,
Turin

*135 *Tiger (Tigre).* 1981
Mixed media on canvas, 110 1/4''
× 17' 4 5/8'' (280 × 530 cm.)
Collection Christian Stein, Turin

136 *Temple Snatched from the Abyss
(Tempio rapito dagli abissi).* 1981
Mixed media on canvas, neon tubes
and sculpture with lamp, 118 1/8''
× 19' 8 1/4'' (300 × 600 cm.)
Collection Crex, Zürich

*137 *Cone (Cono)*. 1981
Mixed media on canvas, 98 7/16
× 54 5/16" (250 × 138 cm.)
Collection Giuliana and Tommaso
Setari, Rome

The chorus
The cone
Is the content a portion of
chorus/cone, of a very long conical
calculable leg in the darkness?
Or in the light, immersed towards
an immensely distant vanishing point,
with transparent, osmotic walls easily
crossed by huge elephants a pine
marvelous in its fruits, but placed
upside down for immersion in the
earth.
             THE CONE THE VERY LONG
                               CHORUS

pp. 152-153

138 *Untitled.* 1981
Charcoal and spray paint on linen,
59 1/16'' × 16' 4 7/8''
(150 × 500 cm.)
Courtesy Jean Bernier Gallery, Athens

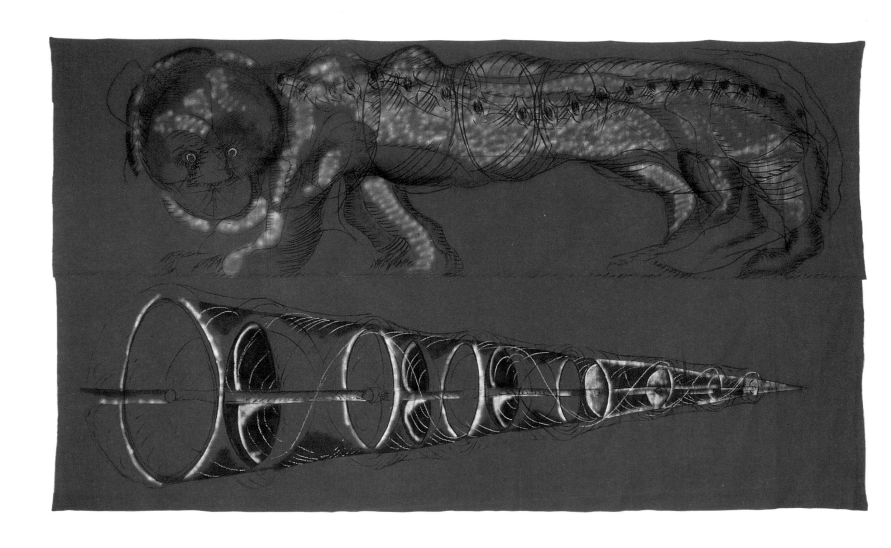

139 *Wandering Songs II*
(Canti errabondi II). 1981
Acrylic, oil and enamel on canvas
and metal tubes, 100 3/8 × 114
3/16 × 8 11/16'' (255 × 290 × 22 cm.)
Collection Sperone Westwater, New
York

141 *Underground (Ipogeo)*. 1981
Bottles, stone, wood and neon tubes,
23 5/8 × 23 5/8 × 15 3/4"
(60 × 60 × 40 cm.)
Collection Dubois, Lausanne; Courtesy
Galleria Lucio Amelio, Naples

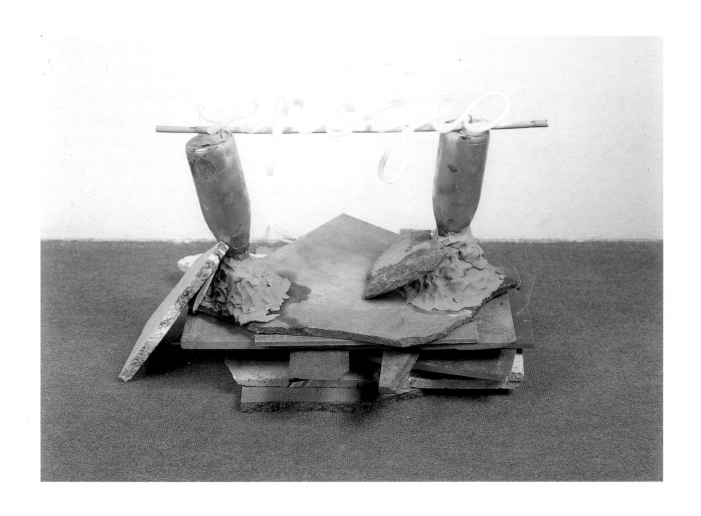

142 *Billiard Hall (Sala dei biliardi).*
1981
Acrylic on canvas, wax and neon
tubes, 78 3/4 × 59' 11/16''
(200 × 1800 cm.)
Collection Staatsgalerie, Stuttgart

*143 *8 Houses (8 case).* 1981-82
Oil, acrylic and charcoal on canvas,
94 1/2'' × 16' 2'' (240 × 492.8 cm.)
The Frito-Lay Collection, Plano, Texas

*144 *If the Form Vanishes, Its Root Is Eternal (Se la forma scompare la sua radice è eterna).* 1982
Metal tubes, wire mesh and neon tubes, structure 70 × 178 × 10''
(178 × 452 × 25.4 cm.); support 23 1/2 × 23 1/2 × 31 1/2''
(59 × 59.7 × 80 cm.)
Courtesy Galleria Christian Stein, Milan and Turin

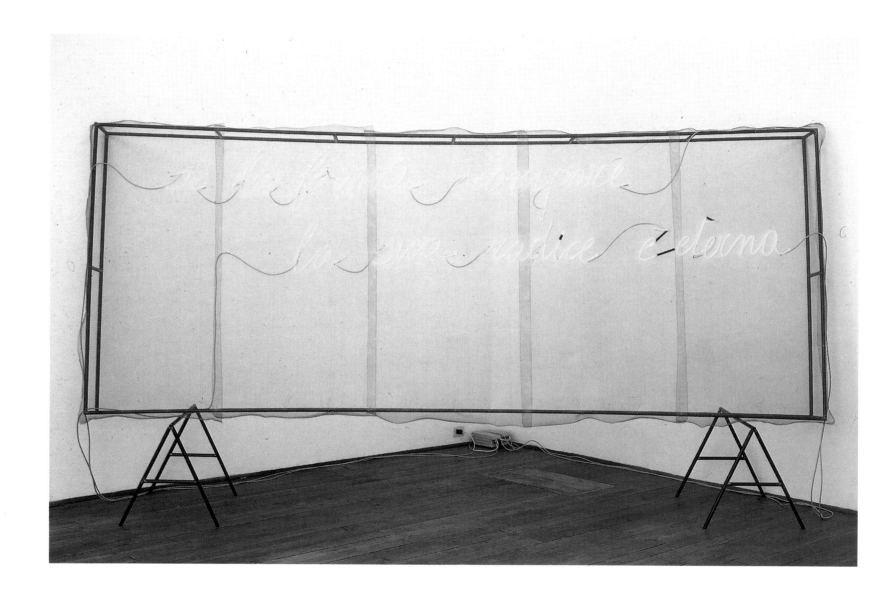

145 *Tasmania*. 1981-82
Oil, acrylic and charcoal on burlap
and neon tubes, 78 3/4 × 17' 3/4"
(200 × 520 cm.); neon 48 1/16"
(122 cm.)
Collection Dallas Museum of Art

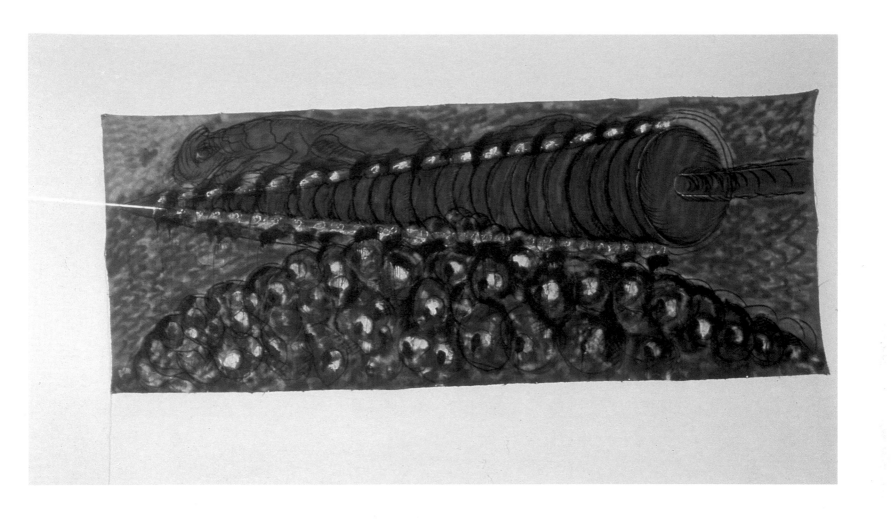

*146 *Bison (Bisonti)*. 1982
Spray enamel, charcoal and pastel on
canvas, and spray enamel and plaster
on cardboard, 79 7/8'' × 18' 9 3/4''
(202.9 × 573.4 cm.); with hooves,
ca. 91 1/2'' h. (232.4 cm.)
Courtesy Sperone Westwater, New
York

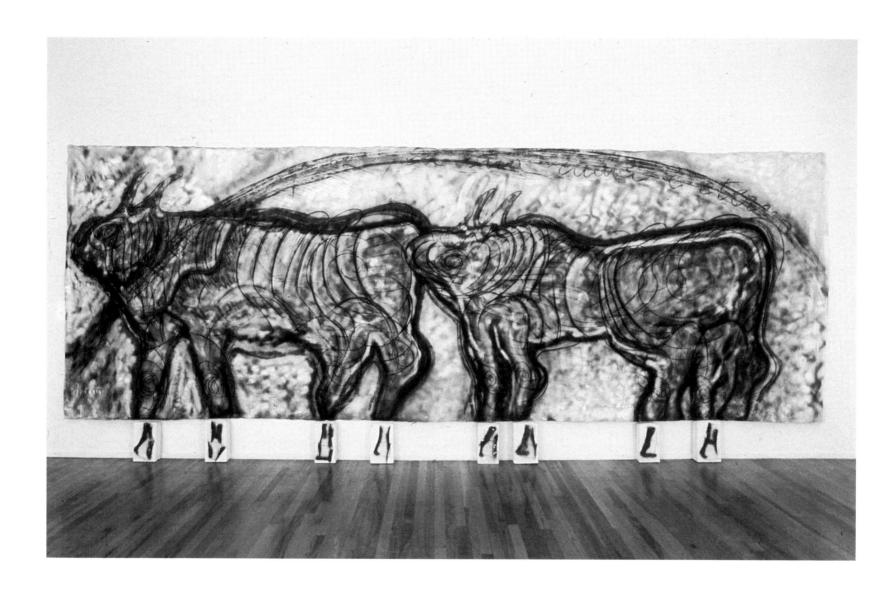

147 *Drops in the Lake (Gocce nel lago).* 1981-82
Oil, acrylic and charcoal on canvas, neon tubes and raincoat, 77 9/16''
× 16' 3'' (197 × 495 cm.)
Private Collection; Courtesy Sperone Westwater, New York

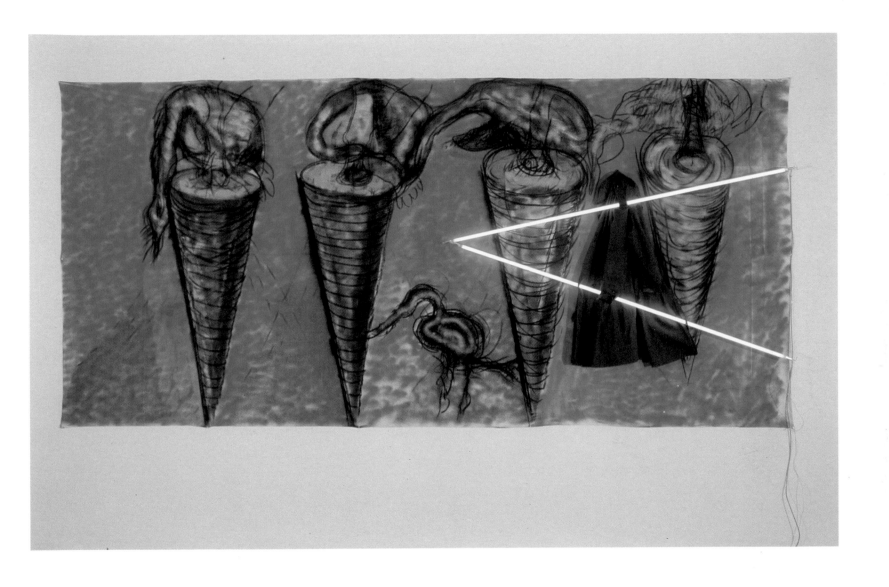

149 *Wandering Songs I (Canti errabondi I).* 1983
Acrylic and oil on canvas, branches
and wax, 111'' × 25' 1 3/16'' × 39 3/8''
(282 × 765 × 100 cm.)
Courtesy Sperone Westwater,
New York

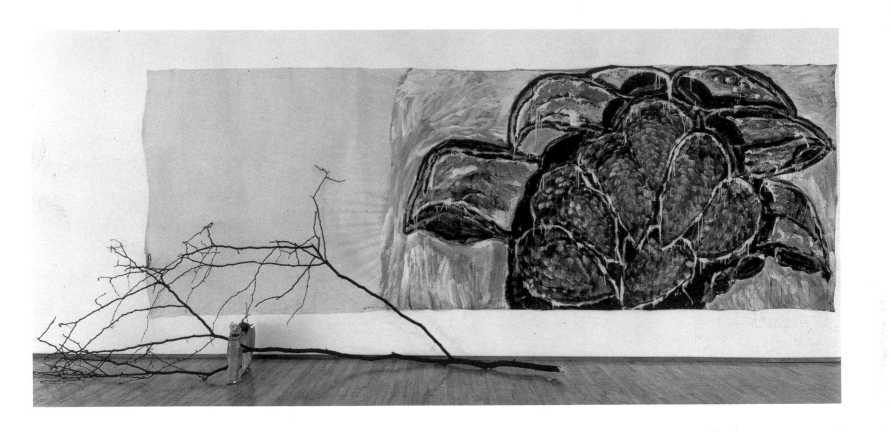

*150 *Spiral Table (Tavola a spirale).*
1982
Aluminum, glass, fruit, vegetables,
branches and wax, 18' d. (549 cm.)
Courtesy Sperone Westwater,
New York

151 Installation, Flow Ace Gallery, Venice, California, August 1982, including clockwise from lower right:
Cat. no. 146 *Spiral Table (Tavola a spirale)*. 1982
Metal tubes, stone, painted stone, bamboo, neon tubes, chalk, fruit, vegetables, branches, wax and bottle, variable dimensions
Collection of the artist
If the Form Vanishes, Its Root is Eternal (Se la forma scompare la sua radice è eterna). 1982
Mixed media on canvas and neon tubes, 98 7/16'' × 26' 3'' × 13 3/4'' (250 × 800 × 35 cm.)
Collection of the artist,
Vegetable Boat (Nave vegetale). 1982
Metal tubes, glass, bamboo and chalk, 118 1/8'' h. × 19' 8 1/4'' d. (300 × 600 cm.)
Collection of the artist
Cat. no. 146 *Bison (Bisonti)*. 1982

152 *Stone Igloo (Igloo di pietra).* 1982
Metal tubes and stone, 78 3/4" h.
× 15' 3 1/2" d. (200 × 480 cm.)
Collection of the artist; Courtesy
Documenta, Kassel, West Germany

*153 *Coniferous Gem (Gemma
conifera).* 1981-82
Oil, acrylic and charcoal on burlap,
78 3/4" × 14' 2" (200 × 431.8 cm.)
Collection Raymond J. Learsy

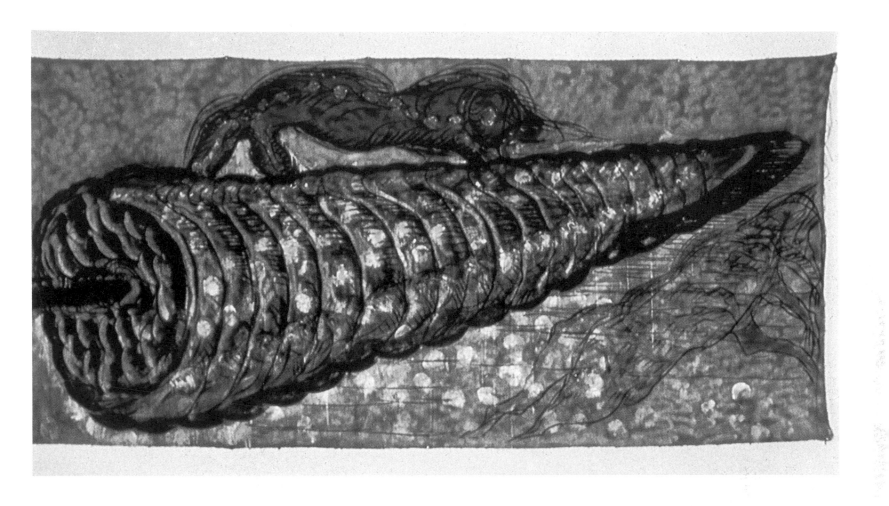

154 Installation, Moderna Museet, Stockholm, February 1983, including from right to left:
Cat. no. 118 *Traveling Animal (Animale in viaggio).* 1980+83
Igloo. 1983
Metal tubes, glass, clamps and neon tubes, 118 1/8'' h. × 19' 8'/4'' d.

(300 × 600 cm.)
Courtesy Moderna Museet, Stockholm
Pink Cloud with Sunset (Nuvola rosa con il tramonto). 1983
Mixed media on canvas, 55 1/8'' × 32'' × 9 11/16'' (140 × 1,000 cm.)
Courtesy Moderna Museet, Stockholm

The Abandoned House (La casa abbandonata). 1977+83
Painted wood and twigs; panels 65 15/16 × 66 1/4; 78 1/8 × 78 5/16; 59 7/16 × 66 1/8; 59 7/16 × 78 5/16'' (167.5 × 168.3; 198.5 × 199; 151 × 168; 151 × 199 cm.)
Courtesy Moderna Museet, Stockholm

*155 *Hoarded centuries to pull up a mass of algae and pearls (Ezra Pound).*
1983
Metal, glass, wire mesh, sulfur and neon tubes, 85 7/16" h. × 13' 1 1/2" d. (217 × 400 cm.)
Courtesy Anthony d'Offay Gallery, London

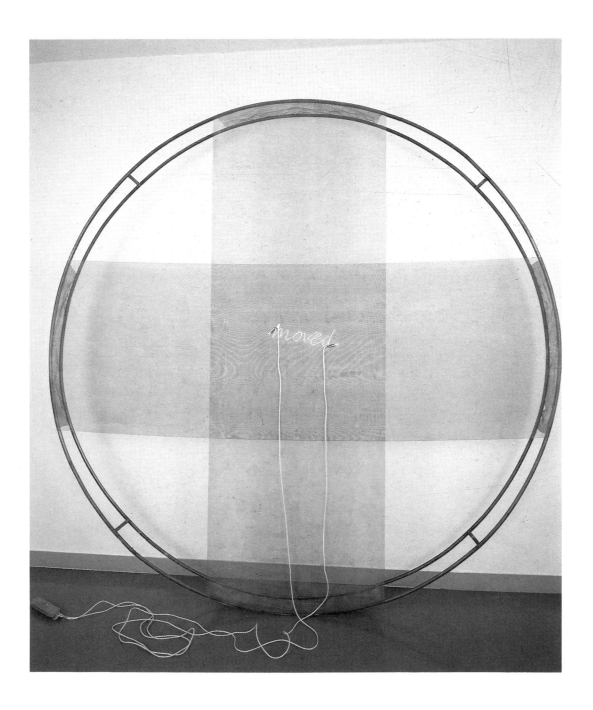

I want to do a portrait immediately. Impossible. But it is possible to hide the portrait in the depths of a forest. Perhaps give it a small table and a stool. The table will be rickety. The stool will soon be moist because of water from the terribly huge plant that towers above it. With the slow descent of a spider towards the decompensated portrait, the painter's brain can start to move. It will be impossible to resolve the question of whether the immense plant and the water, which goes everywhere, will not leave a minimum space for the formation of some approximate but thriving sensation that is present to the sensorial machine of the painter sculptor architect abandoned with the presumption of doing a portrait in the middle of the forest. The violets and the grays will appear and also perhaps forms that are more animal than human. My instruments are an inactive and no longer usable capsule which is ugly but can easily be thought of as being abandoned in the bramble. Charcoal, charcoal, to follow the lines that in some way are the violet so that a heavenly timid being can become the surface of the portrait. The skin of the portrait is obviously becoming animallike, that is, a functioning mechanism and, covering itself with animallike fury, it abandons any semblance of human psychology. Thus, the earth again takes on that which it caused to give birth. And one can write something about doing, that is, forming abandoning a form in order to see the past being transformed and mocked.

pp. 34-35

157 Installation, Palazzo Congressi ed
Esposizioni, Republic of San Marino,
1983, including:
Igloo. 1983
Metal tubes, crystal, stone and clamps,
98 7/16'' h. × 16' 4 7/8'' d.
(250 × 500 cm.)
Untitled. 1983
Automobile, mixed media on canvas
and neon tubes

158 *Sphinx and Chickenlike Predator (Sfinge e rapace gallinaceo).* 1983
Oil, sand and vegetable matter on canvas on metal frame, twigs, neon tubes, wire and branches, 102 3/8'' × 22' 11 9/16'' (260 × 700 cm.)
Private Collection, West Vancouver; Courtesy Vancouver Art Gallery

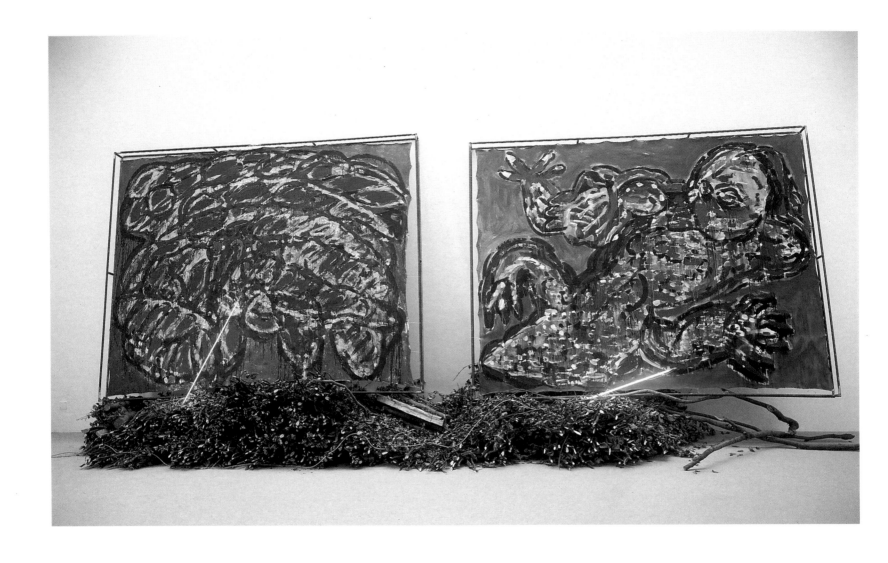

159 *Gecko (Geco)*. 1983
Metal tubes, mixed media on canvas
and tree trunk, 102 3/8'' × 10' 6'' ×
27 9/16'' (260 × 320 × 70 cm.)
Private Collection, Ghent; Courtesy
Galerie Buchmann, Basel

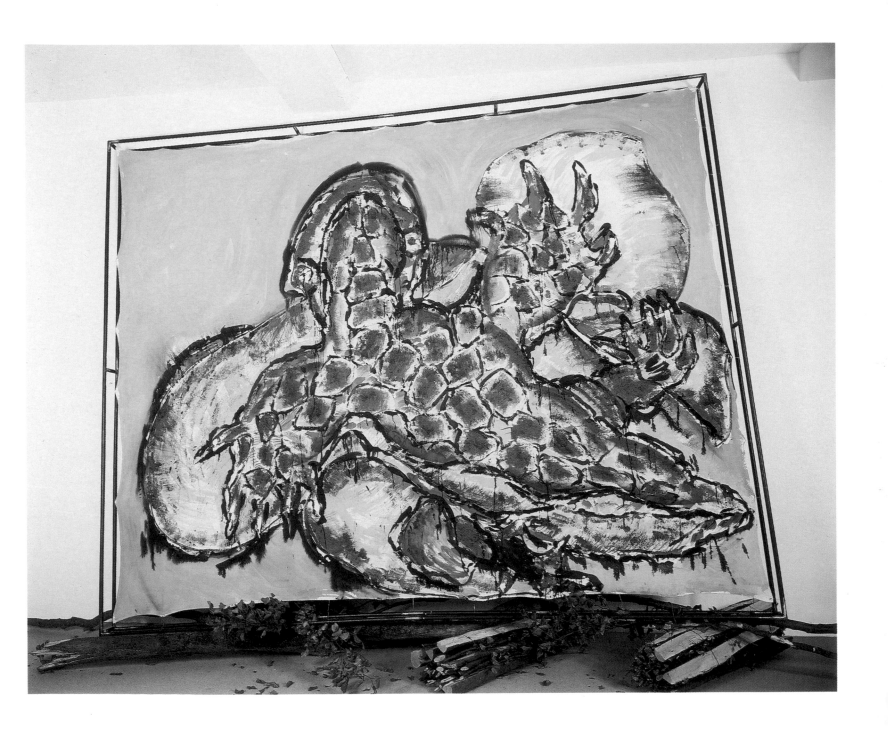

160 *Fibonacci.* 1971+83
Metal tubes, wire mesh, wax, neon
tubes and branches, 118 1/8 × 47 1/4
× 11 13/16'' (300 × 120 × 30 cm.)
Collection Musée d'Art Moderne,
Saint-Etienne

*161 *Hoarded centuries to pull up a
mass of algae and pearls (Ezra Pound).*
1983
Metal, glass, wire mesh, sulfur and
neon tubes, 85 7/16'' h. × 13' 1 1/2'' d.
(217 × 400 cm.)
Courtesy Anthony d'Offay Gallery,
London

162 *Benito Cereno.* 1983
Mixed media on canvas and neon
tubes, 96 1/2'' × 10' (245 × 305 cm.)
Courtesy Galleria Antonio Tucci
Russo, Turin

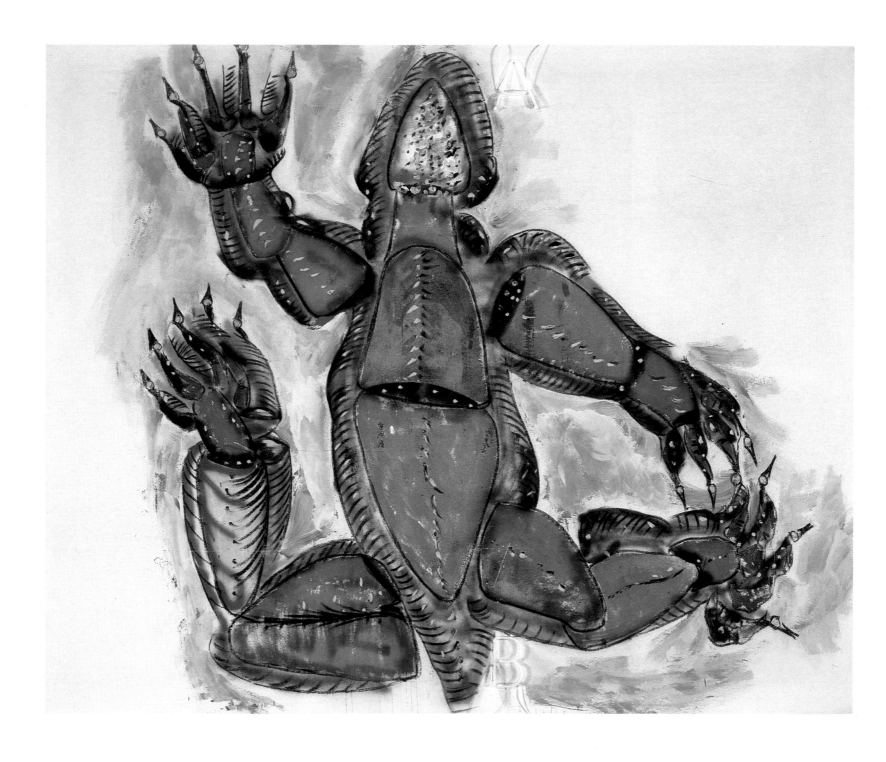

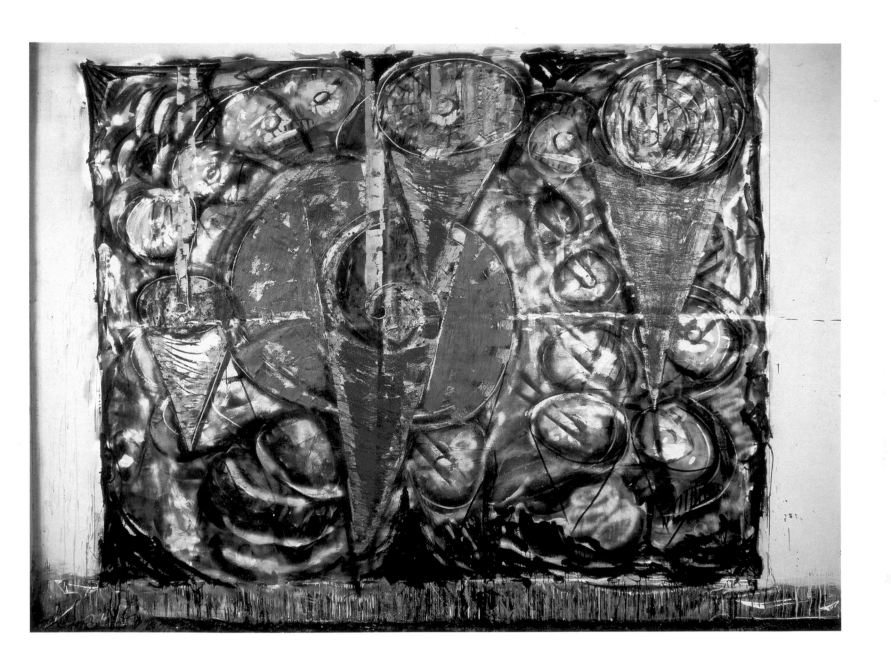

164 *Untitled.* 1983
Oil, acrylic, enamel, charcoal and
spray paint on canvas, enamel on
metal and enamel on spray-painted
plastic, variable dimensions
Courtesy Sperone Westwater,
New York

*165 *The Tree Grows So Many*
Branches and They All Have Common
Sap (L'albero cresce tanti rami e hanno
una linfa comune). 1984
Enamel, charcoal and shell on paper,
69 5/16 × 59 1/16" (176 × 150 cm.)
Collection of the artist

166 *Untitled.* 1984
Neon tubes arranged on the Mole
Antonelliana of Turin, June 12,
daytime

167 *Endless Growth (Crescita senza
fine).* 1984
Oil, enamel, spray paint and neon
tubes on canvas and wood, 109 7/16''
× 15' 11 5/16'' (278 × 486 cm.)
Collection Christian Stein, Turin;
Courtesy Galleria Christian Stein,
Milan and Turin

168 *Igloo.* 1984
Metal tubes, wax and metal, 78 3/4'' d.
(200 cm.)
Courtesy Konrad Fischer, Düsseldorf

169 *From Honey to Ashes (Dal miele
alle ceneri).* 1984
Metal tubes, wax, pinecones, stuffed
antelope head, aluminum and muslin,
95 11/16'' d. (243 cm.)
Courtesy Sperone Westwater,
New York

170 *Untitled.* 1984
Wicker, metal tubes, twigs, stones,
dirt and electric lamp, 118 1/8''
× 13' 1 1/2'' × 98 7/16''
(300 × 400 × 250 cm.)
Courtesy Galerie Pietro Sparta,
Chagny, France

171 Installation, Galerie Pietro Sparta,
Chagny, France, October 1984,
including:
L'Autre Côté de la lune. 1984
Metal tubes, glass, stone, vegetables
and fruit, 27 9/16'' × 11' 5 13/16''
× 29' 6 3/8'' (70 × 350 × 900 cm.)

Untitled. 1984
Metal tubes, spray paint, oil, metal
and glass on paper and on the wall,
11' 5 13/16'' × 24' 7 1/4''
(350 × 750 cm.)
Courtesy Galerie Pietro Sparta,
Chagny, France

When you do your show at the Solomon R. Guggenheim Museum in New York this year, you will be forced to engage in a dialogue with Frank Lloyd Wright's architecture. You will therefore have to establish a relationship between the fluid situation of the artistic object and the rigid situation of the museum building. How do you intend to cope with that situation, and what problems do you foresee?

First of all, I absolutely have to say that my birth was violated by architecture. That's almost a fact of ancestral psychoanalysis. There is always an ancestral component in a person's work and in what he does. I remember feeling a kind of love-hate when I saw grass amid rocks, and I thought: That is life. When I didn't see grass amid rocks, I felt a sense of sadness. I am not trying to make an ecological statement, I simply want to give you a glimpse into my mind. A lot of children don't notice the grass, they prefer biking – which also happened with me. But I had a sense of doubleness, of subdivision between architecture and what is ultimately called life. And I always wondered why human beings invented that whole thing known as architecture.

It's an action of placing stone upon stone.

Yes. Something I've never really understood. Yet at the same time, it may be humanity's greatest invention, because the placing of stone upon stone actually created a sense of refuge. The human being created a world for himself, which estranges him from the organic. Even a car is architecture, so is a plane, and so was a boat – they're perfect architecture with the possibility of having everything, including movement. That was what my bicycle meant for me: using a device that becomes architecture. Vittorio Gregotti talks about the importance of the design of the bicycle. It's true, it's important for an architect, and I felt the same way, in that I saw architecture as an element of violence against the organic. There are rather violent transitions between inside and outside, which I feel strongly, even in a fine architect.

Then, I revolted and made up my mind in art: I would make the problem between inside and outside dialectical, by creating architecture within architecture: the hemisphere, which was then called "igloo" in the more ecological and also more superficial sense of the word. But it is real architecture,

like a beehive – an intrinsically simple architecture. And that is the very reason why I want to make it complex, for instance, by using glass shards or similar things in the igloo – elements coming from outside. Thus, once again, the problem is art history, the painting. Whenever you enter a church and you see a painting, which is central, the icon, you wonder: what came first – the painting or the stone and the architecture? Those are two elements that mutually support each other. And in the case of this work, I feel that the details will be of great interest since this is a general systematization. Frank Lloyd Wright's Guggenheim in particular seems to be a totality, a thorough overall synthesis; yet the details are important in that they create an internal landscape. My problem will be to create an internal landscape. My internal landscape will be superimposed upon an internal landscape that already exists – that of the museum and that of Frank Lloyd Wright.

Like a fresco added to the temple?

Exactly like a fresco. And if I like the fresco, it becomes a mosaic, with its fabulous ability to be architecture. For instance the mosaic floor of the Romans was exceptional in that it represented things: it was architecture per se. So was the Byzantine mosaic. I am attempting to do something similar. Not putting the object in view, or rather not placing the object as an artwork, but instead positing it as an architectural project, the very essence of architecture.

I am close to architecture, but I don't want to emphasize it. I want to create an inside architecture, the one done by Wright – maximal, radicalized. I don't want to place an emphasis on architecture, it's not necessary because it's already history. And since it's history, emphasizing it would be boring. It's better to radicalize the presence of art in such a way that it can become history.

The igloo is an architectural structure that resorts to frail and ephemeral materials, such as glass shards and twigs, stucco and neon. It therefore opposes the absoluteness of Wright's architecture. We are in the actual contact of two epidermises: one is soft, nervous and cutting, the other secure, linear and affirmative.

I have to accept my fresco, my psychopathic existence. I have to accept the fact that today's world creates psychopaths, not

straight, linear people. Straightness is [intrinsic to] the machine, but the human being inserted into the gears is really very twisted. We have an inner body and an outer body. Ultimately the inner body is more important than the outer one.

In seeking analogies with the past, can one say that your intention is to weld (your Welder *painting was done during the fifties) together two architectural structures, the igloo and the museum?*

I recall the sight of the young grass, the moss emerging almost against its will between two rocks. Even today I still remember how fascinating it was – I was almost scared of it.

One night, while going through the deserted city, I saw two men, and instead of seeing them like normal workers doing a normal hard job – welding – I saw them as new beings who were adding something – not sociologically, but in a much larger sense, like the human being who works with an object, the blowtorch, that does not belong to the day. An object that produces sparks: I am talking about the oxy-hydrogen flame.

I then felt that this oxy-hydrogen flame should enter my world. It was something that I felt I had to paint. Even though it created problems for me, because the oxy-hydrogen flame is one thing and painting is another. But I abandoned the idea of finding a solution to the issue of painting, and I put that nocturnal phantom directly into the picture: the man working on the trolley wheel with the blowtorch flame. This inspired me not to be afraid of taking qualitative leaps: jumping from a painterly order so as to embrace a presence that brings disorder. Painting is basically a treasure-trove of order, but sometimes it's overwhelmed with external elements that eventually cause it to lose its order. And that was sort of the adventure I embarked on.

From the psychological viewpoint of the work, your relationship to Europe and Italy is different from your relationship to America or Japan – I mean, with regard to language and focus. These two relationships are two different territories. Do you feel that your emotional or psychopathic reactions are constantly transferred, or do you have a different way of reacting? I am referring, say, to the twig landscapes of Zürich or the Chapelle Saint-Louis de la Salpêtrière in

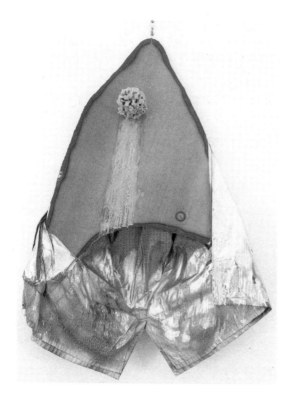

172 *The Architect (L'architetto).* 1984
Steel, pinecones, wax, spray paint and
raincoat, 55 1/8 × 31 1/2 × 11 13/16"
(140 × 80 × 30 cm.)
Courtesy Sperone Westwater,
New York

Paris – both of which are part of a European landscape.

I believe it will be very difficult to place them within the context of the Guggenheim. It will be impossible, because America rejects certain poetic attitudes, making us feel unfavored by fortune. It is the problem of surviving in a complex world. In some places there are favorable elements; in others there are none.

The problem of architecture is that of external and internal. Even in America architecture confronts the geography of the country; it is not true that architecture is total. Even in New York, when I take a walk on my own, I see that it's like being on a boat, you go from east to west and from south to north. You feel the geography of the rock on which the works, the skyscrapers, are built. I don't feel as if I were in the belly of the Big Apple, I feel like I'm on a ship or in a spaceship, where life keeps going on. If I see it in those terms, I can then include Central Park in my work. But it will be different from what I did in Switzerland, where the carpet of twigs evoked the local countryside. Central Park exists on this ship, which is New York, and I don't regard Central Park as a place where I can go to read my newspaper – I think of it as architecture. Its form is architecture, and I'm interested in the organisms that constitute the outside of that total architecture that is Manhattan.

That's why you see Central Park as a different edifice, in the sense that it is not the Swiss landscape or the Italian landscape.

Central Park is Central Park, and it can't be mistaken for the trees you see in Switzerland or Italy. The twigs have to become the Central Park of my work at the Guggenheim, they can't be a repetition of what I did in Europe – above all, because of the meaning that Central Park has for this total architecture that is New York. The idea of the indefinite park does not exist. Central Park is truly Central Park, it has an architectural definition.

At the Salpêtrière in Paris, you used the twigs to create a small park inside the glass igloo, so that the wooden confessionals and the church pews became architectural structures surrounding the architecture of the igloo, which was isolated in its park of twigs.

In Manhattan I see those skyscrapers, which are not isolated from one another,

they are points. They form a complex of mutually dependent architectural structures. My work is very similar to that situation. An organic element leans on an inorganic element, which becomes the other's opposite in both color and meaning. This opposition is fundamental for me. I would say that I am repeating the analogy of the grass between the rocks. My twigs will be placed in a stone architecture, they will grow unwittingly, like the grass, in the cement cavity of the Guggenheim. The same thing is bound to happen with the electricity, whose presence I make obvious in the flow of neon light. This too is an organic element, a natural energy that moves freely through space, crossing things and objects, the igloo and the tables.

Hence, the neon lance that penetrates things is similar – so far as you are concerned – to the twigs or to the glass that enters the stucco?

In a certain sense, yes. By putting everything together, I touch remote poles: a bundle of twigs, a piece of wood, a glass shard and the electrode. To cover that distance I have to make a tremendous effort. This is the foundation of my work.

Because I had to react to both Minimalism and figurative art – not because I didn't want them, but because it was necessary for me to react, so that art could survive, not only for me, but also for others.

A survival that I could bring about only by stretching my arms far apart and touching two widely separated poles with one finger each. That is the foundation of my work.

Do the two poles produce a vitalizing discharge?

Instead of a single line, they create an electric arc that produces a palpable tension. The person who doesn't feel it is used to the idea of an art with a precise value. In my art I did the opposite: I counterpoised two mutually remote values.

I also did painted canvases in order to experiment with the possibility of going against objectality. At a certain point objectality became a canon – which made it dangerous. I therefore preferred placing the canvas inside the igloo. And even inside that snail, Wright's hollow, I saw a being that could happily flit about inside it. And inside that vacuum I hope to place a painted canvas that traverses an igloo, that is both inside and outside. A being that is inside

*173 *Very Slowly (Pianissimo).* 1984
Wax, pinecone, plexiglass, steel and
aluminum, 102 × 31 1/2 × 23 1/2''
(259.1 × 80 × 59.7 cm.)
Courtesy Sperone Westwater,
New York

*174 *Painter in Africa (Pittore
in Africa).* 1984
Metal tubes, wire mesh and neon
tubes, 118 1/8 × 102 3/8 × 14 9/16''
(300 × 260 × 37 cm.)
Collection Haags Gemeentemuseum,
The Hague
Refabricated for present exhibition

and outside an architectural structure, even inside and outside itself. This brings back my idea of psychopathy, or of the nervous being that sustains its nervousness inside and outside life.

Can Wright's upside-down cone be thought of as an igloo seen from below?
The ceiling is its base. It's a powerful feeling, the same thing I felt around certain big trees. It's something majestic, it's not dark, it responds to powers that are inside the human being – for instance enlarging the lungs in order to breathe better. Here the architecture creates the feeling of the sky above the earth.

Do you feel analogies with your painted or interwoven cones?
The cone derives from violence (the head of the lance), an intrinsic violence. But I don't play with violence, I play with equilibrium. There is the cone that transfixes and there is the cone that rises: two elements that interpenetrate one another by playing diverse roles.
The lance is an element that preceded the igloo. A major factor in my work. These are not real lances, they are rising cones. Elements of lightness. Wright's edifice has majesty as well as lightness. It's not only religious, it's also based on a Socratic idea, the idea of Socraticness.

Your work has always included the notion of a theater of life, which has to be renewed constantly. Even the same structure becomes a different igloo. Take your idea of instability, your entrance with an unstable mosaic into the stability of architecture. How do you see this mechanism, which could be a weakness, but isn't, because it contains an enormous strength? How do you explain it?
There are two possibilities: the matter can be resolved with an extremely rigorous aesthetics or with an extremely energetic aesthetics. Both solutions are radical, because you don't know where maximum energy comes from, but you do know the source of maximum rigor. The problem is a historical one. Human beings are accustomed to rigor because they have drawn maps of the entire earth, they have traced lines from east and west and the whole segmentation of human life. Schedules are elements of rigor. Human beings are accustomed to both rigor and energy. They use energy as a living thing. Yet often energy is made to rest and it's tranquilized by the

terms of rigor. Today rigor is reactionary. The public is more accustomed to representing rigor than to representing energy. The latter is something that came with the Futurists, who sided with energy against rigor. The metaphysics of de Chirico reproposed tranquility, silence, organization. I have to choose, and it is a dialectical choice, and even though I know both parts, I have to accept the improvisation of the energy element, the unknown that it involves. Naturally, perils exist. One has to go against oneself and not be argued into anything else. The public does not argue with me. The public, acting as a single entity, is reactionary. It actually sees art as a pause. Yet there are moments in the history of art, brief moments, when the public is virtually eliminated, and its thoughts are unimportant.
If I were to think that the public were suddenly here, I would no longer feel free to pursue my experiments.

175 *The Gold that We Are Able (L'oro che possiamo)*. 1984
Oil, enamel and spray paint on canvas and wood, 108 1/4 × 107 1/2''
(275 × 273 cm.)
Courtesy Galleria Christian Stein,
Milan and Turin

*176 *The Gardener's House (La casa del giardiniere)*. 1983-84
Metal tubes, wire mesh, oil and acrylic on canvas, wax, metal, shells and pinecones, 78 3/4'' h. × 158'' d.
(200.6 × 401 cm.)
Courtesy Sperone Westwater,
New York

177 Installation, Kunsthaus Zürich,
April 1985, including:
Cat. no. 132 *Khadafi's tent (Tenda
di Gheddafi).* 1981
Cat. no. 125 *Double Igloo (Doppio
Igloo).* 1979+81

178 Installation, Galleria Christian
Stein, Milan, October 1985, including:
Untitled. 1985
Mixed media on canvas and tree
trunks, 114 3/16'' × 36' 1 1/16''
× 35 7/16'' (290 × 1100 × 90 cm.)
Collection of the artist

179 Installation, Leo Castelli Gallery in collaboration with Sperone Westwater Gallery, New York, November 1985, including:
Four Tables in the Shape of Magnolia Leaves (Quattro tavole in forma di foglie di magnolia). 1985
Wax and mixed media on welded steel tables, sixteen sections, total 29" × 65' 3" × 60" (73.7 × 1981 × 152.4 cm.)
Courtesy Sperone Westwater, New York

Bateau ivre. 1983
Acrylic, spray paint and charcoal on canvas, 102 3/8" × 76' 1 3/8" (260 × 2320 cm.)
Courtesy Sperone Westwater, New York

180 *Everything Flows, Heraclitus
(Tutto scorre, Heraclite).* 1985
Clay blocks and neon tubes on
linoleum, each block 5 15/16 × 7
1/16'' (15 × 18 cm.), total 11
13/16'' × 26'3'' (30 × 800 cm.)
Courtesy Galerie Vera Munro,
Hamburg

*181 *Igloo.* 1984-85
Metal tubes, wire mesh, neon tubes,
plexiglass, glass and wax, 39 1/4 h.
× 78 1/2" d. (99.7 × 199.4 cm.); base
four pieces, total 91" × 9' 10 1/4"
(231 × 300.4 cm.)
Collection Gerald S. Elliott, Chicago

182 *853.* 1985
Metal tubes, glass, clamps, twigs and
neon tubes; *Objet cache-toi* in center
of largest structure, igloos 26' 3'' d.;
16' 4 7/8'' d.; 118 1/8'' d.
(800; 500; 300 cm.)
Collection of the artist

183 *Places Without Streets (Luoghi senza strada)* detail. 1987
Metal tubes, wire mesh, stone, twigs and neon tubes, 78 3/4" × 13' 1 1/2" d. (200 × 400 cm.)
Collection of the artist

Following pages:
*184 *Do We Walk Around Houses or Do Houses Walk Around Us? (Noi giriamo intorno alle case o le case girano intorno a noi?).* 1985
Metal tubes, stone, glass and electric light; igloo 102" h. × 16' 4 7/8" d. (259 × 500 cm.); tunnel 24" × 19' 6" × 40" (61 × 600 × 102 cm.)
Courtesy Anthony d'Offay Gallery, London

185 *Towards the Zenith (Verso lo zenith).* 1985
Iron, wood, wax and steel wool,
90 9/16'' h. × 118 1/8'' d.
(230 × 300 cm.)
Courtesy Galleria Mario Pieroni,
Rome

186 *Untitled.* 1985
Chalk, charcoal, wax wood and steel
wool, 157 1/2 × 118 1/8''
(400 × 300 cm.)
Courtesy Galleria Mario Pieroni,
Rome

187 Installation, Museo di
Capodimonte, Naples, April 1987,
including:
The River Appears (*Il fiume appare*).
1986
Newspapers, glass, neon tubes, iron
plates and metal tubes, 19' 8' 1/4''
× 91' 10 3/8'' (600 × 2800 cm.)
Collection Ceat-Cavi, Turin

188 *The River Appears (Il fiume appare).* 1986
Mixed media on canvas and tracing paper, neon tubes, newspapers, iron plates and canvas, 39' 4 7/16''
× 118 1/8'' (1200 × 300 cm.)
Courtesy Galleria Antonio Tucci Russo, Turin

189 *The River Appears (Il fiume appare)*. 1986+88
Mixed media on canvas and tracing paper, neon tubes, newspapers, iron plates, canvas, metal tubes and glass, 39' 4 7/16'' × 118 1/8'' (1200 × 300 cm.); triangular structures each 22' 11/16'' × 29' 6 3/8'' × 13' 11 5/16'' (700 × 900 × 425 cm.)
Collection The Rivetti Art Foundation, Turin; Courtesy Galleria Antonio Tucci Russo, Turin

190 *Une ouvrée, une mésure de terre qui donne un portrait bien terrestre.*
1986
Twigs, paving stones, wax, metal tubes, neon tubes and plywood,
11' 5 13/16'' × 31' 2'' × 24' 7 1/4''
(350 × 950 × 750 cm.)
Courtesy Galerie Pietro Sparta, Chagny, France

191 *Une ouvrée, une mésure de terre
qui donne un portrait bien terrestre.*
1986
Twigs, paving stones, wax
and chimney caps, 14' 9 3/16''
× 13' 9 3/8'' (450 × 420 cm.)
Courtesy Galerie Pietro Sparta,
Chagny, France

192 *The Drop of Water* (*La goccia d'acqua*). 1987
Metal tubes, glass and neon tubes; igloo 39' 4 7/16'' d. (1200 cm.);
Collection of the artist; Courtesy CAPC/Musée d'Art Contemporain, Bordeaux

193 *Fontaine*. 1987
Metal tubes, glass, neon tubes and
fountain; igloo 32' 9 11/16'' d. (1000
cm.); triangular structure 31 1/2''
× 86' 7 3/8 × 14' 7 3/16''
(80 × 2640 × 445 cm.)
Collection of the artist; Courtesy
CAPC/Musée d'Art Contemporain,
Bordeaux

Following pages:
194 Installation, Nationalgalerie,
Berlin, June 1988, of works by Jannis
Kounellis and Merz, including in
center:
*The Drop of Water (La goccia
d'acqua)*. 1987
Metal tubes, glass and neon tubes;
igloo 39' 4 7/16'' d. (1200 cm.)
Collection of the artist; Courtesy
Nationalgalerie, Berlin

195 *Celui qui est en plomb.* 1987
Metal tubes, wire mesh, lead, wood,
wax and canvas, 118 1/8" d. (300 cm.)
Collection Musée de Nîmes; Courtesy
CAPC/Musée d'Art Contemporain,
Bordeaux

196 *Untitled*. 1984+87
Wicker, metal tubes, glass and stone,
cone 13 1/2" h. × 78 3/4" d.
(400 × 200 cm.); table 29.6
3/8" × 11.5 13/16" × 29 1/2
(900 × 350 × 75 cm.)
Collection Sparta, Chagny, France;
Courtesy Galerie Pietro Sparta,
Chagny, France

Following pages:
197 *Unreal City* (*Città irreale*). 1987
Gouache, watercolor and ink
on paper, 78 3/4 × 12' 1 7/8"
(200 × 370.5 cm.)
Courtesy Anthony d'Offay Gallery,
London

*198 *Untitled.* 1988
Iron, pillow, telephone and neon
tubes, 82 11/16 × 51 3/16 × 43 5/16''
(210 × 130 × 110 cm.)
Courtesy Galerie Pietro Sparta,
Chagny, France

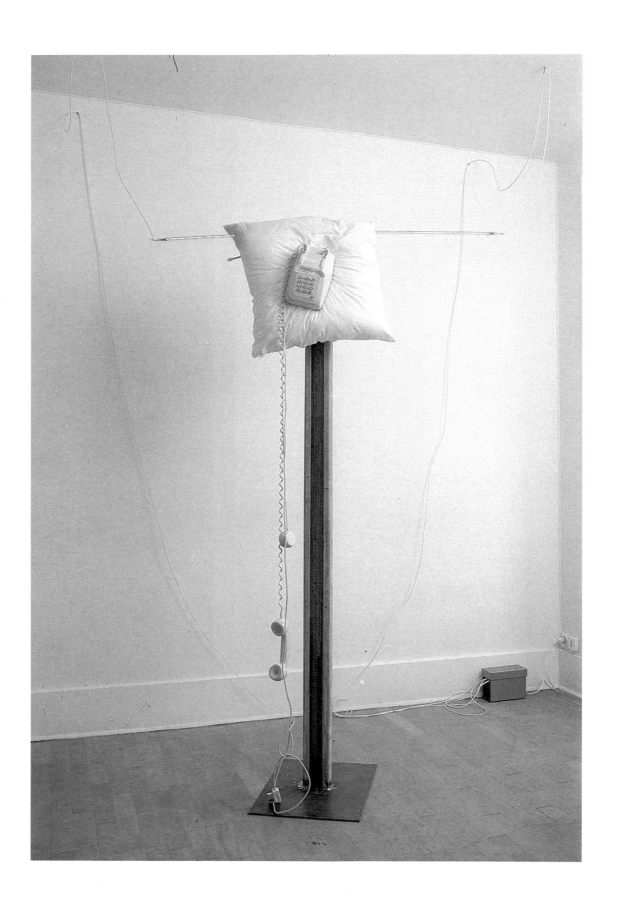

199 *Turbine (Turbina)*. 1988
Mixed media on canvas, raincoat, neon
tube, stone and music stand, 16'4 7/8''
× 11'5 13/16'' (500 × 350 cm.)
Collection of the artist

201 Installation, Kunstmuseum
Saint-Gallen, 1988, including:
*Untitled. ("Everything Is Connected,"
Hölderlin) ("Tutto è connesso,"
Hölderlin)*. 1988
Metal tubes, clamps, glass, stone and
neon tubes, 90 9/16" × 17' 4 11/16"
× 18' 1/2" (230 × 530 × 550 cm.)
Collection H. Emanuel Schmid, Zürich

202 *Virgilius, Futurist Memory*
(*Virgilius, memoria futurista*). 1988
Metal tubes, metal and wax, 13'
1 1/2'' × 78 3/4'' (400 × 200 cm.)
Courtesy ICA/Institute of
Contemporary Art, Nagoya

203 Installation at Louisiana Museum of Modern Art, Humlebaek, Denmark, 1988, including:
*Spiral Table and Igloo (Spiraltisch und Igloo). 1981+88
Metal tubes, glass, twigs, neon tubes and wax; igloo 51 3/16″ h × 78 3/4″ d. (130 × 200 cm.); table 25 9/16″ × 23′ 7 7/16″ × 10 7/16″ (65 × 720 × 880 cm.)
Gallery Jean Bernier, Athens
*Cat. no. 88 Panthers on Cone (Pantere sul cono). 1978
Persecuted Crocodile (Coccodrillo perseguitato). 1981
Mixed media on canvas and metal

204 Installation, Museum of
Contemporary Art, Los Angeles,
February 1989, including:
Untitled. 1989
Glass, steel, clay, sheet metal, neon
tubes, rocks, mortar, wax and clamps.
Courtesy Museum of Contemporary
Art, Los Angeles

*205 *Madame de Lafayette.* 1988
Oil, clay, newspaper, stuffed alligator
and putty on paper and neon tube,
11' 1 7/8'' × 102 3/8'' × 47 1/4''
(340 × 260 × 120 cm.)
Collection of the artist

206 *House in the Forest*
(*Casa sulla foresta*). 1989
Metal, wire mesh, rubber, wax, twigs
and neon tubes, 40 1/8 × 102 3/8
× 47 1/4'' (102 × 260 × 120 cm.)
Collection of the artist

207 *If the Form Vanishes, Its Root Is Eternal (Se la forma scompare la sua radice è eterna)*. 1982(89)
Neon tubes
Collection of the artist

Works in the catalogue

*Indicates work in the exhibition.

Dimensions are not given for room-size and outdoor installations. As most of the works are irregular, dimensions are approximate.

Dating:
A hyphenated date, for example 1966-67, indicates that the object was worked on for the duration of time cited; the appearance of a plus mark, 1966+67, indicates that the object was altered at the later date; the use of parentheses, 1966(85), indicates that the object was refabricated at the later date.

Exhibition histories:
It is often difficult to determine the precise exhibition histories of individual objects because of the ephemeral nature of Mario Merz's work and the scarcity of definitive records. Therefore we have assumed that works were included in an exhibition if they are illustrated in the catalogue for that exhibition and not otherwise documented.
Information under exhibitions and references is abbreviated. For full citations see the selected exhibitions lists and bibliography in this catalogue. References with only a city, date, catalogue and/or page number signify the catalogue produced for the exhibition in question; full data for these catalogues are given in the exhibitions lists rather than the bibliography.

*1 *Leaf (Foglia)*. 1952
Oil on wood, 37 7/16 × 55 1/8'' (95 × 140 cm.)
Private Collection
Exhibitions: Turin, 1954; Turin, 1962, repr. p. 4; Modena, 1982, repr. p. 78; Pisa, 1983, repr. p. 78; Turin, 1983, repr.; Bologna, 1983; Zürich, 1985, cat. no. 2
Reference: San Marino, 1983, cat. no. 10, repr. p. 25

2 *Untitled*. 1953
Oil on canvas, 39 3/8 × 29 1/2'' (100 × 75 cm.)
Private Collection, Turin

*3 *Seed in the Wind (Seme nel vento)*. 1953
Oil on Masonite, 32 11/16 × 39'' (83 × 99 cm.)
Private Collection, Turin
Exhibitions: Turin, 1983, repr. (as *Senza titolo*); Bologna, 1983; San Marino, 1983, cat. no. 11, repr. p. 27; Zürich, 1985, cat. no. 1
Reference: Rovereto, 1989, repr. p. 162

4 *Tree (Albero)*. 1953
Oil on canvas, 28 × 39 1/2'' (71 × 100.3 cm.)

Private Collection, Turin
Exhibitions: Turin, 1962; Münster, 1982, repr. p. 19
References: ARC/Musée d'Art Moderne de la Ville de Paris, 1981, repr.; Vienna, 1983, p. 140, repr. p. 83; San Marino, 1983, cat. no. 15, repr. p. 30; Rovereto, 1989, repr. p. 164

*5 *Gypsy Wagon (Carrozzone)*. 1953
Oil on canvas, 70 7/8 × 79 1/8'' (180 × 201 cm.)
Collection Udo and Anette Brandhorst
Exhibitions: Turin, 1954; San Marino, 1983 (not in cat.)
Reference: Rovereto, 1989, repr. p. 163

6 *Flower (Fiore)*. 1953-54
Mixed media on wood, 39 × 27 3/16'' (99 × 69 cm.)
Collection Marcello Levi, Turin

*7 *The Welder (Il saldatore)*. 1956
Oil on canvas, 39 3/16 × 27 3/8'' (99.5 × 69.5 cm.)
Collection Museo Civico di Torino, Galleria d'Arte Moderna, Turin
Exhibitions: Milan, 1957; Turin, 1985, repr. p. 275; Turin, 1987, cat. no. 201, repr. p. 211
Reference: San Marino, 1983, cat. no. 17, repr. p. 32

*8 *Spiral Leaf (Foglia spirale)*. 1955
Enamel, oil and dirt on canvas, 43 3/8 × 49 1/4'' (110.5 × 125 cm.)
Collection of the artist

*9 *Red and Green Face (Faccia rossa e verde)*. 1955
Enamel and oil on wood, 46 7/16 × 48'' (118 × 122 cm.)
Collection of the artist

10 *Composition (Composizione)*. 1954
Oil on canvas, 40 1/8 × 30 15/16'' (102 × 77 cm.)
Collection Valla, Turin
Exhibition: Turin, 1954

*11 *Untitled*. 1952
Enamel and oil on canvas, 51 × 35 1/2'' (129.5 × 90.1 cm.)
Collection of the artist

*12 *Untitled*. 1958
Mixed media on canvas, 63 × 35 7/16'' (160 × 90 cm.)
Collection of the artist; Courtesy Galleria Antonio Tucci Russo, Turin

*13 *The Stone (Il sasso)*. 1959
Oil on canvas, 78 1/2 × 59 1/4'' (199.4 × 150.5 cm.)
Collection Liliane and Michel Durand-Dessert, Paris

14 *Untitled*. 1959-60
Oil on wood, 39 3/8 × 50 3/8'' (100 × 128 cm.)
Collection Ezio Gribaudo, Turin

15 *Untitled*. 1960
Oil on wood, 39 3/8 × 27 9/16'' (100 × 70 cm.)

Collection Renata Novarese, Turin

16 *Untitled*. 1963
Mixed media and watercolor on paper, 39 3/8 × 27 9/16'' (100 × 70 cm.)
Private Collection

17 *Untitled*. 1965
Mixed media on wood, 44 7/8 × 41 3/4'' (114 × 106 cm.)
Collection Giampaolo Prearo, Milan

18 *Untitled*. 1966
Wood, burned wicker and nylon netting, 53 1/8 × 78 3/4 × 29 1/2'' (135 × 200 × 75 cm.)
Collection of the artist; Courtesy Gian Enzo Sperone, Turin
Reference: San Marino, 1983, cat. no. 20, repr. p. 35

*19 *Small Salami (Salamino)*. 1966-67
Blanket and neon tube, 37 7/16 × 100'' (90 × 254 cm.)
Private Collection, Turin
Exhibitions: Turin, Deposito d'Arte Presente, 1967-69 (exhibited 1968); Paris, 1969, repr. (dated 1966); Rome, 1976; Zürich, 1985, cat. no. 6
Reference: San Marino, 1983, cat. no. 30, repr. p.45

20 *Horse Theater (Teatro Cavallo)*. 1967
Plastic tubes, neon tubes and pillow, 98 7/16 × 118 1/8 × 9 11/14'' (250 × 300 × 50 cm.)
Sonnabend Collection, New York
Exhibitions: Turin, 1968, repr.; Düsseldorf, 1968; Paris, 1969, repr. (as *Il teatro*); Turin, 1976; Madrid, 1987, repr. p. 216 (dated 1966, without pillow); Bordeaux, 1988, repr. p. 232 (dated 1966, without pillow); Berlin, Hamburger Bahnhof, 1988 (dated 1966, without pillow); Rome, 1989, repr. p. 139 (dated 1966, without pillow)
References: Venice, 1978, fig. 179, repr. p. 164; Essen, 1979, cat. no. 15, repr. p. 32 (dated 1963, without pillow); ARC/Musée d'Art Moderne de la Ville de Paris, 1981, repr. (as *Teatrocavallo*); San Marino, 1983, repr. p. 44; *Parkett*, 1988, repr. inside cover (dated 1966, without pillow)

*21 *Horse Theater (Teatro cavallo)*. 1967
Plastic tubes and neon tubes, 98 7/16 × 118 1/8 × 19 11/16'' (250 × 300 × 50 cm.)
Collection Museo Civico di Torino, Galleria d'Arte Moderna, Turin
Exhibitions: Turin, Galleria Civica d'Arte Moderna, 1967, repr. p. 110; Turin, 1985, repr. p. 273
References: Essen, 1979, cat. no. 4,

repr. p. 12 (dated 1962-63); San Marino, 1983, cat. no. 21, repr. p. 37

*23 *Untitled*. 1966-67
Murano bottle, glasses, spray paint and neon tube, 40 1/2 × 13 3/8 × 27 9/16'' (103 × 35 × 70 cm.)
Collection Marcello Levi, Turin
Exhibitions: Turin, Galleria Gian Enzo Sperone, 1968; San Marino, 1983 (not in cat.); Milan, 1989, repr. p. 100

24 *Bottle (Bottiglia)*. 1966-67
Bottle, neon tube and spray paint, 35 7/16 × 19 11/16 × 19 11/16'' (90 × 50 × 50 cm.)
Collection Pierluigi Pero, Milan
Exhibition: Turin, Galleria Gian Enzo Sperone, 1968
References: Essen, 1979, cat. no. 11, repr. p. 28 (dated 1962); San Marino, 1983, cat. no. 22, repr. p. 38

25 *Cone (Il cono)*. 1967
Wicker, 7 7/8 - 39 3/8'' h. × 78 3/4'' d. (20 - 100 × 200 cm.)
Collection Städtisches Museum Abteiberg, Mönchengladbach
Exhibitions: Düsseldorf, 1968; Amalfi, 1968; Paris, 1969, repr. (as *Cestone di vimini*, dated 1966, with boiling water inside cone); Essen, 1979 (not in cat.); Düsseldorf, 1979; London, Whitechapel Art Gallery, 1980; London, Anthony d'Offay Gallery, 1983; Rotterdam, 1988
References: ARC/Musée d'Art Moderne de la Ville de Paris, 1981, repr. (dated 1969); Vienna, 1983, repr. p. 98

*26 *Hamper (Cestone)*. 1967
Wicker basket, 53 1/8 × 78 3/4 × 29 1/2'' (135 × 200 × 75 cm.)
Courtesy Galerie Liliane et Michel Durand-Dessert, Paris
Exhibitions: Turin, Galleria Christian Stein, Galleria Gian Enzo Sperone and Galleria Il Punto, 1967; Turin, 1968, repr.; Düsseldorf, 1968, cat. no. 1, repr.; Amsterdam, 1969 (as *Vimini*, dated 1966); Tokyo, 1970; Zürich, 1985, cat. no. 8, repr. vol. 2 (dated 1968); Nîmes, 1987, cat. no. 48
References: Essen, 1979, cat. no. 16, repr. pp. 32-33 (dated 1964); ARC/Musée d'Art Moderne de la Ville de Paris, 1981, repr.; San Marino, 1983, repr. p. 44

*27 *Raincoat (Impermeabile)*. 1967
Raincoat, wax, wood and neon tube, 49 3/16 × 66 15/16 × 15 3/4'' (125 × 70 × 40 cm.)
Collection Christian Stein, Turin
Exhibitions: Milan, 1967; Turin, 1968, repr.; Rome, 1976; Frankfurt, 1985, cat. no. 1, repr. p. 64 (dated 1966); London, 1989, repr. p. 218; Milan, 1989, repr. p. 99
References: Essen, 1979, cat. no. 12, repr. p. 29 (dated 1963); ARC/Musée d'Art Moderne de la Ville de Paris,

1981, repr. (dated 1963); San Marino, 1983, cat. no. 26, repr. p. 41; Sauer, *Die Sammlung FER-The FER Collection*, 1983, pp. 107, 185, repr. p. 106; Bonn, 1983, repr. p. 15 (dated 1966); Silverthorne, *Parkett*, 1988, repr. p. 70 (dated 1963); Rovereto, 1989, repr. p. 165

*28 *Umbrella (Ombrello)*. 1967(77)
Umbrella, neon tube and spray paint, 24 × 78 × 28'' (61 × 198.1 × 71.1 cm.)
Collection Giuliana and Tommaso Setari, Rome
References: Essen, 1979, cat. no. 13, repr. p. 30 (dated 1963); Linz, 1980, repr. p. 448 (dated 1963); Vienna, 1983, p. 140, repr. p. 86; San Marino, 1983, cat. no. 24, repr. p. 39; Rovereto, 1989, repr. p. 168

*29 *Untitled*. 1966+84
Glass-top table, neon tube, glass and ivy, 28 3/4 × 40 1/8 × 28 5/16'' (73 × 102 × 72 cm.)
Private Collection

30 Installation, Galleria Gian Enzo Sperone, Turin, January 1968, including:
* *Lance (Lancia)*. 1967
Plexiglass and painted wood, 112 3/16 × 25 9/16 × 9 13/16'' (285 × 65 × 25 cm.)
Private Collection, Genoa
Exhibitions: Turin, 1968; Zürich, 1985, cat. no. 7
Reference: San Marino, 1983, repr. p. 38
Untitled. 1966-67
Plexiglass, Murano bottle, glasses and neon tubes, 13 3/4 × 27 9/16 × 27 9/16'' (35 × 70 × 70 cm.)
Collection Marcello Levi, Turin

31 *Giap Igloo – If the Enemy Masses His Forces, He Loses Ground; If He Scatters, He Loses Strength (Igloo di Giap - Se il nemico si concentra perde terreno, se si disperde perde forza)*. 1968
Metal tubes, wire mesh, neon tubes and dirt, 118 1/8'' d. (300 cm.)
Collection of the artist
Exhibitions: Turin, Deposito d'Arte Presente, 1967-69 (exhibited 1968); Rome, 1968; Düsseldorf, 1968; Amsterdam, 1969, cat. no. 2; Turin, 1970, repr.; Rome, 1972, p. 379; Philadelphia, 1973, repr.; Krefeld, 1981, cat. no. 10, repr. p. 21; Amsterdam, 1982, cat. no. 1, repr. p. 68; Perugia, 1984, repr. p. 87
References: Essen, 1979, cat. no. 22, repr. p. 39; Paris, Musée National d'Art Moderne, 1981, repr. p. 293; ARC/Musée d'Art Moderne de la Ville de Paris, 1981, repr.; San Marino, 1983, cat. no. 33, repr. p. 47; Vienna, 1983, p. 140, repr. pp. 79, 129, 133

*32 *Giap Igloo – If the Enemy Masses His Forces, He Loses Ground; If He Scatters, He Loses Strength (Igloo di*

Giap – Se il nemico si concentra perde terreno se si disperde perde forza). 1968 (82)
Metal tubes, wire mesh, wax, plaster and neon tubes, 47 1/4 h. × 78 3/4'' d. (120 × 200 cm.)
Collection Musée National d'Art Moderne, Centre Georges Pompidou, Paris
Exhibitions: Zürich, 1985, cat. no. 9 (dated 1968), repr. vol. 2; Paris, 1986, cat. no. 249, repr. p. 218 (dated 1968); Chambéry, 1987, cat. no. 25, repr. p. 30 (dated 1968)
References: Oslo, 1986, repr. (dated 1968); Vienna, 1986, repr. p. 47 (dated 1968); Silverthorne, *Parkett*, 1988, repr. p. 72

*33 *Sitin*. 1968 (71)
Metal tubes, wire mesh, wax, neon tubes and glass, 11 13/16 × 35 7/16 × 28 1/2'' (30 × 90 × 72.4 cm.)
Collection Marisa Lombardi, Milan

*34 *What's To Be Done? (Che fare?)*. 1968
Metal pot, wax and neon tubes, 5 7/8 × 17 11/16 × 7 1/16'' (15 × 45 × 18 cm.)
Collection Giulio Einaudi Editore SpA, A.S., Turin
Exhibitions: Turin, Deposito d'Arte Presente, 1967-69 (exhibited 1968); Paris, 1969; Turin, Galleria Gian Enzo Sperone, 1976; Krefeld, 1981, cat. no. 12, p. 38, repr. p. 22; Zürich, 1985; cat. no. 13; Chambéry, 1987; Lille, 1987; La Roche-sur-Yon, 1987, cat. no. 26, repr. p. 70 (dated 1969); Munich, 1988, cat. no. 157, repr. p. 247
References: Essen, 1979, cat. no. 6, repr. p. 18 (dated 1969); Linz, 1980, repr. p. 446 (dated 1969); San Marino, 1983, cat. no. 13, repr. p. 28; Silverthorne, *Parkett*, 1988, repr. p. 62

35 *Solitary Solidarity (Solitario solidale)*. 1968
Terra-cotta pot, wax and neon tubes, 5 7/8 × 19 11/16 × 7 7/8'' (15 × 50 × 20 cm.)
Collection Museum Haus Lange, Krefeld
Exhibitions: Turin, Deposito d'Arte Presente, 1967-69 (exhibited 1968); Düsseldorf, 1968; Paris, 1969, repr.; Krefeld, 1981, cat. no. 11, repr. p. 22; Krefeld, 1983, cat. no. 238, repr. p. 183
References: Essen, 1979, cat. no. 18, repr. p. 35; ARC/Musée d'Art Moderne de la Ville de Paris, 1981, repr.; San Marino, 1983, cat. no. 31, repr. p. 35

*36 *Never Has Stone Been Raised on Stone (Mai alzato pietra su pietra)*. 1968 (82)
Metal tubes, wire mesh, cloth and neon tubes, 39 3/8 h. × 78 3/4'' d. (100 × 200 cm.)
Collection Udo and Anette Brandhorst
Exhibitions: Zürich, 1985, cat. no. 10,

repr. vol. 2 (dated 1968); Krefeld, 1985, cat. no. 35, repr. p. 47 (dated 1969)
References: Venice, 1978, repr. p. 45, fig. 99 (dated 1969); *Dalla natura all'arte, dall'arte alla natura*, repr. p. 163; *Artenatura*; Linz, 1980, repr. p. 449

*37 *Objet cache-toi*. 1968(86)
Metal, wire mesh, cloth and neon tubes, 43 5/16 h. × 82 3/4'' d. (110 × 210 cm.)
Sonnabend Collection, New York
Exhibitions: Madrid, 1987, repr. p. 219 (dated 1968); Bordeaux, 1988, repr. p. 235 (dated 1968); Berlin, Hamburger Bahnhof, 1988 (dated 1968); Rome, 1989, repr. p. 141 (dated 1968)
Reference: Grüterich, *Parkett*, 1988, repr. p. 46

*38 *Wax and Rubber (Cera e gomma)*. 1968
Metal, rubber, incandescent lamp and wax, 27 1/2 × 53 × 86 1/2'' (69.9 × 134.6 × 219.7 cm.)
Sonnabend Collection, New York
Exhibitions: Düsseldorf, 1968; Amsterdam, 1969, cat. no. 3 (dated 1969); Paris, 1969, repr.; Madrid, 1987, repr. p. 217; Bordeaux, 1988, repr. p. 233; Berlin, Hamburger Bahnhof, 1988; Rome, 1989, repr. p. 138
Reference: Essen, 1979, cat. no. 5, repr. p.16

*39 *Hagoromo*. 1968
Metal tubes, wire mesh, wax and neon tubes, 11 × 78 3/4 × 18 1/4'' (27.9 × 200 × 46.4 cm.)
Courtesy Sonnabend Gallery, New York
Exhibitions: Turin, Deposito d'Arte Presente, 1967-69 (exhibited 1968); Krefeld, 1981, cat. no. 9, p. 38, repr. p. 20 (dated 1967-69)
References: San Marino, 1983, cat. no. 35, p. 49; Nagoya, 1988, repr. p. 60

*40 *Unreal City (Città irreale)*. 1968
Metal tubes, wire mesh, wax and neon tubes, 78 3/4 × 66 1/8 × 9 7/16'' (200 × 168 × 24 cm.)
Collection Stedelijk Museum, Amsterdam
Exhibitions: Amsterdam, 1969 (not in cat.); Amsterdam, 1982, repr. on cover, cat. no. 2, repr. p. 16; Zürich, 1985, cat. no. 11; Munich, 1988, cat. no. 154, repr. p. 245; London, 1989, repr. p. 217
References: San Marino, 1983, cat. no. 36, repr. p. 49; Silverthorne, *Parkett*, 1988, repr. p. 72

*41 *Nugget (Lingotto)*. 1969(81)
Metal tubes, wood, wax and twigs, structure 80 × 72 × 15 1/2'' (203 × 183 × 39.4 cm.); twigs 98'' h. (249 cm.)
Courtesy Anthony d'Offay Gallery, London
Exhibitions: Krefeld, 1981, cat. no. 13,

repr. p. 23 (dated 1969); London, Anthony d'Offay Gallery, 1983; Zürich, 1985, cat. no. 18 (dated 1969); London, 1988

42 *Nugget (Lingotto)*. 1969
Metal tubes, wood, wax and twigs, 103 1/8'' × 12' 3 1/4'' × 44 7/8'' (262 × 374 × 114 cm.)
Courtesy Galerie Liliane et Michel Durand-Dessert, Paris

43 Installation, Galleria L'Attico, Rome, 1969, including from right to left:
Igloo with Tree (Igloo con albero). 1969
Metal tubes, glass, plaster and branch, 59 1/16 h. × 98 7/16'' d. (150 × 250 cm.); with branch 10' 6'' h. (320 cm.)
Collection of the artist; Courtesy Galleria Christian Stein, Milan and Turin
Exhibitions: Rome, 1969; Bern, 1969 (as *Acqua scivola*); Turin, 1970, repr.; Munich, 1988, cat. no. 155, repr. p. 256 (as *Igloo-objet cache-toi*); Berlin, Hamburger Bahnhof, 1988, repr. (as *Igloo-che fare?*); Milan, 1989, repr. p. 101
References: Essen, 1979, cat. no. 44, repr. p. 72; Paris, Musée National d'Art Moderne, 1981, repr. p. 284; Bordeaux, 1982, repr.; Vienna, 1983, repr. p. 42; Zürich, 1985, repr. on cover, pp. 10, 14, 24, 32, 34, 42, 48, 52, 60, 62, 72, 82, 88, 95, 96, vol. 1.; Vienna, 1986, repr. p. 45; Spoleto, 1987, repr. p. 144; Silverthorne, *Parkett*, 1988, repr. p. 72; Rovereto, 1989, repr. p. 167

Automobile Pierced by Neon (Automobile trapassata dal neon). 1969
Simca 1,000, neon tubes, 14' 9 3/16'' × 59 1/16 × 78 3/4'' (450 × 150 × 200 cm.)
Collection of the artist

44 *Relationships of growth within the development of a tree outlined in an unbroken line according to the Fibonacci series*. 1970
Neon tubes and wire, variable dimensions
Courtesy Sonnabend Gallery, New York
Exhibitions: New York, 1970; Zürich, 1985, cat. no. 27
References: Essen, 1979, cat. no. 24, repr. p. 42; San Marino, 1983, cat. no. 46, repr. p. 60

45 *Propped (Appoggiati)*. 1970
Glass, plaster and neon tubes
Courtesy Galleria Civica d'Arte Moderna, Bologna
Exhibitions: Bologna, 1970; New York, 1970; Lucerne, 1970, repr.; Turin, 1970, repr.; Rome, 1970, repr.
References: Vienna, 1971, repr. (as *Vetri Fibonacci*, dated 1969); ARC/Musée d'Art Moderne de la Ville de Paris, 1981, repr.; Nagoya, 1988, repr. p. 64

46 *Objet cache-toi*. 1968 (77)
Metal tubes, glass, clamps, wire mesh, bottles and neon tubes, 157 1/2" d. (400 cm.)
Sonnabend Collection, New York
Exhibitions: Chicago, 1977; repr.; Cologne, 1981; Zürich, 1985, cat. no. 14
References: Essen, 1979, cat. no. 32, repr. p. 58; Linz,1980, repr. p. 449 (dated 1968); ARC/Musée d'Art Moderne de la Ville de Paris, 1981, repr.; Münster,1982, repr. pp. 11, 13; Stockholm, 1983, repr. p. 32 (dated 1968); Vienna, 1983, p. 139, repr. p. 71;San Marino, 1983, cat. no. 14, repr. p. 28

47 *Untitled*. 1969(78)
Bales of hay and neon tube, 47 1/4 × 15 3/4 × 15 3/4" (120 × 40 × 40 cm.)
Collection Lia Rumma, Naples
Exhibition: Naples, 1978
Refabricated for present exhibition

48 Installation, Sonnabend Auxilliary Space, New York 1970, including from right to left:
Igloo-Cancelled Numbers (Igloo-numeri cancellati). 1970
Metal tubes, wire mesh, wax, Perspex containers and neon tubes, 118 1/8" d. (300 cm.)
Exhibitions: New York, 1970; Rome, 1970, repr.; Vienna, 1971, repr.
Reference: San Marino, 1983, repr. p. 64

cat. no. 45 *piopped (Appagati)*, 1970

*49 *Igloo Fibonacci*. 1970
Copper, aluminum and marble, 72 × 96 × 96" (182.9 × 243.8 × 243.8 cm.)
Sonnabend Collection, New York
Exhibitions: New York, 1970; Lucerne, 1970; Essen, 1979, cat. no. 25, cat. no. 47 (as *Igloo Fibonacci su pezzi di terra*, supported by blocks of earth), repr. p. 78; Bonn, 1983, repr. p. 14; Zürich, 1985, cat. no. 25; Madrid, 1987, repr. p. 218; Bordeaux, 1988, repr. p. 234; Berlin, Hamburger Bahnhof, 1988; Rome, 1989, repr. p. 140
References: Linz, 1980, repr. p. 445; ARC/Musée d'Art Moderne de la Ville de Paris, 1981, repr.; Münster, 1982, repr. p. 15; San Marino, 1983, cat. no. 45, repr. p. 59; Berlin, Nationalgalerie, 1988, repr. p. 42

*50 *Fibonacci Progression (Progressione di Fibonacci)*. 1971
Neon tubes arranged along the inner spiral of the Guggenheim Museum, New York
Refabricated for present exhibition
Exhibition: New York, Solomon R. Guggenheim Museum, 1971
References: Rome, 1973, p. 365; Essen, 1979. fig. 26, repr. p. 44; San Marino, 1983, cat. no. 57, repr. p. 57; New York, Solomon R. Guggenheim Museum, 1985, cat. no. 105, repr. p. 165

*51 *Untitled*. 1971
Raincoat, neon tubes, spray paint, wood and snail shell, 86 5/8 × 63 × 15 3/4" (220 × 160 × 40 cm.)
The Arthur and Carol Goldberg Collection
Exhibitions: ARC/Musée d'Art Moderne de la Ville de Paris, 1981 (Basel venue only, as *Chiocciola con impermeabile*); Buffalo, Albright-Knox Art Gallery, 1984, cat. no. 1, repr. p. 3

52 Installation at Sonnabend Gallery, New York, 1971, including from right to left:
* *Aprons = Natural Numbers (Grembiali = numeri naturali)*. 1971
Metal tubes, wire mesh, neon tubes and plastic, variable dimensions
Sonnabend Collection, New York
Exhibitions: New York, Sonnabend Gallery, 1971
Reference: Vienna, 1983, p. 140, repr. p. 87
1+1=2. 1971
Metal tubes, neon tubes and wire mesh, 39 3/8 × 78 3/4" (100 × 200 cm.)
Courtesy Galleria Mario Pieroni, Rome
Exhibitions: New York, Sonnabend Gallery, 1971; New York, John Weber Gallery, 1972; Zürich, 1985, cat. no. 29
References: Paris, ARC/Musée d'Art Moderne de Ville di Paris, 1981, repr.; San Marino, 1983, cat. no. 53, repr. p. 65; Vienna, Galerie nächst St. Stephan, 1984, repr. p. 87; New York, Solomon R. Guggenheim Museum, 1985, repr. p. 163.

53 *Fibonacci Proliferation (Proliferazione di Fibonacci)*.
1973 Wire, neon tubes and plants, variable dimensions
Collection of the artist;
Courtesy Galleria Gian Enzo Sperone, Turin

*54 *610 Function of 15 (610 funzione di 15)*. 1971
Glass, newspapers and neon tubes, 11' 5 13/16" × 63 × 26 3/4" (350 × 160 × 68 cm.)
Refabricated for present exhibition

*55 *Iguana*. 1971
Stuffed iguana and neon tubes, 86 5/8 × 6 3/8" (219.7 × 16.5 cm.)
Courtesy Thomas Ammann, Zürich
Exhibitions: Minneapolis, 1972, cat. no. 7; New York, 1972, repr. p. 5; Vienna, 1983, p. 140, repr. p. 105
References: ARC/Musée d'Art Moderne de la Ville de Paris, 1981 repr.; Nagoya, 1988, repr. p. 66

56 Installation, Walker Art Center, Minneapolis, January 1972, including from right to left:
Fibonacci Igloo. 1972

Metal tubes, cloth, wire and neon tubes, 39 3/8 × 78 3/4" (100 × 200 cm.)
*cat no. 55 *Iguana*. 1971
Function of Fibonacci, from 8 to 28657, detail. 1972 Neon tubes

*57 *Acceleration = Dream, Fibonacci Numbers in Neon and Motorcycle Phanton (Accelerazione = sogno, tubi di Fibonacci al neon e motocicletta fantasma)*. 1972
Motorcycle, waterbuck horns and neon tubes, dimensions unknown
Collection of the artist
Refabricated for present exhibition
Exhibitions: Kassel, 1972; Los Angeles, 1984; Venice, 1986, repr. p. 45
References: Essen, 1979, cat. no. 34, repr. p. 62; ARC/Musée d'Art Moderne de la Ville de Paris, 1981, repr. (as *Motocicletta*, not dated); San Marino, 1983, cat. no. 71, repr. p. 85; Nagoya, 1988, repr. p. 67

58 Merz during installation of *Fibonacci Unit* at Sonnabend Gallery. New York, April 1970

59 Installation, Walker Art Center, Minneapolis, January 1972

*60 *Untitled (A Real Sum Is a Sum of People)*. 1972
Black and white photographs and argon tubes, 24" × 16' 7 1/4" × 5 1/8" (61 × 506.1 × 13 cm.)
Collection The Museum of Modern Art, New York, Mrs. Armand P. Bartos Fund, 1974
Reference: Merz, *Fibonacci 1202*, Turin, 1972, repr.

61 *it is possible to have a space with tables for 88 people as it is possible to have a space with tables for no one*. 1973
Wood tables and neon tubes; modular tables from 39 3/8" × 39 3/8" to 16' 4 7/8" × 16' 4 7/8" (100 × 100 to 500 × 500 cm.)
Courtesy John Weber Gallery, New York
Exhibitions: New York, 1973, repr.; Perugia, 1984, repr. p. 86
References: Paris, Musée National d'Art Moderne, 1981, repr. p. 437 (as *Tables*, dated 1974); San Marino, 1983, cat. no. 66 and cat. no. 72, repr. p. 87

62 Installation, Haus am Lützowplatz, Berlin.
March 1974, including from front to back:
Black Igloo (Igloo nero). 1974
Metal tubes, wire mesh and concrete, 39 3/8 h. × 78 3/4" d. (100 × 200 cm.)
Courtesy DAAD, Berlin
Exhibition: Berlin, 1974
References: Essen, 1979, cat. no. 46, repr. p. 76 (dated 1967); San Marino, 1983, cat. no. 76, repr. p. 92

Untitled. 1974
Mixed media on canvas and neon tubes
Courtesy DAAD, Berlin

63 *Progressive Closet (Armadio progressivo)*. 1974
Wood, glass and neon tubes
Courtesy DAAD, Berlin
Exhibitions: Berlin, 1974; Essen, 1979, cat. no. 45, repr. p. 74 (dated 1972)
Reference: San Marino, 1983, cat. no. 75, repr. p. 91

*64 *Zebra and Fibonacci (Zebra e Fibonacci)*. 1973
Stuffed zebra head and neon tubes, 110 1/4" × 12' 1 11/16" (280 × 370 cm.)
Collection Museo d'Arte Contemporanea, Palazzo Reale, Milan
Exhibitions: Milan, 1974; Frankfurt, 1985, repr. p. 177; Venice, 1986, *Wunderkammer*, repr. p. 45

*65 *Boards with Paws Become Tables (Tavole con le zampe diventano tavoli)*. 1974
Ink on canvas, two parts, total 17' 3/4" × 50' 2 3/8" (520 × 1530 cm.)
Collection Rijksmuseum Kröller-Müller, Otterlo
Exhibitions: Tortona, 1974 (executed in situ); Milan, 1974; Basel, 1975, repr.; London, 1975; Paris, Musée National d'Art Moderne, 1981, repr. p. 437
References: Essen, 1979, cat. no. 29, repr. p. 50; Linz, 1980, repr. p. 450; ARC/Musée d'Art Moderne de la Ville de Paris, 1981, repr.; Vienna, 1983, p. 139, repr. p. 67; San Marino, 1983, cat. no. 66, repr. 79; Nagoya, 1988, repr. p. 69

*66 *For the Tables (Per li tavoli)*. 1974
Mixed media on canvas, 110 1/4" × 12' 1 11/16" (280 × 370 cm.)
Collection Angelo Baldessarre, Bari
Exhibitions: Venice, 1975; Zürich, 1985, cat. no. 32 (as *Ohne Titel [Tischprogression mit Tassen]*, dated 1975), repr. vol. 2
Reference: San Marino, 1983, cat. no. 78, repr. p. 98

67 *Untitled*. 1974
Mixed media on canvas, 110 1/4 × 145 11/16" (280 × 370 cm.)
Private Collection
Exhibitions: Venice, 1975; Zürich, 1985, cat. no. 33 (as *Ohne Titel [Tischprogression]*, dated 1975)
Reference: San Marino, 1983, cat. no. 79, repr. p. 99

68 *The Number Grows (Like) the Fruits of Summer and the Abundant Leaves 1, 1 ,2, 3... (Il numero ingrassa [come] i Frutti d'estate e le foglie abbondanti 1, 1, 2, 3...)*. 1974(85)
Painted wood
Courtesy Promenades, Parc Lullin, Geneva
Exhibition: Geneva, 1985

69 *When the Plants Invade the World (Quando le piante invaderanno il mondo)*. 1975
Mixed media on canvas, neon tube and terra-cotta vase
Courtesy Gian Enzo Sperone, Turin

70 *Untitled*. 1976
Metal tubes, stone, fruit, vegetables, glass and branches
Courtesy Galleria Mario Pieroni, Rome
Exhibition: Pescara, 1976
References: Rome, 1981, cat. no. 181, repr. p. 153; Venice, 1983, repr. p. 66 (as *L'isola della frutta*); San Marino, 1983, cat. no. 83, repr. p. 108

71 *Untitled*. 1976
Neon tubes arranged on the facade of the Antiche Prigioni in Pescara
Courtesy Galleria Mario Pieroni, Rome
Exhibition: Pescara, 1976
Reference: Modena, 1988, cat. no. 117, repr. p. 135 (as *Proliferazione di Fibonacci*)

*72 *Stopgap Leaves (Foglie tappabuchi)*. 1976
Mixed media on canvas, 59 1/16'' × 12' 9 9/16'' (150 × 390 cm.)
Courtesy Galleria Antonio Tucci Russo, Turin
Exhibition: Nice, 1985, cat. no. 50, repr. p. 50

73 *Spiral Table for Banquet of Newspapers Dated the Day of the Banquet (Tavolo a spirale per festino di giornali datati il giorno del festino)*. 1976
Metal tubes, glass, fruit, vegetables, twigs, crystal, stone, newspapers and neon tubes; spiral table maximum 26' 3'' d. (800 cm.)
Courtesy Galleria Antonio Tucci Russo, Turin
Exhibition: Turin, 1976
References: Essen, 1979, cat. no. 1, repr. p. 2; Sydney, 1979, repr.; Linz, 1980, repr. p. 451; ARC/Musée d'Art Moderne de la Ville de Paris, 1981, repr.; Bologna, 1982, repr. on cover; Stuttgart, 1982, repr. p. 134; Vienna, 1983, p. 140, repr. p. 123 (as *6765*); Cologne, 1983, repr. p. 66; Los Angeles, 1984, repr. p. 89 (as *6765*); Nagoya, 1988, repr. p. 71

74 *Fibonacci, 1975*. 1975
Stuffed ibex head and neon tubes, variable dimensions
Collection Peppino Di Bernardo, Naples

*75 *The Island of Fruit (L'isola della frutta)*. 1975
Color photographs and neon tubes, 118 1/8 × 196 7/8'' (300 × 500 cm.)
Collection Galleria Mario Pieroni, Rome

76 *Tables (Tavoli)*. 1976
Painting in copper sulfate and sulfur, and dirt

Collection of the artist
Exhibition: Venice, 1976
References: Essen, 1979, cat. no.33, repr. pp. 60-61;Bologna, 1982, repr. pp. 6-7 (as *La casa fantasma*, dated 1978); San Marino, 1983, cat. no. 81, repr. p. 103; Naples, 1986, repr. pp. 6-7 (as *La casa fantasma*); Modena, 1988, cat. no. 183, repr. p. 202 (as *Pittura di solfato di zolfo su muro stonacato ai Padiglioni*); Nagoya, 1988, repr. p. 70

77 *Untitled*. 1976
Mixed media on canvas and snail shell
Courtesy Annemarie Verna Galerie, Zürich

78 *Snail (Chiocciola)*. 1976
Mixed media on paper and snail, 27 9/16 × 39 3/8'' (70 × 100 cm.)
Courtesy Galleria Mario Pieroni, Rome

79 *Untitled*. 1976
Mixed media on canvas and snail shell, 28 3/8 × 40 13/16'' (72 × 102 cm.)
Collection Jean-Paul Jungo, Morges

80 *Nature Is the Art of the Number (La natura è l'arte del numero)*. 1976
Metal tubes, glass, clamps, plaster, crystal, stone, neon tubes, fruit, vegetables, twigs and newspapers, variable dimensions
Courtesy, Konrod Fischer, Düsseldorf
Exhibition: Düsseldorf, Galerie Konrad Fischer

80a *Nature Is the Art of the Number (La natura è l'arte del numero)*. 1976
Metal tubes, glass, clamps, plaster, crystal, stone, neon tubes, fruit, vegetables, twigs and newspapers, variable dimensions
Courtesy Museo Aragona Pignatelli, Naples
Exhibition: Naples, 1976
References: Essen, 1979, cat. nos. 36, 37, repr. pp. 64-65; Münster, 1982, repr. p. 20

81 *Prehistoric Wind from the Frozen Mountains (Vento preistorico dalle montagne gelate)*. 1977
Mixed media on canvas and twigs, 98 7/16 × 70 7/8'' (250 × 180 cm.)
Collection F.E. Rentschler, Laupheim
Exhibitions: Zürich, 1977; Rome, 1978
References: Essen, 1979, cat. no. 48, repr. p. 82 (dated 1978); San Marino, 1983, cat. no. 93, repr. p. 125;Sauer, *Sammlung FER-The FER Collection*, 1983, cat. no. 2, p. 185, repr. p. 107 (dated 1976); Zacharopoulos, *Parkett*, 1988, repr. p. 97

*82 *The Bridge of the Big Mother Round Trip (Il Ponte della Gran Madre Andata e Ritorno)*. 1977
Mixed media on canvas, 56 1/16'' × 16' 1/2'' (150 × 489 cm.)
Collection Guido Accornero; Courtesy Galleria Antonio Tucci Russo, Turin

83 *Fibonacci Drawing*. 1977
Drawing in chalk on Louis Sullivan's Chicago Stock Exchange Quotation Board at The Art Institute of Chicago, each board 11' 3'' × 16' 9'' (342.9 × 510.5 cm.); total 35' 6'' × 16' 9'' (1082 × 510.5 cm.)
Destroyed
Courtesy The Art Institute of Chicago
Exhibition: Chicago, 1977
References: ARC/Musée d'Art Moderne de la Ville de Paris, 1981, repr.; San Marino, 1981, repr.;Vienna, 1983, repr. p. 106

84 *Igloo-Paving Stones and Broken Glass from the Destroyed House Reactivated by Art in a Gallery/ in a Museum (Igloo-pietre del selciato e vetri rotti della casa distrutta riattivati per l'arte in una galleria/in un museo)*. 1977
Metal tubes, glass, clamps, stone, plaster and lamp, 22' 11 5/8 × 165 3/8 × 82 11/16'' (700 × 420 × 210 cm.)
Exhibitions: Milan, 1977; Basel, 1982, repr. p. 35
References: ARC/Musée d'Art Moderne de la Ville de Paris, 1981, repr. (as *La casa corre con il mondo*, dated 1976); San Marino, 1983, cat. no. 85, repr. p. 111

*85 *Fountain (Fontana)*. 1978
Neon tubes, metal can, metal tubes and fountain pump, 92 × 32 × 6'' (233.7 × 81.3 × 15.2 cm.)
The Arthur and Carol Goldberg Collection
Exhibition: Athens, 1978

*86 *Raincoat (Impermeabile)*. 1978
Raincoat, wood and neon tubes, 63 1/2 × 65'' (141.2 × 165 cm.)
Collection Rijksmuseum Kröller-Müller, Otterlo
Reference: Wagemans, *Sculptures in the Rijksmuseum Kröller-Müller*, 1981, cat. no. 460, repr. p.159

87 *Untitled*. 1978
Mixed media on canvas, 31 1/8 × 55 1/8'' (79 × 140 cm.)
Collection Ippolito Simonis, Turin

*88 *Panther on Cone (Pantere sul cono)*. 1978
Mixed media on canvas, two parts, each 78 3/4'' × 13'1 1/2'' (200 × 400 cm.)
Courtesy Konrad Fischer, Düsseldorf
Exhibition: Humlebaek, 1988 (without lightbulbs)

*89 *Nine Vegetables (Nove verdure)*. 1978
Mixed media on canvas and vegetables, 70 7/8 × 118 1/8'' (180 × 300 cm.)
Metzeler Collection, Düsseldorf
Exhibitions: Bologna, 1978; Eindhoven, 1980
References: San Marino, 1983, cat. no. 135, repr. p. 173; Nagoya, 1988, repr. p. 72

90 *Prehistoric Wind from the Frozen Mountains (Vento preistorico dalle montagne gelate)*. 1965+78
Wood, oil on canvas, neon tubes and twigs, 79 1/8 × 78 3/4 × 23 1/4'' (201 × 200 × 59 cm.); neon 10' 2 3/4'' × 1'' (312 × 2.5 cm)
Collection Rijksmuseum Kröller-Müller, Otterlo
Exhibition: Paris, 1986, cat. no. 246
Reference: ARC/Musée d'Art Moderne de la Ville de Paris, 1981, repr.; Wagemans,*Sculptures in the Rijksmuseum Kröller-Müller*, 1981, cat. no. 459, repr. p. 157

91 *If the hoarfrost grip thy tent thou wilt give thanks when night is spent*. 1978
Metal tubes, wire mesh and neon tubes, 13' 1 1/2'' d. (400 cm.)
Collection Annick and Anton Herbert, Ghent
Exhibitions: Athens, 1978; Genazzano, 1979, repr.; Ghent, 1980; Eindhoven, 1984, repr. p. 75; Zürich, 1985, cat. no. 40, repr. vol. 2; Graz, 1986, cat . no. 59, repr. p. 107
References: ARC/Musée d'Art Moderne de la Ville de Paris, 1981, repr. (as *If the hoarfrost grip thy tent thou wilt give thanks when night is spent [Ezra Pound]*); Münster, 1982, repr. p. 14; Stockholm, 1983 (as *If the hoarfrost grip thy tent thou wilt give thanks when night is spent [Ezra Pound]*), repr. p. 33; San Marino, 1983, cat. no. 94, repr. p. 127

92 *Evidence of 987 (Evidenza di 987)*. 1978
Metal tubes, glass, clamps, car door, metal objects, canvas, branches, painted canvas, burned branches and neon tubes, 19' 8 1/4'' d. (600 cm.)
Courtesy Galleria Antonio Tucci Russo, Turin
Exhibition: Turin, 1978
References: Essen, 1979, cat. no. 43, repr. pp. 70-71; ARC/Musée d'Art Moderne de la Ville de Paris, 1981, repr.; Madrid, 1982, repr. p. 80 (as *Iglu de vidrios rotos*, dated 1967-77); San Marino, 1983, cat. no.12, 92, repr. p. 124; Los Angeles, 1984, repr. pp. 34, 90-91

*93 *Old Bison on the Savannah (Vecchio bisonte nella savana)*. 1979
Mixed media on canvas, neon tube, branches and bottles; canvas 12' × 13' 6'' (304.8 × 411.5 cm.); branches 53 × 90 × 110'' (134.6 × 228.6 × 279.4 cm.)
Private Collection, Sydney
Exhibitions: New York, 1980; Omaha, 1981, repr.; Buffalo, Hallwalls, 1984, cat. no. 14; Turin, Mole Antonelliana, 1984, cat. no. 2, repr. p. 70; Washington, D.C., 1984, repr. p. 116
Reference: San Marino, 1983, cat. no. 117, repr. p. 154

*94 *Rhinoceros (Rinoceronte)*. 1979

Mixed media on canvas and neon tube, 114 9/16'' × 14' 1 5/16'' (291 × 430 cm.)
Private Collection; Courtesy Galleria Christian Stein, Milan and Turin
Exhibitions: New York, 1980; London, 1981, p. 221, repr. p. 101; Turin, Mole Antonelliana, 1984, cat. no. 3, repr. p. 70
References: Vienna, 1983, p. 140, repr. p. 90; San Marino, 1983, cat. no. 118, repr. p. 154

*95 *Lizard (Lucertola)*. 1979
Oil and charcoal on cloth and neon tube, 108 1/4 × 92 15/16'' (275 × 236 cm.)
Courtesy Willy D'Huysser Gallery, Brussels and Knokke, Belgium
Exhibitions: New York, 1980; London, Anthony d'Offay Gallery, 1983; Zürich, 1985, cat. no. 45, repr. vol. 2; Humlebaek, 1988; London, 1989, repr. p. 220
References: Essen, 1982; repr. p. 18 (as *Coccodrillo*, dated 1978); San Marino, 1983, cat. no. 116, repr. p. 153

96 *Round Legs (Gambe rotonde)*. 1979
Oil on canvas, metal tubes and branches, 98 7/16'' d. (250 cm.); canvas 57 1/16'' × 12' 9 1/2'' (145 × 390 cm.)
Collection Egidio Marzona, Düsseldorf
Exhibitions: Bern, 1980; Stuttgart, 1985; Humlebaek, 1988

*97 *Untitled*. 1976+79
Leather jacket, painted plexiglass, neon tube and twigs, 39 3/8 × 47 1/4 × 11 13/16'' (100 × 120 × 30 cm.)
Collection Udo and Anette Brandhorst

*98 *The Sum in Your Pocket (La cifra in tasca)*. 1974
Jacket, wood, spray paint and neon tubes, 39 3/8 × 59 1/16 × 9 3/16'' (100 × 150 × 25 cm.)
Collection Elisabeth and Ealon Wingate, New York

*99 *Crocodile in the Night (Coccodrillo nella notte)*. 1979
Oil, metallic paint, charcoal on canvas and neon tubes, 108 1/2'' × 14' 3'' (275.6 × 434.3 cm.)
Collection Art Gallery of Ontario, Toronto
Exhibitions: New York, 1980; Omaha, 1981, repr.; Buffalo, Albright-Knox Art Gallery, 1984, cat. no. 2, repr. p. 9
References: Essen, 1982; repr. p. 13 (dated 1978); Vienna, 1983, p. 140, repr. p. 72 (dated 1980)

100 *Irritable Irritated (Irritabile irritato)*. 1979
Mixed media on canvas, plaster and neon tube, 110 1/4'' × 17' 4 11/16'' (280 × 530 cm.)
Courtesy Annemarie Verna Galerie, Zürich
Exhibition: Zürich, 1979
References: ARC/Musée d'Art Moder-

ne de la Ville de Paris, 1981, repr.; San Marino, 1983, cat. no. 99, repr. p. 135; Silverthorne, *Parkett*, 1988, repr. p. 68

*101 *Fall of the House of Usher (La caduta della casa di Usher)*. 1979
Oil, metallic paint and charcoal on canvas, neon tube and rock, 11' 8 1/2'' × 14' 3/4'' (356.9 × 428.6 cm.)
Collection The Museum of Modern Art, New York, Anne and Sid Bass Fund, 1981
Exhibition: London, 1981, p. 221, repr. p. 102

102 *Do Houses Walk Around Us or Do We Walk Around Houses? (Le case girano intorno a noi o noi giriamo intorno alle case?)*. 1979
Bamboo, glass, plaster, lamp and paint on tracing paper, 3' 13/14'' × 12' 11/16'' × 13 1 1/2'' (360 × 370 × 400 cm.)
Collection Museum Van Hadendaagse Kunst, Ghent
Exhibitions: Paris, 1979; Ghent, 1980; Lisbon, 1985
Reference: San Marino, 1983, cat. no. 102, repr. p. 139

103 Installation, Museum Folkwang, Essen,
January 1979, including from right to left
Raincoat (Impermeabile), 1979
Spiral with Bottle (Spirale con bottiglia). 1979
Metal tubes, wire mesh, bottle, neon tubes and basins of sand, variable dimensions
Collection of the artist
References: ARC/Musée d'Art Moderne de la Ville de Paris, 1981, repr.; Bonn, 1983, repr. p. 14 (as *Solitario solidale*)

104 *Places Without Streets (Luoghi senza strada)*. 1979
Metal tubes, wire mesh, bitumen and neon tubes, 78 3/4'' d. (200 cm.)
Collection Stedelijk Van Abbemuseum, Eindhoven
Exhibitions: Essen, 1979; London, Whitechapel Art Gallery, 1980; Zürich, 1985, cat. no. 31, repr. vol. 2
References: San Marino, 1983, cat. no. 97, repr. p. 132; Nagoya, 1988, repr. p. 73

105 Installation, Galleria Franco Toselli, Milan, October 1979, including from right to left:
Untitled. 1979
Mixed media on canvas and neon tube, 98 7/16'' × 12' 5 5/8'' (250 × 380 cm.)
Courtesy Galleria Franco Toselli, Milan
Three (Tre). 1979
Metal stubes, mixed media on canvas, neon tubes, twigs and bottle, 78 3/4 × 78 3/4 × 46 5/16'' (200 × 200 × 25 cm.)

Courtesy Konrad Fischer, Düsseldorf
Silver Crocodile (Coccodrillo d'argento). 1980
Mixed media on canvas and neon tube, 13' 9 3/8'' × 78 3/4'' (420 × 200 cm.)
Private Collection, Courtesy Stedelijk Van Abbemuseum, Eindhoven

106 *Double Igloo (Doppio igloo)*. 1979
Outer structure: metal tubes, clamps, glass and hat; inner structure: metal tubes, wire mesh, dried mud and neon tubes, 118 1/8'' h. × 19' 8 1/4'' d. (300 × 600 cm.)
Courtesy Museum Folkwang, Essen
Exhibitions: Essen, 1979 (not in cat.); New York, Sperone Westwater Fischer Gallery, 1979; London, Whitechapel Art Gallery, 1980; Bern, 1980, repr. (as *Iglu*); 1980; London, Hayward Gallery, 1980; repr. p. 109
Reference: Linz, 1980, repr., p. 449

107 *The wind my home*. 1979
Metal tubes, glass, clamps, plaster, branches and neon tubes, variable dimensions
Courtesy Institute of Modern Art, Brisbane
Exhibition: Brisbane, 1979

108 *The refuse of newpapers or the refuse of nature or the refuse of body of the snail have in themselves the spiral or the continuity in time of power of space*. 1979
Mixed media on canvas, newspapers, glass, neon tubes, bottle, branches and pinecones
Collection Gino di Maggio, Milan; Courtesy National Gallery of Victoria, Melbourne
Exhibition: Melbourne, 1979

109 *Prehistoric Wind from the Frozen Mountains (Vento preistorico dalle montagne gelate)*. 1966+79
Canvas, neon tube and twigs, 118 1/8 × 98 7/16 × 31 1/2'' (300 × 250 × 80 cm.)
Courtesy Museum Folkwang, Essen
Exhibitions: Naples, 1978 (without neon numbers); Essen, 1979, repr. p. 82
References: Kassel, 1982, repr. p. 32 (as *Senza titolo*, dated 1965); Nagoya, 1988, repr. p.73; Silverthorne, *Parkett*, 1988, repr. p. 65

110 *Untitled*. 1979
Metal tubes, mixed media on canvas and neon tubes, 11' 5 13/16'' d. (350 cm.)
Collection U. Hodel, Zürich
Exhibitions: Genazzano, 1979; Rome, 1979; Turin, Mole Antonelliana, 1984, cat. no. 7, p. 172, repr. p. 74
Reference: Toronto, 1985, cat. no. 1, p. 327, repr. pp. 138-139

111 Installation, Castello Colonna, Genazzano, November 1979 including from front to back:

Untitled. 1979
Metal tubes, clamps, stone and neon tubes, igloo 118 1/8'' h. × 19' 8 1/4'' d. (300 × 600 cm.); circular structure 11' 5 13/16'' d. (350 cm.)
Collection of the artist
110 *Untitled*, 1979

112 *Reflections on the Table in December 1979 (Riflessi sul tavolo nel dicembre 1979)*. 1979
Spray-painted tables, poles covered with metal shavings attached to lumps of plaster, neon tubes and cups, variable dimensions
Collection Salvatore Ala, New York; Courtesy Galleria Salvatore Ala, Milan
Exhibition: Milan, 1979

113 Installation, Galerie Albert Baronian, Brussels, 1980, including:
Près de la table. 1980
Spray-painted tables, poles covered with metal shavings attached to lumps of plaster, neon tubes, cup, branches and canvas, variable dimensions
Collection Arnold Forde, Los Angeles
Exhibitions: Schaffhausen, 1984; Humlebaek, 1988
References: ARC/Musée d'Art Moderne de la Ville de Paris, 1981 (as *Le scimmie sono in movimento verso altre scimmie*); San Marino, 1983, cat. no. 115, repr. p. 152; Nagoya, 1988, repr. p. 76

114 *Billiards (Biliardo)*. 1981
Mixed media on canvas and neon tube, 78 3/4'' × 19' 8 1/4'' (200 × 600 cm.)
Collection Christian Stein, Turin
Exhibition: Turin, Galleria Christian Stein, 1980, repr.
Reference: San Marino, 1983, cat. no. 113, repr. p. 150

115 *Tincta purpura tegit fuco roseo conchyli*. 1980
Metal tubes, wire mesh, stone and neon tubes
Courtesy Kunsthalle Basel
References: ARC/Musée d'Art Moderne de la Ville de Paris, 1981; San Marino, 1983, cat. no. 134, repr. p. 171

116 Installation, Stedelijk Van Abbemuseum, Eindhoven, April 1980, including from front to back:
Cat. no. 120 *Untitled*. 1980
Anatomy Lesson (Lezione di anatomia). 1979
Oil and crayon on canvas mounted on steel frame, steel tables and neon tube: canvas and metal frame 102 3/8 × 16' 5 1/2'' × 13'' (260 × 500 × 33 cm.); tables, each 35 × 55 × 98 1/2'' (89 × 139.7 × 250.2 cm.)
Collection Bonnefantenmuseum, Maastricht, The Netherlands
Exhibitions: Bern, 1980; Eindhoven, 1980; Düsseldorf, 1981; ARC/Musée d'Art Moderne de la Ville de Paris, 1981 (not in cat.); Nîmes, 1987, repr.

p. 107 (as *Respirazione*)
References: San Marino, 1983, cat. no. 68, repr. p. 80; New York, 1984, repr.

117 *From the Overturned Bottle (Dalla bottiglia rovesciata)*. 1980
Metal tubes, neon tubes, bottle, spray-painted crystal and soup plate
Collection of the artist
Exhibition: Venice, 1980
References: ARC/Musée d'Art Moderne de la Ville de Paris, 1981, repr.; San Marino, 1983, cat. no. 119, repr. p. 156

118 *Traveling Animal (Animale in viaggio)*. 1980+83
Mixed media on canvas and metal tubes, 98 7/16'' × 16' 5 5/8'' (250 × 502 cm.)
Collection Berjer, Stockholm
Exhibitions: London, Hayward Gallery, 1982, repr. p. 169 (as *Animale feroce*), 1981; Stockholm, 1983 (with wood bases); Helsinki, 1983, vol. 1, cat. no. 115, repr. p. 153 (as *Una porta verso nordest*), 1983; Stockholm, 1983, repr. on cover and cat. no. 103, repr. p. 28; Madrid, 1985, repr. p. 91
References: Vienna, 1983, p. 139, repr. p. 59; New York, 1984, repr.

119 *Running Legs (Gambe che corrono)*. 1967+80
Mixed media on canvas, neon tubes, twigs and wicker hamper
Private Collection, Hamburg.
Courtesy Konrad Fischer, Düsseldorf
Exhibitions: London, Whitechapel Art Gallery, 1980 (as *Bianca cappella e tubi al neon in sostituzione dei numeri al neon*); Eindhoven, 1980 (as *Bianca cappella*); ARC/Musée d'Art Moderne de la Ville de Paris, 1981 (as *Gambe che coriono*, with basket and branches)
Reference: San Marino, 1983, cat. no. 110, repr. p. 148

120 *Untitled*. 1980
Metal tubes, twigs, stone, bottle, neon tube and wicker cone
Exhibitions: Eindhoven, 1980; Turin, Mole Antonelliana, 1984, cat. no. 6, repr. p. 73; Madrid, 1985, cat. no. 66, repr. p. 83

121 *Cervidi*. 1980
Mixed media on canvas and twigs, 12' 3 5/8'' × 13' 1 1/2'' (375 × 400 cm.)
Courtesy ARC/Musée d'Art Moderne de la Ville de Paris
Exhibition: ARC/Musée d'Art Moderne de la Ville de Paris, 1981
Reference: Essen, 1982, repr. p. 25

122 *Untitled*. 1980
Wood, clay, terra-cotta, rubber, leather, bottle, glass and neon tube, 10' 100'' × 55'' × 55'' (330,2 × 139,7 × 139,7 cm.)
Courtesy Barbara Gladstone Gallery, New York
Exhibition: New York, 1986

123 *The Painting Is Long and Swift (La*

pittura è lunga e veloce). 1980
Canvas, metal tubes, stone, twigs, glass and clamps; canvases 78 3/4'' × 26' 3''; 78 3/4 × 118 1/8''; 78 3/4'' × 13' 1 1/2'' (200 × 800; 200 × 300; 200 × 400 cm.)
Collection Salvatore Ala, New York
Exhibitions: Milan, 1980; Bologna, 1982 (with three canvases on the wall); Zürich, 1985, cat. no. 47
References: ARC/Musée d'Art Moderne de la Ville de Paris, 1981 (with three canvases on the wall and a different spiral table); San Marino, 1983, cat. no. 133, repr. p. 170; Siracusa, 1986, cat. no. 33, repr. p. 51

124 *The Painting Is Long and Swift (La pittura è lunga e veloce)*. 1980+82
Oil on canvas; canvases 78 3/4'' × 26' 3''; 78 3/4 × 118 1/8''; 78 3/4'' × 13' 1 1/2'' (200 × 800; 200 × 300; 200 × 400 cm.)
Collection Salvatore Ala, New York

125 *Double Igloo (Doppio igloo)*. 1979+81
External structure: metal tubes, glass, clamps and hat; internal structure: metal tubes, wire mesh, dirt and neon tubes, 19' 8 1/4'' d. (600 cm.)
Collection Staatsgalerie Stuttgart
Exhibitions: ARC/ Musée d'Art Moderne de la Ville de Paris, 1981, repr. (as *Un doppio igloo*, with red neon); Stockholm, 1983, repr. p. 33 (as *Dubbeligloo*); Venice, 1983, cat. no. 69, repr. p. 65 (as *Igloo*, with red neon); Zürich, 1985, cat. no. 43, repr. vol. 2 (with red neon); London, 1989 (with red neon), repr. p. 221
References: Münster, 1983, repr. p. 14; Vienna, 1983, p. 140, repr. p. 108; San Marino, 1983, cat. no. 123, repr. p. 160; Nagoya, 1988, repr. p. 80 (dated 1968-81)

126 *Prehistoric Wind (Vento preistorico)*. 1981
Mixed media on canvas, 94 1/2'' × 16' 4 7/8'' (240 × 500 cm.)
Courtesy Galerie Buchmann, Saint-Gallen
Exhibitions: ARC/Musée d'Art Moderne de la Ville de Paris, 1981 (with branches); Turin, Galleria Christian Stein, 1981
Reference: San Marino, 1983, cat. no. 114, repr. p. 151

127 Installation, Kunsthalle Basel, July 1981, including from right to left:
Prehistoric Wind (Vento preistorico). 1981
Mixed media on canvas, 98 7/16'' × 19' 8 1/4'' (250 × 600 cm.)
Courtesy Kunsthalle Basel
Far-Seeing Igloo (Igloo lungimirante). 1981
Metal tubes, clamps and stone, 118 1/8''-19' 8 1/4'' d. (300-600 cm.)
Courtesy Kunsthalle Basel

Reference: Vienna, 1983, p. 140, repr. p. 78 (dated 1969-81)

128 Installation, *Mario Merz-Morgen*, Studio ORF, Salzburg, 1981, including:

Igloo. 1981
Metal tubes, glass and twigs
The process of creating the igloo was videotaped by Austrian radio-television

*129 *Mountain Lion (Leone di montagna)*. 1981
Mixed media on canvas and neon tubes, 98 7/16'' × 18' 8 7/16'' (250 × 570 cm.)
Courtesy Galleria Antonio Tucci Russo, Turin
Exhibitions: Turin, Galleria Antonio Tucci Russo, 1981; London, 1982, repr. p. 168; Nice, 1985, cat. no. 51a, repr. p. 50; Zürich, 1985, cat. no. 57; Berlin, Akademie der Kunst, 1988
References: Essen, 1982, repr. p.19; Gibellina, 1983, repr. p.85; San Marino, 1983, cat. no. 126, repr. p. 164

130 *The Musicians (I musicanti)*. 1981
Mixed media on canvas and neon tubes, 11' 10 15/16'' × 13' 6'' (363 × 412 cm.)
Collection H. Emanuel Schmid, Zürich
Exhibitions: Turin, Galleria Antonio Tucci Russo, 1981; Rome, 1982, repr.p. 82; Bologna, 1982; Lyon, 1983
Reference: San Marino, 1983, cat. no. 126, repr. p. 164

131 *Igloo with Vortex (Igloo con vortice)*. 1981
Mixed media on canvas, twigs, bottle and neon tube, 110 1/4 × 106 5/16 × 19 11/16'' (280 × 270 × 50 cm.)
Private Collection, Turin
Exhibition: Turin, Galleria Christian Stein, 1981

*132 *Khadafi's Tent (Tenda di Gheddafi)*. 1981
Metal tubes and acrylic on burlap, 98 7/16'' h. × 16' 4 7/8'' d. (250 × 500 cm.)
Collection Castello di Rivoli, Museo d'arte Contemporanea, Rivoli (Turin)
Exhibitions: Paris, Musée National d'Art Moderne, 1981 (not in cat.); Venice, 1983, cat. no. 70, repr. p. 65 (as *Igloo*); San Marino, 1983, cat. no. 139, repr. p. 180; Zürich, 1985, cat. no. 55, repr. vol. 2
References: Vienna, 1983, p. 139, repr. p. 56; Venice, 1983, repr. p. 65, fig. 70 (as *Igloo*); Modena, 1988, cat. no. 210, repr. p. 229 (as *La casa di Gheddafi*); Silverthorne, *Parkett*, 1988, repr. p. 72; Rovereto, 1989, repr. p. 170

133 *Untitled*. 1981
Mixed media on canvas, neon tubes, spray-painted bottle and glass, 94 1/2'' × 102 3/8'' (240 × 260 cm.)
Collection Museum Ludwig, Cologne
Exibitions: Turin, Galleria Antonio

Tucci Russo, 1981; Modena, 1982, repr. p. 79
Reference: Madrid, 1985, repr. p. 84

*134 *Architecture Built by Time, Architecture Demolished by Time (Architettura fondata dal tempo, architettura sfondata dal tempo)*. 1981
Metal tubes, painted glass, canvas, mixed-media on canvas, neon tubes and twigs; igloo 118 1/8' h. × 19' 8 1/4'' d. (300 × 600 cm.); canvas on metal frame 102 3/8'' × 15' 6 1/4'' × 7 7/8'' (260 × 473 × 20 cm.); table 13 3/4 h. × 116'' d. (35 × 295 cm.)
Collection The Rivetti Art Foundation, Turin
Exhibitions: Galleria Antonio Tucci Russo, Turin, 1981; Bordeaux, 1987
References: Rome, Mura Aureliane da Porta Metronia a Porta Latina, 1982; *Avanguardia-transavanguardia*, repr. p. 81; Essen, 1982; repr. p. 7; Modena, Galleria Civica, 1983, repr. p. 79; London, Institute of Contemporary Arts, 1982, repr.p. 167; Gibellina, 1983, repr. p. 83; Bonn, 1983, repr. p. 14; Florence, 1983, repr. p. 61 (as *Scuola d'anatomia)*; Vienna, 1983, p. 140, repr. p. 73 (dated 1961); San Marino, 1983, cat. no. 128, repr. p. 167; Los Angeles, 1984, repr. p. 93; Siracusa, 1986, repr. p. 59 (dated 1983); Grüterich, *Parkett*, 1988, repr. p. 53

*135 *Tiger (Tigre)*. 1981
Mixed media on canvas, 110 1/4'' × 17' 4 5/8'' (280 × 530 cm.)
Collection Christian Stein, Turin
Exhibitions: ARC/Musée d'Art Moderne de la Ville de Paris, 1981 (not in cat.); Berlin, 1982, repr. (dated 1982); Bologna, 1982; Turin, 1982

136 *Temple Snatched from the Abyss (Tempio rapito dagli abissi)*. 1981
Mixed media on canvas, neon tubes and sculpture with lamp, 118 1/8'' × 19' 8 1/4'' (300 × 600 cm.)
Collection Crex, Zürich
Exhibitions: Turin, Galleria Christian Stein, 1981; Rome, 1982, repr. p. 80; Schaffhausen, 1984; Madrid, 1985, cat. no. 73, repr. p. 89
References: Münster, 1982, repr. p. 17; San Marino, 1983, cat. no. 138, repr. p. 179

*137 *Cone (Cono)*. 1981
Mixed media on canvas, 98 7/16 × 54 5/16'' (250 × 138 cm.)
Collection Giuliana and Tommaso Setari, Rome

138 *Untitled*. 1981
Charcoal and spray paint on linen, 59 1/16'' × 16' 4 7/8'' (150 × 500 cm.)
Courtesy Jean Bernier Gallery, Athens

139 *Wandering Songs II (Canti errabondi II)*. 1981
Acrylic, oil and enamel on canvas and metal tubes, 100 3/8 × 114 3/16 ×

8 11/16'' (255 × 290 × 22 cm.)
Collection Sperone Westwater, New York
Exhibition: Chicago, 1984, repr. p. 38

*140 *The Lombard Plain (Pianura Padana)*. 1981
Metal tubes, mixed media on canvas and twigs, 110 1/4'' × 17' 4 5/8'' (280 × 530 cm.)
Courtesy Konrad Fischer, Düsseldorf
Exhibitions: Düsseldorf, 1981; Madrid, 1985, cat. no. 72, repr. p. 88; Humlebaek, 1988 (without branches or neon numbers)
References: Essen, 1982; repr. p. 14; San Marino, 1983, cat. no. 120, repr. p. 157; New York, 1984, repr. (without branches or neon numbers)

141 *Underground (Ipogeo)*. 1981
Bottles, stone, wood and neon tubes, 23 5/8 × 23 5/8 × 15 3/4'' (60 × 60 × 40 cm.)
Collection Dubois, Lausanne; Courtesy Galleria Lucio Amelio, Naples
Exhibitions: Naples, 1981; Herculaneum, 1984, repr. p. 114
Reference: Izzo, *lapis/arte*, 1981, repr. pp. vii, viii, xvi

142 *Billiard Hall (Sala dei biliardi)*. 1981
Acrylic on canvas, wax and neon tubes, 78 3/4'' × 59' 11/16'' (200 × 1,800 cm.)
Collection Staatsgalerie Stuttgart
Exhibitions: Düsseldorf, 1981; Essen, 1982, repr. p. 21
Reference: San Marino, 1983, cat. no. 149, repr. p. 194

*143 *8 Houses (8 case)*. 1981 + 82
Oil, acrylic and charcoal on canvas, 94 1/2'' × 16' 2'' (240 × 492.8 cm.)
The Frito-Lay Collection, Plano, Texas
Exhibitions: Turin, Galleria Christian Stein, 1981; Sperone Westwater Fischer Gallery, New York, 1982
References: Essen, 1982, repr. p. 11; Vienna, 1983, p. 140, repr. p. 74

*144 *If the Form Vanishes, Its Root Is Eternal (Se la forma scompare la sua radice è eterna)*. 1982
Metal tubes, wire mesh and neon tubes, structure 70 × 178 × 10'' (178 × 452 × 25.4 cm.); support 23 1/2 × 23 1/2 × 31 1/2'' (59,7 × 59,7 × 80 cm.)
Courtesy Galleria Christian Stein, Milan and Turin
Exhibition: Venice, California, 1982 (affixed to mixed media painting); Paris, Chapelle Saint-Louis, 1987
References: Nagoya, 1988, repr. p. 81; *Parkett*, 1988, repr.

145 *Tasmania*. 1981-82
Oil, acrylic and charcoal on burlap and neon tubes, 78 3/4'' × 17' 3/4'' (200 × 520 cm.); neon 48 1/16'' (122 cm.)
Collection Dallas Museum of Art

Exhibitions: Essen, 1982 (not in cat.); Buffalo, Albright-Knox Art Gallery, 1984, cat. no. 4
Reference: Madrid, 1985, repr. p. 84

*146 *Bison (Bisonti)*. 1982
Spray enamel, charcoal and pastel on canvas, and spray enamel and plaster on cardboard, 79 7/8'' × 18' 9 3/4'' (202.9 × 573.4 cm.); with hooves, ca. 91 1/2'' h. (232.4 cm.)
Courtesy Sperone Westwater, New York
Exhibition: Venice, California, 1982

147 *Drops in the Lake (Gocce nel lago)*. 1981-82
Oil, acrylic and charcoal on canvas, neon tubes and raincoat, 77 9/16'' × 16' 3'' (197 × 495 cm.)
Private Collection; Courtesy Sperone Westwater, New York
Exhibitions: Sperone Westwater Fischer Gallery, New York, 1982; Buffalo, Albright-Knox Art Gallery, 1984, cat. no. 3, repr. p. 22; Chicago, 1984, p.19, repr. p. 37
References: Essen, 1982, repr. p. 27; Los Angeles, 1984, repr. p. 92 (without raincoat)

*148 *Giant Woodsmen (I giganti boscaiuoli)*. 1981-82
Oil, acrylic and charcoal on canvas, 94'' × 18' 4'' (238.8 × 558.8 cm.)
Courtesy Sperone Westwater, New York
Exhibitions: Turin, Galleria Antonio Tucci Russo, 1981 (with two pieces of slate, as *I Boscaiuoli*); New York, Sperone Westwater Fischer Gallery, 1982; Essen, 1982, repr. pp. 16-17 (Stuttgart venue only); London, Anthony d'Offay Gallery, 1983; Chicago, 1984, p. 19, repr. p. 37
References: Rome, Mura Aureliana da Porta Metronia a Porta Latina, 1982; repr. p. 80; Essen, 1982, repr. p. 16; Gibellina, 1983, repr. p. 84; San Marino, 1983, repr. p. 192; Turin, Mole Antonelliana, 1984, repr. p. 156; Madrid, 1985, repr. p. 84

149 *Wandering Songs I (Canti errabondi I)*. 1983
Acrylic and oil on canvas, branches and wax, 111'' × 25' 1 3/16'' × 39 3/8'' (282 × 765 × 100 cm.)
Courtesy Sperone Westwater, New York
Exhibition: Chicago, 1984, p. 19, repr. p. 39

*150 *Spiral Table (Tavola a spirale)*. 1982
Aluminum, glass, fruit, vegetables, branches and wax, 18' d. (549 cm.)
Courtesy Sperone Westwater, New York

151 Installation, Flow Ace Gallery, Venice, California, August 1982, including clockwise from lower right:

cat. n. 146 *Bison (Bisonti)*. 1982
Spiral Table (Tavola a spirale). 1982
Metal tubes, stone, painted stone, bamboo, neon tubes, chalk, fruit, vegetables, branches, wax and bottle, variable dimensions
Collection of the artist
Vegetable Boat (Nave vegetale). 1982
Metal tubes, glass, bamboo and chalk, 118 1/8'' h. × 19' 8 14'' d. (300 × 600 cm.)
Collection of the artist
If the Form Vanishes, Its Root Is Eternal (Se la forma scompare la sua radice è eterna). 1982
Mixed media on canvas and neon tubes, 98 7/16'' × 26' 3'' × 13 3/4'' (250 × 800 × 35 cm.)
Collection of the artist

152 *Stone Igloo (Igloo di pietra)*. 1982
Metal tubes and stone, 78 3/4'' h. × 15' 3 1/2'' d. (200 × 480 cm.)
Collection of the artist; Courtesy *Documenta*, Kassel, West Germany
Exhibition: Kassel, 1982
References: Madrid, 1982, repr. p. 81 (as *Iglu con arroyo*); Münster, 1982, repr. pp. 11, 14; San Marino, 1983, cat. no. 141, repr. p. 184; Stockholm, 1983, repr. p. 32; Turin, Mole Antonelliana, 1984, cat. no. 4, repr. p. 71; Madrid, 1985, cat. no. 69, repr. p. 85; Davvetas, *Parkett*, 1988, repr. p. 88

*153 *Coniferous Gem (Gemma conifera)*. 1981-82
Oil, acrylic and charcoal on burlap, 78 3/4'' × 14' 2'' (200 × 431.8 cm.)
Collection Raymond J. Learsy
Exhibitions: Turin, Galleria Antonio Tucci Russo, 1981; New York, Sperone Westwater Fischer Gallery, 1982; Essen, 1982, repr. p. 20
References: Vienna, 1983, p. 140, repr. p. 75; Madrid, 1985, repr. p. 84

154 Installation, Moderna Museet, Stockholm, February 1983, including from right to left:
cat. no. 118 *Traveling Animal (Animale in viaggio)*. 1980 + 83
Igloo. 1983
Metal tubes, glass, clamps and neon tubes, 118 1/8'' h. × 19' 8 1/4'' d. (300 × 600 cm.)
Courtesy Moderna Museet, Stockholm
Exhibitions: Stockholm, 1983, Cat. no. 105, repr. pp. 24, 27, 28-30 (as *Oscuro chiaro chiaro oscuro*); Helsinki, 1983. vol. 2, cat. no. 114, repr. pp. 31-32, 152-153 (as *Oscuro chiaro chiaro oscuro*); San Marino, 1983, cat. no. 131, repr. p. 168
Pink Cloud with Sunset (Nuvola rossa con il tramonto). 1983
Mixed media on canvas, 55 1/8'' × 32' 9 11/16'' (14 × 1000 cm.)
Courtesy Moderna Museet Stockholm
Exhibitions. Stockholm, 1983, cat. no. 106, repr. pp. 24, 26, 28; Madrid 1985

References: San Marino, 1983, cat. no. 130, repr. p. 168; New York, 1984, repr.
The Abandoned House (La casa abbandonata). 1977 + 83
Panted wood and twigs; panels 65 15/16 × 66 1/4; 78 1/8 × 78 5/16; 59 7/16 × 66 1/8''; 59 7/16 × 78 5/16'' (167.5 × 168.3; 198.5 × 199; 151 × 168; 151 × 1909 cm.)
Courtesy Moderna Museet, Stockholm
Exhibions: Münster, 1982, two panels, cat. no. 74, repr. p. 57 (as *ohne Titel*, dated 1978) and cat. no. 69, repr. p. 58 (as *ohne Titel*, dated 1977); Stockholm, 1983, panels, cat. nos. 1-4, repr. pp. 38-41, total work, repr. pp. 24, 25, 27, 28, 29, 42
Reference: San Marino, 1983, cat. no. 131, repr. p. 168

*155, 161 *Hoarded centuries to pull up a mass of algae and pearls (Ezra Pound)*. 1983
Metal, glass, wire mesh, sulfur and neon tubes, 85 7/16'' h. × 13' 1 1/2'' d. (217 × 400 cm.)
Courtesy Anthony d'Offay Gallery, London
Exhibitions: London, 1983; London, Anthony d'Offay Gallery, *About Sculpture*, 1987; Bordeaux, 1987; London, Anthony d'Offay Gallery, *Mario Merz*, 1988, repr.; Humlebaek, 1988
References: Siracusa, 1986, repr. p. 51; Grüterich, *Parkett*, 1988, repr. p. 43; Florence, 1989, repr.

*156 *Moved*. 1983
Metal tubes, wire mesh and neon tubes, 96 1/16 × 96 1/16 × 8 11/16'' (244 × 244 × 22 cm.)
Collection Raymond J. Learsy
Exhibitions: Rome, 1983; Arnhem, 1986

157 Installation, Palazzo Congressi ed Esposizioni, Republic of San Marino, 1983 including:
Igloo. 1983
Metal tubes, crystal, stone and clamps, 98 7/16'' h. × 16' 4 7/8'' d. (250 × 500 cm.)
Exhibitions: San Marino, 1983 (not in cat.); Turin, Mole Antoneliana, 1984
References: Vienna, 1983, repr. p. 47; New York, 1984, repr.
Untitled. 1983
Automobile, mixed media on canvas and neon tubes
Exhibitions: San Marino, 1983 (not in cat.); Turin, Mole Antonelliana, 1984, cat. no. 8, repr. p. 75 (as *Senza titolo*)
References: Vienna, 1983, p. 139, repr. p . 47; New York, 1984, repr.

158 *Sphinx and Chickenlike Predator (Sfinge e rapace gallinaceo)*. 1983
Oil, sand and vegetable matter on canvas on metal frame, twigs, neon tubes, wire and branches, 102 3/8'' × 22' 11 9/16'' (260 × 700 cm.)

Private Collection, West Vancouver; Courtesy Vancouver Art Gallery
Exhibition: Basel, 1983, repr. pp. 12-13, 30-31
References: Vienna, 1983, p.139, repr. p. 47; Siracusa, 1986, cat. no. 28, repr.

159 *Gecko (Geco)*. 1983
Metal tubes, mixed media on canvas and tree trunk, 102 3/8'' × 10' 6'' × 27 9/16'' (260 × 320 × 70 cm.)
Private Collection, Ghent; Courtesy Galerie Buchmann, Basel
Exhibition: Basel, 1983, repr. pp. 6, 27, 29
References: Vienna, 1983, p. 139, repr. p. 44; Siracusa, 1986, cat. no. 27, repr.

160 *Fibonacci*. 1971+83
Metal tubes, wire mesh, wax, neon tubes and branches, 118 1/8 × 47 1/4 × 11 13/16'' (300 × 120 × 30 cm.)
Collection Musée d'Art Moderne, Saint-Etienne
Exhibitions: Rome, 1978; San Marino, 1983, cat. no. 52, repr. p. 65 (without branches, dated 1971); Chambéry, 1987 (without branches), cat. no. 28, p. 70, repr. p. 71
References: Vienna, 1983, p. 139, repr. p. 40 (with branches); New York, 1984, repr. (with branches)

161 see cat. no. 155

162 *Benito Cereno*. 1983
Mixed media on canvas and neon tubes, 96 1/2'' × 10' (245 × 305 cm.)
Courtesy Galleria Antonio Tucci Russo, Turin

163 *Untitled*. 1984
Oil, enamel and spray paint on canvas, 98'' × 10' 6'' (249 × 320 cm.)
Courtesy Galerie Vera Munro, Hamburg
Exhibitions: Hamburg, 1985; Turin, Castello di Rivoli, 1984

164 *Untitled*. 1983
Oil, acrylic, enamel, charcoal and spray paint on canvas, enamel on metal and enamel on spray-painted plastic, variable dimensions
Courtesy Sperone Westwater, New York

*165 *The Tree Grows So Many Branches and They All Have Common Sap (L'albero cresce tanti rami e hanno una linfa comune)*. 1984
Enamel, charcoal and shell on paper, 69 5/16 × 59 1/16'' (176 × 150 cm.)
Collection of the artist

166 *Untitled*. 1984
Neon tubes arranged on the Mole Antonelliana of Turin, June 12, daytime
References: Madrid, 1985, cat. no. 76, repr. p. 92 (as *Senza titolo [serie di Fibonacci]*); New York, 1985, repr. p. 126; Oslo, 1986, repr.

167 *Endless Growth (Crescita senza fine)*. 1984
Oil, enamel, spray paint and neon tubes on canvas and wood, 109 7/16'' × 15' 11 5/16'' (278 × 486 cm.)
Collection Christian Stein, Milan and Turin; Courtesy Galleria Christian Stein, Turin
Exhibitions: Turin, Galleria Christian Stein, 1984; Zürich, 1985, cat. no. 67, repr. vol. 2
Reference: Toronto, 1985, cat. no. 2, repr. pp. 140-141

168 *Igloo*. 1984
Metal tubes, wax and metal, 78 3/4'' d. (200 cm.)
Courtesy Galleria Konrad Fischer, Düsseldorf
Exhibition: Humlebaek, 1988

169 *From Honey to Ashes (Dal miele alle ceneri)*. 1984
Metal tubes, wax, pinecones, stuffed antelope head, aluminum and muslin, 95 11/16'' d. (243 cm.)
Courtesy Sperone Westwater, New York
Exhibitions: Turin, Mole Antonelliana, 1984, cat. no. 10, p. 172, repr. p. 77; Madrid, 1985, cat. no. 70, repr. p. 86

170 *Untitled*. 1984
Wicker, metal tubes, twigs, stones, dirt and electric lamp, 118 1/8'' × 13' 1 1/2'' × 98 7/16'' (300 × 400 × 250 cm.)
Courtesy Galerie Pietro Sparta, Chagny, France
Exhibition: Chagny, 1984, repr.

171 Installation, Galerie Pietro Sparta, Chagny, France, October 1984, including:
L'Autre Côté de la lune. 1984
Metal tubes, glass, stone, vegetables and fruit, 27 9/16'' × 11' 5 13/16'' × 29' 6 3/8'' (70 × 350 × 900 cm.)
Exhibition: Chagny, 1984, repr.
Reference: Venice, 1987, repr. pp. 364-365 (as *Tavolo di Chagny*)
Untitled. 1984
Metal tubes, spray paint, oil, metal and glass on paper and on the wall, 11' 5 13/16'' × 24' 7 1/4'' (350 × 750 cm.)
Courtesy Galerie Pietro Sparta, Chagny, France
Exhibition: Chagny, 1984, repr.

172 *The Architect (L'architetto)*. 1984
Steel, pinecones, wax, spray paint and raincoat, 55 1/8 × 31 1/2 × 11 13/16'' (140 × 80 × 30 cm.)
Exhibition: New York, 1984

*173 *Very Slowly (Pianissimo)*. 1984
Wax, pinecone, plexiglass, steel and aluminum, 102 × 31 1/2 × 23 1/2'' (259.1 × 80 × 59.7 cm.)
Courtesy Sperone Westwater, New York
Exhibitions: New York, 1984; Turin, Mole Antonelliana, 1984, cat. no. 1, repr. p. 69

*174 *Painter in Africa (Pittore in Africa)*. 1984
Metal tubes, wire mesh and neon tubes, 118 1/8 × 102 3/8 × 14 9/16'' (300 × 260 × 37 cm.)
Collection Haags Gemeentemuseum, The Hague
Refabricated for present exhibition
Exhibition: Turin, Castello di Rivoli, 1984, cat. no. 65, repr. pp. 116-117
Reference: New York, 1984, repr.

175 *The Gold that We Are Able (L'oro che possiamo)*. 1984
Oil, enamel and spray paint on canvas and wood, 108 1/4 × 107 1/2'' (275 × 273 cm.)
Courtesy Galleria Christian Stein; Milan and Turin
Exhibition: Turin, Galleria Christian Stein, 1984

*176 *The Gardener's House (La casa del giardiniere)*. 1983-84
Metal tubes, wire mesh, oil and acrylic on canvas, wax, metal, shells and pinecones, 78 3/4'' h. × 13' 1 1/2'' d. (200.6 × 401 cm.)
Courtesy Sperone Westwater, New York
Exhibitions: Zürich, 1985, cat. no. 65, repr. (as *Vento preistorico dalle montagne gelate*, without wax, with neon); New York, Sperone Westwater Gallery and Leo Castelli Gallery, 1985; Bordeaux, 1987
Reference: Nagoya, 1988, repr. p. 83

177 Installation, Kunsthaus Zürich, April 1985, including:

cat. no. 132 *Khadafi's Tent (Tenda di Gheddafi)*. 1981;
cat. no. 125 *Double Igloo (Doppio igloo)*. 1979+81

178 Installation, Galleria Christian Stein, Milan, October 1985, including:
Untitled. 1985
Mixed media on canvas and tree trunks, 114 3/16'' × 36' 1 1/16'' × 35 7/16'' (290 × 1100 × 90 cm.)
Collection of the artist
Reference: Siracusa, 1986, cat. no. 24, repr. p. 49

179 Installation, Leo Castelli Gallery in collaboration with Sperone Westwater Gallery, New York, November 1985, including:
Four Tables in the Form of Magnolia Leaves (Quattro tavole in forma di foglie di magnolia). 1985
Wax and mixed media on welded steel tables, sixteen sections, total 29'' × 65' 3'' × 60'' (73.7 × 1981 × 152.4 cm.)
Courtesy Sperone Westwater, New York
Exhibitions: New York, Sperone Westwater Gallery, 1985
Reference: Silverthorne, *Parkett*, 1988, repr. p. 69
Bateau ivre. 1983

Acrylic, spray paint and charcoal on canvas, 102 3/8'' × 76' 1 3/8'' (260 × 2320 cm.)
Courtesy Sperone Westwater, New York

180 *Everything Flows, Heraclitus (Tutto scorre, Heraclite)*. 1985
Clay blocks and neon tubes on linoleum, each block 5 15/16 × 7 1/16'' (15 × 18 cm.), total 11 13/16'' × 26' 3'' (30 × 800 cm.)
Courtesy Galerie Vera Munro, Hamburg
Exhibition: Hamburg, 1985

*181 *Igloo*. 1984-85
Metal tubes, wire mesh, neon tubes, plexiglass, glass and wax, 39 1/4 h. × 78 1/2'' d. (99.7 × 199.4 cm.); base, four pieces, total 91 1/4'' × 9'10 1/4'' (231 × 300.4 cm.)
Collection Gerald S. Elliott, Chicago
Exhibitions: Zürich, 1985, cat. no. 66, repr. vol. 2; New York, 1986; New York, 1989

182 *853*. 1985
Metal tubes, glass, clamps, twigs and neon tubes. In center of largest structure *Objet cache-toi*, igloos 26' 3'' d.; 16' 4 7/8'' d.; 118 1/8'' d. (800; 500; 300 cm.)
Collection of the artist
Exhibitions: Zürich, 1985, cat. no. 68, repr. vol. 2; Paris, Chapelle Saint-Louis, 1987

183 *Places Without Streets (Luoghi senza strada)* detail. 1987
Metal tubes, wire mesh, stone, twigs and neon tubes, 78 3/4'' × 13' 1 1/2'' d. (200 × 400 cm.)
Collection of the artist
Exhibitions: Paris, Chapelle Saint-Louis, 1987
References: Nagoya, 1988, repr. p. 85; Szeemann, *Parkett*, 1988, repr. p. 91

*184 *Do We Walk Around Houses or Do Houses Walk Around Us? (Noi giriamo intorno alle case o le case girano intorno a noi?)*. 1985
Metal tubes, stone, glass and electric light; igloo 102'' h. × 16' 4 7/8'' d. (259 × 500 cm.); tunnel 24 × 236 × 4033' 5 9/16'' long (1020 cm.)
Courtesy Anthony d'Offay Gallery, London
Exhibitions: Paris, Chapelle Saint-Louis, 1987; London, 1988; Humlebaek, 1988
References: Nagoya, 1988, repr. p. 84; Grüterich, *Parkett*, 1988, repr. p. 47; Szeemann, *Parkett*, 1988, repr. p. 90

185 *Towards the Zenith (Verso lo zenith)*. 1985
Iron, wood, wax and steel wool, 90 9/16'' h. × 118 1/8'' d. (230 × 300 cm.)
Courtesy Galleria Mario Pieroni, Rome
Exhibitions: Rome, 1985, repr.; Munich, 1986

186 *Untitled*. 1985
Chalk, charcoal, wax, wood and steel
wool, 157 × 118 1/8'' (400 × 300 cm.)
Courtesy Galleria Mario Pieroni, Rome
Exhibition: Rome, 1985, repr.

187 Installation, Museo di Capodimonte, Naples, April, 1987 including:
The River Appears (Il fiume appare).
1986
Newspapers, glass, neon tubes, iron
plates and metal tubes, 19' 8 1/4'' × 91'
10 3/8'' (600 × 2800 cm.)
Collection Ceat-Cavi, Turin
Exhibitions: Turin, 1986; Naples,
1987; Bordeaux, 1987; Paris, Chapelle
Saint-Louis, 1987

188 *The River Appears (Il fiume appare)*. 1986
Mixed media on canvas and tracing
paper, neon tubes, newspapers, iron
plates and canvas, 39' 4 7/16'' × 118
1/8'' (1200 × 300 cm.)
Courtesy Galleria Antonio Tucci Russo, Turin
Exhibition: Turin, 1986 (without triangular structure or glass, with bitumen
strips); Prato, 1988 (with triangular
structure and glass), repr. pp. 144-145
(with asphalt strips)

189 *The River Appears (Il fiume appare)*. 1986+88
Mixed media on canvas and tracing
paper, neon tubes, newspapers, iron
plates, canvas, metal tubes and glass,
39' 4 7/16'' × 118 1/8'' (1200 × 300
cm.); triangular structures each 22'
11/16'' × 29' 6 3/8'' × 13' 11 5/16''
(700 × 900 × 425 cm.)
Collection The Rivetti Art Foundation,
Turin; Courtesy Galleria Antonio Tucci Russo, Turin
See cat. no. 188 for exhibition history

190 *Une ouvrée, une mésure de terre
qui donne un portrait bien terrestre*.
1986
Twigs, paving stones, wax, metal tubes, neon tubes and plywood, 11' 5
13/16'' × 31' 2'' × 24' 7 1/4'' (350 ×
950 × 750 cm.)
Courtesy Galerie Pietro Sparta, Chagny, France
Exhibitions: Chagny, 1987; Nîmes,
1987, cat. no. 49, repr. p. 109 (dated
1987)
Reference: Grüterich, *Parkett*, 1988,
repr. p. 41

191 *Une ouvrée, une mésure de terre
qui donne un portrait bien terrestre*.
1986
Twigs, paving stones, wax and chimney
caps, 14' 9 3/16'' × 13' 9 3/8'' (450 ×
420 cm.)
Courtesy Galerie Pietro Sparta, Chagny, France
Exhibition: Chagny, 1987

192 *The Drop of Water (La goccia
d'acqua)*. 1987

Metal tubes, glass and neon tubes; igloo
39' 4 7/16'' d. (1200 cm.)
Collection on the artist; Courtesy
CAPC/Musée d'Art Contemporain,
Bordeaux

193 *Fontaine*. 1987
Metal tubes, glass, neon tubes and
fountain; igloo 32' 9 11/16'' d. (1000
cm.); triangular structure 31 1/2 × 86'
7 3/8 × 14' 7 3/16'' (80 × 2640 × 445
cm.)
Collection of the artist; Courtesy
CAPC/Musée d'Art Contemporain,
Bordeaux
Exhibitions: Bordeaux, 1987; Nîmes,
1987, repr. p. 108

194 Installation, Nationalgalerie, Berlin, June 1988, featuring works by
Jannis Kounellis and Merz, including
in center:
The Drop of Water (La goccia d'acqua).
1987
Metal tubes, glass and neon tubes; igloo
39' 4 7/16'' d. (1200 cm.)
Collection of the artist; Courtesy Nationalgalerie, Berlin,
Exhibition: Berlin, 1987
Reference: Berlin, Nationalgalerie,
1988, repr. p. 50

195 *Celui qui est en plomb*. 1987
Metal tubes, wire mesh, lead, wood,
wax and canvas, 118 1/8'' d. (300 cm.)
Collection Musée de Nîmes; Courtesy
CAPC/Musée d'Art Contemporain,
Bordeaux
Exhibitions: Düsseldorf, 1987; Bordeaux, 1987

196 *Untitled*. 1984+87
Wicker, metal tubes, vglass and stone,
cone 13' 1 1/2'' h. × 78 3/4'' d.
(400 × 200 cm.); table 29' 6 3/8'' × 11'
5 13/16'' × 29 1/2'' (900 × 350 × 75
cm.)
Collection Sparta, Chagny, France;
Courtesy Galerie Pietro Sparta, Chagny, France

197 *Unreal City (Città irreale)*. 1987
Gouache, watercolor and ink on paper,
78 3/4 × 12' 1 7/8'' (200 × 370.5 cm.)
Courtesy Anthony d'Offay Gallery,
London
Exhibition: London, 1988

*198 *Untitled*. 1988
Iron, pillow, telephone and neon tubes,
82 11/16 × 51 3/16 × 43 5/16'' (210 ×
130 × 110 cm.)
Courtesy Galerie Pietro Sparta, Chagny, France

199 *Turbine (Turbina)*. 1988
Mixed media on canvas, raincoat,
neon tube, stone and music stand,
16' 4 7/8'' × 11' 5 13/16'' (500 × 350
cm.)
Collection of the artist

200 *Pouring of Remote Times, Here,
Now (Versamento di tempi lontani, qui,
ora)*. 1988

Stone, fluorescent light, laser, chalk,
bamboo, water and canvas, 65' 7 1/2'' ×
42' 7 7/8'' × 106 5/16'' (2000 × 1300 ×
270 cm.)
Courtesy ICA/Institute of Contemporary Art Nagoya
Exhibitions: Nagoya, 1988, repr. on
cover, pp. 49-53

201 Installation, Kunstmuseum Saint-Gallen, 1988, including:
*Untitled ("Everything Is Connected,"
Hölderlin) ("Tutto è connesso," Hölderlin)*. 1988
Metal tubes, clamps, glass, stone
and neon tubes, 90 9/16'' × 17' 4
11/16'' × 18' 1/2'' (230 × 530 × 550
cm.)
Collection H. Emanuel Schmid, Zürich

202 Installation, Louisiana Museum of
Modern Art, Humlebaek, Denmark,
1988, including:
*Spiral and Igloo (Spiraltisch und
Igloo)*. 1984+88
Metal tubes, glass, twigs, neon tubes
and wax; igloo 51 3/16'' h. × 78 3/4''
d. (130 × 200 cm.); table 25 9/16'' ×
23' 7 7/16'' × 10 7/16'' (65 × 720 ×
880 cm.)
Exhibition: Humlebaek, 1988
Courtesy Jean Bernier Gallery, Athens
*Cat. no. 88 *Panther on Cone (Pantere
sul cono)*. 1978
Persecuted Crocodile (Coccodrillo perseguitato). 1981
Mixed media on canvas and metal

203 *Virgilius, Futurist Memory (Virgilius, memoria futurista)*. 1988
Metal tubes, metal and wax, 13'
1 1/2'' × 78 3/4'' (400 × 200 cm.)
Courtesy ICA/Institute of Contemporary Art, Nagoya
Exhibition: Nagoya, 1988, repr. pp. 54,
58

204 Installation, Museum of Contemporary Art, Los Angeles, February
1989
Untitled. 1989
Glass, steel, clay, sheet metal, neon
tubes, rocks, mortar, wax, clamps

*205 *Madame de Lafayette*. 1988
Oil, clay, newspaper, stuffed alligator and putty on paper and neon tube,
11' 1 7/8'' × 102 3/8'' × 47 1/4''
(340 × 260 × 120 cm.)
Collection of the artist

206 *House in the Forest (Casa sulla
foresta)*. 1989
Metal, wire mesh, rubber, wax, twigs
and neon tubes, 40 1/8 × 102 3/8 ×
47 1/4'' (102 × 260 × 120 cm.)
Collection of the artist

207 *If the Form Vanishes, Its Roots Is
Eternal (Se la forma scompare la sua
radice è eterna)*. 1982 (89)
Neon tubes
Collection of the artist

The following works are in the exhibition but are not included in the
catalogue:

Tree (Albero). 1953
Oil on canvas, 28 × 39 1/2'' (71 ×
100.3 cm.)
Private Collection, Turin

Unreal City (Città irreale). 1968
Metal tubes, wire mesh, wax and neon
tubes, 110 1/4'' × 55 1/8'' × 9 13/16''
(280 × 140 × 25 cm.)

Fibonacci. 1971
Metal tubes, wire mesh, wax and neon
tubes, 31 1/2'' × 12' 7 3/16'' × 8
11/16'' (80 × 384 × 22 cm.)
Collection Musée d'Art Moderne,
Saint-Etienne

Untitled. 1976
Suede coat, enamel, plastic tube, neon
tube and branch, 38 × 45'' (96.5 × 114
cm.)
Private Collection, Antwerp

Yellow Crocodile (Coccodrillo giallo).
1987
Paper, newspaper and pigment, six
sections, total 182 1/8'' (463 cm.)
Collection of the artist

Alligator with Fibonacci Numbers.
1989
Stuffed alligator, metal and neon tubes
Collection of the artist; courtesy Stein
Gladstone Gallery, New York
Installation on exterior of Guggenheim
Museum, New York

Untitled. 1989
Metal, lead and wire mesh 59' h. ×
118'' d. (150 × 300 cm.)
Collection of the artist; Courtesy Stein
Gladstone Gallery, New York

Untitled. 1989
Metal, glass, twigs, rubber and stone;
igloos 16' 4 7/8'' × 32' 8'' d.; 157 3/8''
h. × 26' 3'' d.; 98 7/16'' h. × 16' 4 7/8''
d. (500 × 1000 × 800; 250 × 500 cm.)
Collectioin of the artist; Courtesy Stein
Gladstone Gallery, New York

Drawing (Disegno). 1970-77
Spray paint, charcoal, crayon, scratchings and pasted paper on transparent
paper, 17 1/2'' × 21 3/4'' (44 × 55 cm.)
Private Collection, Turin

Drawing (Disegno). 1970-77
Spray paint, charcoal, crayon and pasted paper on transparent paper, 16
1/2'' × 21 1/4'' (42 × 55 cm.)
Private Collection, Turin

Drawing (Disegno). 1970-77
Spray paint, charcoal, crayon and pasted paper on transparent paper, 18 × 21
1/2'' (46 × 55 cm.)
Private Collection, Turin

Drawing (Disegno). 1970-77
Spray paint, charcoal, crayon, scratchings and pasted paper on transparent paper, 17 1/2'' × 22 1/2'' (45 × 55 cm.)
Private Collection, Turin

Drawing (Disegno). 1970-77
Charcoal, spray paint and pasted paper on transparent paper, 17 1/2'' × 21 1/2'' (43 × 55 cm.)
Private Collection, Turin

Drawing (Disegno). 1970-77
Charcoal, crayon, spray paint and pasted paper on transparent paper, 17 1/2'' × 21 1/2'' (44 × 55 cm.)
Private Collection, Turin

Drawing (Disegno). 1970-77
Charcoal, spray paint and pasted paper on paper, 19 × 26 (48 × 66 cm.)
Private Collection, Turin

Drawing (Disegno). 1970-77
Spray paint, charcoal and pasted paper on transparent paper, 38 3/16'' × 22 1/4'' (56.5 × 97 cm.)
Private Collection, Turin

Drawing (Disegno). 1970-77
Spray paint, charcoal and pasted paper on transparent paper, 41 5/16'' × 21 5/8'' (105 × 55 cm.)
Private Collection, Turin

Drawing (Disegno). 1970-77
Spray paint, charcoal, crayon, pensil and pasted paper on transparent paper, 35 1/4'' × 21 5/8'' (89 × 55 cm.)
Private Collection, Turin

Drawing (Disegno). 1970-77
Spray paint, charcoal, crayon, cork, tape and scratchings on transparent paper, 18 × 25 3/8'' (46 × 65 cm.)
Private Collection, Turin

Drawing (Disegno). 1978
Spray paint, crayon, cork, tape and scratchings on transparent paper, 18 × 25 3/8'' (46 × 65 cm.)
Private Collection, Turin

Drawing (Disegno). 1978
Spray paint, crayon, charcoal, cork, tape and scratchings on transparent paper, 18 × 25 3/8'' (46 × 65 cm.)
Private Collection, Turin

Drawing (Disegno). 1978
Spray paint, steel wool, tape, crayon and charcoal on transparent paper, 18 × 25 3/8'' (46 × 65 cm.)
Private Collection, Turin

Drawing (Disegno). 1978
Cork, tape, charcoal and ink on transparent paper, 18 × 25 3/8'' (46 × 65 cm.)
Private Collection, Turin

Drawing (Disegno). 1978
Steel wool, spray paint, charcoal and tape on transparent paper, 28 1/2'' × 18'' (73 × 46 cm.)
Private Collection, Turin

Drawing (Disegno). 1979
Steel wool, spray paint, charcoal and tape on transparent paper, 17 1/2'' × 24 1/2'' (44 × 61 cm.)
Private Collection, Turin

Drawing (Disegno). 1979
Steel wool, charcoal, spray paint and tape on transparent paper, 25 × 18'' (63 × 46 cm.)
Private Collection, Turin

Drawing (Disegno). 1979
Steel wool, spray paint, charcoal and tape on transparent paper, 25 1/2'' × 18'' (64 × 46 cm.)
Private Collection, Turin

Drawing (Disegno). 1979
Steel wool, charcoal and tape on transparent paper, 17 1/2'' × 24 1/2'' (44 × 61 cm.)
Private Collection, Turin

Drawing (Disegno). 1979
Spray paint, charcoal, dried flower, tape and scratchings on transparent paper, 18 × 25 1/2'' (46 × 64 cm.)
Private Collection, Turin

Drawings with Plant Remains Gathered in the Garden of Woga-Woga Australia (Disegni con reperti di vegetali raccolti nel giardino di Woga-Woga, Australia). 1979
Charcoal, pencil, leaves and tape on paper, fourteen sheets, each 30 × 22'' (76 × 55.8 cm.)
Private Collection, Turin

Painting is Long and Fast (La pittura è lunga e veloce). 1980
Oil on burlap, 100 1/4'' × 21' 5'' (255 × 655 cm.)
Courtesy Galleria Salvatore Ala, Milan and New York

Painting is Long and Fast (La pittura è lunga e veloce), 1980
Oil on burlap, 100 1/4'' × 18' 7'' (255 × 570 cm.)
Courtesy Galleria Salvatore Ala, Milan and New York

Wright Igloo. 1989
Metal tubes, glass and twigs, 59 1/16'' h. × 118 1/8'' d. (150 × 300 cm.)
Collection of the artist; Courtesy Stein Gladstone Gallery, New York

Untitled (Senza titolo). 1989
Metal tubes, wax and mixed media, 59 1/16'' h. × 118 1/8'' d. (150 × 300 cm.)
Collection of the artist; Courtesy Stein Gladstone Gallery, New York

Biography
Selected Bibliography
Selected Exhibitions

1925-40

Mario Merz was born on January 1, 1925, in Milan. His father was an engineer and inventor who designed engines for Fiat; his mother was a music teacher. He has one sister. During his early childhood, the family moved to Turin, where he attended the scientific lycée. Later he enrolled at the medical school of the Università degli Studi di Torino and remained there for two years. Before World War II Merz briefly experimented with concrete poetry, an activity that prefigured both his evocative written statements that parallel his visual art and the neon script found in many of his later works.

1941-45

In 1944 Merz made drawings in which he did not lift his pencil from the paper until the drawing was complete. He did these while sitting in a field and referred to the technique as drawing in progression or proliferation. During the war Merz joined the anti-Fascist group Giustizia e Libertà (Justice and Liberty). His participation in this organization involved distributing leaflets at the University. In 1945 he was arrested for such political activities and sent to the Carceri Nuove, a prison in Turin. While in jail he began to draw incessantly on whatever materials he could find, such as letters, bread or cheese wrappers and the like. Once his father started to pressure him to select a profession after his release from prison, Merz fled to Paris where he worked as a truck driver in Les Halles while pursuing political activities. He visited the city's art museums, the Louvre in particular, but focused on contemporary painters such as Jean Dubuffet, Jean Fautrier and Jackson Pollock. He also read the works of Jean-Paul Sartre.

1946-49

Upon his return to Italy Merz began to read the writings of Franz Kafka, Cesare Pavese (*Paesi tuoi*), Karl Marx, John Steinbeck (*Of Mice and Men*), Eugenio Montale (*Ossi di seppia*) and Leonardo da Vinci, particularly his writings on drawing. In Rapallo he saw Ezra Pound, whose work became an important inspirational source for Merz's art. He befriended the Italian painters Mattia Moreni, Ennio Morlotti and Luigi Spazzapan. With the guidance of Brother Pontino, a professor of art history and Italian, he became well acquainted with the work of Pablo Picasso, Georges Braque, Giorgio Morandi and Francesco Casorati. He traveled from Turin to Rome on a bicycle. In 1949 he returned to his method of drawing in progression, again working outdoors.

1949

Luciano Pistoi, an art historian and critic whom Merz met while in jail,

published a drawing by the artist in the Communist newspaper *L'Unità*. The drawing illustrates Merz's face, rendered in a stylized manner with geometrical configurations. He considers this drawing a transitional work, for it marked a break from his previous, more realistic style. Its appearance in newsprint was prescient in that Merz would later use stacked and crumbled newspapers as socially and politically charged components of his work.

1950-59

Merz began painting with oil on canvas, creating powerful but relatively dispassionate images in an attempt to distance himself from the Italian and French Informel movement of the early to mid-1950s. Employing a vocabulary of abstract imagery loosely derived from nature, Informel was dominated by the individuality of the artist's direct interaction with the canvas. To counter this sensibility, Merz utilized industrial materials such as enamel and spray paint, which he applied in his early canvases with a compressor. Even though he based these images on organic forms – as did the Informel artists – Merz considers them synedochic codes for the entire ecological system. These paintings were exhibited in Merz's first one-man show, organized by the art historian and critic, Luigi Carluccio, and held in 1954 at Galleria La Bussola, Turin. Around this time Merz became acquainted with the artists Emilio Vedova and Pinot Gallizio. At the end of the decade he met his future wife, Marisa, who is also an artist. They traveled to Switzerland, where he continued to paint and draw from nature. In Switzerland he decided to use tree branches in his work.

1960-65

Upon returning to Italy, the couple lived near Pisa in an old farmhouse, where Merz began experimenting in his painting with increased scale and using excessive amounts of pigment. In 1963 Merz bought all the tubes of oil paint in the city of Pisa and applied their contents to a single canvas. Believing that painting has a life of its own, that it is a dynamic, unending process, Merz returned to his early canvases, covering their surfaces with numerous layers of paint. One painting from this period, worked on for an entire year, was purportedly five and seven-eighths inches thick. At that time, the spiral emerged as a motif in his work. Merz's second one-man exhibition, which featured paintings, was held at the Galleria Notizie: Associazione Arti Figurative, Turin, in the spring of 1962. During these years, Turin was steadily evolving as an international art center. In 1964 Merz began to experiment with shaped canvases and sculpture.

1966-68

By 1966 Merz had shifted away from painting and started making irregularly shaped blank canvases penetrated by thin neon tubes. The interpenetration of such disparate elements – material and light – created, for Merz, a discrete, unified object with provocative spatial and poetic possibilities. Beginning in 1967 he pierced bottles, umbrellas, worn raincoats, and other items with ribbons of neon, visible currents of energy that symbolically transform, but do not destroy, the objects. These assemblages, including *Horse Theater (Teatro cavallo)* and *Carrier Cone (Cono portante)*, were exhibited at Galleria Gian Enzo Sperone, Turin, in 1968. Before this solo show opened, Merz had embarked on an association with several artists based in Turin – Giulio Paolini, Gilberto Zorio, Jannis Kounellis, Luciano Fabro, Giuseppe Penone, Alighiero Boetti, Michelangelo Pistoletto and Giovanni Anselmo – that has endured to the present. Through regular discussions among themselves as well as with critics, writers, philosophers and political activists, they collectively formulated an antielitist aesthetic. In defiance of the dehumanizing aspects of industrialization and consumer capitalism then emerging in northern Italy, they embraced an art of humble materials drawn from everyday life and the organic world.

Named Arte Povera by Germano Celant on the occasion of a group exhibition in 1967 at Galleria Bertesca in Genoa, this loosely defined and eclectic movement sought a radical but regenerative art.

1968

Merz adopted his signature motif, the igloo, this year. In an effort to produce a surface independent from the wall, but not traditionally sculptural, Merz created a hemisphere that rests on the floor as an absolute space in itself. The igloo is a metaphorical form embodying Merz's belief that art is transitory and ever-changing, yet inexorably bound to the earth, specifically its local environment. Merz associates the artist with the nomad, constantly in motion, at home everywhere, in touch with both nature and culture. Constructed with segmented, metal armatures, the hemispherical structures are covered with a net and followed by fragments of clay, wax, mud or glass, or bundles of twigs. Political or literary references in neon script often span the domes. The earliest example, *Giap Igloo (Igloo di Giap)* bears a slogan in neon letters attributed to the North Vietnamese military strategist, General Vo Nguyen Giap: *Se il nemico si concentra perde terreno se si disperde perde forza* ("If the enemy masses his forces, he loses ground; if

he scatters, he loses strength.") The contradiction expressed in this phrase captures Merz's conception of the igloo – momentary shelter shifted from place to place so that, despite its temporality, it remains a constant. To symbolize the nomadic essence of the igloo, as well as its references to a simple, human-scale economic system close to nature, Merz uses materials indigenous to the sites of his exhibitions. For a show in Australia in 1979, for instance, he used eucalyptus leaves to blanket an igloo. And in his installation at the Museum of Contemporary Art in Los Angeles in 1989, he used granite from San Fernando Valley quarries and local palm fronds.

Three other works from this period, comprised of melted wax in metal containers with neon words, have explicit political references related to the uprisings of May 1968: *What Is To Be Done? (Che fare?)* and *Solitary Solidarity (Solitario solidale)*. Merz saw the phrase *"Solitaire solidaire"* scrawled as graffiti on a wall in Paris. *Che fare?* is a translation of the title of *Chto delat?*, a 1912 speech by Lenin (later published in pamphlet form), which analyzes class political consciousness and the proletariat in Russia. The phrase had also been adopted for the title of an avant-garde critical journal published in May and November 1967 in Milan. During these years Merz was included in important international exhibitions featuring Conceptual, process and Minimalist art, such as *Prospect 68* in Düsseldorf, *Arte povera + azioni povera* in Amalfi, *Op Losse Schroeven: Situaties en cryptostructure* in Amsterdam and *Live in Your Head: When Attitudes Become Form* in Bern.

1970
Since 1970, Merz has incorporated the Fibonacci formula of mathematical progression into his works. Originally conceived by the medieval monk Leonardo da Pisa (known as Fibonacci) and explicated in his *Liber Abacci* of 1202 and 1228, the formula requires that each numeral cited equal the sum of the two numbers that precede it: 1, 1, 2, 3, 5, 8, 13.... His observations were based on the reproduction of rabbits beginning with one pair and expanding, ultimately, to infinity. Corresponding to biological, spatial and temporal dimensions, Fibonacci proportions relate to the proliferation and growth of organic materials – leaves, reptile skins, deer antlers, pinecones, seashells, iguana tails – items or images that Merz incorporates into his art. An early work, *Propped (Appoggiati)*, of 1970, consisted of panes of glass leaned against a wall; to these panes were attached neon numbers in Fibonacci progression. The piece was shown at *Gennaio 70, III Biennale internazionale della giovane pittura* along with Merz's videotape of a violinist playing chords corresponding to the Fibonacci sequence. For *10 Tokyo Biennale '70: Between Man and Matter* in 1970, Merz created *Proliferation of a Plant (Proliferazione di una pianta)*, in which he analyzed and projected the proliferation of pine branches on the wall of the gallery with a sequence of neon numbers connected by cords.

1971-72
In 1971 Merz made his second videotape, *Lumaca* (produced by Gerry Schum), which is based on the Fibonacci proportions found in the spiral of snails' shells. For the *Guggenheim International Exhibition 1971*, Merz laced the interior of the Museum's ascending spiral with neon Fibonacci numerals in accordance with the structural progression of the Frank Lloyd Wright design. In 1972 Merz had his first one-man exhibition in the United States at the Walker Art Center, Minneapolis. At this time he introduced stacked newspapers, archetypal animals, motorcycles, and photographs with neon into his increasingly complex iconography. This year also marked the emergence of the table as a central motif. Similar in meaning to Merz's igloo, the table has evolved historically from specific social requirements to become a locus of human activity. The photographic series *A Real Sum Is a Sum of People* of 1972, exhibited that year at the Jack Wendler Gallery, London, documents the seating arrangements of people in The George IV, a pub in Kentish Town, London, following the Fibonacci progression from one to fifty-five.

1973-77
For his one-man exhibition at the John Weber Gallery in New York in 1973, Merz constructed wooden tables titled *It is possible to have a space for 88 people as it is possible to have a space with tables for no one*. In 1974 Merz created long triangular tables, similar in shape to his earlier lances, which stood alone or intersected igloos. Later, glass tables were conceived in a spiral format, circling around themselves and the fruits, vegetables and branches they supported. Merz won a DAAD (Deutscher Akademischer Austauschdienst) grant in Berlin in 1974. He had his first one-man museum exhibition in Europe at the Kunsthalle Basel in 1975, followed by a show in the same year at the Institute of Contemporary Art, London.

1977-89
By 1977, Merz had enthusiastically returned to painting, the activity with which he began his career. He continued to employ three-dimensional motifs and the Fibonacci sequence and concurrently developed a rich iconographic painting style. Primarily figurative yet intensely abstracted, the paintings depict mythological beasts – lizards, crocodiles, lions, rhinoceroses, bison – with convoluted and exaggerated anatomies. These vigorously gestural, brightly colored images are often combined with accumulations of branches, traversed by neon or draped over igloos. The theme of the *Painter in Africa (Pittore in Africa)*, of an artist who travels to a fantastic place to paint fabulous animals, emerged in 1981. Merz also began constructing double igloos and then triple igloos, one inside the other, utilizing the property of transparency in order to display the layered structures. Subsequent installations were increasingly multifarious, combining tables, igloos, paintings, fruits and vegetables, newspapers, stuffed crocodiles and neon. In 1981 Merz won the Arnold Bode prize of the city of Kassel, West Germany, and in 1983 he was awarded the Oskar Kokoschka prize by the city of Vienna.

Recent exhibitions have offered Merz the opportunity to respond directly to the architectural environment in which his works are seen, much in the spirit of his 1971 Guggenheim installation. In 1984 he placed neon numbers, in ascending Fibonacci sequence, on the spire of the Mole Antonelliana in Turin. In 1987 Merz was invited to create an installation at the Salpêtrière in Paris, a seventeenth-century compound which once housed Jean Martin Charcot's neurological clinic, where early studies of hysteria were conducted. The Chapelle Saint-Louis, also on this site, is still used today. Merz's installation in the chapel, which included a monumental glass igloo and a linear proliferation of Fibonacci numbers running along the floor under metal arches, acquired new metaphoric dimensions in such an environment. The infinitude suggested by the Fibonacci series and the transparency of the igloo corresponded to the metaphysical trappings of the church architecture. Concurrently and subversively, the heightened subjectivity – the Nietzschian air of Merz's program – evoked the hidden memory of Charcot's asylum. Using a few central motifs, but recreating and transforming them in response to each environment in which he exhibits, Merz produces a theater of meaning particular to each of his installation sites.

Bibliography

Bibliography, exhibition lists
and exhibition histories by
Ida Gianelli, Luisa De Vettor
and Jennifer Blessing

I. Books

Udo Kultermann, *Nuove dimensioni della scultura*, Milan, Feltrinelli, 1967

Germano Celant, *Arte povera*, Milan, Gabriele Mazzotta Editore, 1969; *Art Povera*, New York, Praeger, 1969

Udo Kultermann, *Nuove forme della pittura*, Milan, Feltrinelli, 1969; *The New Painting*, trans. Gerald Onn, New York, Praeger, 1969

Udo Kultermann, *I contemporanei*, Milan, Mondadori, 1970

Renato Barilli, *Dall'oggetto al comportamento: la ricerca artistica 1960-1970*, Rome, Ellegi, 1971

Achille Bonito Oliva, *Il territorio magico: comportamenti alternativi dell'arte*, Florence, Centro Di, 1971

Ursula Meyer, *Conceptual Art*, New York, Dutton, 1972

Grégoire Müller, *La nuova avanguardia*, Venice, Alfieri, 1972; *The New Avant-garde: Issues for the Art of the Seventies*, New York, Praeger, 1972

Gillo Dorfles, *Ultime tendenze nell'arte d'oggi: dall'informale al concettuale*, 2nd ed., Milan, Feltrinelli, 1973

Lucy Lippard, *Six Years: The Dematerialization of the Art Object from 1966 to 1972*, New York, Praeger, 1973

Germano Celant, *Senza titolo 1974*, Rome, Bulzoni, 1974

Renato Barilli, "L'arte povera" in *Arte moderna*, Milan, Fabbri, 1975

Germano Celant, ed., *Precronistoria 1966-69: minimal art, pittura sistemica, arte povera, land art, conceptual art, body art, arte ambientale e nuovi media*, trans. Germano Celant, L. Costa, Florence, Centro Di, 1976

Achille Bonito Oliva, *L'ideologia del traditore*, Milan, Feltrinelli, 1976

Achille Bonito Oliva, *Europe/America: the different avant-gardes*, ed. Corinna Ferrari, Milan, Deco, 1976

Germano Celant, *Ambiente/Arte dal futurismo alla body art*, Venice, La Biennale di Venezia, 1977

Germano Celant, *Offmedia, nuove tecniche artistiche: video disco libro*, Bari, Dedalo libri, 1977

Edward Lucie-Smith, *Arte oggi: dall'Espressionismo Astratto all'Iperrealismo*, Milan, Arnoldo Mondadori Editore, 1976; *Art now: from Abstract Expressionism to Superrealism*, New York, Morrow, 1977

Achille Bonito Oliva, *Autocritico automobile – Attraverso le avanguardie*, Milan, Il Formichiere, 1977

Renato Barilli, *Informale, ogetto, comportamento*, vol. I: *La ricerca artistica negli anni '50 e '60*, vol. II: *La ricerca artistica negli anni '70*, Milan, Feltrinelli, 1979

Renato Barilli, ed., *L'arte in Italia nel secondo dopoguerra*, Bologna, Società editrice il Mulino, 1979

Pierre Restany, *L'altra faccia dell'arte*, Milan, Editoriale Domus, 1979

Paolo Mussat Sartor, *Fotografo 1968-1978: Arte e artisti in Italia*, Turin, Stampatori Editore, 1979

Mario Abrate, Giancarlo Bergami, Paolo Bertoldi, Enzo Bottasso, Caorsi Gigi et al., *Torino città viva, da capitale a metropoli, 1880-1980*, 2 vols., Turin, Centro Studi Piemontesi, 1980

Jole de Sanna, *Breve storia dell'arte italiana dal 1895 al 1980*, Milan, Casa degli artisti, 1980

Barbara Maestri, *L'arte di Mario Merz*, thesis, Università degli Studi di Bologna, 1980-81

Giorgio de Genova, *Generazione anni venti*, Bologna, Bora, 1981

A.F. Wagemans, *Sculptures in the Rijksmuseum Kröller-Müller*, trans. Patricia Wardle, Otterlo, Rijksmuseum Kröller-Müller, 1981

Giorgio de Marchis, "L'arte in Italia dopo la seconda guerra mondiale" in *Storia dell'arte italiana*, vol. 7, Turin, Einaudi, 1982

Mariano Apa, *Arte moderna e contemporanea*, Rome, Studio Bazin, 1983

Renato De Fusco, *Storia dell'arte contemporanea*, Rome, Laterza, 1983

Christel Sauer, *Die Sammlung FER – The FER Collection*, ed. Paul Maenz, trans. Radka Donnell, Cologne, Gerd de Vries, 1983

Centre d'Art Contemporain, Genève 1974-1984, Geneva, Centre d'Art Contemporain, 1984

Maurizio Calvesi, *Le due avanguardie: dal Futurismo alla Pop Art*, 2nd ed., Rome-Bari, Laterza, 1984

Mario Diacono, *Verso una nuova iconografia*, Reggio Emilia, Collezione Tauma, 1984

Arturo Carlo di Quintavalle and Vittorio Corna, *Italian Art 1960/80*, preface Thomas M. Messer, trans. Howard Rodger MacLean, New York, Banca Commerciale Italiana, 1984

Germano Celant, *Arte Povera, Storie e protagonisti/ Art Povera, Histories and Protagonists*, ed. Ida Gianelli, trans. Paul Blanchard, Milan, Electa, 1985

Germano Celant, *Autotattoo*, Milan, Automobilia, 1986

Germano Celant, *Arte dall'Italia*, Feltrinelli, 1988

Marlis Grüterich, "Mario Merz" in *Künstler: Kritisches Lexikon der Gegenwartskunst*, vol. 3, Munich, Weltkunst und Bruckmann, 1988

II. Periodicals

Angelo Dragone, "Torinesi che espongono," *Il Popolo Nuovo* (Turin), February 2, 1957

Germano Celant, "Nuove tecniche d'immagine: Arte ricca e arte povera," *Casabella* (Milan), no. 319, October 1967, pp. 60-62

Carlo Guenzi, "Nuove tecniche d'immagine: Impegno ed evasione," *Casabella* (Milan), no. 319, October 1967, pp. 59-60

Germano Celant, "Arte povera – Appunti per una guerriglia," *Flash Art*, no. 5, November-December 1967

Germano Celant, "Giovane scultura italiana," *Casabella* (Milan), no. 322, January 1968, pp. 46-47

Antonia Del Guercio, "Arte povera," *Rinascita* (Rome), March 29, 1968

Tommaso Trini, "Merz: vedere attraverso/Merz: Look Through," *Bit* (Milan), vol. 2, April 1968, pp. 27-29

Lea Vergine, "Torino '68 – Nevrosi e sublimazione," *Metro*, no. 14, June 1968, pp. 128-143

Piero Gilardi, "Primary Energy and the 'Microemotive Artists,'" *Arts Magazine*, vol. 43, September-October 1968, pp. 48-51

Alberto Boatto, "Evento come avventura," *Cartabianca* (Rome), November 1968

Piero Gilardi, "Micro-emotive Art," *Museumjournaal*, vol. 13, no. 4, 1968, pp.198-202

Tommaso Trini, "Nuovo alfabeto per corpo e materia," *Domus*, no. 470, January 1969, pp. 45-51

Tommaso Trini, "L'imaginazione conquista il terrestre," *Domus*, no. 471, February 1969, pp. 43-50

Gillo Dorfles, "Arte concettuale o arte povera?," *Art International*, vol. 13, March 1969, pp. 35-38

Pierre Restany, "Povertà dell'arte povera," *Corriere della Sera* (Milan), May 15, 1969

Germano Celant, "Sensorio, sensazionale, sensitivo, sensibile, sentimentale, sensuoso," *Senza Margine*, no. 1, May 1969

Grégoire Müller, "Vielfältigkeit, Überfluss," *Kunstnachrichten*, vol. 9, June 1969

Harald Szeemann, "Vorwort," *Kunstnachrichten*, vol. 9, June 1969

Dino Buzzati, "Ecco l'arte povera," *Corriere della Sera* (Milan), February 9, 1970, p. 3

Mario De Micheli, "Candidi naturalisti e apprendisti stregoni," *L'Unità* (Turin), February 25, 1970

Maurizio Calvesi, "Schermi al posto dei quadri," *L'Espresso Colore* (Rome), March 15, 1970

Achille Bonito Oliva, "Le chiffre de l'homme," *Opus International*, no. 16, March 1970, pp. 30-33

Gillo Dorfles, "Milan, Turin, Rome," *Opus International*, no. 16, March 1970, pp.16-17

Marisa Volpi Orlandini, "L'art pauvre," *Opus International*, no. 16, March 1970, pp. 39-43

Dino Buzzati, "Gli enigmi dell'arte concettuale," *Corriere della Sera* (Milan), October 15, 1970, p. 3

Ricky E. Comi, "I procedimenti mentali di Merz e Boetti," *NAC* (Milan), no. 2, November 1970, p. 17

Mirella Bandini, "Twombly, Dibbets, Merz," *NAC* (Milan), no. 5, May 1971, pp. 35-36

Germano Celant, "Mario Merz," *Domus*, no. 499, June 1971, pp. 47-52

Renato Barilli, "Commento su Merz," *Data*, vol. 1, September 1971, pp. 24-25

Achille Bonito Oliva, "Process, Concept and Behaviour in Italian Art," *Studio International*, vol. 191, January-February 1976, pp. 3-10

Angelo Dragone, "Immaginazione e realtà," *Stampa Sera* (Turin), April 13, 1976

Marlis Grüterich, "Mario Merz," *Data*, no. 21, May-June 1976, pp. 54-59

Marlis Grüterich, "Mario Merz – Die Bio-Logik von Mario Merz – Kunst aus gesellschaftlichem Anlass," *Kunstforum International*, vol. 15, 1976, pp. 146-156

Mirella Bandini, "La frutta di Merz," *Data*, no. 25, February-March 1977, pp. 14-15

Enzo Siciliano, "Maestri del '900 e un po' di arte povera," *Corriere della Sera* (Milan), March 1978

Mirella Bandini, "La mia casa è il vento," *Avanti!*, April 22, 1979

Angelo Dragone, "Fabro, Merz, Paolini, finale 'fortissimo,'" *La Stampa* (Turin), July 8, 1979, p. 8

Bernard Lamarche-Vadel, "L'oeuvre de Mario Merz," *Artistes*, no. 1, October-November 1979, pp. 6-9

Achille Bonito Oliva, "Mario Merz," *Corriere della Sera* (Milan), November 29, 1979

Germano Celant, "Mario Merz: The Artist as Nomad," *Artforum*, vol. 18, December 1979, pp. 52-58

Maurizio Calvesi, "Avanguardia Neo e Post," *L'Espresso* (Rome), vol. 26, January 27, 1980, p. 102

Germano Celant, "20 ans d'art en Italie," *Art Press* (Paris), no. 37, May 1980, pp. 8-9

Jean-Christophe Ammann, "Was die siebziger Jahre von den sechzigern unterscheidet: Der Weg in die achtziger Jahre," *Kunstforum International*, vol. 39, no. 3, 1980, pp. 172-184

Germano Celant, "Die italienische Erfahrung," *Kunstforum International*, vol. 39, no. 3, 1980, pp. 125-133

Bruno Corà, "Texte/ Profile," *Kunstforum International*, vol. 39, no. 3, 1980, pp. 85-104

Bruno Corà, "Profili/ Opere," *A noir, E blanc, I rouge, O vert, U bleu* (Rome), vol. 1, September 1980, pp. 3-27

Marlis Grüterich, "Idylle oder Intensität? Italienische Kunst heute," *Kunstforum International*, vol. 39, no. 3, 1980, pp. 11-18

Marlis Grüterich, "Poetische Aufklärung in der Ikonographie der Alltagskultur," *Kunstforum International*, vol. 39, no. 3, 1980, pp. 20-41

Annelie Pohlen, "Italienische 'Bilder': Kultur, Tradition und Gegenwart," *Kunstforum International*, vol. 39, no. 3, 1980, pp. 105-117

Flaminio Gualdoni, "Mario Merz," *Segno* (Pescara), no. 19, January-February 1981

Bruno Corà, "Mario Merz – Architettura: il problema dello spazio del tempo," *A noir, E blanc, I rouge, O vert, U bleu* (Rome), vol. 2, March 1981, pp. 15-36

Germano Celant, "Mario Merz l'artiste nomade," *Art Press* (Paris), no. 48, May 1981, pp. 13-15

I. Steger, "Übungen zur Befreiung der Phantasie," *Salzburger Nachrichten*, August 19, 1981

Angelo Dragone, "Merz, Il 'primitivo,'" *La Stampa* (Turin), November 29, 1981, p. 21

Francesco Poli, "Mario Merz," *Nuova Società* (Turin), no. 206, December 12, 1981

"Schwebende Frage – Mario Merz, der italienische Beuys, hat sich zum Maler gewandelt," *Der Spiegel*, no. 29, 1981, pp. 131-133

Enzo Bargiacchi, "Mario Merz," *Segno* (Pescara), no. 24, January 1982, pp. 18-20

Angelo Dragone, "Triste Margarethe dai capelli biondi," *La Stampa* (Turin), June 27, 1982

M. Campitelli, "Il fiume scorre lentamente," *Juliet* (Trieste), no. 9, November 1982-January 1983, pp. 15-20

Angelo Dragone, "Merz: la mia pittura è attuale e lontana come un mito," *La Stampa* (Turin), July 23, 1983, pp. 4-5

Beatrice Merz, "Un invito a nascondersi nella trasparenza," *Lo Spazio Umano* (Milan), no. 9, October-December 1983, pp. 45-55

Per Kirkeby, "Caro Mario Merz: Lettera-diario dalla Terry di Peary, estate 1979," *A noir, E blanc, I rouge, O vert, U bleu* (Rome), vol. 4, December 1983, pp. 4-9

Marlis Grüterich, "Merz – Kounellis: Zwei Künstler aus Italien und ihr Werk; Mario Merz – Denken, wie die Natur lebt," *Du*, no. 3, 1983, pp. 26-49

Mirella Bandini, "Mario Merz, il ritorno del mito," *Flash Art* (Italian Edition), no. 117, December 1983-January 1984, cover, pp. 8-15

Angelo Dragone, "Pietre e fuoco per l'arte povera," *La Stampa* (Turin), June 14, 1984, p. 3

Francesco Poli, "Bel ricordo, l'arte povera," *Il Manifesto* (Rome), June 29, 1984

Riccardo Barletta, "Quando le cose giocano con l'assurdo," *Corriere della Sera* (Milan), July 11, 1984

Mirella Bandini, "Dodici esponenti dell'Arte povera," *Avanti!*, July 19, 1984

Enrico R. Comi, "Letter from Milan," *Studio International*, vol. 196, no. 1004, 1984, pp. 52-53

A. Sigrist, "Die menschliche Urbehausung als Kunstform," *Argus* (Basel), March 1985

Gillo Dorfles and Germano Celant, "Decorauto," *Domus*, no. 660, April 1985, pp. 68-71

Jacqueline Burckhardt, "Mario Merz: città irreale," *Parkett*, no. 5, May 1985, pp.75-77, 82-83

Beatrice Merz, "Der Grosse Topf (The Big Pot/La Grande Pentola)," *Parkett*, no. 5, May 1985, pp.78-80, 84-85

Douglas Beer, "Un Prix sous influence?," *La Tribune de Genève*, June 28, 1985

Pier Luigi Tazzi, "Brief aus Paris," *Wolkenkratzer Art Journal* (Frankfurt), no. 8, June-August 1985, pp.52-53

Beatrice Merz, "Mario Merz: Luoghi senza strada," *Domus*, no. 663, July-August 1985, p. 75

Paolo Rizzi, "Il design italiano è il 're' del gusto," *Il Gazzettino* (Venice), October 26, 1985

Mirella Bandini, "Poca vernice, tanta materia," *La Stampa* (Turin), November 9, 1985, p. 7

Carolyn Christov-Bakargiev, "Mario Merz, contare i numeri è un modo per avvicinare l'irrazionalità della vita," *Reporter* (Rome), December 22, 1985, p. 34

Denys Zacharopoulos, "Mario Merz, Solitaire/Solidaire," *Art Studio* (Paris), no. 3, Winter 1986-87, pp. 84-95

Carolyn Christov-Bakargiev, "Arte povera 1967-1987," *Flash Art*, no. 137,

November-December 1987, pp. 52-69

L. L. P., "Lyon des Arts," *Domus*, no. 689, December 1987, pp. 12-13

Démosthenès Davvetas, "Das 'JEN' des Kung Fu-Tse und die MERZISCHE CITÉ/ The Jen of Kung Fu-Tse and The Merzian City," *Parkett*, no. 15, February 1988, pp. 86-89

Marlis Grüterich, "Wege für hier und jetzt an unwegsamen Orten: Mario Merz's Reisebilder 1987/ Paths for Here and Now in Impenetrable Places, Mario Merz's Travel Pictures 1987," *Parkett*, no. 15, February 1988, pp. 38-57

Jeanne Silverthorne, "Mario Merz's Future of an Illusion/ Die Zukunft einer Illusion," *Parkett*, no. 15, February 1988, pp. 58-73

Harald Szeemann, "Präsent-Rätsel-Grössen/Presence-Riddle-Entities," *Parkett*, no. 15, February 1988, pp. 90-91

Denys Zacharopoulos, "Die Gegenwart des Werke/ The Present of a Work," *Parkett*, no. 15, February 1988, pp. 92-97

III. Interviews

Mila Pistoi, "Intervista a Mario Merz," *Marcatré* (Rome), no. 30-33, July 1967, pp. 286-288

Piero Gilardi [Interview with Mario Merz], Turin, January 4, 1968, unpublished

"Intervista," *Data*, vol. 1, September 1971, pp. 20-21

Mirella Bandini, "Torino 1960-1973," *NAC* (Bari), no. 3, March 1973, p. 9

Harald Szeemann, "Raconte-moi tes débuts," *L'Art Vivant* (Paris), no. 53, November 1974

Mirella Bandini, "Mario Merz e Michelangelo Pistoletto: il significato di Gallizio per la nuova generazione" in *Pinot Gallizio e il Laboratorio Sperimentale d'Alba del Movimento Internazionale per una Bauhaus Immaginista (1955-57) e dell'Internazionale Situazionista (1957-60)*, Turin, Galleria Civica d'Arte Moderna, 1974, pp. 27-29

Caroline Tisdall, "Mario Merz: An Interview by Caroline Tisdall," *Studio International*, vol. 191, January-February 1976, pp. 11-17

Lynda Morris and Barbara Reise, "Eine Zahl ist ein Symbol für Wirklichkeit und Wachstum; Interview mit Mario Merz," *Kunstforum International*, no. 15, 1976, pp. 163-166

Giuseppe Risso, "Incontri con...Mario Merz e il numero," *Gazzetta del Popolo* (Turin), March 1, 1978

Francesco Vincitorio, "Il Critico e l'Artista," *L'Espresso* (Rome), vol. 26, July 20, 1980, p. 80

Paul Groot, "Neonbuizen als bliksemschichten: Gesprek met Mario Merz," *NRC/Handelsblad* (Amsterdam), August 1, 1980

Bruno Corà, "Mario Merz – Architettura: il problema dello spazio del tempo," *A noir, E blanc, I rouge, O vert, U bleu* (Rome), vol. 2, March 1981, pp. 15-36

"Declaraciones de Mario Merz: Documenta 7, transavanguardia, postmodernos...," *Vardar* (Madrid), no. 8, November 1982, pp. 2-4

Mirella Bandini, "Intervista a Mario Merz," *Flash Art* (Italian Edition), no. 117, December 1983-January 1984, p. 15

Achille Bonito Oliva, "Mario Merz" in Bonito Oliva, *Dialoghi d'artista*, Milan, Electa, 1984, pp. 256-269

Patrice Bloch and Laurent Pesenti, "Entretien avec Mario Merz," *Beaux-Arts*, no. 24, May 1985, pp. 36-41

Jean Pierre Bordaz, "Entretien avec Harald Szeemann et Mario Merz à propos de l'exposition Mario Merz au Kunsthaus de Zurich," *Neue Kunst in Europa* (Munich), no. 9, July-September 1985, pp. 13-15

Maïten Bouisset, "Bordeaux à l'heure italienne," *Le Matin*, June 8, 1987

Daniel Soutif, "Mario Merz, l'igloo et le glouglou," *Libération* (Paris), June 22, 1987, p. 24

Jacqueline Burckhardt, ed., "Sagt Ich's oder sagt Ich's nicht?! Auszüge aus Gesprächen mit der Redaktion, Dezember/Januar 1987/88/ Did I Say It or Didn't I? Extracts from conversations with the editorial staff of Parkett, December 1987 – January 1988," *Parkett*, no. 15, February 1988, pp. 74-83

Charles D. Scheips, Jr. [Interview], *Artcoast*, May-June 1989, pp. 75-76

IV. By the Artist

The following does not include texts published in exhibition catalogues, which are cited in the exhibition list.

"Parto dall'emozione che mi dà l'ogetto...," in Simonetta Lux, "Tre mostre a Roma," *Cartabianca* (Rome), May 1969

Fibonacci 1202 – Mario Merz 1970, Turin, Sperone Editore, 1970

"La serie di Fibonacci," *Data*, vol. 1, September 1971, pp. 18-19

Fibonacci 1202 – Mario Merz 1972. Una somma reale è una somma di gente, Turin, Galleria Sperone, 1972

"Una domenica lunghissima dura approssimativamente dal 1966 e ora siamo al 1976," *La Città di Riga* (Rome), no. 1, Fall 1976, pp. 7-9

987, Naples, Lucio Amelio, 1976

"La mancanza di iconografia è la nostra

conquista o la nostra dannazione?," *La Città di Riga* (Rome), no. 2, Spring 1977, pp. 13-18

"La serie di Fibonacci..., 1970-72," *Data*, no. 32, Summer 1978, pp. 20-21

"Es waren einmal...," *Kunstforum International*, vol. 39, September 1980, p. 55

"Der grosse Kochtopf des Hauses schmeckt nach Freiheit...," *Kunstforum International*, vol. 39, September 1980, p. 56

"Meine Ungeduld ist ein Schritt ins Auge...," *Kunstforum International*, vol. 39, September 1980, p. 54

"Il castello di foglie," *Domus*, no. 634, December 1982, pp. 68-69

Les fruits, Paris, Editions Baron – Galerie Claudine Bréguet, 1983

"Nella antica terra," *Domus*, no. 648, March 1984, p. 70

"Una poesia di Mario Merz/A poem by Mario Merz," *Lo Spazio Umano* (Milan), no. 2, April-June 1985, pp. 71, 73

"Iglu=Haus (Igloo=House)," *Parkett*, no. 5, May 1985, pp. 77, 84

"Decorauto: 8 Progetti per Renault," *Domus*, no. 663, July-August 1985, p. 67

Beatrice Merz, ed., *Voglio fare subito un libro/Sofort will ich ein Buch machen*, trans. Christina Brunner, Marlis Grüterich, Ingeborg Lüscher, Liselotte Mangels-Giannachi and Harald Szeemann, Aarau, Frankfurt am Main, Salzburg, Verlag Sauerländer, 1985. Published on occasion of *Mario Merz*, Kunsthaus Zürich, 1985

"Project for Artforum: Written leaf," *Artforum*, vol. 24, January 1986, pp. 61-65. Reproduction of artwork

"Senza titolo," *A noir, E blanc, I rouge, O vert, U bleu* (Rome), vol. 7, January-March 1986, p. 72, foldout. Reproduction of artwork

Voglio fare subito un libro, Florence, Hopefulmonster, 1987

"Edition für Parkett/ Edition for Parkett," *Parkett*, no. 15, February 1988, pp. 84-85. Reproduction of etching, sugarlift, drypoint and aquatint on Hahne-Mühle

Tavola, Edinburgh, A Scottish Trust Publication in association with the Richard Demarco Gallery, 1988

I Want To Write a Book Right Now, Florence, Hopefulmonster, 1989

La casa e gli animali, forthcoming, Genoa, Costa & Nolan, 1989

I. Group Exhibitions and Reviews

Milan, Galleria Gissi, *Pittori astratto-concreti*, 1952

Turin, Galleria La Bussola, *Niente di nuovo sotto il sole*, January 4 – 18, 1955

Milan, Galleria Il Milione, *Quattro giovani pittori torinesi: Merz, Soffiantino, Ruggeri, Saroni*, January 8–22, 1957. Catalogue with text by Luciano Pistoi

Turin, Galleria Notizie: Associazione Arti Figurative, *Tre nuovi pittori aformali*, opened January 15, 1957. Catalogue with text by Luciano Pistoi

Turin, Società Promotrice delle Belle Arti, *Quadriennale Nazionale d'Arte*, 1964. Catalogue

Turin, Galleria Civica d'Arte Moderna, *Museo sperimentale d'arte contemporanea*, April – May 1967. Catalogue with texts by Eugenio Battisti, Germano Celant, Luigi Mallé and Aldo Passoni

Milan, Galleria Toselli, *Gilardi, Merz, Piacentino, Pistoletto, Pizzo Greco*, November-December 1967

Turin, Galleria Christian Stein, Galleria Gian Enzo Sperone and Galleria Il Punto, *Con temp l'azione*, opened December 4, 1967. Catalogue with texts by Daniela Palazzoli

Turin, Deposito d'Arte Presente, December 1967 – June 1969

Lugano, Galleria Flaviana, *Con temp l'azione*, opened February 17, 1968

Bologna, Galleria de' Foscherari, *Arte povera*, February 24 – March 15, 1968. Organized in association with Galleria L'Attico, Rome, Galleria La Bertesca, Genoa, and Galleria Sperone, Turin. Catalogue with texts by Renato Barilli, Pietro Bonfiglioli and Germano Celant
– Alberto Boatto, "Arte povera a Bologna," *Cartabianca* (Rome), May 1968
– Francesco Arcangeli, Renato Barilli, Pietro Bonfiglioli, Achille Bonito Oliva, Maurizio Calvesi et al., "Arte povera – La povertà dell'arte," *Quaderni de'Foscherari* (Bologna), no. 1, 1968

Rome, Galleria Arco D'Alibert, *Percorso*, March 23 – April 16, 1968

Alberto Boatto, "9 per un percorso," *Cartabianca* (Rome), November 1968, pp. 15-19

Trieste, Centro Arte Viva Feltrinelli, *Arte povera*, March 23 – April 11, 1968. Catalogue with text by Germano Celant

Düsseldorf, Städtische Kunsthalle, *Prospect 68*, September 20 – 29, 1968. Catalogue

Amalfi, Arsenali dell'Antica Repubblica, *III Rassegna internazionale d'arti figurative: "Arte povera + azioni povere,"* October 4 – 30, 1968. Catalogue with texts by Giovanni M. Accame, Giuseppe Bartolucci, Vittorio Boarini, Pietro Bonfiglioli, Achille Bonito Oliva, Germano Celant et al.
– Angelo Trimarco, "Arte povera e azioni ad Amalfi," *Flash Art*, no. 9, November 1968, unpag.
– Tommaso Trini, "Rapporto da Amalfi," *Domus*, no. 468, November 1968, p. 51

Amsterdam, Stedelijk Museum, *Op Losse Schroeven: Situaties en crypto-structuren*, March 15 – April 27, 1969. Catalogue with texts by Wim A. L. Beeren, Piero Gilardi and Harald Szeemann and "rubate tutto quanto c'è in vista" by the artist and Marisa Merz

Kunsthalle Bern, *Live in Your Head: When Attitudes Become Form: Works – concepts – processes – situations – information*, March 22 – April 27, 1969. Catalogue with texts by Scott Burton, Grégoire Müller, Harald Szeemann and Tommaso Trini. Traveled to Krefeld, Museum Haus Lange, as *Vorstellungen nehmen Form an*, May 9 – June 15, with catalogue with texts by J. Harten, Hans Strelow and Paul Wember; London, Institute of Contemporary Art, as *When Attitudes become form*, August 28 – September 27, with brochure with texts by Charles Harrison, John A. Murphy and Harald Szeeman
– Jean-Christophe Ammann, "Schweizer Brief: 'Live in your Head – When Attitudes become Form,'" *Art International*, vol. 13, May 1969, pp. 47-50
– P.F. Althaus, "Wenn Attitüden Form werden," *Kunstnachrichten*, vol. 9, June 1969
– Hans Heinz Holz, "Die Berner Kunsthalle als Abfallplatz," *Kunstnachrichten*, vol. 9, June 1969
– Tommaso Trini, "Trilogia del creator prodigo/ The Prodigal Maker's Trilogy," *Domus*, no. 478, September 1969, pp. 47-48

Essen, Museum Folkwang, *Verborgene Strukturen*, May 9 – June 22, 1969. Catalogue with text by Wim A. L. Beeren

San Benedetto del Tronto, Palazzo scolastico Gabrielli, *VIII Biennale d'arte contemporanea: "Al di là della pittura,"* July 5 – August 28, 1969. Catalogue with texts by Gillo Dorfles, Luciano Marucci and Filiberto Menna

Turin, Galleria Gian Enzo Sperone, *Disegni e progetti*, opened October 29, 1969

Bologna, Museo Civico, *Gennaio 70, III Biennale internazionale della giovane pittura*, January 31 – February 28, 1970. Catalogue with texts by Renato Barilli, Maurizio Calvesi and Tommaso Trini

Tokyo, Metropolitan Art Gallery, *10 Tokyo Biennale '70: Between Man and Matter*, May 10 – 30, 1970. Catalogue in 2 vols. with text by Yusuke Nakahara. Trans. Joseph Love. Traveled to Kyoto, Municipal Art Museum, June 6 – 28; Nagoya, Aichi Prefectural Art Gallery, July 15 – 26; Fukuoka, Prefectural Culture House, August 11-16

Kunstmuseum Luzern, *Processi di pensiero visualizzati: junge italienische Avantgarde*, May 31 – July 15, 1970. Catalogue with texts by Jean-Christophe Ammann and Germano Celant and "Tracce/ Intervento su intonaco..." and "'Fibonacci' 1202" by the artist – Jean-Christophe Ammann, "Zeit, Raum, Wachstum, Prozesse," *Du*, vol. 30, August 1970, pp. 546-555

Turin, Galleria Civica d'Arte Moderna, *Conceptual Art, arte povera, land art*, June 12 – July 12, 1970. Catalogue by Germano Celant with texts by Germano Celant, Lucy Lippard, Luigi Mallé, Aldo Passoni and the artist
– Mirella Bandini, "Conceptual art, Arte povera, Land art," *NAC* (Milan), no. 1, October 1970, p. 16
– Tommaso Trini, "Arte povera, land art, conceptual art: l'opera sparita e diffusa," *Arte Illustrata* (Milan), no. 34-35-36, October – December 1970, pp. 40-55

Montepulciano, Palazzo Ricci, *Amore mio*, June 30 – September 30, 1970. Catalogue with texts by Achille Bonito Oliva and the artist

Modena, Galleria della Sala di Cultura, Istituti Culturali del Comune di Modena, *Arte e critica '70*, November 14 – December 15, 1970. Catalogue with texts by Giovanni M. Accame, Renato Barilli, Germano Beringheli, Vittorio Boarini, Alberto Boatto et al.

Rome, Palazzo delle Esposizioni, *Vitalità del negativo nell'arte italiana 1960/70*, November 1970 – January 1971. Catalogue by Achille Bonito Oliva with texts by Giulio Carlo Argan, Alberto Boatto, Achille Bonito Oliva, Maurizio Calvesi, Gillo Dorfles et al.

Innsbruck, Galerie im Taxispalais, February 9 – March 4, 1971, *situation concepts*. Catalogue with texts by Mel Bochner, Ricky Comi, Joseph Kosuth, Sol LeWitt and Peter Weiermair. Trans. Sonja Bahn and Ricky Comi. Traveled to Vienna, Galerie nächst St. Stephan, March 15 – April 10

New York, Solomon R. Guggenheim Museum, *Guggenheim International Exhibition 1971*, February 12 – April 11, 1971. Catalogue with texts by Edward F. Fry, Thomas M. Messer and

Diane Waldman and "The Abandonment of a practical space for a theoretical space..." and "Freedom to draw, freedom to read..." by the artist

Nuremberg, Kunsthalle and Künstlerhaus, *II Biennale: Was die Schönheit sei, das weiss Ich nicht. Künstler-Theorie-Werk*, April 30 – August 1, 1971. Catalogue supplement with "L'arco di pietre..." by the artist

Munich, Kunstverein, *Arte Povera*, May 26 – June 27, 1971. Catalogue with texts by Germano Celant

New York, The Museum of Modern Art, *Projects: Pier 18*, June 18 – August 2, 1971

Arnhem, The Netherlands, Park Sonsbeek, *Sonsbeek 71: Sonsbeek buiten de perken*, June 19, 1971 – August 15, 1971. Catalogue in 2 vols. with texts by Wim A.L. Beeren, Cor Blok and P. Sanders and "the page is infinite..." by the artist. Trans. Koos Gräper, J. J. van der Maas, Bob and Geeraldine van Rijn, Ine Rike and Louise van Santen

Buenos Aires, Museo de Arte Moderno, *Arte de sistemas*, July 1971. Catalogue with texts by Jorge Glusberg and "Dignidad única diosa" by the artist

Belgrade, International Theaterfestival-Bitef, *Persona*, opened September 10, 1971. Catalogue with text by Achille Bonito Oliva

Düsseldorf, Städtische Kunsthalle, *Prospect 71 – Projection*, October 8–17, 1971. Catalogue with text by Hans Strelow

New York, John Weber Gallery, *De Europa*, April 29 – May 24, 1972. Organized in association with Galleria Gian Enzo Sperone, Turin, and Galerie Konrad Fischer, Düsseldorf. Catalogue

Venice, *XXXVI Esposizione biennale internazionale d'arte: Il libro come luogo di ricerca; Videonastri; Persona 2; Italia*, June 11 – October 1, 1972. Catalogue in 3 vols. with texts by Francesco Arcangeli, Renato Barilli, Achille Bonito Oliva, Daniela Palazzoli, Gerry Schum et al.

Kassel, Museum Fridericianum, *Documenta 5: Befragung der Realität, Bildwelten Heute – Prozesse*, June 30 – October 8, 1972. Catalogue with texts by Jean-Christophe Ammann, Ursula Barthelmess, Ingolf Bauer, Hans-Henning Borgelt, Bazon Brock et al.

Berlin, Ausstellungshallen am Funkturm, April 8 – May 1, 1973

Rome, Palazzo delle Esposizioni, *X Quadriennale: La ricerca estetica dal 1960 al 1970*, May 22 – June 30, 1973. Catalogue by Mario Quattro Ciocchi and Filiberto Menna

Berlin, Akademie der Künste und Stadtgebiet, *Aktionen der Avantgarde 1973/ADA*, September 9 – October 3, 1973. Catalogue with texts by the artist

Museum of Philadephia Civic Center, *Italy Two: Art Around '70*, November 2 – December 16, 1973. Catalogue with texts by Alberto Boatto and Filiberto Menna

Rome, Parcheggio di Villa Borghese, *Contemporanea*, November 1973 – February 1974. Catalogue with texts by Pio Baldelli, Giuseppe Bartolucci, Franco Basaglia, Achille Bonito Oliva, Paolo Bertetto et al. Trans. Enic, Rowena Fajardo, Jennifer Franchina, Brigit Kraatz, Romano Mastromattei et al.

Cologne, Kunsthalle, Wallraf-Richartz Museum and Kölnischer Kunstverein, *Projekt '74: Kunst bleibt Kunst: Aspekte internationaler Kunst am Anfang der 70er Jahre*, enlarged ed., July 6 – September 8, 1974. Catalogue with texts by Marlis Grüterich, Brigit Hein, Wulf Herzogenrath, David A. Ross, Manfred Schneckenburger et al. and "Annähern: statische Zeichnungen an dynamische" by the artist

Kunstmuseum Luzern, *Spiralen & Progressionen*, March 16 – April 20, 1975. Catalogue with texts by Jean-Christophe Ammann, Pierre Gaudibert, Christian Geelhaar and Max Wechsler

Ferrara, Galleria Civica d'Arte Moderna, *CAYC 3rd International Open Encounter on Video*, May 25 – 29, 1975. Organized by Center of Art and Communication, Buenos Aires. Catalogue with text by Jorge Glusberg

Venice, Magazzini del Sale alle Zattere, *A Proposito del Mulino Stucky*, September 15 – November 4, 1975. Catalogue with texts by Vittorio Gregotti, Pontus Hultén, Cesare Ripa di Meana, F. Raggi, G. Romanelli and J. Rykwert and "Lo spazio è curvo o dritto" by the artist

Venice, *XXXVII Biennale: Environment, Participation, Cultural Structures – Ambient/Art*, July 18 – October 10, 1976. Catalogue in 2 vols. with texts by Germano Celant

Brescia, Quartiere di Porta Venezia, *Arte-Ambiente*, September 20 – 26, 1976. Catalogue with text by Mirella Bandini and "La vasca da bagno..." by the artist

Düsseldorf, Städtische Kunsthalle, *ProspectRetrospect: Europa 1946-1976*, October 20 – 31, 1976. Catalogue by Jürgen Harten with texts by Benjamin H.D. Buchloh, Konrad Fischer, Rudi Fuchs, John Matheson and Hans Strelow. Trans. Benjamin H. D. Buchloh, John Matheson and Schuldt

Turin, Teatro Gobetti, *Marco Bagnoli, Mario Merz, Giulio Paolini, Remo Salvadori*, opened May 3, 1977. Catalogue

Turin, Galleria Civica d'Arte Moderna, *Arte in Italia 1960-1977*, May – September 1977. Catalogue with texts by Renato Barilli, Antonio Del Guercio and Filiberto Menna

Kassel, Orangerie, *Documenta 6*, June 14 – October 14, 1977. Catalogue in 3 vols., *Handzeichnungen/ Utopisches Design/ Bücher* (vol. 3) with text by Wieland Schmied

Wrexham, Wales, Festival of the Celtic People, *Joseph Beuys, Jannis Kounellis, Mario Merz, Marisa Merz*, Summer 1977

Art Institute of Chicago, *Europe in the Seventies: Aspects of Recent Art*, October 8 – November 27, 1977. Catalogue with texts by Jean-Christophe Ammann, David Brown, Benjamin H.D. Buchloh, Rudi Fuchs and James Speyer. Traveled to Washington, D.C., Hirshhorn Museum and Sculpture Garden, Smithsonian Institution, March 16 – May 7, 1978; San Francisco Museum of Modern Art, June 23 – August 6; Fort Worth Art Museum, September 24 – October 29; Cincinnati, Contemporary Art Center, December 1, 1978 – January 31, 1979

Florence, Chiostro di Santa Maria Novella, *Omaggio a Brunelleschi*, opened October 16, 1977

Rome, Galleria dell'Oca, *Mario Merz – Balla, Carrà, De Chirico, De Pisis, Morandi, Savinio, Severini*, opened March 15, 1978

Bologna, Galleria Mario Diacono, *Per una politica della forma: Calzolari, Mario Merz, Kounellis*, April 1978. Brochure with text by Mario Diacono

Gavirate, Chiostro di Voltorre, *Cara morte*, April 1978

Venice, *XXXVIII Biennale: Dalla natura all'arte, dall'arte alla natura – Artenatura*, July 2 – October 15, 1978. Catalogue in several vols., *Artenatura*, with texts by Jean-Christophe Ammann, Achille Bonito Oliva, Antonio Del Guercio and Filiberto Menna. Trans. Marco Cordioli, Alexandra McAdoo and Philip Roberts
– Rosemaria Rinaldi, "Quando la natura fioriva, Mario Merz," *Data*, no. 32, Summer 1978, pp. 19-21
– Klaus Honnef, "Die Biennale Venedig '78: Von der Natur zur Kunst, Von der Kunst zur Natur," *Kunstforum International*, vol. 27, 1978, pp. 236-256

Milan, Galleria Toselli, *Marisa Merz, Nicola De Maria, Mario Merz*, opened October 20, 1978

Naples, Galleria Lucio Amelio, *Città irreale*, opened November 18, 1978

Zürich, InK (Halle für internationale neue Kunst), *Poetische Aufklärung in der europäischen Kunst der Gegenwart bei Joseph Beuys, Marcel Broodthaers, Daniel Buren, Jannis Kounellis, Mario Merz, Gerhard Richter – Geschichte von heute und morgen*, November 26, 1978 – January 21, 1979. Catalogue with texts by Marlis Grüterich and interview with the artist by Marlis Grüterich
– Marlis Grüterich, "Poetische Aufklärung in der europäischen Kunst der Gegenwart," *Kunstforum International*, vol. 30, 1978, pp. 203-208

Krefeld, Museum Haus Lange, *Die Erweiterung des Wirklichkeitsbegriffs in der Kunst der 60er und 70er Jahre*, January 12 – March 18, 1979. Catalogue with text by Gerhard Storck

New York, Hal Bromm Gallery, *New Works: Boetti/ Caro/ Merz/ Paolini/ ZaZa*, March 10 – April 7, 1979
– R. B. Roufberg, "The Best Little Galleries in SoHo," *Time Off* (New York), May 2 – 8, 1979, p. 9
– Tiffany Bell, "Five Italian Artists," *Arts Magazine*, vol. 53, May 1979, pp. 33-34

Sydney, The Art Gallery of New South Wales, *European Dialogue, The Third Biennale of Sydney*, April 14 – May 27, 1979. Catalogue with texts by Laszlo Beke, Georges Boudaille, Pontus Hultén, Elwyn Lynn, John McEwen et al. and "the fruit is here!..." by the artist. Trans. Pat Angly, K. B. Beaton, Rudi Krausmann, Lindsay Moloney, Liz Snowden and Jane Thynne
– Nick Waterlow, "Biennale of Sydney: European Dialogue," *Flash Art*, no. 90-91, June – July 1979, p. 16

Melbourne, National Gallery of Victoria, June 1979

Turin, Galleria Christian Stein, *Quodlibet – Fabro, Merz, Paolini*, opened July 5, 1979

Munich, Städtische Galerie im Lenbachhaus, *Kunst der 70er Jahre, Werke aus der Sammlung Crex*, September 13 – October 7, 1979. Catalogue with texts by Christel Sauer

Düsseldorf, Galerie Konrad Fischer, *Palermo, Merz, Richter*, October 2 – 23, 1979

Zürich, InK (Halle für internationale neue Kunst), *Merz, Penck, Baumgarten, Penone*, November 12, 1979 – January 6, 1980. Documented in *Dokumentation 5*, Zürich, InK, 1979, publication by Christel Sauer with texts by Peter Blum, Patrick Frey, Dieter Hall, Christel Sauer and Christoph Schenker.

Trans. Patrick Frey and Peter Pasquill

Genazzano, Castello Colonna, *Le Stanze*, November 30, 1979 – February 29, 1980. Catalogue with text by Achille Bonito Oliva and "L'arte povera (dicono)..." by the artist
– Corinna Ferrari, "Le Stanze del Castello (The Rooms of the Castle)," *Domus*, no. 604, March 1980, p. 55

Milan, Galleria Salvatore Ala, *Fabro, Kounellis, Merz, Paolini*, December 1979

Milan, Galleria Salvatore Ala, *Fabro, Kounellis, Merz, Paolini*, February 1980

Kunsthalle Bern, *Fabro, Kounellis, Merz, Paolini: Materialen zu einer Ausstellung*, February – April 7, 1980. Brochure with texts by Johannes Gachnang, Per Kirkeby and Jannis Kounellis and "Ein sehr langer Sonntag dauert annähernd seit 1966 und jetzt sind wir im Jahr 1976" by the artist
– Marlis Grüterich, "Idylle oder Intensität: Beispiel 'Città de Riga,'" *Kunstforum International*, vol. 39, no. 3, 1980, pp.42-47

Karlsruhe, Badischer Kunstverein, *Kunst seit 1960 – Werke aus der Sammlung Crex*, March 18 – May 4, 1980. Catalogue with texts by Christel Sauer
– Irmela Franzke, "Beispiele aus der Sammlung Crex, Zürich im Badischen Kunstverein Karlsruhe," *Kunstforum International*, vol. 38, no. 2, 1980, pp. 248-249

London, Hayward Gallery, *PIER + OCEAN: Construction in the Art of the Seventies*, May 8 – June 22, 1980. Catalogue with texts by Germano Celant, Gerhard von Graevenitz et al. and "For the House" and "Concepts of Space" by the artist. Traveled to Otterlo, Rijksmuseum Kröller-Müller, July 13 – September 8, 1980

Ravenna, Pinacoteca Comunale, *Ut pictura poesis*, May 1980. Catalogue with texts by Mirella Bandini

Venice, *XXXIX Biennale: L'arte negli anni '70*, June 1 – September 30, 1980. Catalogue with texts by Achille Bonito Oliva, Michael Compton, Martin Kunz and Harald Szeemann
– P.F. Althaus, "Zur Biennale in Venedig 1980, Subjektive Bemerkungen und Exkurse," *Kunstnachrichten*, no. 6, November 1980, p. 150
– Bice Curiger, "Biennale in Venedig – Eine Ausstellung fur Kunsttouristen," *Kunst-Bulletin*, no. 9, 1980, p. 4

Lyon, ELAC (Espace Lyonnais d'Art Contemporain), *Europe 80*, June 6 – September 6, 1980. Catalogue with texts by Alain Charre and the artist

Ghent, Museum van Hedendaagse Kunst and Centrum voor Kunst en Cuultur, *Kunst in Europa na '68*, June 21 – August 31, 1980. Catalogue with texts by Alexandra Beaton, Germano Celant, Johannes Cladders, Sandy Nairne et al.
– Laszlo Glozer, "Rauchspuren im Museum – Europalia Gent: Die nicht unterbrochene Poesie in der Kunst nach 1968," *Süddeutsche Zeitung*, August 9-10, 1980

Linz, Österreichisches Institut für visuelle Gestaltung, *Forum Design: Design ist unsichtbar*, June 27 – Öctober 5, 1980. Catalogue with texts by Friedrich Achleitner, Christopher Alexander, Giulio Carlo Argan, Carl Auböck, Gregory Battock, Liesbeth Waechter-Böhm et al.
– Mario Merz, "Mario Merz at 'Forum Design': Pensando si può eseguire...," *Domus*, no. 610, October 1980, p. 49

Dublin, School of Architecture in University College – National Gallery of Ireland, *Rosc '80: the Poetry of Vision, An International Exhibition of Modern Art and Chinese Painting*, July 6 – September 30, 1980. Catalogue with "Look for the First House" by the artist. Trans. Denys Ropp-Zacharopoulos

Turin, Galleria Gian Enzo Sperone, *Giovanni Anselmo, Mario Merz*, opened November 18, 1980

London, Royal Academy of Arts, *A New Spirit in Painting*, January 15 – April 18, 1981. Catalogue with text by Christos M. Joachimides

Rome, Palazzo delle Esposizioni, *Linee della ricerca artistica in Italia 1960-1980*, February 14 – April 15, 1981. Catalogue in 2 vols. with texts by Maurizio Calvesi, Constantin Dardi, Vittorio Fagone, Filiberto Menna, Arturo Carlo Quintavalle and Franco Solmi

Krefeld, Museum Haus Lange, *Kounellis, Merz, Nauman, Serra: Arbeiten im 1968*, March 15 – April 26, 1981. Catalogue with texts by Marianne Stockebrand and Gerhard Storck
– Marlis Grüterich, "Gekochte und halbrohe Mythen des 20. Jahrhunderts – 'Arbeiten um 1968,'" *Kunstforum International*, no. 44-45, May – August 1981, pp. 290-297

Kunstverein Hamburg, *Kunst der 70er Jahre, Werke aus der Sammlung Crex*, April 11 – May 31, 1981. Catalogue with texts by Christel Sauer

Cologne, Rheinhallen, Messegelände, *Westkunst: Zeitgenössische Kunst seit 1939*, May 30 – August 16, 1981. Catalogue with texts by H. Borger, L. Glozer, K. Koenig and K. Ruhrberg

Max Wechsler, "Westkunst," *Kunst-Bulletin*, no. 7-8, July – August 1981, p. 2-9

Paris, Musée National d'Art Moderne, Centre Georges Pompidou, *Identité italienne: L'art en Italie depuis 1959*, June 25 – September 7, 1981. Catalogue by Germano Celant with texts by Maurizio Calvesi, Germano Celant, Carla Lonzi and Alberto Asor Rosa and "Vento preistorico dalle montagne gelate" by the artist. Trans. Jean Georges d'Hoste and Fabio Palmiri

Marie Luise Syring, "Journal ... Frankreich: Italienische Identität," *Du*, no. 9, 1981, p. 108
– Jean-Christophe Ammann, "Identité Italienne: Una scelta per Parigi," *Domus*, no. 621, October 1981, p. 57
– Achille Bonito Oliva, "Così Celant tutti," *Domus*, no. 621, October 1981, pp. 58, 62
– Pierre Restany, "O tempora, o mores!," *Domus*, no. 621, October 1981, p. 58
– Tommaso Trini, "Ricominciare dall'Europa," *Domus*, no. 621, October 1981, pp. 62-63
– Marlis Grüterich, "Italienische Identität oder reiche arme Kunst," *Kunst-Bulletin*, no. 2, February 1982, pp. 2-9

Middletown, Connecticut, Wesleyan University, *No Title: The Collection of Sol Le Witt*, October 21 – December 20, 1981. Organized in association with Wadsworth Atheneum, Hartford. Catalogue with texts by John T. Paoletti, Stephen L. Shriver et al.

Acireale, Palazzo di Città, *XV Rassegna Internazionale d'Arte: Mostra d'Arte*, November 15 – December 31, 1981. Catalogue with text by Achille Bonito Oliva. Trans. Alessandra Bonatti

Canberra, Australian National Gallery at the Australian National University, *Landscape=Art: Two Way Reaction*, December 15 – March 12, 1981. Catalogue with text by Grazia Gunn

Bordeaux, capc/Centre d'Arts Plastiques Contemporains, *Arte povera, antiform: Sculptures 1966-1969*, March 12 – April 30, 1982. Catalogue with texts by Germano Celant
– Xavier Girard, "Arte povera, antiform," *Art Press* (Paris), no. 60, June 1982, p. 34

Amsterdam, Stedelijk Museum, *'60 – '80: attitudes/ concepts/ images*, April 9 – July 11, 1982. Catalogue in 2 vols. with texts by Wim Beeren, Cor Blok, Antje von Graevenitz, Dorinne Mignot, Ad Peterson et al. and "Da almeno due secoli..." by the artist. Trans. Marijke van der Glas, Patty Krone, Yvonne Limburg, J. J. van der Maas, M. E. Muntz et al.

– Jörg Zutter, "Eine der bewegtesten Perioden in der Kunst unseres Jahrhunderts," *Kunstforum International*, no. 51, July 1982, pp. 147-148
– Paul Groot, "Reviews...Amsterdam: '60 – '80: attitudes/ concepts/ images, Stedelijk Museum," *Artforum*, vol. 21, October 1982, pp. 78-79

Rome, Mura Aureliane da Porta Metronia a Porta Latina, *Avanguardia transavanguardia*, April – July 1982. Catalogue with text by Achille Bonito Oliva

Essen, Museum Folkwang, *Mario Merz, Vettor Pisani, Ettore Spalletti*, May 21 – July 4, 1982. Catalogue for each artist with text by Zdenek Felix. Trans. Stephen Reader. Traveled to Stuttgart, Staatsgalerie, August 8 – September 12

Modena, Galleria Civica, *Forma Senza Forma*, May 22 – July 11, 1982. Catalogue by Enzo Bargiacchi. Trans. Charles Lambert and David Ward. Traveled to Pisa, Palazzo Lanfranchi, July 24 – September 19
– Dwight V. Gast, "Galleria Civica: putting the 'mod' in Modena," *Rome Daily American*, June 11, 1982, p. 5

Turin, Galleria Christian Stein, *Anselm Kiefer, Jannis Kounellis, Mario Merz*, opened June 3, 1982

Stuttgart, Württembergischer Kunstverein, *Vergangenheit – Gegenwart – Zukunft. Teil II: Schöpfungsgeschichtliche Grunderfahrungen*, June 9 – August 22, 1982. Catalogue with texts by T. Osterwold et al.

Kassel, Museum Fridericianum, *Documenta 7*, June 19 – September 28, 1982. Catalogue in 2 vols. with texts by Saskia Bos, Coosje van Bruggen, Germano Celant, Johannes Gachnang, Walter Nikkels and Gerhard Storck and "Da sind die Dinge, die man erleidet" (vol. 1) and "Wenn ich auf meine Handfläche..." (vol. 2) by the artist
– Corinna Ferrari, "Mostre – Documenta 7," *FMR*, no. 6, September 1982, pp. 22-23
– Craig Owens, "Bayreuth '82," *Art in America*, vol. 70, September 1982, pp. 131-138, 191
– Chantal Pontbriand, "Commentaires/Reviews – Documenta 7," *Parachute*, no. 28, September – November 1982, pp. 30-32
– Harald Szeemann, Pierre Restany, Jean-Christophe Ammann, Achille Bonito Oliva, Zdenek Felix et al., "Kassel Academy – Documenta 7," *Domus*, no. 632, October 1982, pp. 67-74

Kunsthalle Basel, *Werke aus der Sammlung Crex*, July 18 – September 12, 1982. Catalogue by Christel Sauer with texts by Jean-Christophe Ammann et al. and the artist

New York, The Museum of Modern Art, *New Work on Paper 2 (Borofsky, Clemente, Merz, Penck, Penone)*, July 29 – September 21, 1982. Catalogue with text by Bernice Rose and "from ancient men/the proliferation of eyes" by the artist
– John Russell, "Art: Drawings, Reticent and Bold, at the Modern," *The New York Times*, July 30, 1982, p. C24
– Roberta Smith, "Drawing Fire," *The Village Voice*, vol. 27, August 17, 1982, p. 74
– Kay Larson, "The Powers of Paper," *New York*, vol. 15, August 23, 1982, pp. 74, 76
– Kate Linker, "New Work on Paper 2," *Artforum*, vol. 21, November 1982, pp. 76-77

Ridgefield, Connecticut, Aldrich Museum of Contemporary Art, *PostMINIMALism*, September 19 – December 19, 1982. Catalogue with text by Richard E. Anderson

London, Institute of Contemporary Art and Hayward Gallery, *Arte italiana, 1960-1982*, October 12 – 24, 1982, and October 20, 1982 – January 9, 1983. Organized by Commune di Milano. Catalogue with texts by Guido Ballo, Renato Barilli, Flavio Caroli, Roberto Sanesi and Caroline Tisdall

Berlin, Martin-Gropius-Bau, *Zeitgeist*, October 15, 1982 – January 16, 1983. Catalogue by Christos M. Joachimides and Norman Rosenthal with texts by Walter Bachaurer, Thomas Bernhard, Karl-Heinz Bohrer, Paul Feyerabend, Christos M. Joachimides et al. and "Agli animali/ To the Animals" by the artist. Trans. Jeremy D. Adler, Ulrike Bleicker, Martha Humphrey, David R. McLintock and Mark A. Smith
– Wolfgang Max Faust, Franco Toselli, Corinna Ferrari, "'Zeitgeist' lo spirito dei tempi," *Domus*, no. 634, December 1982, pp. 72-73
– Wolfgang Max Faust, "The Appearance of the Zeitgeist," *Artforum*, vol. 21, January 1983, pp. 86-93

Long Island City, New York, Institute for Art and Urban Resources, P.S. 1, *Beast: Animal Imagery in Recent Painting*, October 17 – December 12, 1982. Catalogue with text by Richard Flood

Madrid, Palacio de las Alhajas, *Correspondencias – 5 Arquitectos, 5 Escultores*, October 19 – November 15, 1982. Catalogue with texts by Santiago Amón, Juan Muñoz and Fran Nelson and "El iglú es el vacio, el iglú es el lleno" by the artist. Trans. Alfonso Lucini and Everett Rice
– Francisco Calvo Serraller, "Las 'correspondencias' entre arquitectura y

escultura, expuestas en las obras de 10 artistas contemporaneos," *El Pais* (Madrid), October 20, 1982, p. 35

Cleveland, New Gallery of Contemporary Art, *New Italian Art*, January 14 – February 12, 1983

Gibellina, Museo Civico d'Arte Contemporanea, *Tema celeste*, January 22 – March 30, 1983. Catalogue with text by Demetrio Paparoni. Trans. Jole Cartia Assennato, Iris Maria Carulli, Henry Meyric Hughes and Anna Eleonore Huth Pignatelli

Milan, Galleria Toselli, *Merz, Paladino, Penck, Vedova*, opened January 29, 1983

Bonner Kunstverein, *Concetto-Imago: Generationswechsel in Italien*, March 18 – May 1, 1983. Catalogue with texts by Zdenek Felix and Margarethe Jochimsen and interview with the artist by Germano Celant

Venice, Chiesa di San Samuele, *Artisti italiani contemporanei 1950-1983*, April 15 – July 15, 1983. Catalogue with text by Achille Bonito Oliva. Trans. Cristopher Huw Evans

Comune di Pescara, *L'Avanguardia Plurale, Italia 1960-70*, April 1983. Catalogue by Roberto Giuseppe Lambarelli

New York, Solomon R. Guggenheim Museum, *Recent European Painting*, May 20 – September 4, 1983

Turin, Accademia Albertina di Belle Arti di Torino, *Arte a Torino 1946/1953*, May 30 – July 17, 1983. Catalogue with texts by Giulio Carlo Argan, Giorgio Auneddu, Mirella Bandini, Giuseppe Mantovani, Francesco Poli et al.

Fiesole, Palazzina Mangani, *Il Grande Disegno*, June 4 – July 24, 1983. Catalogue with text by Vanni Bramanti

Lyon, ELAC (Espace Lyonnais d'Art Contemporain), *Adam la terra*, June 14 – October 18, 1983. Catalogue with text by Alain Charre

Bologna, Galleria d'Arte Moderna, *L'informale in Italia, mostra dedicata a Francesco Arcangeli*, June – September 1983. Catalogue with texts by Francesca Alinovi, Adelaide Auregli, Adriano Baccilieri, Renato Barilli, Alberto Bertoni et al.

Turin, Galleria Christian Stein, *Anselmo, Kounellis, Merz*, opened July 1, 1983

Benevento, Museo del Sannio, *Arcaico Contemporaneo con Tony Cragg, Mario Merz, Bill Woodrow, nella Terra dei Sanniti*, September 3 – October 8,

1983. Catalogue by Ricky Comi
– Enrico R. Comi, "Arcaico Contemporaneo," *Lo Spazio Umano* (Milan), no. 9, October – December 1983, pp. 57-66

London, Tate Gallery, *New Art at the Tate Gallery 1983*, September 14 – October 23, 1983. Catalogue with text by Michael Compton

Cologne, Kölnischer Kunstverein, *Eine Kunst – Geschichte in Turin 1965-1983*, October 8 – November 13, 1983. Catalogue with texts by Germano Celant, Marlis Grüterich and Wulf Herzogenrath

Helsinki, Ateneumin Taidemuseo, *Ars 83, Helsinki*, October 14 – December 11, 1983. Catalogue in 2 vols. with texts by Mats B., Yrjänä Levanto, Barbara J. London, J.O. Mallander and Leena Peltola. Trans. Gaber Abrahamsen, Maria Ahlmén, Harald Arnkil, Susanne Lehtinen, Marjatta Levanto et al.

New York, Solomon R. Guggenheim Museum, *Trends in Postwar American and European Art*, November 8 – 27, 1983

Krefeld, Kaiser Wilhelm Museum, *Sammlung Helga und Walther Lauffs im Kaiser Wilhelm Museum*, November 13, 1983 – April 8, 1984. Catalogue with texts by Julian Heynen, Marianne Stockebrand, Gerhard Storck and Paul Wember

Musée d'Art Moderne de la Ville de Paris, *Electra: l'électricité et l'électronique dans l'art au XXᵉ siècle*, December 10, 1983 – February 15, 1984. Catalogue with texts by Marie-Odile Briot, Frank Popper et al. Trans. Erika Abrams, Anne Barrault, Suzanne de Conninck, Marie-Dominque Dupret, Dagmar Fregnac et al.

Madrid, Casa del Monte, *La Imagen del Animal: Arte Prehistórico, Arte Contemporáneo*, December 1983 – January 1984. Catalogue with texts by Julio Caro Baroja, Joseph Beuys, Ramón Bilboa, Manuel Martín Bueno, Juan Muñoz et al. and "Agli animali!/ A los animales!" by the artist. Trans. Mar Erice, David Reher and Caridad Torres

Los Angeles, California State University, Northridge, Otis Art Institute of Parsons School of Design, Los Angeles Institute of Contemporary Art, University of California, Los Angeles, University of Southern California; Irvine, University of California; Newport Harbor Art Museum; Santa Monica College, *Il Modo Italiano*, January 19 – February 19, 1984. Organized by Los Angeles Contemporary Exhibitions. Catalogue in 2 vols. with texts by Germano Celant and Pier Luigi Tazzi. Trans. Murta Baca

– Christopher Knight, "The blitzkrieg takes hold in L.A.'s art world," *Los Angeles Herald Examiner*, January 8, 1984

Turin, Over Studio, *Que Reste-t-Il*, opened March 23, 1984. Documented in Alain Burnett, "Que reste-t-il," *Panda's Over* (Turin), no. 5, Summer 1984

Brescia, Galleria Massimo Minini, *Dieci Anni*, March 1984

Nice, Villa Arson, Centre National des Arts Plastiques, *Écritures dans la peinture*, April – June 1984. Catalogue in 2 vols. with texts by Jean de Benjy, Michel Giroud, Bernard Lamarche-Vadel, Jean-Clarence Lambert, Gilbert Lascault et al.

Cologne, Galerie Karsten Greve, *Italien (1968) Das Soziale und das Pathos*, May 3 – July 31, 1984. Documented in Irene Saxinger, ed., *Premieren 3.-5.5.84 30 Kölner Galerien und die Museen der Stadt Köln*

Schaffhausen, Switzerland, Hallen für Neue Kunst, *Kunst auf drei Etagen*, opened May 5, 1984. Catalogue with text by Christel Sauer

Paris, Galerie Liliane et Michel Durand-Dessert, *Sculptures italiennes (Anselmo, Fabro, Kounellis, Manzoni, Merz, Pascali)*, May 9 – July 13, 1984
– D. Doebbels, "Sculptures italiennes, Fabro, Anselmo, Penone, Manzoni, Merz et Tutti gli altri plongent en pleine déprime. Plouf!," *Libération* (Paris), June 18, 1984

Kunsthaus Zürich, *Internationale Neue Kunst aus der Sammlung des MGB (Migros-Genossenschafts-Bund)*, May 11 – June 17, 1984. Catalogue with text by Christel Sauer

Turin, Mole Antonelliana, *Coerenza in coerenza: dall'arte povera al 1984*, June 12 – October 14, 1984. Catalogue with text by Germano Celant, chronology edited by Giovanna Castagnoli, Ida Gianelli, Floriana Piqué and "Castello di foglie..." by the artist
– Beatrice Merz, "L'arte povera alla Mole Antonelliana," *Lo Spazio Umano* (Milan), no. 12, July-September 1984, pp. 81-82
– Luciana Rogozinski, "Reviews: Turin – 'Coerenza in coerenza: dall'arte povera al 1984,' Mole Antonelliana," *Artforum*, vol. 23, December 1984, pp. 96-97

Antwerp, Kattendijkdok Westkaai, *Torens van Babel*, June 16 – September 13, 1984. Catalogue with text by the artist

Chicago Public Library Cultural Center in collaboration with Chicago Council on Fine Arts and The Renaissance Society at the University of Chicago,

Contemporary Italian Masters, June 30 – September 8, 1984. Catalogue with texts by Henry Geldzahler and Judith Russi Kirchner

Herculaneum, Villa Campolieto, *Terrae Motus*, July 6 – December 1984. Organized by Fondazione Amelio Istituto per l'Arte Contemporanea, Naples. Catalogue by Michele Bonuomo with texts by Lucio Amelio, Giulio Carlo Argan, Joseph Beuys, Achille Bonito Oliva and Giuseppe Galasso, "Architettura fondata dal tempo/ Architecture built by time" by the artist and interview with Mario Merz by Bruno Corà. Trans. Bruno Arpaia, Diego Cortez, Maria Grazia D'Eboli, Hilary McCann and Alex Simotas
– J. Behrens, "Beherrschte Beben im Palast," *Wolkenkratzer Art Journal* (Frankfurt), no. 4, September – October 1984, pp. 10-15
– Ida Panicelli, "Reviews – Naples: 'Terrae Motus,' Villa Campolieto," *Artforum*, vol. 23, Summer 1985, p. 120

Perugia, Rocca Paolina, Palazzo dei Priori, Palazzo del Capitano del Popolo, *Attraversamenti: linee della nuova arte contemporanea italiana*, September – November 1984. Catalogue by Maurizio Calvesi and Marisa Vescovo

Washington, D.C., Hirshhorn Museum and Sculpture Garden, Smithsonian Institution, *Content: A Contemporary Focus, 1974-1984*, October 4, 1984 – January 6, 1985. Catalogue with texts by Howard N. Fox, Miranda McClintic and Phyllis Rosenzweig and "I Start My Work..." by the artist

Maison de la Culture de Rennes, *Ars+Machina 3: la création artistique et les nouvelles technologies*, October 31 – December 2, 1984. Catalogue with texts by Jean-Christophe Bailly, Dan Flavin, Antonio Guzman, John G. Hanhardt, Pierre Restany et al. and "En pensant on peut exécuter – exécuter n'est pas penser..." by the artist
Joël Benzakin, "Expositions, Rennes – 'Ars + Machina 3' Maison de la Culture," *Art Press* (Paris), no. 88, January 1985, p. 58

Lyon, Musée Saint-Pierre, *Collection 84*, October 1984. Catalogue in 2 vols.

Knokke-le Zoute, Belgium, Garden House, and Brussels, Galerie Albert Baronian, *Il Disegno in dialogo con la terra*, opened November 10 and November 13, 1984, respectively. Catalogue by Beatrice Merz

Eindhoven, Stedelijk Van Abbemuseum, *L'Architecte est absent: works from the collection of Annick and Anton Herbert, répertoire*, November

23, 1984 – January 6, 1985. Catalogue by Rudi H. Fuchs and Jan Debbaut with "Tu giri intorno alle case, o le case girano intorno a te?" by the artist. Trans. Trait d'union, Eindhoven

Turin, Castello di Rivoli, *Ouverture: Arte Contemporanea*, December 18, 1984 – late 1986. Catalogue with text by Rudi H. Fuchs. Trans. Francesco Ciafaloni
– U. A., "Assalto al castello," *Il Giornale dell'Arte* (Turin), vol. 3, January 1985, pp. 18-19
– Leo Van Damme, "Castello di Rivoli – 'Ouverture,'" *Artefactum* (Antwerp), vol. 3, April – May 1986, pp. 14-18, 64-65

Paris, Galerie Antiope France, *L'arte povera et les Anachronistes*, December 21, 1984 – late January 1985
– Anne Dagbert, "Expositions, Paris – L'Arte Povera et les anachron'istes' Galerie Antiope-France," *Art Press* (Paris), no. 89, February 1985, p. 64

Zürich, Annemarie Verna Galerie, *In Exitum Cuiusdam*, December 1984 – January 1985

Düsseldorf, Galerie Mayer Hahn, *Tutti Frutti*, 1984

Madrid, Palacio de Velásquez and Palacio de Cristal, *Del Arte Povera a 1985*, January 24 – April 7, 1985. Catalogue by Germano Celant with texts by Germano Celant, Ida Gianelli and Carmen Giménez and "En la 'Mole Antonelliana'" and "En cambio" by the artist. Trans. Rita de Nardo
– J. Soler, "El arte povera es una Energia," *Diario* (Madrid), January 25, 1985
– Francisco Calvo Serralier and F. Huici, "Arte povera," *El País* (Madrid), January 26, 1985
– Liliana Albertazzi, "Expositions, Madrid – Arte Povera, Palacio Velásquez, Palacio de Cristal," *Art Press* (Paris), no. 92, May 1985, p. 55

Musée d'Art Contemporain de Montréal, *Les Vingt ans du Musée à travers sa collection*, January 27 – April 21, 1985. Catalogue with texts by Paulette Gagnon and Pierre Landry. Trans. Josée Bélisle, René Blouin, Lucette Borchard, Sylvie Gilbert, Gilles Godiner et al.

Toronto, The Art Gallery of Ontario, *The European Iceberg: Creativity in Germany and Italy Today*, February 8 – April 7, 1985. Catalogue by Germano Celant with texts by Giovanni Anceschi, Giuseppe Bartolucci, Vittorio Boarini, Nicoletta Branzi, Bazon Brock et al. Trans. Joachim Neugroschel and Leslie Strickland
– John Bentley Mays, "Reviews, Toronto – 'The European Iceberg,' Art

Gallery of Ontario," *Artforum*, vol. 23, May 1985, p. 116

Frankfurter Kunstverein, *Italienische Kunst 1900-1980: Hauptwerke aus dem Museo d'Arte Contemporanea, Mailand*, February 22 – April 8, 1985. Catalogue with texts by Mercedes Garberi, Flaminio Gualdoni, Marco Meneguzzo, Elena Pontiggia and Peter Weiermair

Tübingen, Kunsthalle, *7000 Eichen*, March 2 – April 14, 1985. Catalogue by Heiner Bastian. Traveled to Bielefeld, Kunsthalle, June 2 – August 11

Lisbon, Fundação Calouste Gulbenkian, Centro de Arte Moderna, *Exhibition-Dialogue: Exposiçao-diálogo*, March 28 – June 16, 1985. Catalogue with texts by Wim A.L. Beeren and René Berger and "Imagination is something that exists/ A imaginação é uma coisa que existe" by the artist. Trans. Cor Blok, Mariada Conceiço, Sousa Macedo Estameja, John Gabriel, Ruth Koenig et al.

Paris, Grande Halle de la Villette, *Nouvelle Biennale de Paris, 1985*, March 28 – June 16, 1985. Catalogue with texts by Achille Bonito Oliva, Georges Boudaille, Pierre Courcelles, Jean-Pierre Faye, Gérald Gassiot-Talabot et al. and "Musée naturel/ Museum of nature..." by the artist. Trans. Catherine Amidon-Kayoun, Elizabeth Chenet-Muñoz, Raymonde Coudert, Anne Dagbert, Simonetta Greggio et al.
– Chantal Béret, "L'architecture vue de l'intérieur," *Art Press* (Paris), no. 90, March 1985, p. 14
– Achille Bonito Oliva, "Eclectique et internationale," *Art Press* (Paris), no. 90, March 1985, pp. 9-10
– Georges Boudaille, "Des oeuvres qui dialoguent avec l'espace," *Art Press* (Paris), no. 90, March 1985, pp. 7-8
– Gérald Gassiot-Talabot, "Une biennale volontariste," *Art Press* (Paris), no. 90, March 1985, pp.11-12
– Alanna Heiss, "Une rétrospective," *Art Press* (Paris), no. 90, March 1985, pp. 10-11
– Kasper Koenig, "Un moment transitoire," *Art Press* (Paris), no. 90, March 1985, pp. 8-9
– Philippe du Vignal, "Les mises en scène du son," *Art Press* (Paris), no. 90, March 1985, pp. 12-13
– Lucia Spadano, "Nouvelle Biennale de Paris," *Segno* (Pescara), no. 46, May 1985, pp. 20-29
– Denys Zacharopoulos, "Reviews – Paris: Nouvelle Biennale de Paris, Grand Halle de la Villette," *Artforum*, vol. 24, September 1985, pp. 133-134

Milan, Galleria Franco Toselli, April 22, 1985

Geneva, Parc Lullin, *Promenades*, June

8 – September 8, 1985. Organized by Centre d'Art Contemporain, Geneva. Catalogue by Adelina von Furstenberg with texts by Bruno Corà, Adelina von Furstenberg and Denys Zacharopoulos. Trans. Henry Daussy and Giovanni Polito
– Corinna Ferrari, "En plein air/ 'Promenades' a Ginevra," *Domus*, no. 664, September 1985, pp. 90-91

Nice, Centre Nationale d'Art Contemporain, Villa Arson, *L'Italie d'Aujourd'hui/Italia Oggi*, June 14 – October 14, 1985. Catalogue in 2 vols. with texts by Achille Bonito Oliva, Michel Butor, Maurizio Calvesi, Antonio Del Guercio and Filiberto Menna

Esslingen am Neckar, West Germany, Galerie der Stadt, *Sein und Sehnsucht: 10 italienische Künstler der 60er und 70er Jahre*, July 19 – August 25, 1985. Organized by Galerie Tanit, Munich. Catalogue with texts by Ingrid Rein and Alexander Tolnay. Traveled to Kunstverein Kassel, October 1985

Krefeld, Museum Haus Lange and Museum Haus Esters, *Dreissig Jahre durch die Kunst*, September 15 – December 1985. Catalogue in 2 vols. with texts by Britta Buhlmann, Julian Heynen, Christian Nagel, Gerhard Storck and Paul Wember

Long Island City, New York, Institute for Art and Urban Resources, P.S. 1, *The Knot: Arte Povera at P.S. 1*, October 6 – December 15, 1985. Catalogue by Germano Celant with texts by Germano Celant. Trans. Joachim Neugroschel
– Monica Amari, "Cinquemila metri quadri di arte povera," *Il Sole 24 Ore* (Milan), September 22-23, 1985
– "Le Mostre: Al P.S. One: L'arte povera e la ricca New York: la mostra più impegnativa dei 12 artisti italiani," *Il Giornale dell'Arte* (Turin), vol. 3, September 1985, p.8
– Tommaso Trini, "I 'Poveri' Italiani a New York," *Epoca* (Rome), vol. 36, October 3, 1985, p. 64
– Mario Albertazzi, "'Prima' di rilievo in Usa dell'Arte Povera Italiana," *Il Progresso*, October 13, 1985
– Grace Glueck, "Conceptual Art, Italian Style Makes a Statement at P.S. 1," *The New York Times*, October 13, 1985, Sect. 2, p. 29
– Vivien Raynor, "Art: From Italy, a Show of 12 Called 'The Knot,'" *The New York Times*, October 18, 1985, p. C26
– "Pioggia di mostre a New York," *Libertà* (Piacenza), October 21, 1985
– Paolo Rizzi, "Arte povera italiana nelle ricca New York," *Il Gazzettino* (Venice), October 22, 1985
– Kenneth Baker, "New York is rich in 'Poor Art,'" *San Francisco Chronicle*,

October 29, 1985
– Gary Indiana, "Now, Voyager," *The Village Voice*, October 29, 1985
– Enrico R. Comi, "Luci sull'Arte Povera," *Lo Spazio Umano*, October – December 1985, pp. 80-92
– E. C., "New York, riflettori sull'Italia," *La Stampa* (Turin), November 7, 1985, p. 3
– Kay Larson, "Hard hats, soft heads," *New York*, vol. 18, November 11, 1985, pp. 122, 124
– Alan Jones, "The Knot: Arte Povera à P.S.1, New York," *Galeries Magazine*, no. 7, November 1985, pp. 17-23. Trans. Marie-France Azar
– Iseki Masaaki, "A review of Arte Povera," *Bijutsu Techo*, no. 553, November 1985, pp. 60-69
– Robert Nickas, "The Knot – Arte Povera at P.S. 1," *East Village Eye* (New York), November 1985
– Renato Barilli, "Poveri ma belli," *L'Espresso* (Rome), vol. 31, December 1, 1985, pp. 191-192
– David Bourdon, "Italian Alchemy: The riches of 'poor art,'" *Vogue* (New York), December 1985
– Michèle Cone, "New York – The Knot Arte Povera, PS1," *Flash Art*, no. 125, December 1985-January 1986, p. 42
– Lucio Pozzi, "Italiani poveri e poveri americani," *Il Giornale dell'Arte* (Turin), vol. 3, December 1985, p. 30
– "Mostre – The Knot," *Il Giornale dell'Arte* (Turin), vol. 3, December 1985
– Henriette Väth-Hinz, "Gordischer Knoten," *Wolkenkratzer Art Journal* (Frankfurt), no. 10, Winter 1985/86, pp. 69-71
– Jane Bell, "Arte Povera, P.S. 1," *Art News*, vol. 85, January 1986, pp. 131-132
– Jeanne Silverthorne, "Reviews: 'The Knot: Arte Povera at P.S. 1,'" *Artforum*, vol. 24, January 1986, pp. 90-91
– Barry Schwabsky, "Reviews, New York – 'The Knot *Arte Povera*' at PS 1," *Artscribe*, no. 56, February – March 1986, p. 75
– Tsipi Ben-Haim, "The Knot – Arte Povera," *Sculpture*, March – April 1986
– Stephen Westfall, "Anything, Anytime, Anywhere: Arte Povera at P.S. 1," *Art in America*, vol. 74, May 1986, pp. 132-137, 169

Paris, Galeries Nationales du Grand Palais, *Anciens et Nouveaux*, 1985

New York, Solomon R. Guggenheim Museum, *Transformations in Sculpture: Four Decades of American and European Art*, November 22, 1985 – February 16, 1986. Catalogue with text by Diane Waldman

Rome, Galleria Mario Pieroni, *Mario Merz – Sol Lewitt*, December 1985. Catalogue with text by Bruno Corà
– Luigi Mango, "Alberi e piramidi per un duetto tra pittori," *Paese Sera* (Rome), December 30, 1985, p. 7
– Demetrio Paparoni, "Sentiero per qui. Mario Merz," *Tema Celeste* (Siracusa), no. 8, May 1986, pp. 18-21, 53-54
– Tommaso Trini, "LeWitt (Abitare l'Abisso) Merz," *Tema Celeste* (Siracusa), no. 8, May 1986, pp. 22-28, 54-56
– Pier Luigi Tazzi, "Reviews – Rome: Sol LeWitt and Mario Merz, Galleria Mario Pieroni," *Artforum*, vol. 24, Summer 1986, p. 134

Turin, Castello di Rivoli, *Il Museo Sperimentale di Torino: Arte Italiana degli Anni Sessanta nelle collezioni della Galleria Civica d'Arte Moderna*, December 1985 – February 1986. Catalogue with texts by Mirella Bandini, Maria Teresa Roberto and Rosanna Maggio Serra

Alsace, F.R.A.C. et locales de Cédric Selestat, *Acquisitions 1984*, 1985

Lagège-Innôpole, France, Centre Régional d'art Contemporain, *Collection du F.R.A.C. Midi-Pyrénées*, 1985

Lille, Musée de l'Hospice Comtesse, *Collection du F.R.A.C. Nord-Pas-de-Calais*, 1985

Lyon, Musée Saint-Pierre, *Collection 1985*, 1985

Frankfurter Kunstverein, *1960-1985 Aspekte der italienischen Kunst*, January 17 – February 23, 1986. Catalogue with texts by Renato Barilli, Flavio Caroli and Concetto Pozzati. Traveled to Berlin, Haus am Waldsee; Hannover Kunstverein; Bregenz, Kunstverein Kunstlerhaus – Palais Thurn und Taxis; Vienna, Hochschule für augewandte Kunst. Trans. Fried Rosenstock

Siracusa, Sicily, Chiesa dei Cavalieri di Malta, *Mater Dulcissima*, January 18 – February 19, 1986. Catalogue with texts by Michelangelo Castello and Demetrio Paparoni and "Castello di foglie/ Castle of Leaves," "Pensando si puó eseguire/ Thinking one can execute" and "Per la Pittura del Torrente/ To Paint a Torrent" by the artist. Trans. Giuseppina Carveni, Lucia Davies, Alexandra Miletta and Emma Sessa

Milan, *Triennale di Milano*, January 1986

New York, Barbara Gladstone Gallery, *Alighiero Boetti, Luciano Fabro, Jannis Kounellis, Piero Manzoni, Mario Merz, Giulio Paolini, Pino Pascali, Michelangelo Pistoletto*, March 8 – 29, 1986. Organized in association with Galerie Rudolf Zwirner, Cologne

London, Hayward Gallery, *Falls the Shadow: Recent British and European Art*, April 9 – June 15, 1986. Catalogue with texts by Barry Barker and Jon Thompson

Oslo, Kunstnernes Hus, *Fra Usikkerhet til Samlet Kraft...*, April 26 – June 8, 1986. Individual catalogues for each of 6 artists included in exhibition; *Mario Merz* with text by Beatrice Merz and "la terra/il mare/l'aria," "Se la nostra cara orecchia è.../If our beloved ear is..." and "Scendendo il fiume/Going downstream in the river" by the artist. Trans. Eddie Allen and Wenche Gulbransen

Chicago, Rhona Hoffman Gallery, *Giovanni Anselmo, Luciano Fabro, Jannis Kounellis, Mario Merz, Giulio Paolini, Gilberto Zorio*, May 16 – June 28, 1986

Vienna, Wiener Festwochen im Messepalast, *De Scultura*, May 16 – July 20, 1986. Catalogue by Rudi Fuchs with texts by Rudi Fuchs

Arnhem, The Netherlands, Park Sonsbeek, *Sonsbeek 86: Internationale Beelden Tentoonstelling = International Sculpture Exhibition*, June 18 – September 14, 1986. Catalogue in 2 vols. by Saskia Bos and Jan Brand with texts by Saskia Bos, Marianne Brouwer and Antje von Graevenitz (vol. 1) and "brief te midden van de bomen/ letter in between the trees" (vol. 2) by the artist. Trans. Michael Gibbs, Barbara Fasting et al.
– Pier Luigi Tazzi, Paul Groot and Annelie Pohlen, "Sculpture in Review, Critics & Curators: What is today's sculpture? Three views," *Artforum*, vol. 25, September 1986, pp. 149-152

Ghent, Abbaye Saint-Pierre, *Initiatief 86*, June 21 – September 21, 1986. Catalogue

Ghent, Museum van Hedendaagse Kunst, *Chambre d'Amis*, June 21 – September 21, 1986. Catalogue with text by Jan Hoet and "Tavola che diventa scultura..." by the artist. Trans. Anita Buysse, Maria Negroni, Godfried Van Calbergh and Sabine Visser
– Paul Groot, "Chambres d'Amis," *Wolkenkratzer Art Journal* (Frankfurt), no. 13, June – July – August 1986, pp. 74-79
– Rony Heirman, "Chambres d'Amis – Gent," *Artefactum*, (Antwerp), vol. 3, September – October 1986, p. 48
– Johanne Lamoureux, "Chambres d'amis/ Le Biennale de Venise," *Parachute*, no. 44, September – October – November 1986, pp. 57-60

Bari, Gipsoteca del Castello Svevo, *Sculture da Camera, Chamber Sculptures*, June 1986. Organized by Galleria Marilena Bonomo. Catalogue by Valentina Bonomo and Attilio Maranzano with texts by Francesco Vincitorio. Trans. Myriam Bellini and Magda Bonomo

Venice, *XLII Biennale: Arte e Scienza – Wunderkammer: artisti di oggi e Camere delle meraviglie; Arte e alchimia*, June – September 1986. Catalogue in 4 vols.: *Wunderkammer* by Adalgisa Lugli, *Arte e alchimia* by Arturo Schwarz. Trans. Loredana Bolzan, Silvia Bortoli, Licia Fiandesio, Geraldine Ludbrook, Salvatore Mele et al.

Paris, Musée National d'Art Moderne, Centre Georges Pompidou, *Qu'est-ce que la sculpture moderne?*, July 3 – October 13, 1986. Catalogue by Margit Rowell with texts by Benjamin H.D. Buchloh, Jean-Pierre Criqui, Thierry de Duve, Rosalind Krauss, Franz Meyer et al. Trans. Pierre Bourlis, Nathalie Brunet, Jean-Pierre Criqui, Didier Don, Claude Gintz et al.
– Michael Brenson, "A Show in Paris Asks what Makes Modern Sculpture Distinct," *The New York Times*, July 20, 1986, Sect. 2, pp. 29-30

Genazzano, Castello Colonna, *Sogno Italiano: La collezione Franchetti a Roma*, July 5 – October 31, 1986. Catalogue by Achille Bonito Oliva

Munich, Städtische Galerie im Lenbachhaus, *BEUYS zu Ehren*, July 16 – November 2, 1986. Catalogue by Armin Zweite with texts by Lucio Amelio, Johannes Cladders, Klaus Gallwitz, Laszlo Glozer, Georg Jappe et al. Trans. Johanna Eltz, Helmut Friedel, Lucia Luger-Stock, John Ormrod and Claudia Schinkievicz

Cologne, Museum Ludwig, *Europa/ Amerika: die Geschichte einer Künstlerischen Faszination seit 1940*, September 6 – November 30, 1986. Catalogue by Siegfried Gohr and Rafael Jablonka with texts by Craig Adcock, Dore Ashton, Alberto Boatto, John Cage, Henning Christiansen et al.

Philadelphia Museum of Art, *Philadelphia Collects: Art Since 1940*, September 28 – November 30, 1986. Catalogue with texts by Mark Rosenthal and Amy Ship

Marseilles, Galerie Roger Pailhas, *Inauguration: Daniel Buren, Toni Grand, Jannis Kounellis, Sol LeWitt, Mario Merz, Bruce Nauman*, October 15 – November 22, 1986
– Marc Partouche, "Expositions, Marseilles: Kounellis, Merz, Buren, Nauman, Grand, LeWitt, Della-Noce, Galerie Roger Pailhas," *Art Press* (Paris), no. 110, January 1987, p. 72

Los Angeles County Museum of Art, *The Spiritual in Art: Abstract Painting 1890-1985*, November 23, 1986 –

March 8, 1987. Catalogue with texts by Carel Blotkamp, John E. Bowlt, Charlotte Douglas, Charles C. Eldredge, Robert Galbreath et al. Traveled to Chicago, Museum of Contemporary Art, April 17 – July 19; The Hague, Haags Gemeentemuseum, September 1 – November 22

Zürich, Annemarie Verna Galerie, *Open-House of the Zürich Galleries*, November 1986

Milan, Padiglione d'Arte Contemporanea, *Il Cangiante*, December 4, 1986 – January 25, 1987. Catalogue by Corrado Levi

Dunkerque, F.R.A.C. Nord Pas-de-Calais, Musée des Beaux-Arts, *Selection d'oeuvres*, 1986

Graz, Austria, Stadtmuseum, *Die Wahlverwandtschaften-Zitate*, 1986. Catalogue by Peter Pakesch with texts by Elechi Amadi, Alberto Boatto, Konrad Bayer, Elias Canetti, Daniil Charms et al. and "Cerca la prima casa..." by the artist
– Lidia Reghini di Pontremoli, "Die Wahlwerwandtschaften-Zitate, Stadtmuseum, Graz," *Tema Celeste* (Siracusa), no. 10, January – March 1987, pp. 67-68, 89-90

Grenoble, F.R.A.C. Rhone-Alpes, *Uno sguardo: Un régard de Bruno Corà sur les oeuvres du F.R.A.C. Rhone-Alpes*, 1986

Opéra de Lille, *Sculpture et musique*, 1986

Macon, Ecole Régionale des Beaux-Arts, *Anselmo, Merz, Zorio*, 1986. Catalogue

Paris, Galerie Liliane et Michel Durand-Dessert, *Arte povera: 1965-1971*, January 10 – February 28, 1987
– F. Huser, "Jeu de ficelle, jeu de vilain," *Nouvel Observateur* (Paris), January 23, 1987
– Ph. Dagen, "Arte povera," *Le Monde*, January 24, 1987, p. 19
– Maïten Bouisset, "Arte povera: le whose's who de la pauvreté," *Le Matin*, January 31, 1987
– Maïten Bouisset, "Douze apôtres de l'ultra-minimalisme," *Le Matin*, January 31, 1987
– Pierre Cabanne, "Les riches heures de la pauvreté," *Le Matin*, January 31, 1987
– Gilles de Bure, "Riche art pauvre," *Vogue Homme*, February 1987, p. 65
– Michel Nuridsany, "Art Pauvre: l'insignifiant manifeste," *Le Figaro*, February 17, 1987, p. 27

London, Anthony d'Offay Gallery, *About Sculpture*, January 28 – March 5, 1987. Catalogue

Venice, Palazzo Grassi, *Effetto Arcimboldo: The Arcimboldo Effect: Transformations of the Face from the Sixteenth to the Twentieth Century*, February 15 – May 31, 1987. Catalogue with texts by Sven Alfons, Massimo Cacciari, Jean Clair, Salvador Dali, Paolo Fabbri et al. Trans. Lisa Clark, Patrick Creagh, Margaret Kunzle, Robert Mann, Crispin Mason et al.
– "Le Mostre – Palazzo Grassi – Dopo Arcimboldo, Tinguely che andrà a Torino," *Il Giornale dell'Arte* (Turin), vol. 5, February 1987, p. 18
– "Le Mostre – Arcimboldo, effetto polemica," *Il Giornale dell'Arte* (Turin), vol. 5, March 1987, pp. 19-20
– Corinna Ferrari, "Lo spazio è Merz: tre eventi," *Domus*, no. 685, July – August 1987, pp. 9-10

Chambéry, Musée Savoisien, *Turin 1965-1987: De l'Arte Povera dans les collections publiques françaises*, March 7 – May 11, 1987. Catalogue with texts by Gérard Labrot and Bernard Marcadé and interview with Germano Celant by Daniel Soutif. Trans. Gaudenzio D'Alessandro and Luigiano Zecchin. Traveled to Lille, Musée de l'Hospice Comtesse, June 13 – August 30; Musée d'Art la Roche-sur-Yon, September 21 – November 16
– Elisabeth Bozzi, "A Chambéry: Turin 1965-1987, De l'arte povera dans les collections publiques françaises," *New Art International* (Lausanne), no. 3-4, May 1987, pp. 52f.

New York, Barbara Gladstone Gallery, *Alighiero Boetti, Luciano Fabro, Pier Paolo Calzolari, Jannis Kounellis, Mario Merz*, March 7-28, 1987
– Daniela Salvioni, "Reviews: New York...Arte Povera, Barbara Gladstone," *Flash Art*, no. 135, Summer 1987, p. 106

Ravenna, Loggetta Lombardesca, *Disegnata: Percorsi del disegno italiano dal 1945 ad oggi*, March 21 – May 31, 1987. Catalogue by Concetto Pozzati with Silvia Evangelisti with texts by Alberto Boatto, Silvia Evangelisti, Concetto Pozzati and Eduardo Sanguineti

Chicago, Rhona Hoffman Gallery, *Light Works*, March 27 – April 25, 1987

Paris, Galeries Nationales du Grand Palais, *Terrae Motus, Naples, tremblements de terre*, March 28 – May 11, 1987. Coorganized with Fondazione Amelio – Istituto per l'Arte Contemporanea, Naples. Catalogue by Michele Bonuomo and Ramon Tio Bellido with texts by Giulio Carlo Argan, Ramon Tio Bellido Joseph Beuys, Achille Bonito Oliva, Michele Bonuomo and Giuseppe Galasso and "Architettura fondata dal tempo..." by the artist. Trans. Tania Bitan, Eve Dayre, Maria Grazia D'Eboli, Joan Olivar, Cathérine Routelli et al.

London, Anthony d'Offay Gallery, *Drawings*, May 1 – 29, 1987

Turin, Galleria Eva Menzio, opened May 6, 1987

Paris, Musée National d'Art Moderne, Centre Georges Pompidou, *L'époque, la mode, la morale, la passion: Aspects de l'art d'aujourd'hui 1977-1987*, May 21 – August 17, 1987. Catalogue with texts by Bernard Blistène, Bernard Ceysson, Jean-François Chevrier, Serge Daney, Catherine David et al.

Erice, La Salerniana, ex Convento S. Carlo, *Incrocio*, June 6 – July 12, 1987. Catalogue with texts by Rudi Fuchs and Johannes Gachnang

Westfälischen Landesmuseum für Kunst und Kulturgeschichte in der Stadt Münster, *Skulptur Projekte in Münster 1987*, June 14 – October 4, 1987. Catalogue by Klaus Bussmann and Kasper König with texts by Marianne Brouwer, Benjamin H.D. Buchloh, Antje von Graevenitz, Thomas Kellein, Hannelore Kersting et al. and "Die optische Ebene" and "Draussen" by the artist. Trans. Klaus Bussmann, Edith Decker, Georg Jappe and Brigitte Kalthoff

Milan, Galleria Christian Stein, *Anselmo, Boetti, Kounellis, Paolini, Penone, Zorio*, Summer 1987

Spoleto, Chiesa di San Nicolò, *L'Attico 1957 – 1987, 30 anni di pittura, scultura, musica, danza, performance, video*, July 1 – August 30, 1987. Catalogue with texts by Renato Barilli, Alberto Boatto, Achille Bonito Oliva, Maurizio Calvesi, Luciano Giaccari, et al.

Nîmes, Musée d'Art Contemporain, *Italie Hors D'Italie*, July 10 – September 30, 1987. Catalogue by Johannes Gachnang with texts by Rudi Fuchs, Johannes Gachnang, Remo Guidieri, Alessandra Lukinovich and Jole de Sanna. Trans. Evelyne Giumelli, Alessandra Lukinovich and Madeleine Rousset

Turin, Galleria Civica d'Arte Moderna, *1945-1965 Arte italiana e straniera*, July – October 1987. Catalogue with texts by Paolo Fossati, Marco Rosci and Rosanna Maggio Serra

Lyon, Musée Saint-Pierre, *Sol LeWitt + Mario Merz*, October 9 – November 23, 1987. Brochure with anonymous text

Madrid, Centro de Arte Reina Sofia, *Colección Sonnabend: 25 años de selección y de actividad*, October 30, 1987 – February 15, 1988. Conceived by capc/Musée d'Art Contemporain de Bordeaux. Catalogue, in language of each venue, with texts by Achille Bonito Oliva, Michel Bourel, Germano Celant, Jean-Louis Froment, Michel Guy et al. Traveled to capc/Musée d'Art Contemporain de Bordeaux, May 6 – August 21; Berlin, Hamburger Bahnhof, December 7, 1988 – February 26, 1989; Rome, Galleria Nazionale d'Arte Moderna e Contemporanea, April 14 – October 2
– Barbara Tosi, "Exhibitions: Sonnabend Collection," *Contemporanea*, July-August 1989, vol. 2, p. 94

Turin, Galleria Eva Menzio, *Ritrattare*, opened December 9, 1987. Catalogue by Achille Bonito Oliva
– "Ritrattare," *Flash Art* (Italian Edition), no. 137, February – March 1987, p. 82

New York, Barbara Gladstone Gallery, *Pier Paolo Calzolari, Jenny Holzer, Joseph Kosuth, Mario Merz, Bruce Nauman, Keith Sonnier*, March 12 – April 2, 1988

Munich, Bayerische Staatsgemäldesammlungen and Ausstellungsleitung Haus der Kunst, *Mythos Italien-Wintermärchen Deutschland: die italienische Moderne und ihr Dialog mit Deutschland*, March 24 – May 29, 1988. Catalogue by Carla Schulz-Hoffmann with texts by Achille Bonito Oliva, Germano Celant, Maurizio Fagiolo dell'Arco, Zdenek Felix, Helmut Friedel et al.

Zürich, Annemarie Verna Galerie, *Gallery Group Exhibition*, March – April 1988

New York, The Museum of Modern Art, *Contemporary Print Acquistions 1986-88*, March 24 – July 19, 1988

Milan, Galleria Christian Stein, *Andre, Fabro, Kounellis, Long, Merz, Nauman, Weiner*, opened June 16, 1988

Berlin, Hamburger Bahnhof, *Zeitlos: Kunst von Heute im Hamburger Bahnhof, Berlin*, June 22 – September 25, 1988. Catalogue supplement with text by Markus Brüderlin
– John T. Paoletti, "Letter from Germany," *Arts*, vol. 64, October 1988, pp. 106-109
– Tony Godfrey, "Report from Germany: A Tale of Four Cities," *Art in America*, vol. 76, November 1988, pp. 33-41

Berlin, Nationalgalerie, *Positionen heutiger Kunst*, June 23 – September 18, 1988. Catalogue with texts by Germano Celant, Bruno Corà, Wulf Herzogenrath, Dieter Honisch, Katherina Schmidt and Hans Strelow. Trans. Isolde Eckle and Verena Listl

Prato, Museo d'Arte Contemporanea,

Europa oggi: arte contemporanea nell'Europa occidentale/ Europe Now: Contemporary Art in Western Europe, June 25 – October 20, 1988. Catalogue by Amnon Barzel with texts by Carlo Bertelli, Achille Bonito Oliva, Bruno Corà, Gillo Dorfles, Helmut Draxler et al. and "un sasso è bene/ a rock is good" by the artist

Rotterdam, *Rotterdam 88, la città: un palcoscenico*, Summer – October 1, 1988
– Reyn Van Der Lugt, "Rotterdam: la città delle sculture," *Domus*, no. 697, September 1988, pp. 4-5

Pecetto, Giardini pubblici, *Sotto le antenne del cielo*, July 1988

Turin, Galleria Ippolito Simonis, *Anselmo, Boetti, Festa, Mainolfi, Merz*, September 15 – October 31, 1988

Frankfurt, Städtische Galerie im Städelschen Kunstinstitut, *Disegno Italiano: Italienische Zeichnungnen 1908/1988*, September 22 – November 6, 1988. Catalogue with texts by Carlo Bertelli, Vittorio Fagone, Ada Masoero, Edwald Rathke and Margret Stuffmann. Heide Röhrscheid and Annette Seemann. Traveled to Berlin, Staatliche Museen Preussischer Kulturbesitz and Kupferstichkabinett, December 10, 1988 – February 19, 1989; Kunsthaus Zürich, March 3 – May 7

Maastricht, The Netherlands, Bonnefantenmuseum, *Accademia*, October 2, 1988 – January 9, 1989

Paris, Galerie Liliane et Michel Durand-Dessert, *Nature Morte*, November 24, 1988 – January 14, 1989

Milan, Studio Guenzani, *Neon Light: Pier Paolo Calzolari, Dan Flavin, Joseph Kosuth, Mario Merz, Keith Sonnier*, December 1, 1988 – January 1, 1989

Mönchengladbach, West Germany, Städtisches Museum Abteiberg, *Kunst der Gegenwart, 1960 bis Ende der 80er Jahre*, 1988

London, Royal Academy of Arts, *Italian Art in the 20th Century: Painting and Sculpture 1900-1988*, January 14 – April 9, 1989. Catalogue by Emily Braun with texts by Paolo Baldacci, Carlo Bertelli, Emily Braun, Germano Celant, Alberto Asor Rosa et al. Trans. David Britt, John Mitchell, Meg Shore and Shara Wasserman

Milan, PAC/Padiglione d'arte contemporanea, *Verso l'arte povera: Momenti e aspetti degli anni sessanta in Italia*, January 20 – March 27, 1989. Catalogue with texts by Marco Meneguzzo and Paolo Thea. Trans. Howard Rodger MacLean. Traveled to Lyon, ELAC (Espace Lyonnais d'Art Con-

temporain), June 24 – September 6

Rovereto, Palazzo dell'Istruzione, *I monti pallidi*, January – May 1989. Catalogue with texts by Marlis Grüterich

New York, Barbara Gladstone Gallery, *Jannis Kounellis/Mario Merz: Selected Works*, February 2 – 25, 1989

Paris, Galerie Liliane et Michel Durand-Dessert, *Hommage aux collections particulières en France*, March 2 – April 18, 1989

Bari, Santa Scolastica, *Collections du Fonds Régional d'Art Contemporain Nord Pas-de-Calais*, March 15 – April 26, 1989. Catalogue with texts by Martine Buissart, Jo Coucke, Claude Courtecuisse, Caroline David and Gérard Durozoi. Trans. Angela Casone

Elisabeth Bozzi, "Du Nord au Sud," *New Art International*, no. 3, May 1989, pp. 60-63

Musée Cantonal des Beaux-Arts de Lausanne, *Collection FCM: Mario Merz, Jannis Kounellis, Giuseppe Penone, Enzo Cucchi*, Spring 1989. Brochure with text by Jacqueline Burckhardt. Trans. Diana de Rham Jotterand

Cologne, Rheinhallen, *Bilderstreit*, April 8 – July 2, 1989. Catalogue
– Lucille Beyer, "Reviews...Germany – Bilderstreit, Rheinhallen Fair Center, Cologne," *Flash Art*, no. 147, Summer 1989, p. 154

Turin, Salone del Libro – Torino Esposizioni, *Allestimento di opere di arte povera*, May 12 – 18, 1989

Paris, Musée National d'Art Moderne, Centre Georges Pompidou, and La Villette, *Magiciens de la Terre*, May 18 – August 14, 1989. Catalogue with texts by Homi Bhabha, Mark Francis, Pierre Gaudibert, Aline Luque et al. and "Liberté de Lecture en prison..." by the artist. Trans. Jeanne Bouniort, Christian-Martin Diebold, Sylvia Fernandez and Elisabeth Galloy

Basel, Galerie Littmann, June 8 – October 15, 1989, *Stücki 1*, June 9 – September 10, 1989

Turin, Parco Michelotti, *Hic sunt leones*, July 1 – September 3, 1989

Turin, Arboreto dell'Orto Botanico, *Hortus artis*, opened September 14, 1989

II. Solo Exhibitions and Reviews

Turin, Galleria La Bussola, opened June 8, 1954
– M. Bernardi, "Mostre d'arte – Mario Merz," *La Stampa* (Turin), June 9, 1954
– Luciano Pistoi, "Mario Merz alla Bussola," *L'Unità* (Turin), June 10, 1954
– Luigi Carluccio, "Mario Merz," *Gazzetta del Popolo* (Turin), June 17, 1954

Turin, Galleria Notizie: Associazione Arti Figurative, *Dipinti di Merz*, April 11, 1962. Catalogue with text by Carla Lonzi
– Angelo Dragone, "Il caso Merz," *Stampa Sera* (Turin), April 16-17, 1962

Turin, Galleria Gian Enzo Sperone, January 19 – February 8, 1968. Catalogue with text by Germano Celant

Rome, Galleria L'Attico, *Che fare?*, opened February 5, 1969

Turin, Galleria Gian Enzo Sperone, opened March 1969

Paris, Galerie Sonnabend, opened April 22, 1969. Catalogue with text by Michael Sonnabend

Düsseldorf, Galerie Konrad Fischer, *Igloo Fibonacci*, March 7 – 31, 1970

New York, Sonnabend Gallery and Sonnabend Auxiliary Space, April 25 – May 14, 1970

Milan, Galleria Françoise Lambert, *Sciopero generale azione politica relativa proclamata relativamente all'arte*, October 1 – November 3, 1970

Turin, Galleria Gian Enzo Sperone, opened March 27, 1971

New York, Sonnabend Gallery and John Weber Gallery, December 11, 1971 – January 5, 1972

Minneapolis, Walker Art Center, January 29 – March 19, 1972. Brochure with interview with the artist by Richard Koshalek
– Carter Ratcliff, "New York Letter," *Art International*, vol. 16, February 1972, pp. 32-34, 52-56

London, Jack Wendler Gallery, *A real sum is a sum of people*, May 2 – 16, 1972

New York, John Weber Gallery, *it is Possible to Have a Space with Tables for 88 people as it is Possible to Have a Space with Tables for No One, Tables from Drawings of Mario Merz*, November 10 – December 5, 1973. Catalogue with "Projected Table for a House..." by the artist, published by John Weber Gallery, New York and Jack Wendler Gallery, London, 1974

Berlin, Haus am Lützowplatz, DAAD (Deutscher Akademischer Austausch-

dienst), *Mario Merz*, March 19 – April 20, 1974. Catalogue with texts by Karl Ruhrberg and Wieland Schmied, "Was ist der Unterschied zwischen Professor-Sein und Nicht-Professor-Sein?," "Do the houses turn around you or do you turn around the houses," and "L'immaginazione vivente è in movimento continuo..." by the artist and interview with the artist by Michael Haerdter
– Heinz Ohff, "Mario Merz," *Das Kunstwerk*, vol. 27, May 1974, p. 67

London, Jack Wendler Gallery, June 14 – July 5, 1974

Florence, Galleria Area, opened October 5, 1974

Tortona, Cascina Ova, *Mario Merz*, October 1974. Catalogue with "Tavole con le zampe diventano tavoli" by the artist, published by Edizioni Toselli, Milan

Milan, Galleria Toselli, *Mario Merz*, November – December 1974

Kunsthalle Basel, *Mario Merz*, January 11 – February 16, 1975. Catalogue with text by Carlo Huber and "Die Fibonacci – Zahlen und die Kunst," "Mann kommt nicht um die Tatsache der Zahlen herum...," "Der Betrag, den der Neue Berliner Kunstverein dem eingeladenen Künstler zur Verfügung stellt...," "Der Hund ist in Bewegung zu anderen Hunden...," "Die Zahlen sind prähistorisch," "Drohungen – Bedroht der viereckige Raum den runden Raum?," "Im Steinbogen entfaltet sich die imaginäre Spirale," "Kann Man Raum und Raum zusammenzählen?," "Das Haus," "Genesis," "Für das Haus," "Ein Gedicht," "Die Lebende Einbilding (das heiss Die Visionen) ist in Bewegung," "Theorie für eine Ausstellung – Der Integrierte Verdacht – Wider die Tautologien" and "Wenn ich zum Vorschlag, über das Thema 'Kreative Strategien' etwas zu schreiben...." by the artist
– Fritz Billeter, "Höllenqual und konkrete Utopie, Louis Soutter und Mario Merz in der Kunsthalle Basel," *Tages Anzeiger* (Zürich), January 29, 1975

London, Institute of Contemporary Art, September 3 – October 3, 1975

Stuttgart (Bad Canstatt) and Lauffen am Neckar, Galerie Hetzler, 1975

Rome, Galleria Gian Enzo Sperone, February 20 – April 1976
– Bruno Corà, "Spirali," *Data*, no. 21, May-June 1976, pp. 60-61

Genoa, Galleria Forma, opened February 28, 1976

Turin, Galleria Gian Enzo Sperone, opened April 7, 1976

Pescara, Galleria Mario Pieroni, May

20 – November 20, 1976
– Marlis Grüterich, "Drei Ausstellungs Situationen in der Galerie Mario Pieroni, Pescara, Mittelitalien, 1975-76," *Kunstforum International*, vol. 17, September 1976, pp. 124-133

Turin, Galleria Antonio Tucci Russo, *Tavolo a spirale per festino di giornali datati il giorno del festino*, October 30, 1976 – January 15, 1977

Düsseldorf, Galerie Konrad Fischer, *La natura è l'arte del numero*, November 11 – 27, 1976

Naples, Museo Diego Aragona Pignatelli Cortes, November 20 – December 4, 1976

Milan, Galleria Salvatore Ala, April 6 – May 1977

Zürich, Annemarie Verna Galerie, *Vento preistorico delle Montagne Gelate*, November 16, 1977 – January 10, 1978

Brescia, via delle Battaglie 55a, *La Bottiglia di Leyda*, opened July 1, 1978

Turin, Galleria Antonio Tucci Russo, *Evidenza di 987*, October 18, 1978 – February 15, 1979
– Luciana Rogozinski, "Mario Merz – Tucci Russo, Torino," *Flash Art*, no. 86-87, January-February 1979, p. 8

Athens, Jean and Karen Bernier Gallery, *Evidenza di 10946*, October 26 – November 22, 1978

Essen, Museum Folkwang, *Mario Merz*, January 26 – March 4, 1979. Catalogue with texts by Germano Celant and Zdenek Felix and "Das Haus," "Genesis," "Die Fibonacci-Zahlen und die Kunst," "Für das Haus," "Ein sehr langer Sonntag dauert annähernd seit 1966 – und jetzt sind wir im Jahr 1976," "987 Das Obst ist hier" and "Ist das Fehlen von Ikonographie unsere Eroberung oder unsere Verdammung?" by the artist. Traveled to Eindhoven, Stedelijk Van Abbemuseum (coorganizer) with separate catalogue with texts by Germano Celant and the artist, trans. K. van Ingen-Schenau, April 20 – May 18, 1980
– Marlis Grüterich, "Der Iglu im Zentrum einer Art europäischer Ethnologie: Poetische Aufklärung – Die Ausstellung Mario Merz in Museum Folkwang Essen," *Nürnberger Zeitung*, February 10, 1979
– B. Catoir, "Mario Merz in Essen. Der Künstler sitzt im Iglu: Klause oder Bühne?," *Frankfurter Allgemeine Zeitung*, February 20, 1979, p. 23
– Laszlo Glozer, "Die Symbole sind aus Schlamm – Mario Merz stellt im Folkwang Museum Essen aus," *Süddeutsche Zeitung* (Munich), February 24-25, 1979
– Annelie Pohlen, "Mario Merz," *Heu-*

te Kunst, no. 25, March-April 1979, p. 8
– Peter Winter, "Mario Merz – Museum Folkwang, Essen," *Das Kunstwerk*, vol. 32, April-June 1979, p. 180
– Marlis Grüterich, "Museen und Galerien, Essen: Museum Folkwang Ausstellung, Mario Merz," *Pantheon*, vol. 37, July-September 1979, pp. 198-200
– T. Frenken, "Verbeelding aan de macht," *Eindhovens Dagblad*, May 17, 1980
– Germano Celant, "Een steeds toenemende groei van energie," *Museum Journaal*, vol. 25, June 1980, pp. 154-165

New York, Sperone Westwater Fischer Gallery, March 31 – April 21, 1979
– Harriet Senie, "Igloo Order," *New York Post*, April 7, 1979, p. 29
– Grace Glueck, "Mario Merz," *The New York Times*, April 13, 1979, p. C23
– Valentin Tatransky, "Mario Merz," *Arts Magazine*, vol. 53, June 1979, p. 36
– Carrie Rickey, "Mario Merz, Sperone/Westwater/Fischer," *Flash Art*, no. 90-91, June – July 1979, p. 43
– Carrie Rickey, "Reviews – New York...Mario Merz, Sperone, Westwater, Fischer...," *Artforum*, vol. 17, Summer 1979, pp. 66-67
– Joan Simon, "New York: Mario Merz at Sperone Westwater Fischer," *Art in America*, vol. 67, July-August 1979, pp. 113-114

Brisbane, Institute of Modern Art, *Mario Merz: The Wind My Home*, May 17 – June 4, 1979. Documented in *Bulletin*, May 1979, with "Look for the first dwelling" and "The Structure contains within itself the power of Geometry" by the artist. Trans. Rita Rando

Paris, Galerie Liliane et Michel Durand-Dessert, September 22 – October 24, 1979
Bernard Blistène, "Mario Merz: Galerie Durand-Dessert," *Flash Art*, no. 92-93, October-November 1979, p. 59

Zürich, Annemarie Verna Galerie, *irritabile irritato*, October 9 – November 24, 1979

Milan, Galleria Toselli, opened October 12, 1979
– Barbara Maestri, "Mario Merz," *Flash Art*, no. 94-95, January-February 1980, p. 59
– Isabella Puliafito, "Reviews – Italy...Mario Merz – Franco Toselli Gallery, Milan," *Artforum*, vol. 18, February 1980, p. 108

Rome, Studio d'arte contemporanea di Guiliana De Crescenzo, *6765*, opened December 1, 1979

Turin, OOLP, Libreria Internazionale, opened December 22, 1979

Brussels, Galerie Albert Baronian, *Près de la table*, January 15 – mid-February 1980

London, Whitechapel Art Gallery, *Mario Merz*, January 18 – March 2, 1980. Catalogue with texts by Germano Celant and Zdenek Felix. Trans. Anthony Melville
– Marina Vaizey, "The Simple Skills of the Igloo-maker," *The Sunday Times*, January 27, 1980, p. 39
– W. Feaver, "Marvels of Merz's Millions," *Observer*, January 1980
– B. Hicks, "Gallery Explorations," *The Times*, February 8, 1980
– Waldemar Januszczak, "Mario Merz/ Joel Shapiro," *The Guardian*, February 19, 1980
– Fenella Crichton, "London – Joel Shapiro – Whitechapel Gallery/ Mario Merz – Whitechapel Gallery," *Art & Artists*, vol. 14, March 1980, pp. 42-44

Turin, Galleria Christian Stein, *I rinoceronti*, opened March 14, 1980
Angelo Dragone, "Merz con neon e rinoceronte," *La Stampa* (Turin), April 23, 1980, p. 25

Stuttgart, Galerie Max Hetzler, opened April 20, 1980

New York, Sperone Westwater Fischer Gallery, October 25 – November 18, 1980
– Judith Wilson, "Painting by Numbers," *The Village Voice*, vol. 25, November 12-18, 1980, p. 87
– Hal Foster, "Mario Merz," *Artforum*, vol. 19, January 1981, p. 70

Turin, Galleria Gian Enzo Sperone, opened November 18, 1980

Milan, Galleria Salvatore Ala, *Mario Merz*, opened December 12, 1980

Omaha, Joslyn Art Museum, *1-80 Series: Mario Merz*, March 7 – April 19, 1981. Brochure with text by Hollister Sturges

Düsseldorf, Galerie Konrad Fischer, March 14 – April 18, 1981
– Gislind Nabakowski, "Mario Merz – Grosse Bilder auf Jute und Installationen," *Kunstforum International*, no. 2-3, 1981, pp. 285-286

Warsaw, Studio W Kwietniu, opened April 6, 1981. Brochure with texts by the artist

ARC/Musée d'Art Moderne de la Ville de Paris, *Mario Merz*, May – September 1981. Catalogue with texts by Jean-Christophe Ammann and Suzanne Pagé, "Les nombres qui se multiplient sont aussi réels que les animaux qui se reproduisent/ Zahlen in expansion sind ebenso wirklich wie Tiere, die sich

vermehren," "Les nombres de Fibonacci et l'art/ Die Fibonacci-Zahlen und die Kunst," "La Maison/Das Haus," "Genesis," "L'escargot/ Die Schnecke," "1/La propriété de manger des fruits nous appartient peut-être /1/ Das Recht, Obst zu essen, mag uns eigen sein," "En pensant on peut exécuter.../ Man kann im Denken handeln...," "Projet de tables pour une maison en construction permanente.../ Projekt von Tischen für ein Haus in ständigen Aufbau...," "Combien de temps écoulé à ne rien faire!/ Wieviel Zeit ging mit nichtstun vorüber!," "La peinture est longue et rapide/ Die Malerei ist langsam und schnell" and "L'absence d'iconographie est-elle notre conquête ou notre damnation?/ Ist das Fehlen von Ikonographie unsere Eroberung oder unsere Verdammung?" by the artist and interview with the artist by Jean-Christophe Ammann and Suzanne Pagé. Trans. Annamaria Deplazes, Mariana Hagmann, Sabine Mann and Myriam Tanant. Traveled to Kunsthalle Basel (coorganizer), July 11 – September 13
– E. Neumeister, "Sind wir Vorfahren oder Nachgeborene? Mario Merz in Basel," *Frankfurter Allgemeine Zeitung*, August 14, 1981, p. 25
– Patrick Frey, "Journal – Schweiz: Mario Merz und Jonathan Borofsky in Basel," *Du*, no. 9, 1981, pp. 98, 100
– Patrick Frey, "Mario Merz und Jonathan Borofsky in Basel," *Journal* (Basel), September 1981
– Zdenek Felix, "Merz in Paris – Merz in Basel," *Domus*, no. 621, October 1981, p. 56

Zürich, Galerie Konrad Fischer, June 13 – July 11, 1981

Turin, Galleria Antonio Tucci Russo, *Architettura fondata dal tempo, architettura sfondata dal tempo*, November 9, 1981 – February 15, 1982

Turin, Galleria Christian Stein, *Vento preistorico dalle Montagne Gelate*, opened November 25, 1981

Naples, Galleria Lucio Amelio, *Mario Merz*, December 19, 1981
– Arcangelo Izzo, "Mario Merz: dall'igloo all'ipogeo e viceversa," *lapis/arte* (Salerno), vol. 2, no. 4, 1981, pp. I-XVI

New York, Sperone Westwater Fischer Gallery, February 6-27, 1982
– Vivien Raynor, "Mario Merz," *The New York Times*, February 19, 1982, p. C26
– Kay Larson, "Shotgun Wedding," *New York*, vol. 15, February 22, 1982, pp. 64-65
– Lawrence Eishen, "Mario Merz," *Art/World* (New York), vol. 6, February 22-March 22 1982, p. 6
– Roberta Smith, "Art," *The Village*

Voice, vol. 27, February 23, 1982, p. 60
– William Zimmer, "Mario Merz," *The SoHo News*, vol. 9, February 24-March 2, 1982, p. 46
– Lisa Liebmann, "Reviews – New York... Mario Merz, Sperone, Westwater, Fischer," *Artforum*, vol. 20, Summer 1982, p. 90

Chapel Hill, North Carolina, Ackland Art Museum, *Facets VII: Mario Merz*, February 14 – March 14, 1982

Amsterdam, Galerie Brinkman, March 13 – April 28, 1982

Rome, Galleria Mario Diacono, April 24 – May 22, 1982. Brochure with text by Mario Diacono

Hannover, Kestner-Gesellschaft, *Mario Merz: Disegni / Arbeiten auf Papier*, July 16 – September 12, 1982. Catalogue with texts by Marlis Grüterich and Carl Haenlein. Traveled to Münster, Westfalischer Kunstverein, with separate catalogue with texts by Carl Haenlein and "retro serra..." by the artist, October 29 – December 5
– Annelie Pohlen, "Mario Merz: Kestner-Gesellschaft/Hannover; Folkwang Museum/Essen; Staatsgalerie/Stuttgart," *Flash Art*, no. 109, November 1982, p. 70

Venice, California, Flow Ace Gallery, *Mario Merz: An installation*, August 5 – September 15, 1982
– Christopher Knight, "The In-between World of Mario Merz's Art," *Los Angeles Herald Examiner*, September 1, 1982
– Melinda Wortz, "The Nation – Los Angeles: Mario Merz – Flow Ace," *Art News*, vol. 81, November 1982, p. 158

Hamburg, Galerie Vera Munro, *Mario Merz: Neue Arbeiten*, September 21 – October 1982

Bari, Galleria Marilena Bonomo, November 6 – December 1982
– Santa Fizzarotti, "Mario Merz," *Segno* (Pescara), vol. 6, November 1982-February 1983, pp. 62-63

Bologna, Galleria Comunale d'Arte Moderna, *Esercizi di lettura 8: Mario Merz*, December 18, 1982 – January 14, 1983. Catalogue with texts by Mirella Bandini and "Per la pittura del torrente" by the artist
– Luciana Rogozinski, "Reviews – Bologna: Mario Merz – Galleria d'Arte Moderna," *Artforum*, vol. 21, April 1983, p. 83

Venice, California, Flow Ace Gallery, *Mario Merz: Recent Drawings and Collages*, January 11 – February 5, 1983

Purchase, New York, Neuberger Museum, *Installation/Mario Merz*, January 30 – July 24, 1983

Stockholm, Moderna Museet, *Mario Merz*, February 5 – March 20, 1983. Catalogue with texts by Qlle Granath and Carl Haenlein and "År 1945, när kriget led mot sitt slut, befann jag mig i fängelse av politiska skäl/ In 1945, at the end of the war, when I was in prison for political reasons...," "En Mycket Lång Söndag som Varar Ungefär sedan 1966 och I år är Det 1976/ An Infinitely Long Sunday Has Lasted Approximately from 1966 and Now it is 1976" and "Till Forsen/ To the Torrent" by the artist. Trans. Eva Swartz, Ingrid Weström and Diana W. Wormuth
– Germano Celant, "Italiens Konsthistoria, 1953-1983," *Paletten* (Göteborg), no. 2, April-June 1983, pp. 4-17
– Germano Celant, "Mario Merz," *Moderna Museet* (Stockholm), no. 4, 1982, pp. 22-23

London, Anthony d'Offay Gallery, *Mario Merz*, February 22 – March 23, 1983
– Waldemar Januszczak, "Mario Merz," *The Guardian*, March 4, 1983
– W. Feaver, "Letting Demons Loose," *Observer*, March 6, 1983
– Caroline Collier, "Mario Merz, Anthony d'Offay," *Flash Art*, no. 112, May 1983, p. 68

Rome, Galleria Pieroni, May 29 – July 29, 1983. Invitation with "Voglio fare subito un ritratto" by the artist

Jerusalem, The Israel Museum, *Mario Merz*, July 26 – August 26, 1983. Catalogue with texts by Yona Fischer and Suzanne Landau
– D. Kedar, "Flowers in the Garden," *Al Hamishmar* (Jerusalem), August 5, 1983
– Homar Levy, "Igloo in Jerusalem Summer," *Yediot Acharonot* (Jerusalem), August 5, 1983
– Nizza Maliniak, "Man – Nature – Civilization," *Haaretz* (Jerusalem), August 26, 1983
– Suzanne Landau, "Expositions, Jerusalem – Mario Merz, Israel Museum," *Art Press* (Paris), no. 74, October 1983, p.50

Vienna, Galerie nächst St. Stephan, *Über Mario Merz*, October 27 – November 26, 1983. Catalogue with texts by Gottfried Böhm, Germano Celant, Zdenek Felix, Robert Fleck, Marlis Grüterich, Franz Mrkvicka, Dieter Ronte, Rosemarie Schwarzwaelder, Peter Weibel and Karl Wutt. Trans. Oswald Oberhuber

Basel, Galerie Buchmann, *Mario Merz: ritratto di geco ritratti di rapace gallinaceo e di sfinge che avrebbero dovuto essere fatti 50 000 anni prima del 1983*, November 8, 1983 – January 22, 1984. Catalogue with "Dalle invenzioni alle prospettive degli uccelli e animali/ Von den Erfindungen zu den Aussichten der Vögel und Tiere" by the artist

San Marino, Palazzo Congressi ed Esposizioni, *Mario Merz*, November 18, 1983 – January 22, 1984. Catalogue by Germano Celant with texts by Mirella Bandini, Renato Barilli, Achille Bonito Oliva, Germano Celant, Bruno Corà, the artist et al. and interviews with the artist by Jean-Christophe Ammann and Suzanne Pagé, Mirella Bandini, Germano Celant, Bruno Corà et al. Trans. Rino Ponte, Alex Stenghel and Fulvio Zunino
– Claudio Spadoni, "Come esploratori nell'igloo di Merz," *Il Resto del Carlino* (Bologna), December 4, 1983, p.3
– Mirella Bandini, "Opere di Merz in un percorso dell'immaginario," *Avanti!*, December 8, 1983
– Rolando Zucchini, "Quando l'arte è povera," *Corriere dell'Umbria* (Perugia), December 16, 1983
– Renato Barilli, "Poveri ma elettronici," *L'Espresso* (Rome), vol. 29, December 18, 1983, p. 90
– Mauro Corradini, "L'Arte povera di Mario Merz," *Brescia Oggi*, January 7, 1984, p. 10
– Arturo Carlo Quintavalle, "Mario Merz," *Panorama* (Milan), January 9, 1984, p. 15
– Toti Carpentieri, "Mario Merz," *Quotidiano di Lecce*, January 11, 1984
– Antonello Trombadori, "Ora l'arte va di bene in Merz," *Europeo* (Milan), January 21, 1984, p. 58
– "Merz: mostra interrotta," *Il Giornale dell'Arte* (Turin), vol. 2, January 1984, p. 1
– Laura Maggi, "San Marino: antologica di Mario Merz," *Vogue Italia* (Milan), February 1984
– Michelangelo Castello, "Il numero e la collina," *Tema Celeste* (Siracusa), vol. 2, March 1984, pp. 9-13
– Corinna Ferrari, "San Marino: Mario Merz," *Domus*, no. 648, March 1984, p. 69
– Franco Torriani, "Celant e i suoi 12 apostoli," *Il Giornale dell'Arte* (Turin), vol. 11, May 1984, p. 12

Boston, Institute of Contemporary Art, *Currents: Mario Merz*, January 24 – April 1, 1984. Brochure with text by Elisabeth Sussman and "Architecture built by time..." by the artist. Trans. Alex Simotas

Buffalo, Albright-Knox Art Gallery, *Mario Merz: Paintings and Constructions*, January 28 – March 18, 1984, in conjunction with Hallwalls, Buffalo, *Mario Merz: Drawings*, February 3 – 25. Catalogue with text by Susan Krane and "Suddenly, I feel a shooting pain in the curve of my knee while I talk and drink good evening wine from a glass" and "For the Picture of the Torrent" by the artist

New York, Sperone Westwater Gallery, *Mario Merz: Pittore in Africa*, February 18 – March 17, 1984. Catalogue with photographs by Paolo Mussat Sartor

Düsseldorf, Galerie Konrad Fischer, *Al Torrente*, March 16 – April 15, 1984

St. Gallen in Katharinen, Kunstverein St. Gallen, March 24 – April 21, 1984

Chagny, France, Galleria Pietro Sparta – Pascale Petit, *Mario Merz*, October 28, 1984 – January 30, 1985. Catalogue with texts by Bruno Corà and Beatrice Merz and "Mi ricordo adesso...," "Tempo di niente con i numeri accesi," "Was machen, finalmente contro gli architetti," "Il pieno in elevazione possiede la velocità di essere alto sul piano," "E il trionfo del vuoto sul pieno...," "La Meccanica," "L'impazienza" and "Il Coro, Il Cono" by the artist. Trans. Giorgio Cerruti di Castiglione
– Denys Zacharopoulos, "Reviews – Chagny: Mario Merz, au fond de la cour à droite," *Artforum*, vol. 23, April 1985, p. 103

Turin, Galleria Christian Stein, *Mario Merz*, November 5, 1984 – March 1, 1985

Albi, Musée Toulouse-Lautrec, November 1984

Nantes, Ecole des Beaux-Arts, *Atelier sur l'herbe*, 1984

Kunsthaus Zürich, *Mario Merz*, April 3 – May 27, 1985. Book, Harald Szeemann, ed., *Mario Merz*, with texts by Marlis Grüterich, Ursula Perucchi-Petri and Denys Zacharopoulos and "caro Harald/ Lieber Harald" by the artist, trans. Christine Brunner; catalogue, *Mario Merz*, photographs by Balthasar Burkhard of installation, and checklist; and catalogue, Beatrice Merz, ed., *Voglio fare subito un libro/ Sofort will ich ein Buch machen*, anthology of writings by the artist, trans. Christina Brunner, Marlis Grüterich, Ingeborg Lüscher, Liselotte Mangels-Giannacchi and Harald Szeemann
– Roman Hollenstein, "Wie ein prähistorischer Wind aus vereisten Gebirgen," *Neue Zürcher Zeitung*, April 3, 1985
– Markus Landert, "Iglu-Dorf von Mario Merz im Kunstmuseum," *Der Zürcher Oberländer* (Wetzikon), April 3, 1985
– Wolfgang Bessenich, "Nicht jedes Haus erlaubt das Hausen," *Basler Zeitung*, April 4, 1985
– Jan Marek, "Von der Urform des Wohnens zur urbanen Utopie," *Die Weltwoche* (Düsseldorf), April 4, 1985,

– Charlotte Peter, "Mario Merz im Kunsthaus," *Zuri Woche* (Glattbrugg), April 4, 1985, p. 47
– Robert Schneider, "Eine grandiose Vision von Wachstum und Existenz," *Der Landbote* (Winterthur), April 4, 1985
– Klaus Oberholzer, "Die Iglus von Mario Merz als 'Città irreale,'" *Vaterland* (Lucerne), April 6, 1985
– Inge Sprenger Viol, "Eine Iglu-Stadt im Kunsthaus," *Zuger Tagblatt*, April 6, 1985
– Fritz Billeter, "Haus und Zahl, Zivilisation und Kosmos," *Tages Anzeiger* (Zürich), April 9, 1985
– Irene Meie, "'Irreale' Stadt aus Iglus," *Zürichsee-Zeitung*, (Stäfa), April 9, 1985
– Catherine-France Borrini, "Des iglos de rêve," *L'Hebdo* (Zofingen), April 11, 1985
– Annelise Zwez, "Suche nach Wachstumskraft," *Solothurner Zeitung*, April 11, 1985
– "'Arme Kunst' im Gleichschritt mit dem Wachstum ohne Ende," *Aargauer Tagblatt* (Aarau), April 11, 1985
– John Matheson, "Mario Merz zeigt Iglus – Symbol des absoluten Raumes," *Öltner Tagblatt* (Olten), April 12, 1985
– Kristina Piwecki, "Der Iglu-Atemraum des Menschen," *Neue Zürcher Nachrichten*, April 12, 1985
– "Mario Merz im Kunsthaus Zürich," *Appenzeller Zeitung* (Herisau), April 13, 1985
– Sonia Rügg, "'Città irreale' – eine irreale Stadt," *Appenzeller Zeitung* (Herisau), April 20, 1985
– Irene Stoll-Kern, "Geistige Behausungen eines Nomadenkünstlers," *Der Bund* (Bern), April 20, 1985
– Hanspeter Eggenberger, "Mario Merz: 'Das Leben ist eine Reihe von Strudeln,'" *Berner Zeitung*, April 23, 1985
– Harry Zellweger, "Città reale – Città irreale," *Schaffhauser Nachrichten*, April 25, 1985
– Harry Zellweger, "Surreale Stätte mitten in der Stadt," *St. Galler Tagblatt*, April 26, 1985
– Jean Pierre Bordaz, "Expositions, Zurich – Mario Merz," *Beaux-Arts*, no. 23, April 1985, p. 92
– Harry Zellweger, "Eine Stadt schaut aus dem Fenster," *Stuttgarter Zeitung*, May 2, 1985
– Nik Streiff, "Mehr Mistaufen ins Kunsthaus," *Tages Anzeiger* (Zürich), May 6, 1985
– Jean-Christophe Ammann, "Lieux, événements," *Construire* (Geneva), May 8, 1985
– Reinhard Beuth, "Am Anfang war die Zahl," *Die Welt* (Hamburg), May 14, 1985, p. 27
– Jörg Unger, "Iglus als Gesamtkunst-

werk," *Vorarlberger Nachrichten* (Bregenz), May 17, 1985
– Monique Priscille, "Mario Merz, Louise Bourgeois," *La Suisse* (Geneva), May 20, 1985
– Catherine-France Borrini, "Expositions Suisse – Mario Merz, Kunsthaus Zürich," *Art Press* (Paris), no. 93, June 1, 1985, p. 53
– Oscar Bischoff, "Iglu-Stadt in der Moderne," *Thurgauer Tagblatt* (Weinfelden), June 4, 1985
– Max Wechsler, "Zürich – Mario Merz: Kunsthaus," *Artforum*, vol. 24, September 1985, pp. 134-135

Hamburg, Galerie Vera Munro, *Mario Merz: Neue Arbeiten*, September 17 – October 31, 1985

Münster, Westfälischer Kunstverein, *Mario Merz*, October 5 – November 24, 1985

Stuttgart, Galerie Schurr, *Mario Merz*, October 19 – November 23, 1985

Milan, Galleria Christian Stein, *Mario Merz*, October 25 – December 1985

New York, Sperone Westwater Gallery and Leo Castelli Gallery, *Mario Merz*, November 16 – December 21 and November 23 – December 21, 1985, respectively
– Michael Brenson, "One-man shows will Enrich the Season," *The New York Times*, September 8, 1985, p. 43
– Vivien Raynor, "Mario Merz," *The New York Times*, November 29, 1985, p. C29

Geneva, Musée d'Art et d'Histoire, *Mario Merz*, November 21, 1985 – February 2, 1986. Installation on occasion of Prix de la Banque Hypothécaire du Canton de Genève

Turin, Galleria Antonio Tucci Russo, *Il fiume appare*, March 27 – July 25, 1986
– Maria Teresa Roberto, "Mario Merz, Tucci Russo," *Flash Art* (Italian Edition), no. 134, Summer 1986, p. 62

Chagny, France, Galleria Pietro Sparta – Pascale Petit, *Une ouvrée, une mésure de terre qui donne un portrait bien terrestre*, January 3 – April 28, 1987. Catalogue with texts by Bruno Corà and Beatrice Merz and "Je me rappelle maintenant..." and "Was machen en fin contre les architectes?" by the artist
C. Besson, "Mario Merz," *Plus 1* (Dijon), no. 1, April 1985, pp. 38-42

Düsseldorf, Galerie Konrad Fischer, February 7 – March 7, 1987

Naples, Museo di Capodimonte, *Mario Merz: Onda d'urto*, April 16 – August 13, 1987. Catalogue with texts by Graziella Lonardi Buontempo, Bruno Corà and Nicola Spinosa

– Gabriele Perretta, "Mario Merz, Museo di Capodimonte," *Flash Art* (Italian Edition), no. 139, May-June 1987, p. 64

Bordeaux, capc / Musée d'Art Contemporain – Entrepôt Lainé, *Mario Merz: oeuvres récentes*, May 8 – September 13, 1987. Documented in "Mario Merz, Oeuvres récentes," *Bulletin* (capc / Musée d'Art Contemporain, Bordeaux), no. 13, May-September 1987
– "L'Italie d'hier et d'aujourd'hui," *Sud-Ouest*, May 9, 1987
– Dominique Godfrey, "Une page d'histoire," *Sud-Ouest*, May 10, 1987
– Lieven Van Den Abeele, "Mario Merz bouwt zijn iglo," *Standaart* (Antwerp), May 30, 1987
– Felix Buchmann, "Lettre à Mario Merz," *New Art International* (Lausanne), no. 3-4, May 1987, p. 51
– "L'Arte Povera dans l'actualité française," *New Art International* (Lausanne), no. 3-4, May 1987
– "Mario Merz au CAPC de Bordeaux," *New Art International* (Lausanne), no. 3-4, May 1987, pp. 48-50
– Valérie Briere-Maroger, "Ouverture sur le rêve," *Reforme*, June 19, 1987
– Michel Nuridsany, "Mario Merz, le Généreux," *Le Figaro*, June 30, 1987, p. 31
– M.T., "Expo – Bordeaux: Mario Merz," *Beaux-Arts*, no. 47, June 1987, p. 112
– Geneviève Breerette, "Hommage au constructeur d'igloos," *Le Monde*, July 12-13, 1987, p. 11
– Philippe Piguet, "La Vie des Arts, Musées, Bordeaux: Mario Merz," *L'Oeil* (Paris), no. 384-385, July-August 1987, p. 81
– Francisco Calvo, "Importante muestra en Burdeos de la obra reciente de Mario Merz," *El Pais* (Madrid), August 3, 1987
– Liliana Albertazzi, "Mario Merz," *Galeries Magazine*, August-September 1987, p. 64
– M. Bruch, "Mario Merz," *L'Amateur d'Art*, September 1987
– Rafael Marquez, "Mario Merz, un clásico de la vanguardia europea," *El Medico* (Madrid), September 4, 1987
– Anne Dagbert, "Igloos, ligatures," *Art Contemporain*, September 11, 1987
– Geneviève Breerette, "Merz et l'art pauvre," *Le Monde*, September 17, 1987, p. 22
– Maïten Bouisset, "Mario Merz – L'année en France d'un nomade du temps présent," *Art Press* (Paris), no. 119, November 1987, pp. 43-45
– Geneviève Breerette, "La maison des métaphores," *Le Monde*, December 10, 1987, p. 17

Frankfurt, Galerie Herbert Meyer-Ellinger, *Mario Merz: Arbeiten auf Papier*, July 2 – September 5, 1987

Musée d'Art Contemporain de Montréal, *Mario Merz: Triple Igloo*, September 6 – October 25, 1987. Catalogue with text by Paulette Gagnon. Trans. Helena Scheffer

Paris, Chapelle Saint-Louis de la Salpêtrière, *Festival D'Automne à Paris, La Planète Merz*, November 16, 1987 – January 3, 1988. Documented in *Libération* supplement, Autumn 1987, with texts by Demosthenes Davvetas, Hervé Gauville and Marlis Grüterich and interview with the artist by Germano Celant
– Salvatore Licitra, "Mario Merz: Intervento nella Salpêtrière, Parigi," *Domus*, vol. 22, May 1988, pp. 80-84

London, Anthony d'Offay Gallery, *Mario Merz*, February 5 – March 5, 1988
– A. Robertson, "Mario Merz," *Time Out* (London), February 10, 1988, p. 30
– "Avant-Garde Igloo," *International Herald Tribune*, February 19, 1988, p. 7
– James Hall, "Mario Merz, Anthony d'Offay," *Artscribe*, no. 69, May 1988, pp. 72-73

Turin, Galleria in Arco, *Mario Merz, Opere su carta*, February – March 1988. Catalogue with "Quando aperta, la bocca è aperta..." by the artist

Nagoya, Institute of Contemporary Art, *Mario Merz*, April 23 – June 19, 1988. Catalogue with texts by Germano Celant and Demosthenes Davvetas, "Tu giri intorno alle case o le case girano intorno a te?" by the artist and interview with the artist by Fumio Nanjo. Trans. Tsutomu Mizusawa, Haruki Morokawa, James Roberts, Meg Shore, Ryoko Sugio et al.

Edinburgh, Richard Demarco Gallery, April 1988

Humlebaek, Denmark, Louisiana Museum of Modern Art, *Mario Merz*, May 28 – July 3, 1988
– Demosthenes Davvetas, "Planeten Merz," *Louisiana Revy* (Humlebaek), no. 3, May 1988, pp. 10-12
– Steingrim Laursen, "Mario Merz," *Louisiana Revy* (Humlebaek), no. 3, May 1988, p. 3
– Albert Mertz, "Mertz om Merz," *Louisiana Revy* (Humlebaek), no. 3, May 1988, pp. 6-9

Milan, Galleria Christian Stein, *Mario Merz*, December 1, 1988 – January 15, 1989
– Angela Vattese, "Nell'incontro natura-civiltà," *Il Sole 24 Ore* (Milan), no. 315, December 4, 1988, p. 26
– Jole de Sanna, "Reviews – Mario Merz, Galleria Christian Stein," *Artforum*, vol. 27, February 1989, p. 143

Los Angeles Museum of Contemporary

Art, *Mario Merz*, February 25 – June 18, 1989
– Elizabeth Venant, "Merz Knocks Traditional Statuary Off Its Pedestal," *Los Angeles Times*, February 18, 1989, Pt. VI, p. 6
– Christopher Knight, "Merz on the move at MoCA: But project runs out of gas too soon," *Los Angeles Herald Examiner*, March 10, 1989
– William Wilson, "The Mario Merz Environment: Artist offers healing vision of man reintegrated with nature," *Los Angeles Times*, March 12, 1989, pp. 90, 93
– Kenneth Baker, "Too-Sterile Setting for 'Arte Povera,'" *The San Francisco Chronicle*, April 16, 1989, pp. 1(?), 15
– Steven Appleton, "Encirclements and Progressions," *Artweek* (Oakland), April 29, 1989, p. 1
– Bruno Corà, "Mario Merz: L'eredità dinamica dello spazio di veduta," *New Art International* (Lausanne), no. 3, May-June 1989, pp. 28-31
– Ben Marks, "A dome decreed: the mythological landscapes of Mario Merz," *Artcoast*, May-June 1989, pp. 74-75
– Kenneth Baker, "Reviews...Los Angeles – Mario Merz, Museum of Contemporary Art," *Artforum*, vol. 27, Summer 1989, pp. 150-151

Villeurbanne, France, Le Nouveau Musée, *Mario Merz, dessins*, June 9 – September 10, 1989

Florence, Fortezza da Basso, *Pitti Immagine Uomo*, June 30 – July 3, 1989. Brochure with "I am doctor Merz/ Io sono il dottor Merz," and "I began working on the first igloo in 1967.../ Ho lavorato al primo igloo durante l'anno 1967..." by the artist

Paris, Galerie AmelioBrachot "Pièce Unique," *Déclaration des droits de l'Homme et du Citoyen*, July 11, 1989 – October 10, 1989